IN THE LAND OF OZ

Fiction

Coming From Behind
Peeping Tom
Redback
The Very Model of a Man
No More Mr. Nice Guy
The Mighty Walzer
Who's Sorry Now?
The Making of Henry
Kalooki Nights
The Act of Love
The Finkler Question
Zoo Time

Nonfiction

Shakespeare's Magnanimity (with Wilbur Sanders)
Roots Schmoots: Journeys Among Jews
Seriously Funny: From the Ridiculous to the Sublime
Whatever It Is, I Don't Like It

IN THE LAND OF OZ

Howard Jacobson

BLOOMSBURY

NEW YORK · LONDON · NEW DELHI · SYDNEY

Published by Bloomsbury USA, New York

All papers used by Bloomsbury USA are natural, recyclable products made from
wood grown in well-managed forests. The manufacturing processes conform
to the environmental regulations of the country of origin.

LIBRARY OF CONGRESS CATALOGING-IN-PUBLICATION DATA HAS BEEN APPLIED FOR

Paperback ISBN: 978-1-60819-895-5

First published in 1987 by Hamish Hamilton
First published by Bloomsbury in 2011
This paperback edition published in 2013

1 3 5 7 9 10 8 6 4 2

Typeset by Hewer Text UK Ltd, Edinburgh

Printed and bound in the U.S.A. by Thomson-Shore Inc., Dexter, Michigan

To all those who, knowing what we were about, spared no pains to ease our way – but especially to Geoff and Carole Gibbs, Ron Wise, Mayor Finlayson, Stanley Brown, Angela and Colin Davis, Leanne Cook, Judith Coleman, and Neil Batt – this book is affectionately dedicated.

PREFACE TO THE NEW EDITION

It is hard to believe, fondly turning these pages again, that the journey it records – all around Australia and then up through the middle – was made twenty-five years ago. It was the adventure of my life, though in truth I took no risks in the sense that adventurers take risk; but I gave myself up to continuous discomfort, bad roads, the bullying babble of long-distance Australian bus drivers, the uncertainties of cheap motels, venomous spiders, the monologues of racists, and the difficulty of making sense of a country that was at one and the same time magnanimous and cruel, sophisticated and suspicious, self-righteous and free-spirited.

I fell for Australia when I first went there as a young man to teach at Sydney University. On the morning I left, three years later, I sat on a bench in a little park overlooking the Harbour and wept. My passion for the place returns the moment the sun comes out in England. At the first hint of warmth, I smell Australia and long to be back there. This journey, undertaken twenty years later, tried – unsuccessfully – to shake off some of that sentimentality, while endeavouring to broaden my interest in the country, which up until then had been Sydney-centred. The consequence was a fiercer passion still, this time for outback and small-town Australia, the thousand greens of the bush, the deep quiet of the desert, the skies filled with parrots, and the intense intimacies which Australians encourage at the very moment of meeting.

My companion for most of this journey was my then wife, Rosalin Sadler, an Australian herself, a perceptive, funny and indefatigable conversationalist, and the instigator of many of the more challenging treks we made, both of body and of mind. I am not an intrepid traveller. I cannot abide isolation. Nor can I abide silence. For me, to travel is to talk, and it would have been untrue to the journey not to have told what we talked about.

The book is not a history of Australia, nor is it an analysis of the Australian character, though it is impossible to travel in the far north or west of the country without walking straight into the heartbreak of white Australian/Aboriginal relations. Watching *Ghostbusters* on television in the Aboriginal community of Areyonga, a paradisal ruin 200 kilometres or so west of Alice Springs, was the funniest and saddest experience of the whole journey. Faced with the realities of Aboriginal squalor, you have no choice but to think politically.

As I travelled I recorded, sitting in the back of a camper van or in a motel room every night, writing down everything I'd seen and heard. Where possible I took public transport. You don't learn much about a place by flying over it. My most vivid memory is of sitting in buses for days at a time, stopping at roadhouses from which I never expected to escape alive, listening to one driver after another enunciate his philosophy of manliness and mateship, encountering Australians of every age and with every reason for being on the road themselves, watching the eagles glide and the earth turn red. There is no more variously beautiful country. This book is a record of the near anguish I felt the whole time I was there. The only way I can describe that briefly is to say it stabs the heart.

Howard Jacobson, April 2011

CONTENTS

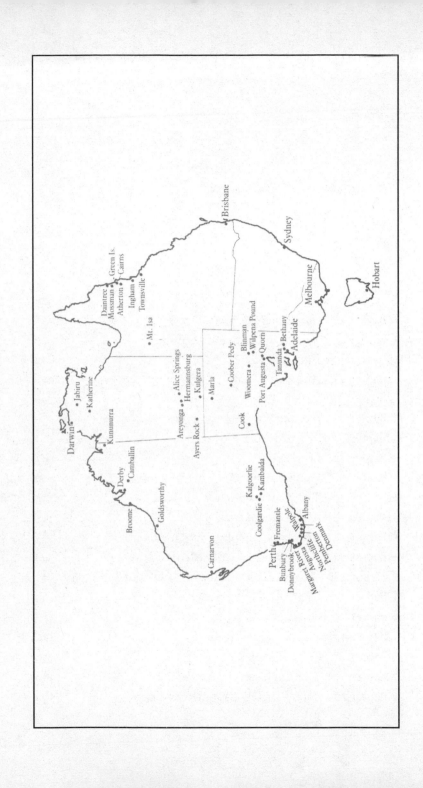

ONE

ON WINGS OF POESY

We knew where we were going. We knew how and even
when we were going. The only thing we weren't entirely sure
about was *why* we were going.

We were loaded down with resolution; what we lacked was
a reason. A publisher's advance could not be called a reason. It
was not elemental enough. And as for this being a double anniversary – twenty-one years exactly since I'd first gone to
Australia, twelve years exactly since my wife had first left it; a
total of thirty-three years almost all of them misspent – well,
that was elemental to excess.

A course between expedience and sentiment somehow
eluded us.

Then we had a stroke of luck. A couple of days before we
were due to leave we ran into the Australian poetess Orianna
Ooi (I have of course slightly changed her name) on the Strand.
We weren't close acquaintances, having only ever met two or
three times before, on each occasion, as chance would have it,
somewhere between Australia House and the Savoy; and we
knew little about her except that she spent the afternoons of her
exile under the chandeliers in the reading room of the Australian

High Commission, combing the literary pages of the Australian newspapers for any mention of her verse. This was the only way, at so great a distance from home, that she could keep abreast with the progress of her reputation. Today, wrapped up extravagantly against the cold – every day had been the coldest day in living memory that winter – she was flushed with excitement: the *Adelaide Advertiser* had just alluded to her dense conceptual invention.

We congratulated her. 'The *Adelaide Advertiser*,' I remarked, 'is not renowned for choosing its words lightly.'

She glowed at us. There might have been snow on the ground, but inside her heart it was suddenly summer. We all three paused to wave to an Australian short-story writer on his way to check what his home newspapers had to say about him.

'He hates it over here,' Orianna confided. 'No one recognizes him. He hasn't signed a single autograph. He has to read about himself in the *Sydney Morning Herald* to remember who he is.'

I must have given some involuntary sigh of sympathy, thinking that very soon now I would be suffering the indignity of anonymity myself, out there in the unheeding heat and dust, because out of the blue Orianna recalled what we'd told her the last time we'd collided on the Strand. 'Aren't you two off any time now?'

'Day after tomorrow.'

'And *you're* going *all* the way round?'

I didn't like the double emphasis. I thought I could hear a request for an exorbitant favour coming; something that would entail our having to look up every Ooi in Australia, or worse, having to search every local outback newspaper for veiled references to this Ooi's effusions. But Rosalin has a less suspicious nature. 'Yes, *all* the way round. Darwin, the Kimberleys, Perth, Kalgoorlie, Alice Springs, the Great Barrier Reef – you name it.'

'Lucky you,' Orianna said, allowing herself just one quick

wintry shiver before she added, 'Look, do you think you could
do me a favour?'

I turned away. I became suddenly engrossed in architectural
niceties I'd never before paid adequate attention to on the Strand;
such as the deeply recessed clerestory fenestration of the building
housing the New South Wales Government, and the ornamentation around the guttering of the Savoy. From the corner of one
eye I could see my poor wife delivering herself of the usual courtesies – 'Certainly . . . Only too delighted . . . If there's any way
we possibly can . . .' – and Orianna rooting around in her hand-
bag. Probably because they are never certain what errand they
are on, whether they are meant to be ladies or bushwhackers,
Australian women carry grotesque handbags. Orianna's was a
sort of sack made from emu feathers and the skin of fruit bat. But
it was what was in it that frightened me. I looked just long
enough to see her produce it – *Jocasta's Jest: Poems of The Domestic
Life* – and to hear her say, 'What I was wondering was whether,
while you're on your travels, you could, you know, pop into
every bookshop you see and check whether they've got stocks of
this.' Then I went back to staring at the Savoy.

When I felt that it was absolutely safe to let my attention
return I discovered that Orianna had gone but that *Jocasta's Jest*
was still with us, in Ros's hand.

'She gave you a copy, then,' I noticed.

There was a degree of hesitation. 'Not exactly.'

'How do you mean, *not exactly*?'

'She didn't exactly *give* it.'

'You're not telling me you nicked it? You didn't mug her for
it, did you?'

I could see that Ros was still thinking over what had occurred.
There seemed to be some uncertainty as to just who had mugged
whom. 'No,' she said at last, 'I appear to have bought it.'

I let it go at that. Since I'd deliberately absented myself I
couldn't really complain about what had happened while I'd

been away. And I'd long ago learnt that there was nothing to gain from being the sort of husband who took attitudes to his wife's purchases. It was only later, when I caught Ros finding space for the poems in her corner of the suitcase, that I raised a query. 'You aren't really, are you?'

'I'm not really what?'

It was too absurd to put into words. I gave one of those backward nods of the head that are meant to suggest previous events in other places – in this case yesterday's encounter on the Strand. 'You know,' I said, adding a forward nod to suggest the next four months and bookshops all over Australia.

Her reply was more prompt than I thought it ought to have been. 'I certainly am,' she said. 'Why shouldn't I? Everybody needs a little project. You've got yours. This is mine.'

'I would have thought we had better things to do out there,' I said.

'Such as?'

She knew she had me there. She knew I'd never been any good when it came to dealing with the big questions. Besides, there was a subtext to this. I'd squandered some of the best years of my life in Sydney and Melbourne in the sixties and early seventies. I'd been back on ghost-laying expeditions several times since, eating too much, drinking too much, fighting with my old friends, and coming home again bemused and disappointed. I was in no position, Ros's question implied, to be talking of 'better things'.

There was another unspoken issue in the room alongside our half-packed cases. Pineapples. I might have adopted Australia but Rosalin had been born there. The last time we'd been back nosing around the ruined sites of our several histories Ros had gone down with a mystery illness which was diagnosed finally as an allergy to her own country. 'It's common,' the doctor told her. 'Many people react badly to where they come from once they've been away. You'll feel better when you leave again.' In the meantime the only comfort available to her in her misery was that afforded by the sight and smell of pineapples. She lay delirious for three weeks in a hotel bed in Manly with a pineapple hanging from each bed post. I sat up through the nights listening to the sharks nibbling at the jetties and waiting for Ros to stir. 'Pineapples,' I had to whisper the moment she opened a bloodshot eye – 'Pineapples, my dear.'

Australia, in other words – even leaving aside what lay curled and ticking in the undergrowth – was a dangerous place for us. Australia contained the past and the past holds more terrors than any jungle. We had to tread carefully. Self-discovery was out. The last thing we wanted to come upon at the end of some five hundred miles of dirt track was ourselves. Any of that and there was a good chance we'd both end up on our backs sniffing pineapples.

Keeping away from our old haunts – the merest whisk around the Eastern cities – would be one way of staying safe. And some simple, selfless project – some course of altruism or utility – would be another.

That's how we came to be flying out of London on the coldest day in recorded history (this detail is important because it explains what we were wearing when we arrived in Darwin on its hottest) with the express purpose of scouring Australia – the Northern Territory, the Western Seaboard, the Goldfields, the Wineries, the Outback, the Rainforests, the Red Centre, the Reef and the ineffable Bush – for copies of Orianna Ooi's latest volume of densely conceptual verse.

From a practical no less than from a poetical point of view, the common or garden flight from London to Sydney or Melbourne via Singapore suffers from the amount of time you are actually in or over Australia before you finally land. You are already sick of the country before you set foot on it. Come in the top way, via Darwin, however, and you arrive as fresh as a daisy and convinced, as you strictly speaking ought to be, that you are still in Asia.

'You sweet?' our steward asked us as we were barely out of Malaysian air-space.

'You sweet?' is Australian stewardese for, 'Is everything absolutely to your requirements, sir?'

We were, I thought, sweet*ish*. 'Perhaps another bottle of Montrose Chardonnay, Mudgee, 1984?' I wondered.

All Australian wines are overeager, impatient to escape the confines of the bottle; but this particular Chardonnay would not sit calmly even in the glass. It sprang to your lips if you so much as nodded to your neighbour. And Trevor was pretty much the same.

He'd been very good with me, spotting me at once as the sort of passenger who appreciated being served in bulk. But he did think it was worth mentioning this time that we would be in Darwin in twenty minutes.

'Twenty minutes?' I couldn't believe it. 'It feels as if we've just left Singapore,' I said.

He shrugged his big broad high effeminate Australian shoulders inside his orange blazer. 'There you are,' he said. He seemed to be letting us in on some well-kept secret as to the real whereabouts of the Top End of Australia.

And there indeed, at a few minutes to four in the morning and with the Chardonnay still fizzing in the bottle, we were. Darwin International Airport. A single shed, as far as we could make out in the dark, constructed of aluminium and corrugated tin. There were no other planes on the runway – assuming this to be a runway that we were on – and the few ground staff we could see stood about rubbing their eyes, as if they wanted us to understand that they'd been dragged out of bed especially for us. Even in the air-conditioned cabin of the jumbo you could smell the damp warm lethargy of the tropics.

'Look,' Ros said, pointing to the open-mouthed passenger

exit being driven slowly in our direction across the steaming tarmac, 'it's coming at us like a wet kiss.'

We experienced the faintest of tremors as the kiss rose and planted itself on the curved body of our craft, then we sat back and waited to be sprayed.

The quarantine officers came aboard yawning. For all the spruceness of their nautical rig – long white socks, navy shorts, short-sleeved white shirts with epaulettes, and deep-sea divers' watches – I wouldn't have wanted to be within a hundred miles of land on any vessel steered by them. And they were bad-tempered as well as half-asleep. They meant to give a hard time of it to a certain Mr Ramsden who was required to proceed to the front of the plane 'with his possessions'.

From the time they took with him I could only suppose he was carrying about his person at least one example of every item you were not allowed to bring into Australia: a snakeskin belt from Venezuela, a woven bamboo basket from Borneo, a rhino horn from Tanzania, the larva of the Abyssinian fruit moth, and signed copies of *Last Exit to Brooklyn* and *Das Kapital*.

Mr Ramsden wasn't our only delay. The quarantine officers refused to walk the length of our plane and back with their cans of deodorizer and disinfectant held aloft until every passenger was in his seat. They drummed on the luggage lockers with their uncontaminated fingers, in order that we should see it was our own time we were wasting, not theirs. They were in no hurry themselves. They'd been tipped out of their warm beds at 3.30 in the morning in order to sanitize us and make us fit for entry and they had nothing else to do now – since planes were few and far between in Darwin – with the entirety of their day. They could wait.

I later learnt that there might have been an element of politics in this show of petulance. Japanese visitors to Australia had been reacting badly to the ritual spraying of their persons, since in their country such an indignity was only ever visited on those whose appearance palpably merited it. Meticulous about their private hygiene they took it ill that they should be presumed to be carrying bugs and bacilli capable of wiping out the entire animal and human population of Australia. An exemption from this hysterical precaution had been requested and, since the first aim of all photogenic countries is to be visited by as many Japanese as possible, the request seemed likely to be granted. Good for the Japanese, good for tourism, but not so good for the self-esteem and future prospects of quarantine officers. It's my belief that they saw the writing on the wall. Soon anyone would be able to breeze into Australia exuding germs and breathing viruses at will. It was unmistakable from the disdain with which they wielded their aerosols at last that they were making us pay for those virulent millions who would one day elude the spray.

Myself, I have to say I think the Japanese response is unimaginative. I love being sprayed. It is a perfect way to begin a journey or a holiday or a new life. It is a physical performance of an emotional requirement – the equivalent of a Turkish bath or a Finnish flagellation, but without the fuss or the pain. A purification. A little symbolical murder of the prior self.

Inside the tin shed that was the terminal they were more concerned with the extermination of the imported fruit fly than the prior self. As we queued to have our passports scrutinized we stood alongside a capacious green bin, gaily decorated with paintings of innocent-seeming apples and oranges and bananas. The bin represented one's last, one's absolutely final, opportunity to get rid of all the apples and oranges and bananas secreted about one's person before they were spotted sticking out of one's pockets by vigilant quarantine and customs men. 'Why risk a fine of $50,000?' the bin asked.

I don't know why I decided to take such an interest in this receptacle. It might have been that the idea of a last-chance fruit depository appealed to something in my theology; or it might just have been inconsequentiality caused by jet-lag or the Montrose Chardonnay. Whatever the reason, I was no sooner through immigration than I wanted to be back out again, where the bin was. I wanted to be sure that I'd got the colour and dimensions right, and that the fine for smuggling in a cherry was indeed $50,000. I knew, of course, that I couldn't really treat immigration as if it were a revolving door; but I didn't think there would be any harm in my standing on tiptoe behind a passport officer's back and jotting down some details in my notebook. It never crossed my mind that such action might look for all the world like espionage – pretty inept and footling espionage (what did they think I was after: the names and birthdays of the passengers I'd flown in with?) but espionage all the same. So I wasn't prepared for the heavy hand that took me suddenly by the shoulder, or the rough inhospitable manner in which I was dispossessed of my notes.

I live in dread of having something taken from me. I am certain that I will fail of the indignation of outraged ownership. I am unable to imagine myself ever calling, 'Stop, thief!' But I did manage, on this occasion, to say, 'Hey, that's my notebook.'

My assailant flicked through it. I think the number of empty pages disconcerted him. That and the total illegibility of the pages that were full. My writing is so bad that it is often taken as shorthand or code.

'What's it for?' he wanted to know. He was red-faced, hot, furious, in that state of apoplexy to which all minor officials reduce themselves when they think they've found a smart-arse. He had a huge belly around which I think I must only have imagined a holster belt and pistol.

But this was holster belt and pistol territory, and holster belt and pistol weather. And I was wearing winter corduroys and Church's shoes.

'I use it to write down my impressions,' I said. I wasn't going to say that I'd had it only one day and that my only impressions so far were of the waste basket and of him.

He took another look in it. I think the idea that people wrote things in notebooks disgusted him.

'Do you know where you are?' he asked me.

'Australia,' I said.

I might have been wrong but I was fairly certain his eyes rolled momentarily with the ecstasy of imagining hitting me. Or of hitting my notebook.

'You're in a customs hall,' he said.

I nodded. We were in a customs hall, all right. And a pretty jumpy one at that. At the far end of the room I could see Ros waiting for our luggage to appear through the hole in the wall. But nearly all those who had their cases were being made to open them. No one was above suspicion in Darwin. One customs official was going through every item of folded under-wear in a bearded teenager's holdall, feeling along the elastic with expert fingers, even checking the hems of his vests for unwonted nodules. It wasn't just apples and bananas they were jittery about in the Territory.

The neuropath who'd collared me drew my attention to a sign high up on the wall above us. It said, CUSTOMS HALL – NO PHOTOGRAPHY.

'D'you see that?'

I said I did.

Our eyes met for an instant. His were a lost, dreamy Australian blue. Then he handed me back my notebook. 'No photography means no writing either,' he said.

I didn't argue. I was in a foreign country. It wasn't for me to go around explaining to the natives what no photography meant.

I went over to where Ros was still waiting for our cases. I ought to have noticed that she was the last one there but I was too full of my own exhilaration. 'This is brilliant,' I said. 'It's a dream start. I've just very nearly had my notebook confiscated.'

'Why is that good?'

'Material,' I said. 'Material. We no sooner land than we're in the shit. It's perfect.'

'In that case you're having an even better start than you realized. They've lost our luggage.'

Remember my mentioning that we'd left London on the coldest day in recorded history? Well, we'd boarded the plane dressed accordingly. Seasoned transcontinental travellers know that that's not how you do it. You are supposed to so juggle your wardrobe that you leave in clothes appropriate to the one climate and arrive in whatever is appropriate to the other. I knew all that myself, but I was keen to circumvent the weight restrictions on our baggage by packing everything that was light and wearing everything that was heavy. 'We might be a trifle uncomfortable on the plane,' I'd said, 'but we can change the minute we hit Darwin.' I still don't think there was anything wrong with my reasoning. I wasn't to know that the airline would misread our labels and confuse Darwin with Java.

We were directed to a lost property and general mishap and balls-up clerk whose offices were located around the side of the sweltering tin terminus. In order to get to him we had to pass empty-handed through customs and out into the night. Already the airport was deserted, all our fellow passengers having been whisked away in their lightweight floral shirts by waiting friends or taxis. Only a few officials remained, looking at their watches and wanting to close before the sun came up.

'No worries,' the clerk said as he filled in 'don't knows' to such questions as, 'Place and date of manufacture of missing suitcase.'

'Big, blue, and heavy,' was the best description I could give him.

He nodded absently and a trifle sceptically, as if he'd heard big, blue and heavy a few too many times before. He was a young, ferrety fellow chosen for his easy charm and lack of sympathy for the sufferings of others. He possessed that twinkling callousness which passes in Australia for calm.

'So you reckon there's a fair chance it will turn up?' I asked him.

'Ah yeah. Should do.'

'Soon?'

'Aw – eventually.'

I had a vague sense that I ought to be demanding firmer assurances, but I was unable to take a harsh tone with him. It wasn't his fault that it was 105 degrees in the dead of night, that the humidity was 100 per cent, and that my wife and I had nothing to wear but the arctic woollens and thermal underwear we stood up in.

I thanked him for his help. He seemed already to have forgotten who we were and what our problem was. But he remembered his manners. 'No worries,' he said.

The people in the Qantas office, to which I repaired in great discomfort later that day, were more forthcoming. Our baggage had not yet been located but they were sure it soon would be. That's provided it hadn't been taken off the plane at Bahrain. (I didn't ask what my chances were if that had happened – there was something about the way they coughed up the word Bahrain that filled me with foreboding.) In the meantime they could offer us twenty-five dollars per person per day to purchase more appropriate apparel. They would, of course, require receipts, and I was to understand that the twenty-five dollars was payable only for each *complete* day the luggage remained missing – thus, if a bag went astray at noon on Monday and was recovered at 11.59 on Tuesday, no pro tem compensation could be expected.

'Just find the case,' I said.

I didn't have time to hang around. Ros was in the hotel – in the shower to be precise – waiting for me to bring back as

much in the way of talcs and cleansers and personal dehumidi-
fiers as I could carry. She had gone into the shower the minute
we'd arrived from the airport and she had remained there, with
only the odd break for sleep, ever since. As she had no intention of coming out until her clothes were found, I had also to
bring her back cans of cold drink, snacks, newspapers, and
descriptions of where we were. Our hotel enjoyed a good view
across The Esplanade to Beagle Gulf but offered no clue as to
the torrid nature of the town itself.

I was disappointed to find the pharmacies in Darwin every
bit as overstocked and glossy as those I was used to in Sydney
and Melbourne. The profession of pharmacist is a highly
glamorous one in Australia and their shops invariably reflect
this prestige. Beautiful women in white coats accost you the
moment you enter, beg to be of assistance and escort you
lingeringly around *parfumerie* or oral hygiene. Going to the
chemist in Australia can be more exciting than going to a
nightclub in Wales. But I had expected something more
indigenous in Darwin. I would have preferred it, frankly, if
they'd laughed in my face when I'd asked for non-contact
roll-on unperfumed anti-perspirant, and recommended spittle
of spayed goanna, instead of showing me a range of over thirty
pretty pots and packages.

And I would have liked it more had there been some distinctive tropical boulevard or bazaar to shop at instead of one of
those tarted-up outdoor arcades that Australians like to refer to
these days as a mall. In the coming months we would see malls
going up (or gone up) all over Australia, many of them in the
most unlikely or undesirable places of business. They were to
become symbols for us of careless and contemptuous free-
wheeling capitalism, the expressions – those in Queensland
especially – of local political insolence, of vandalism initiated at
the very highest level. But at least in Darwin's case it wasn't a
State Premier or Chief Minister who had flattened the old town

to put a mall through; Cyclone Tracy, with an effectiveness that must have made Sir Joh Bjelke-Petersen go green with envy, did that in one single night of spectacular devastation on Christmas Eve, 1974. Thereafter Darwin had become a government town. And that was what I most disliked about Smith Street Mall – for all its attempts to be territorially harmonious, for all its cool enclosures and burgeoning tropical greenery, it felt like the sort of place that public servants from anywhere preferred to shop in. Its dinkiness and petty bourgeois homogeneity seemed specifically designed to lay to rest Darwin's reputation for disorderliness. ('The town is in the hands of Communists!' W. M. Nairn, the Member for Perth, had proclaimed in 1931, after 'Snowy' Mahoney had waved the red flag.) It was a wilful refutation of the town's wild character.

But it hadn't worked. You could give blood (the respectable way) in Smith Street Mall; you could buy flags for charity and every known make of French perfume for your wife; you could sign up to sponsor an African orphan or have your name sealed in a time capsule, for all the world as if you were in a precinct in Cheltenham or Tunbridge Wells. But still the desperadoes were there, men with Robinson Crusoe haircuts and unkempt explorers' beards, wearing solitary silver earrings, horrific scars and menacing tattoos. I'd read about the good old days when Darwin prided itself on being a haven for fugitives from the civil laws or the domestic decencies, and I was pleased to see that, despite the numbers of schoolteachers and welfare workers who had taken the town over, an atmosphere of truancy still prevailed. I saw men in Smith Street Mall who had just crawled in across the desert on their bellies. At one outdoor table, fitted up by the town planners to double as a chess board, half a dozen murderers and rapists sat drinking iced chocolate milk, discussing the merits of the Sicilian defence, and whistling at the girls. One girl, in a cut-away blue singlet and with a skull and crossbones tattooed across her neck, whistled back through broken teeth. There was no doubt in my mind that she'd jumped ship the day before in the Malay Archipelago and swum ashore that morning.

But it was the Aborigines whose presence most defied whatever plans for gentrification the civic architects had dreamed up. They used the Mall as a sort of grand adventure playground. Sociable by instinct and rendered idle by design, they lolled about, sometimes badly drunk but mainly engaging in half-hearted and self-conscious mischief – calling out, laughing, pushing one another, like the street urchins they'd become. You had to be blind not to see at once that purposelessness and inactivity was their problem, not the bottle; and that drink for them was simply the assuagement it always is wherever hope has been extinguished.

Not that I was prepared as yet to face up to the issue of the Aborigines. I would need help with that one. Ros was the guilty Australian, not me. We would confront the race thing together. But just to be going on with I noted that for all their rowdiness they were not threatening. In so far as a Jew can manage not to be frightened by black men, I wasn't frightened by these.

I decided not to wait for my case to turn up but to buy myself at least some thongs and shorts as a temporary measure. A Chinese shop assistant reckoned that I'd look good in pink, so I took his word for it. I was now loaded up with parcels containing abirritants and fungicides and cold drinks and my winter clothes, but I still enjoyed the walk back to the hotel. I loved the sensation I experienced whenever I returned to Australia of being re-acquainted with old and long-forgotten parts of myself – the small of my back, the spaces between my toes, the bristles of my beard, my own perspiration. Your body is simply up to more in Australia, and you are more your body. You drip therefore you are.

I stopped off on the way to buy newspapers. I had no trouble with the *Territorian* but I was naive enough to offer forty cents for a forty cents *Australian*.

'Not up here, mate,' I was told. 'That paper's come three thousand miles and will cost you a dollar eighty.'

I shelled out willingly. I liked the idea of a newspaper as a precious commodity. It made me feel a long way from the usual comforts and amenities. Which was a sensation that Darwin could dismayingly rob you of at any moment. As for example when I read in a shop window that Max Bygraves was in town that night, to open the Darwin Performing Arts Centre at the new five-star Beaufort International Hotel.

I found Ros out of the shower and on the balcony. We stayed there for several hours watching the sun go down over Beagle Bay. The sky flared for a while into a garish adventure novelist's red before shading off into softer romantic Mills and Boon pinks and purples. Then the moon rose like an Arabian Nights scimitar.

We slipped down to the restaurant below and ate buffalo steaks conspicuously. By which I mean that we were conspicuous by virtue of how much we wore – I like to think that we made every effort to compensate for this by eating like normal people. But there is no escaping the attentions of Australians, who are shameless starers at any time. The heaving expectancy under which the whole nation labours means that it is perpetually on the look-out for whoever might come to make it all better, or alternatively whoever might come to take it all away. Messiahs or Antichrists. I don't think we fitted into either category. We just looked bizarre. It is a humiliating experience to be found risible by the worst-dressed people in the world. A girl in a rainbow-coloured tinsel frock almost choked on her pavlova when we came into the restaurant; a fat man in a lemon safari suit laughed off all his buttons. And on top of that the buffalo was no good. Buffalo are a problem in the Top End of the Northern Territory. Brought in by European settlers in the 1830s and subsequently abandoned, they now wander free, damaging vegetation, upsetting water systems, polluting billabongs, rubbing out Aboriginal cave paintings, and disappointing the palate. The toughness of the steak is the snag; unless you pulverize or teriyaki it (in which case you might as well not be cooking with buffalo in the first place), it is likely to turn out tasting like your own footwear, in this instance a heavy winter Church's shoe.

By the time we were back in our room the free electrical entertainment had started. In a cold climate most things that can be called weather happen over your head; in the tropics they take place before you as on a screen. We carried our chairs out on to the balcony to watch. As ever, the Gods proved that their strong suit is not morality but set design. They lit up the sky. They rolled clouds. They sent as many as five lightning strikes at a time sizzling into the sea. Sometimes you could even smell the waters scorching.

I thought it might be worth ringing the airport before bed to see if they had any word of our case. But while I was waiting for someone to answer I came upon a dire warning in the telephone directory. The telephone, it appeared, was highly dangerous in Darwin. During thunderstorms it was a sure-fire source of electric or acoustic shock. *Acoustic* shock? Did that mean it could send your hearing into trauma? 'Use your telephone only for calls of the utmost urgency,' the book warned. 'Keep calls brief. Stay clear of electrical appliances such as stoves, air conditioners, refrigerators and window frames.' I was impressed by the inclusion of window frames in that list. In more temperate countries window frames are not normally considered to be electrical appliances. Then I realized that I had my back to one. And that my right elbow was leaning against the air conditioner. And that the phone itself was sitting on the refrigerator. I dropped the receiver in a panic. I had been brought up to regard the telephone as an instrument of safety. It was what got you out of trouble. Now, suddenly, nothing could be relied upon to help you through. It felt pretty wild out there.

In despite of all my warnings that it was bound to be at least twenty times more lethal than the telephone, Ros insisted on listening to the radio before she went to sleep. I sat cross-legged on the carpet in the middle of the room, making sure that I was in no contact with anything that could be called an appliance. She picked up one of those late-night local call-in programmes in which members of the public are encouraged to disgorge the miseries of their lives in the hearing of complete strangers. (Thereby causing what *I* call acoustic shock.) A man named Greg was describing what it was like being married to a full-blooded Aboriginal woman who beat him up the minute alcohol touched her lips. He was far gone in drink himself – hurt and stupefied and confidential.

'Mate, she's a beautiful person when she's sober,' he explained.

The compère, or whatever you call the harpy who hosts this kind of show, spoke what I can only describe as Wolverhampton Australian. The usual resilient twang had somehow got caught too high in the nasal passages and his words fell in a monotonous emulsoid drip. His morality was gelatinous also. 'Understanding can work wonders, mate,' he said.

'I know that,' Greg said. 'She's a wonderful woman. A full blood. And then she changes. It's terrible. It's good of you to listen to me, mate.'

'I can hear it's helping you to talk about it, mate.'

'That's why I rang you, mate.'

What I could hear were tears and alcohol and confused desire. I'd read about 'Comboism' – the cohabitation of white men and Aboriginal women – in Alfred Searcy's *In Australian Tropics*, published in 1909. And in his account it was all perfectly matter-of-fact:

Nearly all the drovers, cattlemen, and station hands had their black boys (gins) . . . .

These women are invaluable to the white cattlemen, for, besides the companionship, they become splendid horsewomen, and good with cattle. They are useful to find water, settle the camp, boil the billy, and track and bring in the horses in the mornings. In fact, it is impossible to enumerate the advantages of having a good gin 'outback'.

But Greg didn't sound as though he was in it for help with the horses. Listening to him holding back his sobs I thought of Shakespeare's Egypt and Nilus's slime – torpor and crocodiles and the colour of Cleopatra's skin.

'I don't know how it'll finish up,' he went on. 'I don't know. I love her, you see, mate. But I have to ask myself who it is that I love. She's a different woman, mate, a different woman the minute she touches a drop . . .'

'And then apologizes later?'

'That's right, mate. That's right. She promises she'll never do it again. But how long can I . . . ?'

'Well, thanks for talking to us, mate. And don't forget what I said about a little understanding.'

Whatever phlegmy noises were coming from the studio, out there in the darkest reaches of Darwin, life sounded feverish. I smelled blood and bone – the rich, rancid tropical heat of people living at the edges of their sanity.

But the last thought I had before sleep related to Max Bygraves. I wondered how his concert in the new Performing Arts Centre had gone down. And whether he'd had much success getting his audience to join him in a cockney singalong.

TWO

SHIKLONE TROICEE AND AFTER

It is a feature of Darwin plumbing that you can never be certain whether you've turned on the cold tap or the hot, so little difference in temperature is there between what comes out of either. Many was the time, in the week or so we were there, that we scalded ourselves in a shower of cold water.

I discovered the reason for this as we were driving down the Stuart Highway in the company of Tom Winter three days after our arrival. It turned out to be something else to blame the Japanese for. Incensed, as early as 1942, by the persistent refusal of Australian governments to let them in without spraying them, the Japanese – a mite overhasty as always – responded by bombing the bejesus out of Darwin. The Top End of Australia has long been considered the nation's Achilles heel. If the yeller fellers were to get in anywhere they'd get in there. And the temptation just to let them have it must have been very strong. Even in peace time Australians have been trying to get rid of the North. In 1888 a certain Mr J. C. F. Johnson, the Minister for Education and the Northern Territory in the Playford Administration, took one quick look at what he was Minister of and returned proposing that the South Australian boundary be moved north of the MacDonnell Ranges and that what was left be handed back, without any ado, to Britain. But when it comes to possessions countries are as irrational as people: that which they are prepared to give freely they will fight tenaciously to safeguard from plunder. Instead of pulling the few troops who were in Darwin down, the government sent additional troops up. And Darwin being hot and dry, and troops being sweaty and thirsty, the first necessity was water. A new pipe line had to be laid at speed, allowing no time for fancy engineering. So it was built above the ground instead of under it. And there it still stands – an amenity to this day – travelling parallel to the highway and bubbling under the sun.

We were travelling likewise as part of a small group headed towards Kakadu National Park, situated in Arnhem Land – just about – between the Wildman and East Alligator Rivers. We'd heard that Tom Winter was the best man to be taken out by in the Top End, and we had contacted him the moment our luggage was found. (It showed up, by the way, exactly five minutes short of our second twenty-five dollars per person payout, just as in the illustration of our entitlements that the nice people at Qantas had given me. It had, of course, been gone through in some detail by customs. I knew that because everything that had been folded neatly in Ros's corner of the case was now folded neatly in mine. And that included Orianna Ooi's poems. There were clear signs – creased pages, thumbmarks, textual emendations and so on – that her verse had been subject to careful scrutiny.)

The reason we were off to Kakadu for a day trip instead of on one of Tom Winters' more far-flung and extensive safaris was my determination not to stray too far from civilization, at least at this early stage, and not to lie too close to the ground. 'I know it would be fun to live with some Aborigines for a fortnight and to hunt snakes and eat lizards with them,' I said to Ros, 'but we've a long journey ahead of us and there are a lot of other things we have to do.' I wanted it to be understood that I wasn't against eating lizards in principle but that I simply felt it had to take its proper place in the order of priorities. None the less, this was the beginning of some serious disagreement between us as to the nature of travel and curiosity in general and our journey and my nice recusancy in particular. Of which I will have more to say later.

Tom had picked us up from our hotel at about six-thirty in the morning. By seven the little party was complete and well acquainted.

'Hi, I'm Karen,' said Karen from Toronto.

'And we're Carl and Hazel – that's to say he's Carl and I'm Hazel,' laughed Hazel from Washington. It seemed important to Hazel that she should let us all know as soon as possible that she was daffy. It's sweet in Americans, the way they think you need telling.

The other four were June and Brian, and Marion and John, from West Australia. John sold Mitsubishis in Perth and wore a T-shirt that showed four pink palm trees swaying in the wind. Brian told us what he did but because of the strong Scottish accent which still persisted beneath his Australian one it was almost impossible to understand a word he said. It didn't matter. I was so amazed by Brian's similarity to Bob Hawke – and I'm not just referring now to the incomprehensibility – that I wouldn't have been able to hear him anyway. He had the same oiled and weathered sheen, the same deep gouges in his cheeks – like axe marks on an iron visor – and he too seemed not to have brushed his hair but burnished it. The resemblance was so striking that there were moments on the journey when I allowed myself to entertain the wildest of traveller's fantasies.

But I'm pretty sure Brian wasn't Bob Hawke. His sentences were too short for one thing. And he didn't wince when Tom spoke slightingly of the public service domination of Darwin, nor when he resorted to the ultimate Australian insult of comparing it with the nation's capital. 'It might just as well be Canberra. We've only got a thirty-five per cent private sector – that's why I'm so bloody thin.'

Karen was curious to know if public servants came willingly to Darwin and how, if they weren't natives, they coped with the excesses of the climate.

Tom laughed, remembering the days when government men were drafted to Darwin as a punishment. 'If you refused, you got the sack. And, if you stayed, you committed suicide. November and December used to be called the suicide months. The heat and the humidity could prove too much for you if you already didn't want to be here. Which brings me to the Irishman who was taken to Darwin Hospital with forty-nine bruises on his head – he tried to hang himself with an elastic band.'

'I don't get that,' Hazel said.

Tom was not a Top Ender by birth. Few were. He had been up here since the early seventies. He recalled how the town was just installing its first traffic lights when he arrived. 'They'd never seen or heard of such things. They wouldn't stop for a light if it was red, white or purple. The authorities scratched their heads and then came up with the idea of putting an advertisement in the paper, patiently explaining that red meant stop, amber meant prepare to stop, and green meant go as you were going. We were given a ten-day armistice to get used to them, and during that time anyone caught driving through a red light by the police would not be prosecuted. He'd just have it all explained to him again. But even after the ten days no one was taking any notice. You saw a red light and you accelerated. So another advertisement appeared. It said, "Look, these are not bloody Christmas decorations. If you don't do what the buggers tell you you'll be booked!"'

We didn't believe him.

'It's true. I kept both those ads, but they were destroyed by the cyclone.'

By this time we were approaching Humpty Doo (Aboriginal for Nowhere), scene of a notorious rice-growing fiasco. The details of the failure of the project are told and retold with such relish by Australians that you can only suppose the Humpty Dooers were Englishmen. Essentially it is the story of the endless resourcefulness and adaptability of the local magpie geese. Nothing could keep them away from the rice crop, not even scare guns. 'In the end the geese got so used to those guns,' Tom told us, 'that they would fly on to them and peer down the barrels.'

Australians take great pride in the cunning of their native wildlife, particularly when there's some poor Pom on the other end of it.

Tom slowed down his bus and showed us the famous Humpty Doo pub. In the good old days – that's to say the 1970s – the ringers would wander into this pub caked with blood from cutting up buffalo, unwashed for up to ten days on account of the shortage of water, and in need of a drink. They would be only too pleased to engage your company at the bar provided you didn't 'look at them funny'. 'There were only two reasons for going to Humpty Doo in those days,' Tom remembered, 'getting pissed or having a good fight.'

'What's a ringer?' Hazel asked.

Brian helped out. 'Ay's a steckmon or a droovah.'

'Now,' Tom said, 'it's just a domesticated family pub. You can take the kids there on a Sunday.'

He made one ashamed of one's times.

A short way out of Humpty Doo we paused at a well-worn spot for viewing the Cathedral Termite Mounds. We'd seen ant hills in plenty on either side of the road for miles, but these were on a grander scale. Ten-foot-high cellulose shrines with campaniles and flying buttresses and now votaries, they stood witness to the unsurpassed architectural genius of the termites, creatures who could combine navvying with gourmandising, taking in the necessary from one end and passing it out as building material through the other. I wasn't especially impressed myself. I go vacant before the miracle of ants. I find all that stuff about queens and artisans and soldiers hard to take. Perfected social arrangements, especially in the very small, are inimical to all my belief systems. So I didn't fully register everything Tom was saying about the air-conditioning and waste disposal units the termites had installed in their cathedrals. Instead I preferred to look at Tom.

The contradictions in his person fascinated me. He was lean, not tall, but fit. He wore a khaki shirt, embroidered with his name and tour company, over brown walking shorts. A small leather pouch, shaped as if to take a knife, hung at his waist. He didn't favour the knee-length legwear normally worn by territorians going about their business but little ankle socks, white with a couple of nifty pink stripes in them. And these only just protruded from those Australian walking shoes with a tab at the back that I used to know (and love) as Chelsea boots. He was bush-ready in other words, and yet at the same time peacocky. There was a pampered quiff in his hair. He had elegantly shaped and just greying sideburns. And a curly, almost frilly profile, with a small, possibly difficult mouth. A gold chain – the kind sportsmen wear – hung around his neck. And although he told the time off a heavy masculine chronometer, strapped like a weapon to his wrist, he wore two delicate gold rings, one of them with a little roseate stone in it, on the same hand.

Back on the bus he continued to identify wildlife for us, reversing expeditiously if any one of us thought we'd spotted something, getting angry with himself if he confused an eagle with a whistling kite at a distance of five hundred yards, and screeching to a halt whenever some racehorse goanna – the kind of tucker Ros had it in mind for me to learn to spear – went galumphing across the road.

We were now out on the Arnhem Highway, in an area known as the Marrakai Plains. It was wonderful country – spear grass and pandanus palms and water flats. I was surprised to discover in myself a strong attraction to the wet tropical landscape. Fields of daffodils had always left me dead, but a field of wild water lilies – a sudden temporary flotation of impossibly fragile colour – was an irresistible sight. A hundred magpie geese, twisting their necks like periscopes, and our first glimpse of a brolga, hesitant and retiring, uncertain whether we were worthy to watch her mythical dance, confirmed my new passion. Hereafter I was a waterfowl and wetlands man, a floodplains freak, a sucker for storks and swamps. The symbolism is too obvious even to examine. I cannot speak for anybody else, nor do I wish to plunge into the politics of whether women were ever fish, but I can no longer have any doubts in which element I originated.

We stopped for morning tea at the Bark Hut Inn, from which Tom warned us to expect little in the way of service or politeness. We ate toasted ham sandwiches and wandered out into the back gardens where there was a little wire enclosure containing a pair of scraggy emus and a disturbed male wallaroo. As Aborigines do not scruple to observe in their rock paintings, the genitalia of the whole kangaroo family can be of a prodigious size. But this chap was a prodigy among prodigies. He hobbled towards us and extended his penis. I don't know whether he took us for dressed up wallaroos or had simply been forced by the special circumstances of his physique to disregard the niceties of species. Whatever his thinking he put on quite a show for us, fucking the fence, fucking the earth, fucking the grass, and all the while foaming at the nostrils. We weren't too appalled. There seemed to be a specifically Australian fertility about the place. We were to return here for ten minutes on our way back to Darwin. Two dogs would be copulating outside the toilets. And in the main lounge a group of young men, awash with beer and crazed with loneliness, would be foaming at the mouth.

Before we arrived at Nourlangie Rock, to inspect the galleries repainted by the artist Najombolmi, otherwise known to Europeans as Barramundi Charlie, Tom had a few things he wanted to tell us about Aborigines.

'A lot of people say the Aborigine is not a farmer. This is bullshit. The Aborigine farms nature as nature should be farmed. He killed only for what he needed. If he had to take a kangaroo he took the old one. The young were the guarantee of the future. The Aborigine understood regeneration. He never stripped trees bare out of gluttony or greed. He took what was necessary for his immediate survival – no more. And he knew the fluctuations of the seasons. For the Europeans there are only two seasons in the Top End, the Wet and the Dry. The Aborigines recognized six. *Bang-Gerang* – the knock 'em down season. *Yegge. Gunaggarriwulge* – the fire-lighting. *Wurrgeng. Gunumeleng.* How many's that? Oh, yeah, *Gudjewg* – the monsoons. So don't tell me the Aborigine was a dill.'

Any university ecologist or safe city green might have said this, of course, miles from where it mattered or would be likely to be contradicted. But Tom tended his little clearing of reason in the very thick of negrophobia. The people who told him the Aborigines were dills – and that would have been the kindest thing they called them – were his own neighbours, maybe his own friends. He might have been doing his best by his passengers, giving them a good day out, but that was dialogue he was conducting at the wheel of his bus.

'What's a dill?' Hazel asked.

'Ahdollsahfool,' Brian explained.

'Once he's in the country,' Tom went on, 'once he's out here, the Aborigine's a beautiful person.' (I remember wincing at 'beautiful person'; I don't mind it now. You have to take it in the context of all the northern ranting about coons.) 'It's in the town, when he's drunk, that I've no time for him. But I've no time for the white man when he's drunk either.'

The foursome from Perth, John and Marion and June and Brian, wished to concur in this. Yes, yes, indubitably, out here, in the wild as it were, the Aborigines were 'fine people'. But they were just out for trouble and hand-outs in Perth. The half-caste educated ones were the worst. Trying to cash in on land rights and what have you. They would even come up here sometimes, just to stir it.

'If they're given a house they ruin it,' John explained to me. 'They're instantly joined by fifty of their relations from miles around.'

'They're in limbo,' Marion said.

'They won't work,' John said.

But June remembered that there was one who was nice who appeared in town on Saturday mornings and performed bird imitations on his didgeridoo.

Brian's eyes lit up. I suddenly realized that he was about to set his incomprehensibility its most ambitious project yet: *he* was going to render with his voice what the nice Perth-based Aborigine performed on his didgeridoo. The meagre letters of the English alphabet cannot hope to survive a contest between Aboriginal, Scottish, and Australian birdsong, but roughly the noise Brian made was, 'Cay – caw – cooachawahjibli.'

We all sat and ruminated after that until the bus pulled up within a short walk of Nourlangie Rock. On the subject of the spirit-galleries and the rock paintings I intend to remain silent, I don't trust myself on primitivism – the art or the religion – and I am content to leave a proper appreciation of the local creation myth (involving the passage of a couple of giant white-shouldered rock wallabies, cutting crevices as they went) to those whose imaginations swell to such tales. But Nourlangie Rock itself was grand and red and menacing, a wild outcrop of sandstone, and if you must invest a place with spirit this was as good a one to invest in as any. It looked old and ominous – altogether the superior, as a site ministering to superstition, of, say, St Paul's Cathedral or Stonehenge.

And Tom was the best of guides. He discussed the legends, peremptorily dismissed Von Däniken (Kakadu was Dutch spaceman country), and talked to us, as we looked out over the plains to the distant reddening escarpment, about the cruel female circumcision ceremonies of the Aborigines on whose sacred ground we stood. These ceremonies were so brutal and decisive that they once and for all removed the better part of sensation from sexual activity, thereby serving as an efficient if somewhat supererogatory form of family planning. The first white missionaries dissuaded the Aborigines from these barbaric practices whereupon pleasure returned to sex as suddenly and sweetly as a poignant memory. The immediate effect of which, according to Tom, being that the lubras wandered off to follow the white man, leaving the local tribes to fall into atrophy. For him this was just one more instance of the fatal consequences of white interference. He told the story elegiacally, as though it were a modern Garden of Eden myth. 'The white man thought the Aborigine was ignorant,' Tom said. 'But he wasn't.'

On the way down from the rock Brian collared me. 'Trairgic,' he said. 'Ah kees av ahbsahlootlah trairgic mossoondahstahndon.'

We ate lunch in the open-air bar of the Cooinda Hotel/ Motel, an establishment owned by Aborigines but run on a lease, for the time being, by whites. We sat in what was virtually a clearing in the jungle, enjoying the warm afternoon. Underneath a marvellously drooping pandanus palm a group of Aboriginal youths played pool – paradisal pool – using their unchalked cues to shoo away the giant insects which landed, in a spirit of pure and indolent curiosity, on the baize.

I'd noticed that Tom seemed to know everyone here, and I asked him if he was accepted as a friend. He was leaning back in his chair, wholly relaxed, his legs extended, the sun catching the gold chain around his neck. He looked a cross between a buccaneer, an anthropologist, and a male model.

'I've been coming here for about fifteen years,' he said. 'Two or three times a week when I can get through. And I think they are just beginning to trust me. But you have to take it very slowly. They are very patient people, but if you let them down they never forgive you. One mistake and that's that. They can be very unforgiving, even amongst themselves. Don't forget that they used ostracization as a weapon, as a punishment. To be excluded from the safety of the tribe meant that you were without food and water. In three days you'd be dead. Then the white man came along and the ostracized Aborigine would go to him for help, ending up in a kind of limbo, depending on a white society he didn't like, and abandoned by his own. Many found themselves in limbo this way. Many still do. It's just one more way in which the whites altered the balance of black-fellers' justice.'

There was nothing unfamiliar about the idea of social exclusion as punishment – incarceration is just another version of the same. But I saw it as having a peculiarly potent significance for Australia, where even today whites view non-acceptance by the pack with terror. What more melancholy sight is there, in this vast sad country, than a solitary drinker? Listening to Tom, I was struck, as I was to go on being struck, by how many of the deepest anxieties of black culture had seeped silently into the white.

We were interrupted by Hazel. She'd mistaken puddles for goannas and branches for snakes ever since we'd left Darwin. Now she had spotted something lethal high up in the tree above her. 'Oh my, what's that?' she called out.

We all looked. 'That? That's a leaf,' Tom said.

Because the Wet had been rather modest this season the boat which was to take us for a cruise on the Yellow Water Billabong couldn't make it to the jetty. So we had to trudge through boiling amber water, dodging leeches and recalling Katherine Hepburn and Humphrey Bogart, to get to it. I was pleased to see, since one of the purposes of the cruise was to look for crocodiles, that the boat was built of steel. Once aboard we were joined by a party from another tour, amongst whom I recognized a woman who had been on our plane from Bahrain. She had made some impression on us on that occasion because of her jet black Cleopatra wig and lace mantilla, her ability to converse in loud American with one child and even louder Arabic with another, and because she wore a Turkish belly dancer's costume. 'Looks just like Barbra Streisand,' our steward, Trevor, had observed appreciatively. Today she still wore the wig and the mantilla, but had swapped the belly dancer's costume for harem-style Scheherezade pyjamas, worn over tights and, if I read the perfect brittle cones upon her chest correctly, falsies. It wasn't all that long since Ros and I had been a touch overdressed for the tropics ourselves, so we were assiduously uncritical, but there were others aboard whose enjoyment of the wilds of the Yellow Water Billabong was spoiled by this potent reminder of Baghdad and Bloomingdales.

It looked as though we were going to be out of luck as far as spotting crocodiles was concerned. Thirty-five species of waders have been recorded on the wetlands and I think we saw them all. Another brolga refused to do her dance for us. Several magpie geese came to check us out to see if we might be thinking of starting up a rice farm. And every now and then the amazing Jesus bird walked alongside us, on the water. But no sign of any crocs.

I was so satisfied myself of there being no such creatures in these shallows, despite the warnings everywhere, that I idly hung my hand over the side of the slow-moving boat. Then suddenly I felt Ros, next to me, relax. She had been rigid for the last fifteen minutes, not through fear but — and it pains me to say this – through competition. There's no fathoming the universal competitiveness of women. Ever since we had set forth upon the yellow waters of the billabong in search of crocodile, every single woman on the boat – most notably, of course, the Princess Scheherezade – had privately determined to be the first to find one. Even Hazel, starting at each passing twig, was seriously engaged in the subterranean struggle. Ros's sudden relaxation was an expression of pure triumph. 'Over there,' she hardly bothered to raise her voice to say, 'just there – there – about a yard from the bank.'

And there indeed one was, a pair of sleepy malevolent eyes, a long thin bobbled snout, the body suspended in the water in a horrible pretence of weightlessness.

Just as with lovers, your first croc isn't necessarily your best. This one took a slow, languorous look at our steel hull and submerged himself. There was no point waiting. He could stay down longer than we could stay awake. But we would see dozens more before we were through with the north of Australia. We would meet Humpy, who wrestled with them for fun. And we would stand upon the very jetty from which a Queensland girl had tumbled backwards, glass in hand, into a pair of waiting jaws – only her fingernails found in the eighteen-footer's belly when it was shot and gutted after an orgy of vengeance.

Before we started back for Darwin Tom took us on a quick bus tour around Jabiru, service town for the nearby uranium mines. Jabiru is a closed town. You are not permitted casually to spend the night at Jabiru unless you register as a relation of a mine employee and guarantee to stay with him. The official justification for these restrictions is that Jabiru stands on Aboriginal tribal lands, but of course the Mining Companies have reasons of their own for not minding that they're applied.

It looked a dead, ratshit, corporate place, with secrets. Just like other closed and half-closed mining towns we would see.

Funny how malevolent purposes will out in the architecture. Jabiru had clean, deserted streets and shopping precincts, and rows of neat, samey houses which were let out to employees for peanuts. It was the manicured desolation that told you all you needed to know. Had it turned out that sophisticated biological weapons were being manufactured here I wouldn't have been surprised.

As we drove through, Tom told us the story of how the tribal elders had granted a lease to the mining companies on the understanding that they would employ available local Aboriginal labour. This was agreed, but the Aborigines kept their own hours, took rests at times which seemed appropriate to them, and sometimes didn't turn up for work at all. Another agreement was therefore hammered out whereby the mining companies could employ whoever they wanted in return for granting the responsibility for all the town's social services and civic amenities to the Aborigines. No sooner was this ratified by all parties than the elders placed an advertisement in Darwin offering the Jabiru social services and amenities to European tender. 'So who says the Aborigines are simple?' Tom asked.

I wondered how strong local feeling was these days on the question of uranium mining.

Tom didn't hesitate. 'We want it,' he said. 'We all want it. Look, we've already made enough weapons to destroy ourselves a thousand times over. A bit more uranium isn't going to make any difference. The Canadians are at it, and very soon the Chinese will be. They've got more of it, in a purer form, than anyone.'

'And the Aborigines?'

'They want it. They want the revenue. It's only because they're not getting the revenue on the mines the Commonwealth won't allow to operate that they've agreed to the opening up of Kakadu. They prefer mines to tourism, given the choice. Tourism means big mobs of people.'

It wasn't my intention to be provocative but I did want to say that according to all accounts most of the revenue that was meant to go to the Aborigines ended up in the hands of white lawyers and administrators.

'Yes, yes it does. But they'll work it out. It'll take time but the money will get to them. In sixty years they'll be the oil sheikhs of Australia. They'll be rich enough to buy the country back.'

I could see, in the reflection of his driving mirror, how much the idea pleased him, how far it appealed to his sense of symmetry and justice. I hadn't yet learnt how rare it was, in the North, for a white man to accept the idea of an Aborigine having the wherewithal to buy anything, even a beer, let alone the whole of Australia.

'So you reckon Aboriginal Land Rights and uranium is not a burning issue up here?' I asked. 'It's not all still up for debate.'

He couldn't have been more definite. 'It's old hat,' he said. And you can't get much older than that.

But he was wrong. He was speaking only for the calm that was in himself. Out there – outside the rationality of his little bus – it was raging away.

By the time we were back in the outskirts of Darwin we were a softened group. We'd all become chums, and Tom didn't want to see us go. He belonged to the dreaming, yearning school of tour operators. He fell in love with whichever was his latest bus load. He wouldn't have minded if, like the Flying Dutchman, he'd been doomed to take us through the Kakadu National Park for eternity.

Just before he dropped us off he was forced to brake suddenly at the traffic lights. We were all thrown forward. 'Hang on, Tom,' Ros drawled, those aren't bloody Christmas decorations y'know.'

As in art, so in life, no one can resist an echo of the beginning in the end. We laughed and said goodbye with broken hearts.

★ ★ ★

Next morning we went to hand-feed the fish at Doctor's Gully. Never having had much to do with fish myself I didn't at first realize that it was unusual for them to leap out of the water and take slices of French bread from your fingers. But Ros was on her knees, marvelling, at the far end of the pier, and there were notices everywhere warning us not to undo twenty years of hard-won trust by frightening the fish, so I concluded that I was watching something out of the ordinary.

I kept my distance, remembering the crocodiles, and observed the display of personality put on by a young man whose manner and demeanour gave him away at once as an ambisexual Catholic from Melbourne. He made much of wanting to feed certain fish and not others, seeming to find in the water a reflection of a Manichean universe, good bream and evil mullet, the deserving and the otherwise. I was curious to discover the criteria for his preferences, and decided at last that he wished to give only to those who swam alone, the outcasts, the little fishy heroes of the spirit, like himself.

Sometimes he would even reach into the water to retrieve a piece of bread floating towards the wrong beneficiary, but he would squeal if any fish, good or bad, came near him.

'They don't have teeth, you know,' his slight female companion assured him.

'Makes no difference,' he said. He was stylized and witty, a fastidious fairy camping it up on a sultry Saturday morning on the shores of the Timor Sea. 'It's not the pain, it's the principle.'

I am attached to unnaturalness myself. It has a long and honourable tradition. But there is always somebody who has to spoil it for the others.

On our way back into town we passed a canary-yellow Volkswagen, with its top missing – it looked as though it had been opened in a hurry with a can-opener – on the forecourt of a car-hire company. Ros was in one of her Mr Wemmick moods. 'Hello,' she said, 'here's a car. Let's hire it.'

I was wary. I still thought it was too soon to be driving into the bush. 'Why would we want to do that?' I asked.

'Because it's yellow and it matches your shirt. Come on.'

So we drove around Darwin for an hour or so, conspicuous by virtue of our colour, our exposure to the midday sun, and our being very nearly the only vehicle in the Northern Territory that wasn't a Toyota 4-wheel drive, a Mitsubishi 4-wheel drive, or a Holden Jackaroo with Yokohama Super Digger tyres. Until we ended up, partly by design, and partly because that was where the traffic pushed us, in the bohemian suburb of Parap – all bohemias are relative – just in time to catch what was left of the Saturday morning market. The conventional stall-holders had packed up, but the Chinese were caught between wanting to count their takings (which is not how I was brought up to behave on a public market) and needing to sell off the last of their Laotian-style dim sums and Thai noddle soup. And the hippies looked settled in for the afternoon, with fresh herbal coffee on their methane gas rings, and plenty of wholemeal pitta bread sandwiches filled with couscous and capsicum wrapped up waiting in cling film.

The only non-food stall still operating sold Australiana – mainly T-shirts, the most popular of which depicted the nation's symbol of cuddlesomeness and innocence, the koala, being fellated by a beach girl, and bore the legend, How Much Can a Koala Bear? I sometimes think I could have made a living inventing weak and tasteless jokes of this kind because I immediately had an idea for a follow-up – Less Than a Toucan – but I wasn't able to interest anybody in it.

We sat for a while under the trees, eating samosas and listening to the hippies admiring one another's new fluorescent sun glasses – 'Hey, they're *really* nice' – demonstrating their wonderfully relaxed manner with children, and discussing, in preternaturally deep voices, the latest televised episode of *The*

Young Ones. 'It's total anarchy – that's what's so amazing. How do they get away with it. Wow!'

Then we were joined by Alfredo, an elderly Sicilian who wondered whether we came from the south or the east. I didn't want to get into the bother of explaining that Ros came from the west, if we were talking about Australia, and that I came from the north, if we were talking about England, so I simply said, 'London.' He narrowed his eyes and nodded. Yes, he knew where London was, but he'd long since given up thinking about that part of the world. Darwin was his home now. He'd been here years, even before shiklone troicee. Ros and I exchanged glances, but we were of no help to each other. 'Before when?' I asked.

He couldn't believe we were so ignorant. 'Shiklone troicee!' He made a noise with his mouth and a movement with his hands to suggest a great wind and the tops coming off all the houses.

'Oh,' Ros and I said together, 'Cyclone Tracy!'

'Si, si, Shiklone Troicee.'

He'd lost his own property in the disaster but he'd been fortunate – 'I was a lucky' – or provident, more like. Coming from an area that knew to expect nothing but malevolence from Nature, he had built a strong bathroom in the bottom of his house, and there he and his family had sheltered until Troicee had got bored. Now, such reinforced bathroom and shower cubicles were compulsory in all domestic dwellings built in Darwin.

'So if there is another cyclone . . .' I was about to wonder, but he waved away my conditional conjunction.

'No ifs.' He flashed me an irresistible smile, full of spurious European fatalism. 'Only when.'

That was pretty much how I felt on the issue of dispatching our suitcase, though I had a formidable opponent in the girl at the

Greyhound office. Formidable in the sense of difficult to engage with. Every time I asked her a question she backed away. So I tried her with statements. 'We want it to go directly to Perth,' I said. 'On Tuesday.'

Since it contained nothing that could be of any earthly use to us in the heat, there was an argument for sending the case straight back to England, or at least to Melbourne, which amounted to more or less the same thing. But Perth was Rosalin's home town; she had friends and family there still, people she hadn't seen for twenty-five years. It wasn't beyond the bounds of possibility that we would be required to smarten up a bit in Perth. I didn't know at the time, of course, that from the moment of our arrival we would never be out of formal attire, never absent from a first night at the theatre or the ballet, and never far from the august presence of His Honour the Governor of Western Australia. Ros had forgotten to tell me that this was how people passed the time in Perth.

The elusive girl at the Greyhound office said, 'We need advance warning of all unaccompanied baggage consignments.'

'I'm giving you advance warning. We would like it to go on Tuesday.'

'We don't take advance warnings so far in advance,' she said. 'You'll have to tell us the day before.'

'I'm telling you now so that you'll know the day before,' I said.

'I can't do anything with the information. We only take advance warnings on the day itself prior to the day of consignment.'

'Can't I tell you now that I'll be telling you then?' I asked. But I'd forgotten what I'd learnt. Recognizing a question, she backed away.

We comforted ourselves with tea in the gardens of the old Admiralty House, until 1984 the residence of the naval officer commanding whatever there was to command in the northern region, but now functioning as a gallery. It was the kind of small business we knew something about from our own enterprises in Cornwall. We recognized the strains of insufficient capital and a tourist season slow to get started. An atmosphere of anxious self-sufficiency prevailed. The proprietor talked to the only other people there about the problem of snakes. Pinned to a noticeboard was a typed poem about a mother buying a car and driving her children around in the heat. Upstairs, in the gallery itself, was a visitors' book, inviting comment from the public. A visitor from Oxford had written, 'Just more boring art.' And someone else had recently remarked, 'Very nice, but gardens untidy.' This had prompted a reply in handwriting much like that of whoever had written the notices around the place. 'Donate some plants then, critical BARHASTARD!' it said.

We stood on the pleasant timber balcony, looking seaward over the landscaped Esplanade where a group of Aborigines sat partying under the palms, their numbers increasing or diminishing mysteriously by means of that process of Aboriginal materialization which cannot truly be called movement. There wasn't a breath of wind. The only suspirations came from us, sighing over the sameness of things, the indomitable disgruntlement of Europeans, the universal recurrence of their disappointment.

In which temper we wandered over to the Hotel Darwin – the only place in town where you feel you can go troppo in some degree of colonial style – and there, amidst bamboo and fern, and along with all the other louche and lonely with a spare Sunday on their hands in Darwin, we waited for the Glen Baker Quintet and Special Guest Female Vocalist to jazz us into better spirits.

The Special Guest Female Vocalist – hereafter to be referred to as the SGFV – wore a dress the same canary yellow as the Volkswagen we'd hired, though where our car had been altogether without a top the SGFV was uncovered only on one shoulder. She had strong brown legs and nightclub-blonded hair, and was at that age where women are just becoming interesting, where they have memories, not expectation, reflected in their eyes. 'I would now like to perform a number made famous by the late Judy Garland,' she announced. She brought Broadway and Hollywood into the Darwin Hotel; these might have been her friends she was referring to. 'And next, a song sung by the inimitable Marlene Dietrich.' Which didn't stop her attempting the imitation – 'Farhleeng in lahv agayn, nehverr vaahnted to, vaht am I to do, caan't 'elp eet.'

'Somewhere over the Rainbow' had gone down well, but this other anti-family favourite, this breathy multilingual celebration of German incontinence – a song about boys not girls – was received rapturously, uniting in their appreciation the two distinct styles of Australian Ganymede represented at the bar: the butch-brutal in tight blue jeans and sleeveless shirts, with 'Mum' (but never 'Dad') tattooed across the biceps, and the more evanescent, in teased coiffure and little white bunched-up shorts.

As soon as the SGFV had finished what she called her 'set', we rose to take a turn around the gardens. A lush jungle of palms, strung with coloured lights, surrounded the swimming pool. The morals were more conventional out here than inside. Only a few children splashed about in the pool, while their parents sat at white tables and ate prawn and scallop kebab accompanied, as every meal is accompanied in Australia, by slices of tinned beetroot, tinned potato salad, tinned sweetcorn, coleslaw, and grated carrots with sultanas. The company and the cuisine notwithstanding, it was still possible to believe, looking at the sliver of moon through the palm trees, that one was in Asia, in the garden of Raffles, say, waiting to hear if one had been ostracized, for misbehaviour with the natives, from one's club.

On the way back inside we were accosted by an old-style

Aussie in his sixties, a Chips Rafferty with a craggy profile under a slouch hat.

'I've just been called an incorrigible old ratbag,' he said. 'I know what an old ratbag means but I'll have to look incorrigible up in my Collins dictionary.'

He didn't wait for a reply. Australians are masters of throwaway irony and they don't want you handing it back. Later on I caught him throwing it at someone else. '. . . but incorrigible I'll have to go to my thesaurus for,' I heard him say. I noticed that he pretended to be bandy sometimes, as well as slow, as if to make you think that he'd spent his life in the saddle, far from the cunning wiles of civilization. But at the very end of the evening, after the SGFV had finished her special thank-you to Ella and Billie, I spotted him at the bar having his balls squeezed by one of the brutal androgynes with blonded hair. He didn't seem to object to this, or even to make any comical display of covering his parts. He stayed exactly where he was, spinning some stockman's yarn, submitting himself to the vicissitudes of contemporary sociableness. I couldn't make up my mind whether it was desirable that such peace prevailed between the generations in Australia these days. Or whether there was nothing new about it whatsoever. Whether it wasn't, after all, just good old-fashioned mateship in action.

We walked home in the warm night, Ros and I, not quite together, each absorbed in thought. Lightning was still illuminating the sky. Not once, in the five or six nights we'd been here, had the sky been silent or still.

Although the Darwin Performing Arts Centre had already been inaugurally opened to the sound of a not quite capacity audience singing 'You Need Hands', the Beaufort International Hotel which housed it wasn't itself ready to receive guests for another week. We had walked past it almost every day, admiring its daring pastel-pink and baby-blue modernity, and agreeing that it was no bad thing for a hotel to resemble a shopping precinct surrounded by squash courts, especially in Darwin where the prevailing hotel style was a cross between Tower Hamlets residential and Trading Estate functional. But it was not until our last morning in town that we were able to set foot inside it.

We blundered in, seeing as the workmen had now removed the barrier of string and coloured plastic flags from the front entrance, and found ourselves eyeball to eyeball with Paul Everingham, one-time Chief Minister for the Northern Territory, now its Federal Representative, and still very much the presiding genius of the place. He was sitting at a table with the directors and President of the Company financing the Beaufort, drinking early morning champagne and orange juice, and posing for photographers. I watched him as he pretended to sign in, his pen poised above the visitors' book, and I thought how young he looked, and how like a bridegroom, frozen for the cameras with his knife in the cake. He was affable and casual, in shirtsleeves, but he had other engagements. I noticed that as he left he performed a sort of flapper movement with the palms of his hands, much as if he were wiping a window to music. It's even possible that his rotating palms actually made contact with some of the dignitaries he was farewelling. He turned again, as the doors opened for him, to make absolutely certain that he'd left no one out of his elaborately easy-going courtesies – not even Ros and me, standing with our mouths agape in the virgin vestibule – then he was gone, with a final wave and a wipe, a democratic monarch amongst his people.

We looked around the grand reception area with its as yet empty balconies and small plants. There were workmen everywhere putting in finishing touches, affixing signs and straightening acceptably abstract examples of contemporary Australian art. The house and international telephone cubicles were elegantly designed and lacking only telephones. Blank paper rolled off the telex machine. Three very slender Indonesian girls, dressed like air hostesses, stood with fixed smiles behind the desk, waiting for guests.

Not having much to do, now that Mr Everingham had gone, and perhaps supposing, since we were there, that we also were VIPs, the President of the Company came over to shake our hands. A couple of photographers' flash bulbs went off. Did we like what we saw? Oh, enormously. Had we stayed at Beaufort International Hotels before? – the Jimbaran Bay in Bali, for example, or the Tanjung Aru Beach, in Kota Kinabalu? No, no, we didn't think we had, but all other things being equal we thought perhaps we soon should. And would we care to be shown around? We didn't hesitate. Nothing we would care for more, we said.

The person who did the showing was the Assistant Manager, John Girard, on loan from the Hotel Benaktuai, Balikpapan, to 'help out' in Darwin. John Girard was possessed of an assurance which intrigued me on account of its having been emptied of anything that might excite envy. He was easy and even jokey, without being personal or humorous. He had good looks without menacing you with his handsomeness. He was of a stature without being, so to speak, *personally* tall. It was as if he had taken possession of all the desirable attributes as it were on your behalf. I didn't know at which school for hoteliers he had acquired this extraordinary gift, but I wished I'd been to it, even though he made me feel that I had.

The Hotel was high quality, too. I was particularly taken by the Executive Duplex Suites (one room in pinks, one room in greens), yours for $500 per night, and providing a colour T.V. in every room and all manner of electrical gadgets worked with your own specially attributed, unique-to-you, computerized card – 'thrown away the moment you leave, so that no two are ever the same'. You want that.

I wondered if this, then, was the beginning of the first true internationalization of Darwin. There already were Travelodges and so on in town, but they went for a simple-minded ethnicity, with Safari bistros and fake grass ceilings. The Beaufort aspired to an altogether higher and more cosmopolitan ideal of kitsch. It had a Teppanyaki restaurant, 'fitted out from Japan' and fully timbered 'by a famous boat builder from Sydney'. It has drugstores and surface-tension pools, a gourmet diner called Siggi's and a place of entertainment not immediately recognizable to me though Mr Girard assured me, guiding me through it with the merest feather touch beneath my elbow, that it was a typical English pub. And it had a theatre for Max Bygraves to perform in.

The talk that we'd picked up around the town suggested that the Territorians weren't sure what they thought, were reserving their judgement, would wait and see, would certainly pop in for a beer, but suspected the Beaufort didn't quite answer their image of Darwin. I knew how they felt. On the other hand I would very much have liked to put the organization of the rest of my life into the hands of John Girard, that's if I could have persuaded the Indonesians to spare him.

Later on that morning I acquired some interesting statistics relating to the Northern Territory, such as that it contained more lawyers per head of population than anywhere else in Australia, and more people with PhDs. It was Clare Martin, of the local ABC radio station 8DR, who told me this. I'd gone along there, as a Pommy writer passing through, to do a quick interview and be asked how I thought I could get to the bottom of the place if I was passing through so quickly. You are always asked this by Australians. They can't believe that you have come to their country and aren't prepared to give at least seven years of your life to savouring the distinctive flavour, fathoming the peculiar mystery, of every one-horse town the bus happens to spill you out in. And they are no less demanding on themselves. They are all absolutely convinced that there is a *real* Australia out there somewhere, and that they haven't begun to get to know it. And yet they will fly out to Heathrow, sniff the air, declare England, Europe, and indeed the Northern Hemisphere to be 'fucked', and be ready to fly back the same day.

I didn't put this to Clare Martin. It was too hot in the tiny recording studio to get into a brawl. And, besides, there was no reason for me to believe I'd win it. She was a Sydney girl and all the Sydney girls of my experience fight rough. For all her fierce pride in the place she had barely been in Darwin a year herself. She had followed her boyfriend up – she called him her 'man' – after he had followed her down to Canberra and hated it. For some reason this information was enough for me to picture a taciturn sandy-haired surveyor in knee-length khaki shorts. She didn't know who was going to follow whom where next, but wanted to be back in Sydney. 'I'm ambitious,' she explained to me – guiltily, I thought, and with a quick check to make sure the microphones were off, as if the idea of ambition was against the spirit of the Top End. Or the Australian Broadcasting Corporation.

When I mentioned that I'd taken a look at Paul Everingham earlier that morning, she immediately switched the conversation to Bob Collins, the Labour Opposition Leader. Apparently he had come to the far north, like so many other people, to escape the memory of an unhappy love affair. He hadn't had the slightest intention of staying, but had been robbed of all he possessed as he was about to leave, and that was that. You don't argue with an augury. He was now married to an Aboriginal woman and was facing criticism within his own party on the grounds that he associated Labour politics too exclusively with Aboriginal matters. He was alienating many natural white Labour voters, the criticism went.

'Any truth in that?' I asked.

Clare Martin gave me a long, steely, Sydney stare. Had I not known she was Australian I might have thought she came from Sparta. 'What can he do?' she said. 'The national Labour party has reneged on Land Rights and changed its mind about uranium. Where does that leave Collins?'

We both knew where that left Collins. Comprehensively fleeced, for the second time in his life.

The reason for all the lawyers in the Northern Territory, incidentally, was not Aboriginal litigation but the high rate of bankruptcy. People were coming north in the belief that it was a place of boundless opportunity, starting businesses with no know-how, and failing. The two classic but contradictory evaluations of Darwin – that of Captain Phillip Parker King:

It must, at no very distant period, become a place of great trade and that of Thomas Huxley, assistant surgeon aboard *HMS Rattlesnake:*

It is about the most useless, miserable, ill-managed hole in her Majesty's dominions – were still finely poised.

So much for all the lawyers. What all the PhDs were doing up here Clare Martin forgot to tell me.

On our last night in Darwin we watched a television programme dealing with a group which had just formed itself in Katherine, three hundred kilometres down the track. Its name was SPONGE, standing for the Society for the Prevention of Niggers Getting Everything.

'Let's go to Katherine,' Ros said.

She'd fallen for the Northern Territory and didn't want to leave. She believed we should kick around up here a while longer yet, putting our noses into all the trouble spots. I was more for expedition myself, convinced that travel meant covering vast distances at great speed. Perhaps it was racial. Something told me that the best way to keep safe was to keep moving.

But as it happened the bus that was taking us to Kununurra would be calling in at Katherine. 'We'll be there tomorrow,' I said, omitting to add that we'd only be there for an hour, for a lunch stop.

I slept badly that night. I felt that I was letting down everyone and everything that had a woman's name. I was pushing Ros faster than she wanted to go. I wasn't planning to do justice to Katherine. And I hadn't made the slightest effort to order *Jocasta's Jest* from a single bookshop.

THREE

BUNGLE BUNGLE

Our drivers were called Wayne and Clay. Wayne was large and dark and affable, looked to be of Maori descent, and lived in Perth. Clay was brittle and moody, irascibly Anglo-Saxon, and lived in Darwin. It was Clay who did the first stretch of driving and delivered the introductory spiel, a low and often psychopathic routine – misogynistic and homophobic – which turned out to be more or less standard on this particular bus line, and which eventually forced us into finding some other means of transport.

I cannot hope to render the sinewy distaste of this perform-ance, but roughly it went:

'G'day. The name's Clay. The ugly one to my left is Wayne. For those of you who haven't travelled with us before, a few words of caution about the bus. At the very rear you will see a door marked rest room. You'll get no rest there. It is in fact a mobile toilet. Just how mobile you will discover when you sit down in it. You will notice that the door to the mobile toilet opens outwards. Please remember to lock it. This serves two purposes: it activates a light on my dashboard, telling me that you're in there, and it saves you the embarrassment, if I am forced to brake suddenly, of being sent sliding down the aisle with your knickers round your ankles and a rubber rash on each cheek. Rest assured, it happens. The record so far, for your information, is Row 5.

'The curtained partition at the back of the bus is for the relief driver and admission is by invitation only. Yes, I did say invitation. . . . So don't hold your breath, fellers.'

As it fell out, Clay ended up spending most of the journey in this curtained partition himself, in a massive pet occasioned by something Ros said to him. He'd dropped us off at a roadhouse remarkable, even by Australian roadhouse standards, for its lack of anything you might reasonably have called an amenity. Since he was a bloke who clearly enjoyed a joke, Ros congratulated him on his choice as she climbed back into the bus. 'Nice place you found for us, Clay,' she observed. That was sufficient to put him to bed for the day.

Wayne's version of easy-going Australian masculinity was less friable. He sat with his shoulders rounded, staring at the road, chatting to whoever wandered up the bus to talk to him. He was a bit anxious about what was going to happen when double-decker buses were introduced. 'There's talk about them putting stewards on,' he said. 'But they'll probably be poofters like on Qantas. Qantas won't employ you unless you're gay. They reckon poofters treat passengers with more sensitivity and understanding.'

I enjoyed his 'more'.

A runty little West Australian woman with colourless hair joined him for some technical conversation. Dot − I think she said her name was Dot − was the sort of woman who likes to know and talk about what a man likes to know and talk about. She discussed the cost of the bus with Wayne, and its gear system, and its air-cushion suspension. Somehow or other they got on to wildlife. Wayne described a snake he'd driven over the other day. It was stretched across the road and was so big that he could see neither its head nor its tail. 'Ah,' said Dot, 'that'd be a king brown.'

'Could have been,' Wayne agreed.

'It's a good idea,' Dot told him, 'if you're driving along and you hit a king brown to slow down and make sure you see its remains through your rear-view mirror. Otherwise it might have wrapped itself around your differential and will travel home with you. When you park your car it will hop off and come inside your house. I guess you can't blame the snake. It's just self-preservation. I learnt to drive on a 4-wheel drive, which is a good introduction. I think a lot of people just drive to show off.'

'I hate showing off,' Wayne said. 'When I've got passengers, anyway. If I'm going to show off I do it on my own.'

'Right,' said Dot.

Also on the bus was a lean, crazed American, who was carrying about forty paperback thrillers in his rucksack. I'd watched him sorting them out, in order of reading preference and therefore accessibility, at the terminal in Darwin. Already, after only a couple of hours, he'd got through about eight of them. He was wearing very little – just a brief pair of ragged denims and a maroon singlet. Considering how much hair he had growing in his armpits I believed he ought to have worn a shirt. When he raised his arm, to get down another book, I found it necessary to look away. It occurred to me that he might have been Jewish – there was a Saul Bellow somnolence in his eyes – or half-Jewish, half-Puerto Rican, if there was such a thing. I didn't initiate any of the usual secret salutations of brotherhood, though. He'd gone wild, this one. And I don't, as a rule, hit it off with feral Jews.

We stopped for morning coffee at Hayes Creek, a high, quiet, blissful spot, surrounded by red jagged hills. A flock of corellas, disturbed by our arrival, rose from the ground in one movement, pure white like an apparition. It was here, in the warm morning sun, that I first hit upon a method whereby I could personally consecrate places I especially liked, and at the same time acknowledge sundry debts of gratitude and friendship which I felt I owed. Reading the classic accounts of their travels written by the early explorers of Australia, I had been very much taken by the liberality – the munificence, even – with which they gave the names of their acquaintances or benefactors to whichever new feature of the country they happened on. Leichhardt, above all, knew how to repay loyalty or encouragement with punctilious notice:

> I called the brook 'Beames's Brook' in acknowledgment of the liberal support received from Walter Beames Esq., of Sydney. . . . A large flat-topped mountain I called 'Lord's Table Range' after E. Lord Esq., of Moreton Bay; and a sharp needle-like rock, which bore west-by-north, received the name of 'Fletcher's Awl' after Mr John Fletcher, whose kind contribution towards my expedition had not a little cheered me in my undertaking.

Why shouldn't I do the same? It's true that I wasn't exactly exploring virgin territory; that all the brooks and mountain tops and deserts of Australia already had names. But then that was true when Eyre and Sturt and Leichhardt blundered through it, the only difference being that the names they already had were Aboriginal. If they could rechristen, so could I. In accordance with which decision – I made it in the twinkling of an eye, before the ghostly corellas had vanished over the crumbling ridge – I called the place I stood in Christopher Sinclair-Stevenson Creek, after C. Sinclair-Stevenson Esq., of London, who had kindly assisted me in my expedition.

Back on the bus I met Fred Luff, one time tree-engineer, restaurateur, patentee of a highly secret batter for fried fish, and now on his way to Northcliffe, in the far south of West Australia, to take over a public house. Fred had lived in the Northern Territory for nearly twenty years and was leaving it now with some sourness, a casualty, as he saw it, of Aboriginal Land Rights politics. Along, also as he saw it, with the Aborigines themselves. 'We all got on well under the policy of assimilation,' he said. 'It was the idea of self-determination that changed everything.' We were to hear this opinion voiced frequently throughout the north of Australia, but in Fred's case it had the backing of a vivid, personal experience. Fred Luff had lived in paradise one day, and been expelled from it the next. He was, just like any refugee, a passive victim of history.

It had been the sight of a huge goanna, holding up the bus while it crossed the road, that had got Fred talking. 'Very tasty,' he'd said.

I'd leaned towards him so that Ros didn't have to hear. I was trying to avoid all conversation with her on the subject of snake or reptile tucker. 'You've tried it, have you?' I asked, in a low voice.

'Tried it? Lived on nothing else for a couple of years. There aren't many things that taste like a goanna you've speared yourself.'

I was prepared to believe that. But I wondered where Fred had come by his experience. Had he owned a tree-surgery outside Darwin?

He was a small, nuggety man with a bright eye and a bristling moustache. 'Nah,' he said, 'I was with the blackfellers in Arnhem Land.'

And that was how I came to hear about his years in paradise, working as a fire-control officer, and learning to spear goanna with the natives. He'd loved it. So had his wife. 'Every morning, after I'd set off to work, she'd go swimming with the women. She'd swim all day. Then I'd come home and we'd all fish and eat and laugh together. I remember getting back late one night – I'd had to do some burning-off from the air – and finding a party of Frenchmen trying to interest the blackfellers in a few boxes of coloured baubles, plastic beads and mirrors. You have to remember, the blackfellers are very polite people. They smiled and nodded and played with the beads. Then, after the Frenchmen left, they had a big joke about it. "'M cheeky buggers," they said.'

What brought this idyllic existence to an end, according to Fred, was the interference of radicals from the south, politicized blacks imported from America, trouble-makers from the Philippines. 'School teachers started to stir it, too,' he said. 'And then suddenly – overnight – my friends started to go on marches, chanting BLACK IS BLACK, WHITE IS SHIT. My friends!'

This had happened some years ago now. He'd run a seafood restaurant in Darwin since then, and been offered in excess of ten thousand dollars for his patented fish batter. And very soon he'd be back in the south of his home state, at the bar of his own hotel in Northcliffe. But his eyes still flashed with bitterness when he remembered his evacuation. 'Do you know, when we had to leave,' he told me, 'all the Aboriginal women wept. They didn't want us to go. No one in Arnhem Land – no one who *came* from Arnhem Land – wanted any of this. They stood around and cried and pulled their hair. Some of them even attacked themselves with tomahawks.'

He took us to a pub he knew in Katherine for lunch. Five minutes in the street were enough to tell me that I hadn't made any serious mistake, at least as far as my comfort and safety went, giving Katherine a miss. I don't know whether we passed any senior officers of SPONGE but we saw many whites who could have been active members. And the Aborigines, squatting on the nature strip which ran down the middle of the main road, looked angrier than in Darwin, less interested in street mischief, more confrontational. The pub that Fred recommended had an outdoor beer yard where you sat on upturned barrels and avoided eye contact. Next to me a skeletal Aborigine in a leather cowboy hat cleaned his finger nails with a knife, while the woman he was with berated him, with that characteristic rapid raucous click – a fusillade of shrill abuse, coming from high up in the throat – for some obviously minor marital misdemeanour. Through the window to the kitchen I could see the white woman who prepared the steaks standing over the ovens, breathing in the oil and removing wax from her ear. 'Nice here, isn't it?' Fred said. He had his niece with him, a little girl of seven or eight. 'Isn't it?' he repeated, tousling her hair.

We found some way of excusing ourselves, and retraced our steps, moving like a pair of Olympic walkers, in the direction of the service station and takeaway at which the bus had originally dropped us off. It was a murderously scorching day, but unless you are prepared to eat sliced beetroot and lettuce sandwiches you can only ever buy hot fried food in Australia; so we grabbed a half-chicken and some pineapple fritters and sat under the roof of the car wash for shade and with burning fingers ripped the chook apart.

I don't think the hairy American with the Saul Bellow eyes and the Sal Mineo profile bothered about food. He looked upon meal stops as an opportunity to attend to his laundry and rearrange the thrillers in his rucksack. He was always the first off the bus, and before the rest of us were disembarked had his socks and sandshoes and singlet laid out to dry in the dust. At Christopher Sinclair-Stevenson Creek I had watched him throwing pebbles into his sandshoes from a distance of thirty yards. At Katherine he just sat in the dust himself and read the whole of *Answer From a Deadman*.

Sitting drying in the sun must have made him tired, because he curled up and fell asleep – the breeze from his overhead air-conditioner winnowing the hairs under his arms – the minute the bus started moving again. But fifteen minutes out of Katherine

Wayne announced that he had a beaut new video to play us: *The Electric Cowboy*. I don't know whether the movie was based on a paperback that the American had read, or whether he was simply susceptible to titles, but the words, *The Electric Cowboy*, seemed to reach deep into his slumbering pneuma. A solitary paroxysm racked his body and he was instantly bolt upright and wide awake. 'Is it any good?' he asked, without even bothering to rub his eyes.

'Is it any good?' Wayne's confidence in his own critical judgement was unwavering. 'Is the Pope a Catholic?'

The look of uncertainty on the American's face – how should he know *what* the Pope was? – made me wonder again if he might have been Jewish. Though later on, after we'd driven through a plague of locusts on the West Australian border – slaughtering them in their thousands against our windscreen – I peered across at him and found no recognition in his eyes. It was my belief that no two Jews who knew anything of the Old Testament could go through a plague of locusts together without exchanging smiles of quiet satisfaction. On the other hand it was always possible that he had not yet come across the Old Testament in paperback.

Whether or not he was right about the Pope, Wayne couldn't have been more wrong about *The Electric Cowboy*. I watched Robert Redford and Jane Fonda doing their usual thing for about half an hour – exhibiting their neat pin-pricks of conscience about the culture which had made them beautiful and successful – then I gave it away and concentrated on the country outside. We were in termite territory. Their mounds were not as high as those we'd seen on the road to Kakadu, but they were more plentiful – little reddy-brown phallic pillars sprouting like magic mushrooms, for miles on either side. Occasionally the bus would stop, or swerve, to avoid a brumby or a brahmin bull. As we approached the West Australian border the country changed. Gradually the land grew hillier, until we were driving between terraced escarpments of crumbling red sandstone. The rocks had been so evenly worn away that they seemed to be surmounted by a man-made wall, like an ancient but perfectly preserved fortification. At their bases palm trees – Livingstone Palms, Fred told me – huddled for protection from the wet and the heat. Then we crossed the Victoria River – a broad green swathe of water, over which kite hawks hovered. 'This whole area's called the Victoria River District,' Fred said. 'I worked here once. Wonderful, benign country.' I immediately named it the Jeremy Lewis District, after Jeremy Lewis Esq., of London, whose encouragement had not a little fortified me in recent years.

'I was out here on a job a few years ago,' Fred went on, 'entirely on my own, in a 4-wheel drive with radio and rifles in the back. I wasn't expecting any trouble, but it's a good idea to be prepared. I decided to make camp at a little waterhole I knew. I stopped the vehicle and started to get my gear out and suddenly I heard giggles. I looked around. More giggles. Then calling – "Hey, here, over here!" I still couldn't see anyone. Then I looked towards the waterhole and there they were' – he paused here to make sure that his niece was still sleeping, and to lean closer to me across the aisle of the bus – 'three sheilas, three sheilas, stark naked in the water, shouting, "Come on in, come and join us. The water's beaut."'

His face was creased with amusement. He wiped his eyes and towelled down his moustache with a handkerchief.

'So what did you do?' I asked.

'I thought, "Hullo, this looks like trouble", Remember there was no one else around for hundreds of miles – just them in the nuddy and me with my radio and rifles. So I excused myself – politely, of course – and drove up the road a few miles. You know, to cool the situation down.'

'And then what did you do?'

'Made camp and went to sleep,' he laughed. His face danced with wonderful memories.

'What happened to you was what most men fantasize about,' I said.

'I know,' he said. He was doubled up with hilarity now. 'I know.'

An hour or so later we were in Kununurra. We were the only ones breaking our journey. The rest still had another two days travelling ahead of them before they reached Perth, and would stop here just long enough to grab steak, chips, and coleslaw. So we took our farewells, warning Fred that we would call in to see him in his new hotel in Northcliffe, and after settling the issue of our accommodation we ventured out into the town.

Nothing that I had ever seen in Australia before had prepared me for the breathtaking spectacle of sunset in Kununurra. Had I been brought here blindfolded and asked to guess where I was I would have said South America, partly – or perhaps precisely – because I didn't know what South America looked like. Kununurra didn't remind me of anywhere I knew. A crumbling, serrated ridge of hills encircled it. The highest of them, which seemed to be rising from, and indeed about to fall into, the very centre of the town itself, glowed an ochreish red and resembled an utterly exhausted volcano. In the dying sun the hills didn't so much give off colour as palpitate with it. The sky was turquoise, streaked with orange. Silhouetted against it, the palms defined themselves with an extraordinary clarity, so that you could pick out the perfection of every frond. The evening was still and very warm. In the eerie quiet – it was no more than six o'clock – the low-slung town appeared deserted, left entirely to the Aborigines who squatted, as always, wherever there was grass or trees, or who arrived in the back of pick-up trucks, dozens at a time, to collect their grog from the bottle-shops.

As we walked back to the hotel in the fading light – the sky now shot through with electric blues and malarial yellows – we saw the bus pulling out. Clay was at the wheel. We waved, wondering how he would respond. He waved back warmly and tooted his horn. You can't afford to bear grudges in Australia – the country's too big and there aren't enough people in it.

Kununurra is situated just inside the West Australian border in the top eastern corner of the Kimberley Region, and hasn't been there very long. Look on a pre-1960s atlas and you won't find it. Ord River is probably the nearest you will get. And the Ord River is your clue. The reason for the concoction of Kununurra was water: inundation and irrigation. It's very name – as local whites are only too happy to tell you (they love their pidgin, northern whites) – is Aboriginal for 'big mobs of water'. Ever since Alexander Forest took a look around the area in the 1870s, the Kimberleys had been fancied as prime grazing country, but had never found a way of overcoming the problems caused by the extremes of climate, the wet Wet and the dry Dry. As recently as 1945 the possibility of giving the North West of West Australia back to the Commonwealth Government was canvassed – perhaps because it was feared that even the Japanese wouldn't want it. But a certain Dr Oldmeadow, who had been medical officer at Broome for some time, reckoned that settlement of the region was possible for white men providing they left it every three or four years, their wives left it every two years, and their children left it every Wet. It seems to me a pity that such advice was not tendered centuries ago in respect of such settlements as Manchester, Liverpool, or Leeds. It was heeded, anyway, when the Government of West Australia looked into means of developing its extremities; as were the words of the Assistant State Surveyor, who saw the necessity for a massive irrigation scheme in the Ord River Valley but also recommended the establishment of a new town site to service it, since, speaking climatically (and not wanting to put too fine an edge on it), he considered Wyndham – the nearest existing town – 'detestable'. Thus Kununurra; and thus a rather embittered Wyndham, sweating it out without a thank-you where the northern rivers flow into the Timor Sea.

Our interest in the area was not primarily irrigational. Ros wanted to get out into a terrain that was known to be as wild and beautiful as anything in Australia – a country of barely accessible mountain ranges, of marvellous torrential rivers, of remote Aboriginal missions and even leper colonies. And I was keen to visit some of the landmarks made famous – made famous for me, anyway – by George Grey (later to be Governor Grey), whose *Journals of Two Expeditions of Discovery in North-West and Western Australia During The Years 1837, 8 and 9* are neglected classics of comic expeditionary writing. Just as the expeditions themselves are classics of comic expeditioning.

I knew I was never going to get across as far as High Bluff Point, to the south of Brunswick Bay, where Grey first came ashore in order 'to familiarize the natives with the British name and character' but 'not altogether prepared to behold so arid and barren a surface'; though of course I would have loved to be able to stand where he and his landing party of five men and three dogs stood, oppressed with 'thirst and lassitude' and contemplating the two pints of water which was all Grey had thought to bring to Australia to serve the lot of them. I did have hopes, however, of reaching the Prince Regent River, into which Grey had plunged to avoid the spears of natives unimpressed with what they'd so far seen of the British name and character, and where he'd come close to drowning when his military cap filled with water and floated away, thereby all but throttling him with the chin-strap which was still wound around his throat. And I wished, also, to try to find the very vertiginous mountain path responsible for the collapse of Grey's pony – a spot, incidentally, which I had already renamed the Ian MacKillop Ascent, in honour of Ian MacKillop Esq., of Sheffield, a gentleman of soaring intellect but with no head for heights, the very reverse, in other words, of Governor George Grey, whose account of his struggles with his pony I now quote:

> There it lay . . . on a flat rock, 4 or 5 ft wide – a precipice of 150 ft on one side of it, and the projecting rock against which it had struck on the other – whilst I sat upon its head to prevent it from moving. Its long tail streamed in the wind over the precipice; its wild and fiery eye gleamed from its shaggy mane and forelock; and, ignorant of its impending danger, it kicked and struggled violently, whilst it appeared to hang in mid-air over the gloomy depth of this tropical ravine. Anxious as I felt for the safety of my pony, I could not be unconscious of the singular beauty of the scene . . . .

Grey's capacity to find time, in his tribulations, to ponder the beauty of landscape 'as lovely and picturesque as impetuous torrents, foaming cascades, lofty rocks, and a rich tropical vegetation could render it', is an example to all travellers. A lover of Wordsworth myself (the chasmal Wordsworth, anyway), you can see why it was my ambition to go where Grey had been.

But when, on our first morning in Kununurra, we rose with the kookaburra and set off to secure transport and advice on the local conditions, we met with a double disappointment. We were a week or so too early; the Wet was a week or so too late; and all tracks to the inner Kimberleys were impassable. Besides which there were no cars available for hire anyway. They'd all been hired.

I wondered how that could be if there was nowhere you could drive them. But the girl in the town's Visitors Centre treated me to an inscrutable squint. 'Blame the diamond mine,' was all she would say to me.

'Is there a diamond mine here?'

She laughed. 'Largest deposit of diamonds in the world just down the road,' she said.

You have to watch Australians with that 'in the world' clause: they affix it to just about everything their country possesses or produces. But I wasn't going to get into technicalities. The issue wasn't how big the mine was but that they'd hogged the cars.

'They've got all of them, you say?'

'They have today.'

'And there's absolutely no one who would take us out?'

She made a few phone calls. No, no one was prepared to chance their vehicles far-afield. But a girl called Sue – an experienced guide and lovely person – could do us 'A Half-day Agricultural' that afternoon and 'A Full Morning Irrigational' the following day. Alternatively, we could sell everything we owned and hire a plane to fly us over the lost world of Bungle Bungle for twenty minutes. I wondered why we would want to do that. Indescribably beautiful country, apparently. Unreachable by road at any time. Some of the oldest conical sandstone landforms in the world. But don't get too excited because it was always possible that the diamond mine was using all the planes. So we settled for the Afternoon Agricultural, taking a look in the meantime to see if Kununurra came up as well in the daylight as it had in the dark.

It didn't. Without the dying sun on them the surrounding crumbly hills looked undramatic, not so much hills as 'the ruin of hills', to borrow a phrase from Grey. I wasn't pleased, either, to discover that the previous night's spectacular South American peak was known as Kelly's Knob. I immediately changed its name to Gabriel Jacobs Pike, in honour of a friend I hadn't seen for many years. But it was the bungalow modernity of the town – its wholly untropical architectural idiom – which most disappointed. Beneath its inappropriate corrugated roofs the whole place just seemed to cower from the baking heat.

The bottle-shops had not changed from the night before, however. They were still busy supplying the Aborigines who once more turned up in numbers on the backs of trucks. There was drinking going on in the park too, even at this early hour, though it was of a relaxed and friendly nature.

'Yous 'avin a walk-around?' a young Aborigine asked us as we ambled past.

I told him that I'd heard there was a nice boab tree in the park and that we were looking for that.

'A boab tree?' He scratched his head and then fell into earnest conference with his friends. Watching them with their faces close together, deliberating, I felt I'd slipped back a couple of centuries. I wouldn't have been surprised had one of them suddenly leapt up and volunteered to be our guide. Odd, that their sociable instincts should still survive after so much experience of betrayal. Odd and – speaking impersonally – exasperating. They ought to have known better than to smile at a white man by now. It was pleasant for me to be befriended by them, but what did I have to do with anything?

'There's a pretty nice one over there,' the young man said at last, pointing to the far end of the park, while his companions nodded and bewitched us, every one of them, with their smiles.

We drank cappucino in Estelle's and watched someone who might have been Estelle herself making heavy weather of being a white who had perforce to do business with blacks. 'Off! – out!' she shouted at a group of kids who were only very mildly messing around. 'Go walkabout!' When they'd gone she waved a paper bag in the air, wafted the smell of them from under her nose, sprayed the room, sprayed us, sprayed our coffee, and took a cleaning cloth to every surface they might have touched.

Sue picked us up from our hotel on the dot of two o'clock. You could tell at once that she would do most things on the dot. And that what she didn't do on the dot her husband, who was a pilot, would do to the letter. I imagined that they were very close and wore matching uniforms for going jogging or for going to bed. Underneath the pleasantest of manners Sue gave off an air of domestic militarism. She suffered, to boot, from a more than usually serious dose of the sing-song Australian interrogatives. At no time, in the several hours we were to spend in her company, did she address a sentence to us that didn't end in a question mark.

She had no other visitors to Kununurra to show around today but she was taking the opportunity of our unseasonal arrival to train a young woman called Jude in the ins and outs of the Half-day Agricultural. Had we turned up a fortnight later we might have got Jude as our guide. As it was we got them both.

Everyone in Kununurra was a newcomer, but Jude was newer than most. She had come north in the best pioneer tradition – because something dreadful had happened to her in the south. She went in for a more solitary and independent idea of womanhood than Sue. Where Sue's hair fell tidily on her shoulders like an airline receptionist's, Jude's was jagged like a leafleteer's; and, where Sue wore a little sparkling stone in each ear, Jude had a non-concentric pair of gold rings hanging from just one. If I appear to have taken a keen interest in the appearance of these two women that is because I could take no interest at all in what one of them was telling me. Addressing us at all times through her loudspeaker system – although there were only three of us on the bus and we were all sitting right beside her – Sue delivered herself conscientiously of the information we'd paid to hear. She wasn't to know that, of all subjects of least concern in the whole world to me, dams and crops headed the list.

And so I was led, as though in a dream, along the banks of irrigation channels, through peanut farms and fields of sorghum, in and out of water-melon processing and packing plants, and down, down, into a sing-song nightmare of alluvial soils and yields and nitrogen and hectares. I heard – or someone vaguely like me heard – about Black Spot, which I had always thought to be the name of a villainous character in *Treasure Island*, but was in fact (oh God, *fact*) a mango blight brought in from Queensland. And I think I heard of some virus which infects the bloodwood tree and causes it to grow shark fins on its trunk; though that sounds to me now suspiciously like the workings of delirium.

In desperation, after an hour or two of this, I tried to get the women to talk to us about life – real social life, not what peanuts had – in the Kimberleys. Jude swam a lot. Sue liked watching indoor cricket. In fact we were just passing where they played indoor cricket, there, right there. I couldn't see any buildings, only a field.

'We play indoor cricket outdoors in Kununurra,' Sue explained.

'What about the Aborigines?' I asked.

'They don't seem to want to play indoor cricket,' Sue said.

'No, I meant what's it like for them in Kununurra. How do you get on with them?'

It's possible, had I not been sick with sunflower and sorghum, that I might have initiated my enquiries more subtly. But I doubt if I would have got anywhere anyway. Both girls were cautious and non-committal. Jude expressed what I took to be a general pessimism about the future of black/white relations in the area. There was no work for the Aborigines, and although there were many schemes encouraging employers to take them on – generous grants and concessions and so on – few were prepared to do so. Because of her manner of expelling her words – through closed lips and a locked jaw – Jude spoke with a sort of authoritative desolateness. This is very much a style in Australian cities, especially close to the universities. You don't speak, you let off small explosives. Sue, on the other hand, was a country girl. When I brought up the subject of Land Rights – a no-no in Western Australia – she found a quaint pastoral phrase to describe the proliferation of Aboriginal claims. 'They're certainly getting a bit of a spread on,' she said.

Later in the afternoon we drove down to the Ord River, on the way to the Diversion Dam. A party of Aborigines was picnicking under the trees and swimming in the river. Some of the women stood fully clothed, up to their chests in the water. One was absolutely motionless, looking out across the river, lost in thought. She was at least seventy. An old white-haired man bobbed about near her. The rest sat and talked or fished. All the scene lacked to make it paradise was Fred Luff, his face creased with enjoyment.

We were surprised when Sue drove her bus right to the water's edge, into their very midst, so that we could get a better look at them.

'What's the etiquette of this?' Ros asked.

Sue turned her neat little face to us. 'Sorry?' she asked.

Momentary deafness is a fascinating psychological phenomenon. Fear and loathing, I am convinced, lie behind most requests to have a statement repeated.

'Do they like it,' Ros said, 'when you drive so close to them?'

Sue was all smiles now. Her hearing had come back and her voice had found extra lilt. 'Depends. Some are O.K. Especially outside, on the reservations. They like to tell you about themselves and to show you their babies. But in town they're not always delighted. Some of them can be quite rude.'

That last sentence had a question mark before as well as after it, so that it should really be punctuated in the Spanish fashion: '¿Some of them can be quite rude?'

'Fancy that,' Ros said, without interrogatives.

On the way back we stopped off at Hidden Valley, just minutes from the centre of town. It was a series of valleys actually, between low crumbling sandstone rocks, where visitors had been known to go missing for days, beguiled by the beauty of the place, and deceived by its apparent smallness of scale. Sue found us a number of geodes lying about in the dust, and explained how the Aborigines would have ground away at them to extract powder for their paint. I was struck by the contrast between how little she knew, or was prepared to say, about contemporary Aboriginal life, even in her own town, and how informative she'd made herself on the details of their ancient practices. You find this all over Australia: the Aborigine himself somewhere between a petty problem and a pestilence, his arts and customs a matter for reverence and national pride. When George Grey came upon his first examples of Aboriginal art he was as unequivocal in his judgements as Waldemar Januscek. 'I often also found rude drawings scratched upon the trees, but none of these sketches indicated anything but a very ordinary degree of talent, even for a savage.' Say that today and they'd drum you out of Australia.

Seeing Sue with her small face pursed, describing the way the young braves used to sharpen their spears, and watching Ros scanning the orange rocks, imagining corroborees, the idea began to form in my mind that white Australians owed far more than they knew – and certainly far more than many of them would ever willingly acknowledge – to their sable friends, as Ludwig Leichhardt used to call them.

Australians do not, as everybody knows, practise apartheid. But they do post stringent dress requirements – NO THONGS, NO BARE FEET, NO SINGLETS, NO TANK TOPS, NO OUTLANDISH HAIRCUTS – outside their places of refreshment and entertainment, and this works just as well.

It does not, however, mean that the poor Aborigine is compelled to go without his beer. The economy of many a northern country town would immediately collapse if the social security cheques paid to the Aborigines – 'sit-down money', in local parlance – did not promptly make their way back to the white community via the bar and the taxi. (I'll come to the taxi later.) The bar at which they are acceptable – the cheques and the Aborigines – is simply not the one at which we are. We drink in something called the Lounge – in Kununurra it was the Green Room – the Aborigine has either a Workers' or a Sportsmen's. In Kununurra they had a Workmen's, though it was referred to by the locals as the Animal Bar. And through the thin partition that divided us we could hear, day and night, the sounds of unending festivity and riot.

'We're in the wrong place,' Ros remarked, on our first evening in the Green Room.

Looking around at the engineers and public service men, the lackeys of the diamond and mining exploration companies, all in pressed blue shirts and natty shorts and knee-length oatmeal socks, I was inclined to agree with her. But then we fell into conversation with Henri from Mauritius, who did sub-contract work on vehicles owned by the diamond mine, and Charlie who came from Kenya and called himself a pedlar. 'I peddle agricultural machinery,' he told us.

He liked the idea of himself as a poor itinerant, wandering around the whole of Western Australia with a tray of knick-knacks, each one costing about a quarter of a million dollars.

We wondered how business was. 'The trouble with this place,' he said, 'is its isolation. If it was somewhere else it would be a boom town.'

Both he and Henri lived in Perth (Henri pronounced it Pert), some three thousand kilometres down the track, and commuted.

'Yeah, it's a long way to travel to work,' Henri agreed, 'but I make good money. It's my ambition to retire when I'm forty. I'm tirty-eight now.'

He was dark and Frenchified and then Australianized. He had black eyes and a scintillating moist moustache. He was the kind of man who used to be referred to as a handsome devil. And he couldn't say th.

'So what will you do when you retire?' I asked him.

'Fish and drink red wine.'

'Sounds all right,' I said.

He wanted to know whether I liked wine.

I said I did.

'Which colour do you like best?'

I didn't have too many choices but I paused, wanting to get it right. 'Red,' I said.

His face lit up. Had I been a woman I'd have asked him to give me babies. 'Me too,' he said.

'You see, Henri is a typical diamond mines employee,' Charlie said. He waved away Henri's objection that he wasn't employed by the mine but did sub-contract work. 'He takes all his money away from the town. If a farmer gets rich – we call them cockies – he spreads his wealth around the town. Everybody benefits. But a miner takes his money somewhere else. A lot of them never even see the town. They live in camps on the mine itself, and do their drinking there. The diamond mine does nothing for Kununurra.'

There was a fresh, boyish, melancholy colonial air about Charlie. He looked like one of Forster's well-meaning Englishmen, bent on administering the natives firmly but scrupulously. But he wouldn't hear of being referred to as an Englishman. 'I'm a Kenyan,' he told us.

Henri started to up the tempo of our drinking. 'What do you tink of te Americas Cup?' he asked me, after he'd had our glasses changed for bigger ones, and filled.

I wasn't sure just how much irony he wanted of me. I was bored to within an inch of madness by the Americas Cup which was still nearly a year away. On the other hand I had to remind myself that I was now in Western Australia. I laughed. Just a little. 'It is a touch excessive,' I said, leaving out the bored to within an inch of madness stuff.

But I'd missed the point of the question. He wasn't looking for a small amount of irony. He wasn't looking, as it happened, for *any*. What he wanted to know was who I thought would win.

'I fancy England or Italy myself,' he said.

'England?' Shows what I knew. I thought it was only between America and Australia.

'Yep. Dark horse, England.'

'The key to it,' Charlie said, 'is the water between Fremantle and Rottnest. It's a lot trickier than the Americans know or are used to.'

Already this had become too technical for me. I deferred to Ros whose home waters these were. I went vacant and stared into my Swan Lager. From next door, in the Workmen's Bar, came the sounds of the biggest party ever held in Australia, or the world. And they hadn't won a boat race – come to that, they hadn't won anything – for over two hundred years.

I came to when it was my turn to order drinks. 'My shout,' I said, and when I'd paid I tried to do what Charlie and Henri did with their change, leaving it on the bar, like poker money, so that the barman could take from it in response to the faintest nod of the head. I'd always liked this Australian habit of slapping your notes down on the bar and allowing the pile to diminish through the evening; and I noticed that it was even more common in the north, where the heat made fumbling for your wallet in your shorts uncomfortable. I suddenly thought of England and all those white depressed men counting out their pennies from plastic coin trays, and I wanted never to go back there.

'What do you tink of te Adelaide Grand Prix?' Henri asked me.

'Now that,' Charlie said, 'is the way to make money. A lot more people are interested in cars than they are in yachts.'

I fell vacant again.

Towards the end of the evening the name Ernie Bridge cropped up. Ernie Bridge was the Honorary Minister assisting the Minister (that's to say the *real* Minister) for the North-West and Kimberley. He was also an Aborigine. 'He represents this constituency,' Charlie said. 'Doesn't he, Cyril?'

Cyril was the barman and neither knew nor cared who his local state member was. 'I dunno,' he said. 'Maybe.'

'It's amazing,' Charlie said. 'Australians are like that everywhere. Ask them a question about politics and they instantly go vague.'

Henri believed there was time to squeeze in one last beer. 'Tat's te way it should be,' he said. 'It's not right to talk politics while you're drinking.'

Nor, apparently, while you're driving a tourist bus. I tried to get Sue to open up, the following morning, on the subject of the new breed of entrepreneurs who had come to the Kimberleys – people like Frank Camer-Pesci who had arrived as a bricklayer and now owned four modern hotels, and Lord McAlpine, the Treasurer of the Conservative Party, who had a name like a building industry and was at present pumping money and publicity into Broome. But she was unresponsive. 'Some people think they're a bit arrogant,' was the most she would give me.

She became almost radiant, though, on the road to Lake Argyle, when Jude told us that only the week before the police had found the bodies of an Aboriginal woman and a kangaroo floating mysteriously down the River Ord. 'That doesn't sound so good?' she said, her voice at full lilt.

The drive along the Ord to the great Dam at Lake Argyle (where you will find nine times more water than in Sydney Harbour – *nine times!*) was most spectacular. We stopped to look at crocodiles relaxing with their mouths open in the sun, or practising their ghastly weightless droop in the water; and we entered high, silent country where the Ord ran at the bottom of immense ravines, visited by an infinitude of darting swifts and swallows. But no scenery was too wonderful to silence Sue's pedantry. A Morning Irrigation we had paid for, and a Morning Irrigation we received. Volume and weight of water, surface, spillage, seepage, wastage, wantage (was there such a word or had it come to me in a dream of deluge?) – we got the lot.

Later in the morning we arrived at the Argyle Homestead, the home of the famous pioneer family the Duracks (pronounced Durex by Sue), now moved to a new site. Roy Walker, once head stockman for the last of the Kimberley Durex, looked after the place, acting as gardener, curator, guide, admission-ticket collector, identifier of sad Irish faces in photographs ('That's Patrick . . . that's Stumpy'), and general odd-job man. He was stripped to the waist when we turned up, wearing blue jeans and an old drover's hat, and pushing a wheelbarrow. From a distance he could have been taken for an Aborigine; there was the same slowness about his movements, the same melancholy in the set of his features, the same physical attenuation. Close up, though, he had eyes the colour of cornflowers. And the limpid fatigue in them was purely personal, not of the race.

He talked to us about the Aborigines who used to be his friends but who were now gone to ruin in the towns, sniffing petrol, drinking the water from car batteries, eating sandwiches made of boot polish mixed with methylated spirits. 'They'll eat and drink anything up here,' he said, 'even scent, which rots the belly quicker than anything.'

The homestead enjoyed an isolation which made me giddy. The gardens choked in the heat. Spinifex pigeons with rakish crests came to Roy's call. Bower birds busied themselves doing up their bachelor pads. The air swarmed with hosts of butter-flies of enormous size. And the whole time he talked to us a trickle of perspiration ran down Roy's weather-beaten chest. He was getting lonely here. It seemed to me that it was doing him no good, every day raking the ashes not just of someone else's past but also of his own. But he was hopeful of a change.

He had recently been interviewed by a local paper and had been quoted as saying that he wouldn't mind having a woman to live with him up here except that he didn't believe a modern woman could survive the hardship of the bush. Since then he'd had letters from women ready to take up his challenge. He particularly liked the one who simply said, 'I can. I'm forty years old, five feet tall and weigh eight stone.' He'd written back and was expecting her to join him any day.

'With the intention of seeing how you hit it off?' Ros asked.

He wiped the perspiration off his brow and opened his soft blue eyes. 'With the intention of matrimony,' he said.

Since we weren't going to be able to use Kununurra as a base to explore the Kimberleys, I decided that we would try the region from the other end. If we caught the bus after dinner we could be in Derby, eight or nine hundred kilometres away, by four or five o'clock in the morning.

'Derby? What do you want to go to Derby for?' Henri asked when we met again that evening in the Green Room.

He wasn't particularly impressed with any of my reasoning, but when I added that an old childhood friend of Ros's was there, running a hotel and restaurant, his objections lost themselves in simple word association. 'Do you like French food?' he immediately asked me.

'Of course,' I said.

'I'll take you where you can get some in Pert. I know te best chefs. I only eat tere when I know tey're cooking.'

'How do you know when that is?' I asked. Naive bastard.

'I go into the kitchens. I walk straight trough te restaurant and see who's cooking. If tey're not tere, I don't order.'

'I suppose that's the way to do it,' I said.

'Bloody sure. I love good French food and good French wine. Between us, my wife and I can drink tree, four bottles.'

'That's good going,' I said.

Henri rolled his eyes. His moustache was so black and sleek that it actually caught the light. He was, literally, a dazzling man. And he looked so ecstatic, remembering the amount of food and wine he and his wife got through, that I wondered why he didn't think of opening his own restaurant.

'Because I wouldn't have time for fishing.' He looked around him here. I'd noticed that he'd been growing increasingly restive, watching girls coming into the bar. And I had the feeling that he didn't want Ros to hear what he had to say to me next. Which was, 'I'll tell you one ting my wife and I often talk about opening . . . A high-class brottle.'

I got him to repeat this so that I could be certain it was Mauritian/Australian for what I thought it was, and not a perfectly good pronunciation of a word for a Western Australian measure of French wine.

'There are no high-class ones in Perth already?' I asked.

'Yes and no,' Henri said. He was fond of that expression. The night before he'd told us that his wife was pregnant and when we'd asked him if he wanted a son or a daughter he'd employed it then. What he seemed to mean tonight was that there might have been high-class ones *in* Perth, but not where he and his wife had it in mind to open one, which was *off* Perth.

'*Off* Perth?'

He looked around the room again. He didn't want me giving away his idea. 'If you sail six nautical miles out of Pert you can do anyting,' he told me.

I tried to let this information really sink in. 'Anything?'

He nodded. 'Anyting you can tink of.'

While I was failing Henri's test – all I could think of doing six nautical miles off Perth was fishing – Ros had inadvertently blundered into the Australian sex-war zone, patrolled on this occasion by the drivers of the bus we hoped to catch. Calling it a bus had been the first of her mistakes. 'Look, Sheila,' one of them had said, putting his arm around her shoulders and pointing to the passing traffic, 'see that – that's a car. See that – that's a truck. And that, over there, is a coach. On a bus you buy tickets. *I* drive a coach. *I* don't sell tickets.'

'We've already got tickets,' Ros said.

'We?' The arm was still around the shoulder.

'I've got mine, my husband's got his.'

'Oh, your husband. Been keeping him behind the bushes while you do the charming, eh?' He was called John, this one. His mate was Dave. They were a sort of version of Wayne and Clay without the refinement.

From the expression on her face when she returned I could see that she'd been contemplating violence.

'Homicide?' I asked.

'Suicide,' she said.

Charlie tried to calm her down. 'It's just the uniform,' he said. 'It was the same when the coons were given self-government in Kenya. They were suddenly all tin-pot Hitlers. So I played ignorant. It doesn't cost anything to play ignorant.'

It was odd, hearing coon-talk from Charlie. Although it accorded naturally enough with his faint South African/Rhodesian intonation, it was somehow belied by his sympathetic, boyish expression. Had you listened to him only with your eyes you would have believed he was saying something quite different. So here was another example, I told myself, of a person's opinions being the worst and least interesting part of him.

And for some reason Charlie was all opinion tonight. Coons copped it, the diamond mine copped it, even customs officials got it in the neck. 'Do you know,' he said, 'that if they go through your case you can order them to re-pack it exactly as it was? OK, you can say, you took it out, you put it back.'

'Tat's true,' Henri confirmed. 'You can.'

But it was for the local owners of jeeps and Range Rovers and Toyota 4-wheel drives that he reserved his greatest scorn.

'The funny thing is,' he said, 'that nine-tenths of them never drive on anything but bitumen.'

You have to hear a white Kenyan pronounce bitumen in order to realize how much bitch is in it.

Before we left we exchanged addresses and agreed that we would all try to meet up in Perth.

'For a drink,' Ros said.

'For a lot more tan tat,' Henri promised.

We reminded him that his wife was due to give birth at around about the time we'd be in Perth. 'So?' he said. 'We'll take te baby to a French restaurant.'

On the bus to Derby the drivers went through their usual dispiriting routine: mobile toilets, knickers round the ankles, no poofters in the rest area. It occurred to me as I dozed that there was an article to be written dealing with the problems most frequently associated with Aborigines – alcoholism, unsociable behaviour, an inability to be assimilated into polite society, irrational aggression, and so on – except that the subject of the article would be the white Australian male, not the Aborigine. Being a man in Australia, by which I meant being the kind of man who could drive a busload of poofters, sheilas and Abos through the outback in the dead of night, had never looked so precarious to me; for a number of reasons – not the least of which were feminism, androgyny and Land Rights – the Australian bloke appeared to be on the front line of a serious social breakdown.

I didn't do much talking on the bus. I mainly slept. But I did notice that the girl on the seat across the aisle to me was reading Peter Carey's *Illy whacker* and I asked her how she was liking it.

'Aw, not much,' she said. 'I've bought it, so I'll finish it. But I prefer *A Fortunate Life*.'

A Fortunate Life was an endurance story written by an old man who had undergone every known hardship and deprivation but was still able to come up smiling and proud to be an Australian. I had tried to read it, in response to the enormous popularity it was enjoying in the country, but found it unreadable. It seems to me essential that one hold on to the idea of unreadability, as a distinct literary non-quality, an innate thing in itself, even in the face of the evidence of several million readers reading it. *A Fortunate Life* was unreadable because it was unwritten; which unwrittenness, it seemed to me, was the very reason Australians liked it. I had noticed before that Australians preferred their fiction to be unfictional, a mere mode of access to an original, authentic, lived experience. Some of the country's most favoured writers were in fact un-writers and un-wrote with extreme plainness and simplicity, using words only for want of something more elementary. Even the cream of Australia's academic obscurantists, men who could be instantly unintelligible about a single line of poetry, found a new lucidity when they came to be novelists and made little sentences about Frank and Hilda and their embarrassment on their wedding night.

'What's that?' asked Frank, worriedly.

'Blood,' Hilda said, consolingly.

'Aw gee,' Frank said.

'I love you, Frank,' said Hilda, holding him very close.

'I love you, too, Hilda,' Frank said.

As they pledged their troth once more, mysterious noises reached them from the bush.

FOUR

ARSE-END CHARLIE

The saddest and least inviting town-sign you will ever see stands, miles from where any of the visitors it is meant to welcome will ever find it, at the far extremity of Derby, a spot that you neither enter nor leave by, close to where the desolate jetty strays into the rotting waters of King Sound like a half-hearted suicide.

A mere six or seven kilometres away is the Leprosarium; a short sail up the Sound, Point Torment; and, a couple of days' trek through inhospitable country, Mount Disaster. Reach that and you wouldn't be at all far from where the explorer George Grey was speared by natives – his men unable to do much for him, either because they were unable to get their rifles out of their waterproof bags in time, or because they'd dropped down in a dead stupor at their first sighting of the black men they'd come to civilize. 'Oh, God! Sir,' one of Grey's trustiest lieutenants cried out, as the savages advanced. 'Oh, God! Sir, look at them; look at them!' Whereafter he was incapable of delivering a single sensible sentence again until he was transported back to England.

William Dampier, the first white man ever to try his luck

ashore hereabouts — as the melancholy town-sign records — wasn't too impressed by what he saw either. 'Dry and dusty,' he noted in his journal. And as for the inhabitants: the 'Misirablest people in the world'. But, lest you should think that is the beginning and the end of Derby, the home-made hand-painted board proclaims the town's other claims to your attention. As for example its possessing the LARGEST TIDAL VARIATION IN THE SOUTHERN HEMISPHERE; to say nothing of its having landed the LARGEST MUD CRABS and CROCODILES EIGHTEEN AND A HALF FEET LONG. DON'T MISS OUR SUNSETS, you are implored, in case you are still thinking of leaving. And then, as a plaintive afterthought, THE PEOPLE *HAVE* CHANGED.

A hostage to fortune, had fortune ever passed that way.

Things didn't go too well for us in Derby at first. We'd been bundled off the bus in the dead of night, and had booked into a hotel which was a sister establishment to the one we'd stayed in at Kununurra, only to discover in the morning that we were half an hour's walk from the centre of town, assuming there to be a centre of town, and that the walk was more likely to take twice that long in the intense heat. We did it in short bursts, stopping for shelter whenever we found a tree that wasn't itself gasping and leafless. The outskirts of the town were indeed dry and dusty. And flat. And unrelieved. And teeming with small insect and minor reptile activity. Every step we took seemed to disturb a little kingdom of invertebrates. Grasshoppers flicked. Bull ants reared. Tiny lizards darted across our feet. Each blade of grass, each granule of dirt, was alive and chirruping.

Our first object was the Boab Hotel where Ros expected to find her old friend from Perth, Bruce Flower. We were neither of us certain what we wanted from him, over and above a warm handshake and a cold beer, but we shared some essentially unspoken optimism that he would prove to be the element that had been missing from Kununurra, a contact through whom we could meet people knowledgeable about the area, the reason we were going to do much better in the West Kimberleys than we had in the East. So it was a cruel blow to discover that Bruce Flower no longer had any connection with the Boab Hotel, that he no longer lived in Derby, and that it was not the slightest recommendation of us in the bar known as The Waterhole to admit that we knew him.

We took a beer while we were there, and wondered what to do next. I noticed that the present licensee's name was R A (Rosco) Scoro and made ill-tempered anagrams with it for five minutes. A rock band consisting of one Aborigine and one part-Aborigine was practising in the corner. The band was called MANTUS, their speakers bore the maker's name, MANTARBO, and the full Aborigine had the word MANDINGO printed across his T-shirt. All in all there was a lot of MAN about. A lot of irony too. On the wall by the bar was a poster publicizing 1986 as the year of the West Australian Tourist Board's Be Nice To A Visitor Campaign. It depicted, in cartoon form, a number of the very worst kind of holiday-makers looking fat and hot and lost and unhappy in Hawaiian shirts, and it carried the slogan, 'Make a tourist a friend. Give 'em a hand.' This had been altered to, 'Give 'em a hand job.' The men at the bar watched us keenly to see how we responded to Waterhole wit. Just to be on the safe side I permitted a dry rasp to escape my throat.

Once we'd finished our beer we left the pub and made for the Tourist Bureau at the far end of town. With the exception of a few groups of Aborigines partying under the trees, we were the only people on the street not in a car. The sun beat down on us, curling our hair and bleaching the colour out of our clothes. We walked slowly, pausing at one point to observe an Aboriginal family quarrel. A car containing a middle-aged couple had pulled up at one of the extemporized parties, in order to rescue a young girl who had clearly been out all night in company her parents did not consider choice. There was a lot of screaming and shouting, with the father appearing to threaten a heart attack. 'Apart from the bad language and the alcohol,' Rosalin said, 'the scene is not entirely un-Jewish.'

It was too hot for me to rise. And I was hating Derby more with every minute. It seemed to be composed of all the elements that make remote country towns vile anywhere in the world. It possessed none of the natural beauty of Kununurra – no orange hills or hidden valleys – and none of its primitive civic bezazz either. No government buildings that I could see. No bustling shops. Just a tumble of sheds unable to hold their outline in the heat haze. And a long dusty highway with too wide a nature strip in the middle, so that merely crossing the road was a migration. I fell into a slumbering bank to cash a cheque. The bank tellers started at the appearance of another mortal. The name of the one who dealt with me was Stormy Collopy. As I remembered, a collop was an egg fried on bacon, or a thick fold of fatty flesh. Had I been forced to live in Derby I would have changed my name at once to Torrid Rind. Back on the main road I found Ros standing like one of the damned, staring down a side street at the end of which you could see miles of sandflats and in the distance the sea bubbling in the heat. The town centre of Hades must offer an identical prospect.

When we finally found the Tourist Bureau it was closed. A chirpy note informed us that it would be open again in half an hour, though it didn't say in half an hour from when. Suffering from exhaustion, thirst, frustration, and third-degree sunburn, in no particular order, we collapsed into a chicken and chip eatery next door. It's possible to underestimate the subtleties of Australian cuisine. It might be thought that dry stuffed chicken fried in boiling fat would have been the last thing to ease our discomfort, but in fact a scalded stomach can free the mind wonderfully from all other worries. Bleeding internally, we forgot our peeling flesh. And soon our cheerfulness was very nearly restored, although living symbols of determined defeat were all around us.

A big sad girl was being taught how to prepare garlic bread and how to work the till, but seemed unable to distinguish the two activities. Our change came back reeking of garlic. It's possible there was small coinage in the bread. The sweat ran down her face and neck, back into the boiling oil.

An equally sad man sat at the table next to us, presiding over the evidence of a mountainous lunch, the tin-foil carry-home bag in front of him a still-smoking ossuary of chook remains. He took a vague interest in our presence, deriving some comfort, I thought, from our inflammation and fatigue. We seemed to suit the way he felt. Before we fell into conversation he put his face through a variety of wry expressions, smiling and sometimes even mumbling to himself. He was heavy and hapless, his belly hanging like a sack of dead flesh over his blue workman's shorts. He looked central European but spoke his broken Australian with a curious lilt, as if he'd lived for a while in Ireland or Cornwall. He was a seasonal worker, a truck driver who hired himself out as and where there was a need for him. He travelled a million miles a year, he told us, following seasonal demand. But he had contracted a back complaint, which he felt bound to confess to any prospective employer. An expression of slightly crazed honesty passed across his smooth features. 'I must tell,' he said. He didn't really know what had brought him to Derby and didn't have any strong conviction that Derby would have anything to offer him. In the meantime he lived on his own – a single man in a tent – sitting by the hour in this chicken bar, sucking stuffing off his fingers, smiling mirthlessly to himself, and waiting for employment.

'In a good week,' he told us, 'I can make a thousand dollars.' But that was whittled down to no more than a hundred after tax and what he called 'lifestyle expenses'. His work had taken him all over the world, where he had seen things that had bemused him. As for example, the turn around of raw materials. He couldn't understand how or why a thing gets taken out of the ground, exported, changed into another thing, and is then returned to its place of origin at a vastly inflated price, much misery having been caused along the way to the people who have moved and changed it. This wasn't a matter of merely passing perplexity to him; he seemed to have taken all the cruel futility of the process into himself and to have fed upon it. We'd have been quite wrong to suppose he was looking for discussion. Behind his pretend bemusement there was in fact a starry certainty. So when Ros tried to soothe him by wondering if it wouldn't help to see capitalism as a great washing machine, the tumble action being a more encouraging and domestic metaphor than his senseless whirligig of commodities, she was wasting her time. 'I wouldn't know about that,' he said. 'I've no way of ascertaining that.'

What he did know was that a man ought to have his own space to produce the wherewithal to satisfy his own needs. The Chinese Republic looked the best place to him. In the meantime, since everything was inhuman and destructive of man's peace of mind, he couldn't see why we didn't go the whole hog and destroy people. Given that we wanted to make man miserable and full of despair, why did we stop at the dole? Why didn't we mount machine guns to the front of our cars and go out and mow one another down? As for himself he didn't care what happened. Men were better when they lived like beasts and followed the seasons, moving up and down with the snow lines. He likened himself to a bear who wanted to follow the snow.

The phrase 'I wouldn't know about that' was one he resorted to almost every time either one of us said anything. It was part indifference, part personal wariness, but part, too, a refusal to believe that even the most innocently verifiable fact didn't have some explosive hidden away inside it. Thus when we asked him, as a man who drove millions of miles a year, the distance between Derby and Broome, he wouldn't commit himself. 'I wouldn't know about that myself,' he said, 'you'll have to make your own enquiries.'

He stayed in both our minds for days – a modern Australian migrant version of one of those perplexed working-class heroes in Victorian industrial novels, a sort of Stephen Blackpool without the sanctimony and pap, and therefore without the restraints, thinking his way through the major issues of our time, almost without hope, wholly isolated, staring up the skirts of insanity.

We knew it was time to leave him when he brought up the subject of the gas chambers and whether anyone had really been put to death in them. 'I wouldn't know about that myself . . .' We tried the Tourist Information Bureau again. This time it was open. So much for the good news. The news of the other kind was that everything we wanted information about was closed. The Gibb River Road? Impassable. The tracks and turnpikes to the gorges – Derby called itself the Gateway to the Gorges –? Still ungraded. The Wet had done so much damage to the gravel roads that the graders themselves had not yet been able to get through. 'Forget it,' the tourist officer told us when we asked him if there were any local guides or operators who might be prepared to give it a try. 'Forget it,' he told us when we wondered if we could hire a 4-wheel drive to give it a try ourselves. 'My advice to you,' he said, 'is to get the hell out.'

Let me be absolutely clear about something: he was as handsome, helpful, considerate and courteous a tourist information officer as you could hope to find. Benign intention shone from his obliging countenance. The muscular forearms which he folded across his chest in sympathy as we showed our frustration were such as would have plucked a stranger's child from the rapids, or the stranger himself from the jaws of an eighteen-and-a-half-foot crocodile. One small defect only stood between him and his being the best tourist information officer in the business, and that was that he didn't want to give us any tourist information.

'What would you do with a car?' he asked me, when I suggested that he recommend a rental company.

'See the town,' I said.

'See the town? You can see all there is to see in Derby in ten minutes.' He really was upset for us. I thought I even spotted moisture in the corner of his eye. 'In fact, if you've got here you've already seen it.'

There was absolutely nothing we could do to stop him looking in his directory for the times of the next planes out.

Just as he was running his pencil down the page a person called Tony popped in to finalize some travel arrangement. Tony was a peripatetic photographer, specializing in group portraits of families inhabiting remote places. According to Tony the camera had never before been to some of the remote places he took it. Just the person to help us out, you would have thought, except that he was on his way south, to Broome, which was where the man from the bureau immediately decided we should accompany him.

'I won't be leaving until later tonight,' Tony said. 'But you're welcome to join me.'

'I'd snap at that,' the man from the bureau said. 'I wouldn't let an offer like that pass you by.'

Ros and I exchanged bewildered glances. We were neither of us certain how we'd been manoeuvred into looking for a lift out of a town we'd only just got to. 'I'll tell you what,' the photographer said. 'I'll call in at your hotel on the way out. If you're ready to go, fine. If you're not, also fine. No sweat either way. No worries.'

We left it at that and reeled out into the sun. 'You'd be fools not to snap at that,' was the last thing the man charged with welcoming visitors to Derby said to us.

We were both unable to face the walk back to our hotel. I left Ros in the shade and went to look for a phone. As soon as I found one I rang the various local car-hire companies. Most of them were either no longer in business or not answering their phones. Those I did get were uniformly discouraging. One woman had a Suzuki she could let me have but she didn't really feel she could recommend it. 'No air-conditioning in it,' she said. 'And no power. So it's a bit hot, a bit slow and, for what it is, a bit dear.' I said I'd take it. She told me it would be available first thing the following morning. I explained that my wife was at this very moment expiring under a boab tree, that the bakelite of the telephone receiver was at this very moment liquefying in the heat and running molten down my fingers, and that we needed something *right now* to get us back either to our hotel or to the infirmary, whichever happened to be the closer.

'Why don't you try a taxi?' she said.

And that was how we came to fall in with Hector. And to stay in Derby somewhat longer than we'd bargained for.

Ex-Presbyterian-public-schoolboy from Perth (your school is always with you in W.A.), one-time administrator, adventurer and meat inspector, but today looking like a renegade senior auditor who'd run off with his best friend's accounts, Hector Ross in wild and craggy middle age nursed a leg which only didn't trouble him when he was dancing, ferried Aborigines from their alcohol-free townships to the grog shops and back again, and let it be seen that to be a taxi driver out here in the far north-west was to be a species of eccentric, a kind of buccaneer.

It is necessary to conceive, though, of pretty laconic buccaneering.

'That'd be right,' he said, when we told him that we'd had a strange experience in the Derby Disinformation Bureau, just yards from where he picked us up. 'That'd be right,' he repeated, when we told him that we'd been strongly urged to take the first lift out. 'That's what they all get told.'

I asked him if this meant that it wasn't therefore necessarily the case that the roads to the gorges were impassable.

He took his time answering. He drove his car with one hand, rubbing away at his leg with the other. Occasionally he would raise the tips of his fingers above the steering wheel in acknowledgement of the greetings of passing Aborigines. Finally, he pulled into the kerb – I say kerb, but it was a matter only of variation of dust level – and beckoned to one particular Aborigine, a bedraggled make-believe cowboy in drainpipe denims and riding boots. They exchanged a few rapid sentences. Then Hector dismissed him and turned around in his seat. 'Depends where you want to go, of course,' he said. 'But he reckons you can get through. He's just swum across himself to get to the music tonight.'

'There's music tonight?' (That was Ros, not me. I was still picturing the Aborigine dog-paddling across the King Leopold Ranges in his riding boots to have a Friday night on the town.)

Hector took his time answering again. I thought I even caught him checking us out in his rear driving mirror. Choosy place, Derby.

But we must have passed the test, because he eventually said, 'At the Boab.'

'Is it good?' (That was still Ros.)

'Well, I go.'

I mentioned that we'd been along to the Boab ourselves earlier that day in search of Bruce Flower, and that we hadn't, as a consequence, won many friends.

'Bruce Flower? No – that'd be right – I guess you wouldn't have.'

We'd arrived by now at our destination. 'See you later at the Boab, then,' Ros said, entirely to my surprise.

Surprise, however, knew better than to try anything on Hector Ross. 'That's if I'm there,' he said.

Before heading out for the Boab that evening (we didn't so much as mention Broome) we took advantage of HAPPY HOUR AND A HALF at our own hotel, where we briefly talked to Ken Mills, a hospital administrator from Kununurra who was on the point of moving to Kalgoorlie to escape the crippling expense of living in the north. The son of Italian migrants (a good Sicilian name, Mills), himself as angelic as a Raphaelite seraph, with gently throbbing eyes and a soft seraphic beard, Ken addressed us on the subject of Kununurra economics in that grossly exaggerated Australian drawl which only the children of first-generation migrants adopt, presumably as an act of symbolic revolt from the ahshadahpahyahface English of their parents. 'Jeez, the rents. High? What? If they went enny higher they'd be trevelling in bloody Concorde.'

Talking of Kununurra reminded us of the story we'd heard about the Aboriginal woman and the kangaroo found floating down the Ord. We thought Ken would be able to shed some light on this, but in fact it was we who illuminated him. His eyes danced. 'I'm very glad you told me that,' he said. 'I could never work out why the hospital had done an autopsy on a kangaroo.'

I found the reference to dumb animals and dissection a bit untimely myself, given where Ros had decided we were going tonight. Like lambs to the slaughter, I thought, as we trod that same dusty road to the Boab which had broken our spirits earlier in the day. Like fish to the bait. Like moths to the flame.

Pubs that went in for live entertainment had always caused me concern; for some reason not at all worth examining, I associated the combination of music and alcohol with extreme danger. Extreme danger to me. So it was a relief to push open the doors of The Waterhole and discover a perfectly respectable, I might even say clerkly, crowd, clapping their hands to MANTUS, and joining in the words with the lead singer – *I fought the law but . . . the law won.*

Girls who looked like first-year primary teachers or trainee probation officers sat together drinking pineapple juices, dressed in summer frocks their mothers might have posted them from Perth. Young men with beards as soft and seraphic as Ken Mills's stood at the bar and melted us with their warm, welcoming expressions. After several tentative 'How's yer's going?' one of these finally introduced himself. 'Orlando De Biasi,' he said. 'And you?'

It was only when I took his hand that I realized how badly he needed my support. He'd have gone at the knees had I not kept him up. On close inspection I noticed that his eyes were red – not just red-rimmed but red in the very iris, streaked like a Kununurra sunset in the very whites.

'You look worse than my bloody dog,' one of his friends said to him.

The moment he discovered we were travellers he offered to take us fishing. 'I'll pick you up from your hotel at five a.m.,' he said.

I put it to him that he might have trouble making such an early start, given what a good time he was having.

'Bloody will,' he said, blinking his eyes at me and showing us that even his lids were red. There was something of a tyro-musketeer about him, the youngest of the magnificent however many, the one you wouldn't originally take along but would come wholly to rely on in the end. He responded to my implicit challenge to his sobriety by suddenly holding himself very erect and running through an entirely lucid list of the other people who would be accompanying us on the five a.m. fishing expedition, the number of vehicles that would be going, and the precise names of the various creeks and billabongs in which we would be fishing. If I wasn't mistaken in my geography, the last of these necessitated a journey over that same mountain range on which George Grey had paused, while removing Aboriginal spears from his side, in order to wonder at the spectacle of a foaming cataract below him, and to imagine a time when 'civilization would have followed my tracks, and . . . rude nature and the savage would no longer reign supreme'. In which case we really owed it to ourselves to be up and ready in the morning. On the other hand, who on earth *was* Orlando De Biasi?

'How long have we got to decide whether or not we can make it?' I asked him.

He instantly went flexible again – I mean in body and in attitude. 'Tell me at the end of the evening,' he said. 'If you tell me before then I'll forget.'

At which he went off to dance in the small space between the tables with a very fat but breastless girl wearing a cowboy hat fitted with flashing lights – the electric cowgirl.

While we'd been talking to Orlando I'd noticed that Hector had arrived, looking no less authoritative than before, when at the wheel of his taxi, but distinctly spruced up and looking for a good time.

'We've just been offered the chance to go out fishing,' we told him. 'What do you think?'

'Take it! With him? Take it! Snap at it!'

(*Snap at it* was precisely the expression the man from the bureau had used when urging us to accept the lift to Broome. They went in for voicing pretty definite opinions, hereabouts.)

But later on, when Orlando wandered over and explained to Hector that it wasn't fishing on a boat he was planning, but overland travel, Hector changed his mind. 'Give it away,' he said. 'Too uncomfortable. Too hot. Too many mosquitoes. You won't enjoy it.'

It soon became clear to us that where previously, in the harsh light of a Derby afternoon, everybody had been trying to get us out of town, now, in the smoky excitement of a Derby Friday night at the Boab, everybody was competing to see who could give us the better time. At least two more fishing trips came our way. Then Hector proposed a couple of rival schemes of his own. One for putting us in touch with Sam Lovell, a famous local Aborigine whose safaris Hector reckoned to be second to none in Australia. The other for us to travel in the front seat of his taxi with him, through the night, so that we should observe for ourselves the wily character of the blackfeller. Suddenly, after appearing to turn its back on us entirely, Derby was suffocating us in the promiscuity of its embrace.

We suffered some temporary disaffection though – a lovers' tiff, I suppose you might call it – when Hector became over-excited on the subject of Aborigines, what they got up to in his taxi, and what they got up to, come to that, absolutely anywhere else. It began, mildly enough, with his running through the qualities that most typified the Aborigine of his acquaintance – rat-cunning, as I remember, being the one he most frequently returned to. But he somehow moved from that, I hope not with our connivance, to the whole question of Land Rights, and it was then that he began to bang the table. 'It's got no chance in this state. No chance. We'll ship it out.' He had become red in the face and was turning his voice upon us as if it were a cannon. 'We won't give it house room in this state. We won't entertain it. We'll ship it out! Out!'

He took a minute or two to go to the bathroom – I thought maybe to calm himself; but he was even redder when he returned. 'If I may be blunt,' he said, 'this is arse-end Charlie up here. But that doesn't mean we don't know what we're doing. Or what we think. So you tell me this?' – he pointed, unexpectedly, to a spot on the dance floor where the electric cowgirl was setting an example which the primary-school teachers in their Perth frocks were loth to follow – 'What happens if we find minerals or oils there? Right there?'

I tried to joke him out of it. 'Well, first of all I suppose we finish our beers,' I said.

Pathetic, I know. Hector thought so too. He had a way of making me feel that I was a very trivial person. He achieved this partly by looking away, partly by rubbing the pain in his leg, whenever I spoke.

'I'll tell you what happens,' he said. 'We dig. We mine. We get it out. And we all get the benefits. That's what *we* do. But the Abo says the land is his. Coon country. Find uranium or oil on a few hectares he hasn't been near for twenty thousand years and suddenly its sacred coon country. No one else has such rights of private landlordism. Not beyond three metres underground. If I find gold a hundred feet under my house it's not mine by rights. You don't own what's underground. But the Abo thinks he does. I'm telling you – it'll divide the state. You can't have one set of laws for one people and one set of laws for the other.'

I didn't say the obvious thing in response to that last sentence. I'd vowed that I wasn't going to wander round Australia explaining their glaring inconsistencies to Australians. I didn't think that was the right way for a guest to behave. But I had to say something if only to ease my own internal pressure. Just opening my mouth would probably have done; but while it was open I thought I might as well say, 'So Land Rights is still a hot potato?' with it.

He banged the table again, sending spumes of ice-cold beer high into the air. 'Red-hot!' he boomed.

'Wheeeee!' cried the electric cowgirl, tilting her head backwards and catching the beer-spray on her chin.

I can't say that I was especially convinced by the noises either of them was making. The fat girl's good time and Hector's rage seemed to me to belong to the same area of psychological, maybe even purely physiological, compulsion. The need preceded the occasion. There was no reason to suppose that Hector was a confirmed racist, just because he slagged off coons, than to assume that the girl was a dedicated hedonist, just because she was misbehaving on the dance floor. That which we call racism is often merely the expression of a fundamental yearning, akin to thirst or hunger, to speak violence. The object – the particular instance of colour or nationality – is purely arbitrary. It's just tough if you happen to be it.

And, as if to prove that very point, Hector was soon getting the aggression and the competitiveness out of his system on a very different pretext. In order to calm him down, and because she herself was becoming homesick in the heat and the excitement, Ros had begun to talk to him about Perth. Within seconds they'd unearthed a coincidence – of no interest whatsoever to anybody else, but a matter of much hilarity and vehemence for them: Ros's brother and Hector had rowed, respectively, for two of Perth's arch-rival public schools.

'You went to Scotch?'

'Your brother went to Aquinas?'

I couldn't believe my ears. Here in the Boab Hotel in the far West Kimberleys, where eighteen-and-a-half-foot crocodiles patrolled the rivers, in despite of which Aborigines from the northern missions swam down to listen to the wild music of MANTUS, a couple of fully grown adults were standing on chairs and shouting:

'Scotch!'

'Aquinas!'

Although he had something badly wrong with his leg, and would rub away at it whenever I was talking, Hector didn't seem to be at all physically incommoded when it came to dancing with Ros. He threw himself around the little floor, banging into tables, his limbs thrashing, his eyes rolling in his head, while I sat and guarded his purse. You would have said, from the way he jived and bopped and limboed, that here was a man of fifty in the absolute peak of condition; and yet the minute he returned to the table he would start holding his thigh and wincing. At one point, just as I was about to offer some observation on the lateness of the hour, he even howled. 'The doctors say it's a trapped nerve,' he told me. 'But I think the mosquitoes are to blame.'

I didn't tell him what I thought.

It was just after this that the lead singer of MANTUS came over to join us. His name was Rod Drummond and he was a senior welfare worker at an Aboriginal Hostel in town. ('This one's a good one,' Hector whispered to me. 'This one's high caste.')

I asked Rod Drummond what MANTUS meant.

'I shouldn't really say,' he said.

I thought he was joking. 'Go on,' I said. 'I can take it.'

'Well' – he really was reluctant – '*Mantu* means pussy hunting, but with the *us* on the end it means muff diving.'

I marvelled at language variation as subtle as that, but he mistook my wonderment for disapproval. 'I said I shouldn't say,' he said.

At the end of the evening he invited us to come and talk to him at the Hostel before we left Derby. Various others reminded us of our arrangements for the following day. Just as we were leaving Orlando De Biasi fell against us and said something that approximated to 'See you at five in the morning.' And Hector offered to drive us back to our hotel, where there was a late-night disco.

As we were climbing into Hector's taxi a couple of young Aborigines approached us. We never got to find out what they wanted. Hector was on to them in a flash. 'No,' he shouted. 'Oh no – none of that!'

Shocked by the abruptness and violence of Hector's manner,

mindful of the basic respect owing from one race to another, and emboldened by all that the Boab had provided, Ros wound down her window and addressed the youths. 'As a stranger to this town, though not the state,' she said, 'and as a guest of this gentleman's, I regret that I am unable to accord you the courtesy which, in other circumstances and at any other time, I would consider it my pleasure and indeed my bounden duty to . . . ah . . . accord you; not least in the light of the obligations I feel, both for myself and on behalf of others, towards those whose deprivations and disadvantages are such that it would be the grossest discourtesy to compound them in any way – any way, that is, that might . . .'

'Jesus!' Hector said, speeding away, 'that's the longest sentence those bastards will ever have heard. They have enough trouble just handling bloody pidgin.'

We didn't stay long at the disco. Just long enough for me to look after Hector's purse while he did his Fred Astaire routine with Ros and then his Clifford Chatterley with me. Out of the blue – unless it was his leg that reminded him – he brought up the Falklands War. He told me that within hours of the first news of the Argentinian invasion thousands of West Australians with British blood in their veins had volunteered to spill it. There was war fever in the state, he said.

I must have replied with something like, 'How bizarre,' because he was suddenly booming again. 'It is not. It proves the old loyalties are still there. Principle. You fight for principle. And that doesn't change.'

I gave him back his purse. Before he left he reminded us that he'd be calling in the morning.

'That makes about twenty of them,' I said to Ros as I set the alarm clock. We went to sleep worrying not so much which arrangement we should keep but how we could get out of all of them.

But we needn't have fretted. Orlando De Biasi did not wake us at five a.m. and neither did anyone else. By noon the next day we were as friendless and alone in Derby as we'd been the same time the day before. And still without any means of getting about. We sat at the table of an outdoor takeaway joint and watched the dust settle on our spring rolls. A passing Aborigine in a Hawaiian shirt asked us 'ow we were goin', otherwise the streets were deserted. 'I feel like Cinderella,' I said to Ros. 'Last night I was somebody. Now look at me.'

'Do what you did yesterday,' she said.

'What's that?'

'Get a taxi.'

So I did. And that's how we came to fall in with Neil, the tax accountant, and meet Humpy the croc-wrestler, and find an Arab–Israeli war underway on the banks of the Fitzroy River.

FIVE

UMPIE BONG

'Now *that*,' I said, the moment I clapped eyes on my first ever specimen of Boab, 'is what you call a friendly tree.'

I don't think I meant much more than that I was elated to find a tree at last that I could recognize without help, and would, I was sure, on pain of death be able to recognize again. But it's also possible that some profound botanical intuition had worked within me or that there'd been a deep and silent telepathy between plant and man, because I found out later that agreeableness even to benevolence was indeed the crowning virtue of the Boab. It was Ernestine Hill's *The Great Australian Loneliness* which provided the corroborative, if somewhat florid, account:

> A Caliban of a tree, a grizzled, distorted old goblin with a girth of a giant, the hide of a rhinocerous, twiggy fingers clutching at empty air, and the disposition of a guardian angel – such is Kimberley's baobab, friendly ogre of the great North-west. Food for his hunger, water for his thirst, a house to live in, fibre to clothe him, fodder for his flocks, a pot of beer, a rope to hang him, and a tombstone when he is dead – these are the provisions of the

baobab for man. In all nature there is no ally so kindly, with the possible exception of the coconut palm.

(No – in Queensland we had to dodge the coconut palm, in terror of its bounty. Short of sunbathing in a crash helmet, how do you lie on a Queensland beach and 'Beware the falling coconuts'?)

Andansonia gregorii, first cousin to the African monkey-bred, the 'boab', as it is familiarly known, belongs to a zone of 1,000 square miles skirting the coast between Broome and the Victoria River. Magnificent specimens are to be seen in the streets of Derby, and along the banks of the Fitzroy and the Ord, and between those rivers and the sea it grows in profusion, the dominant personality of the bush . . .

Water preserved in its knotted hollows from the wet season is found fresh and clear after weeks, sometimes months, and when that source fails, in the merciless dry, the pith, ripped from beneath the bark and wrung like a cloth into a pannikin, provides a clear draught, cooling and tasteless, that is often the wanderer's eleventh-hour salvation. The rind of the pods, chopped and stirred with water, makes an acrid but nourishing food that the blacks enjoy, and that tides over the tuckerless white man to the next out-camp or station; and the flower, a waxy white bloom, possesses medicinal values, particularly in allaying fever. Stirred with sugar, it makes a refreshing drink. Some of the bushmen have succeeded in concocting spiritu-ous liquors from this mixture, well-fermented, which they insist have a fine 'sting' if made from the flowers of young trees . . .

But it is as first camp and last camp, station homestead, pub, prison, store, post office and bagman's rest that the boab has twined its roots deepest into the history of the country . . .

It was at the Boab Prison Tree in fact, the famous landmark just a few miles out of Derby, that we first talked business – though business wasn't what we called it – to Neil, the second eccentric and buccaneering taxi-driver-who-was-really-something-else we'd met in as many days. Neil had responded promptly to our noontime SOS, coming out of his taxi with an extended arm, a look of friendly calculation under his shaggy beard, and the line, 'So you want to see our fair town?' He was so clean that he actually sparkled in the sun. Sitting beside him in his taxi I could smell the soap he'd used, the deodorant, the shampoo, and maybe even the baby powder.

Seeing the fair town of Derby meant, as the man at the information bureau had warned us, seeing pretty much what we'd seen already. But we did get a look at Dampier's verdict, and the suicidal jetty, and the unsafe sea, and the illimitable marshes throwing up teasing mirages of hope and change. And we did get to find out a lot about Neil. Such as what he thought of the man at the information bureau, what he thought of the state of organized tourism in Derby, what he thought of other members of the business population, and what he thought of himself.

'Let me make one thing clear at the outset,' he told us. 'I only drive this taxi occasionally. I run an accountancy and pharmacy in the town. My partner and I have several million dollars invested in Derby. Which is why I take an interest in your story of how you were advised to leave.'

He was quite a young man to have several million dollars invested in Derby, baby-faced, even, behind his thick glasses and beneath his heavy beard. On the other hand there was something elderly about his deliberation and his pernicketiness. Unlike the man who'd bought the company because he'd liked the razor, Neil had bought the taxi because he'd disliked the company. 'I was sick of getting off planes and into dirty taxis,' he explained. 'I'd fly all the way from Perth without putting a speck on myself, and then after just five minutes in a taxi I'd arrive home filthy. The only way I could be certain of getting into a clean taxi was to buy my own.'

The subject of hygiene must have been what put him in mind to show us Derby's shanty town, an Aboriginal slum just a minute from the centre, though you would have thought, given the dramatic change, that you had been whisked suddenly to the worst of the black townships in South Africa. We were unable to believe our eyes. No photographs of remote or outback Australia ever showed you this – a street of shameful tin shacks in such disrepair that you might have taken each one to be its own rubbish tip; their miserable inhabitants squatting amongst the dereliction, shunning the squalor, to say nothing of the intolerable oven-heat, of their habitations. As we drove past, a dog was shitting on the front steps of an old man's shack. He was vainly trying to shoo it away, but without any expectation of success, his weary, futile loathing compounded by the presence of sightseers. The hand which he raised to the dog he might also have been raising to us, or to some higher authority. The fleeting scene stayed in our minds for months, an image of the utmost misery and hopelessness. We recalled it when the Hon. Malcolm Fraser returned to Australia, after his Eminent Persons' tour of South Africa, breathing righteousness. And we recalled it again when he returned from Memphis, having mysteriously lost his trousers.

'Of course nothing can be done for them,' Neil explained. 'They're vermin. They don't know how to live and they can't be taught. Even when they're given good conditions they turn them into this. They can't handle them. It's not unheard of, you know, for Aborigines to rip up the planks from their verandahs to light the fires in their electric ovens with. They're a good hundred years behind us. I've got some very good Aborigine friends – men I respect professionally, educated men I do business with – but I wouldn't go into any of their houses for fear of what I'd pick up.'

When the Moreton Bay Penal Settlement was moved in 1825 from the Redcliffe Peninsula to what is now Brisbane, the empty buildings were offered as a free gift to the local Aborigines. But they weren't much appreciated. Umpie Bong, the Aborigines called them – Dead Dwellings.

But there seemed no point in trying to talk to Neil about contempt being a double-headed weapon, a spear with a poisoned tip at either end. Though just how many more of his one-way certitudes we would have to swallow was a question that was bound to enter our deliberations when we came to decide on whether or not to accept his offer. Or challenge, I suppose I should call it. Standing by the Boab Prison Tree – a vast, hollowed-out example of my favourite vegetable, used at one time as an overnight lock-up for restraining local malefactors – he had returned to the problem of the man at the tourist bureau, and his 'negative attitude' to tourists. 'Didn't he mention my name,' Neil wanted to know, 'when you asked him whether there was anyone who would be willing to put you an expedition together?'

'Why?' I asked. 'Are you saying that you would have been?'

Neil ran his fingers through his beard and flicked a mite from his shirt front. 'Put it this way,' he said. 'I don't just own a taxi. And I'm not just an accountant. I'm also interested in the tourist prospects for this area. I've got my own heavy-duty Toyota. I'm looking particularly into the field of personalized safaris.'

'So you could have personalized us one?'

'Still can.'

A curious silence descended. I took a stroll or two around the cleft Boab. It was one thing being frustrated because we couldn't get out into the wilds; it was entirely another, it seemed to me, actually agreeing to someone's offer to take us. The more especially when that someone thought that being civilized meant knowing how gadgets work. He'd picked the wrong person to tell that story to, of Aborigines feeding their electric ovens with their verandahs. I was only a sliver of mechanical education away from doing the same. So it was him against us.

On the other hand, no one else was offering. Or, to put that another way, everyone was offering – no one was delivering.

'I'll tell you what,' Neil said, having caught Ros and me exchanging fraught glances, 'why don't you come to my office, I'll make a few telephone calls, and we'll see what we can come up with?'

What he came up with was a two-day personalized safari for a cost commensurate with the principle of personalization. He arrived at this by measuring a map with a ruler and tapping figures into a computer. You would never have guessed, walking bent through the dusty streets of Derby, that they contained such a striking example of twentieth-century office technology. Machines hummed in the background. Phones dialled themselves. Other phones spoke the moment they were spoken to. At one time Neil had three long-distance conversations going while his hands were free to do calculations on a jotter.

Sitting opposite him, in the client's seat, I felt like a man waiting for a mortgage.

Once we'd agreed on a tentative price – it had to be tentative, since there could be no certitude about the roads and therefore about the mileage – Neil proposed that we go out to dinner that night with him and his 'partner'. Actually lifting a phone this time, he rang his 'partner' to check availability, and from his tone of quiet but fretful authority we were able to deduce, correctly, that his 'partner' was female, his girlfriend, and discontented. The machine has yet to be invented that can erase the crackle of domestic stress from a line of communication.

Back at our hotel an amazing change had taken place. Where we had previously been treated with morose indifferentism (not so much rudeness as a sort of regulation Derby discourtesy – wholly impersonal), we were now showered with smiles and solicitations. Our rooms had been cleaned twice. The cost of our accommodation had plummeted.

There could be only one explanation. Although it was a matter of principle with me not to talk about myself as a writer, even less a travel writer, the fact had cropped up in conversation with Neil. It was he, then, who must have flashed a message along the wires, even as we sat with him, to the effect that Derby was under scrutiny. Hereafter the town was on its best behaviour whenever it saw us.

But it was too late. The die had been cast.

Dinner with Neil and his partner, Robin, was a trying experience for all four of us, not so much because they were going through what might best be called a sticky patch in their relationship, but because Robin wanted us to know, and wanted us to know that she knew that we knew, that that was what they were going through. She averted her eyes whenever Neil spoke. She shuttered them whenever Neil spoke to *her*. 'I have a suicidal tendency,' Neil said, suicidally, 'to say the very things that Robin hates to hear.'

'Such as that,' Robin said, somehow managing to pinch her nostrils from the inside, in the way that other people can suck in their cheeks.

'See what I mean?' Neil said.

I noticed that it was the subject of business – how many millions they had invested, and so on – which disturbed Robin most. Not only did she shutter her eyes and pinch her nostrils from the inside when Neil explained that they were on a ten-year plan, and what's more ahead of schedule, she actually succeeded in sucking in the whole of her frame, contracting every part of herself from her shoulder blades to her abdomen, as if in an act of instantaneous anorexia.

'There I go again,' Neil said. He actually took pleasure in it, like a kamikaze pilot.

It was clear that there'd been a time, in the incubation period of Neil's ten-year plan, when they'd had a lot of fun setting up their various businesses, and travelling off every weekend into the bush, a pair of romantic outback Aussies with their heads screwed on. But now they were having fewer and fewer of those bush jaunts. Neil was wired into his machinery seven days a week. Robin was chained to her pharmacy. They worked long hours. They took few holidays. And they weren't wild about their customers. Well, we knew at least what that was like. And for all their present relational disharmony we squeezed one good hour out of the evening, swapping stories about the horrors of seasonal trade, and generally deriving that kind of ghoulish pleasure remembering the vileness of the buying public which is the sole consolation of the small retailer the world over.

It certainly gave us more pleasure than the food or the service. Although the restaurant had a sign at the entrance advising that booking was absolutely essential, only two customers besides ourselves showed up for a meal. But having six people to serve in a restaurant that could seat sixty put pressure on the waitress none the less. She was unable to describe for us a single item on the menu, and was even more surprised than we were when 'Sunrise Potatoes' turned out to be a dollop of ready-mash squeezed through an icing-bag to resemble a meringue or a cow-pat sitting on a slice of orange. Where she was strong, however, was in the etiquette department. Plates crashed to the floor, glasses splintered in our hands, our pepper steaks swam in a thick sweet gravy, but the waitress refused to compromise on the minutiae of ceremony. 'You must always stand by the lady when you serve,' she said. 'It isn't the thing to do it any other way.'

After the meal, Neil ordered Bundaberg rum and coke all round and eased the conversation effortlessly back to coons. 'We had trouble a year or so back,' he said. 'They tried a spot of violence on the streets. It's reasonably calm now, but I'll tell you this: had they raped a white woman I'd have joined a vigilante group.'

I tried to ask whether there'd been any real likelihood of their raping a white woman, but got a bit caught on the absurdity of the phrase. I wasn't able to inject 'white woman' with the appropriate sense of precious, fragile commodity, *and* keep a straight face.

Not that Neil was listening. He just wanted to be able to let a little fire blaze in his eyes and say, 'I'd have shot without hesitation.'

He took us again through the catalogue of Aboriginal incompetence – their hopelessness, their unintelligence, their incomprehension of the idea of property, their economic and moral backwardness. 'What *you* mean,' I said, 'is that they are not able to formulate a ten-year plan.'

I suppose it was hoping for a bit much to get a rise out of him, but I was surprised he didn't so much as blink. 'It won't change either,' he simply went on to affirm. 'It can't change. That's unless we adopt Lang Hancock's suggestion.'

Lang Hancock was the richest man in Australia and went in for that laconic terseness of phrase and moral philosophy which Australians who haven't been to university find appealing. 'And what suggestion would that be?' I asked.

'Poison their waterholes.'

I swallowed down a tumbler of Bundaberg rum myself, forgetting all about the coke, and said, 'Are we to understand that things get pretty dangerous out here?'

But it was Robin who answered. 'Nah,' she said. 'It's much more dangerous in Melbourne. When I go to Melbourne and I'm on my own I lock every door, turn the radio on, and sleep with my brother's Magnum under my pillow.'

'The other way,' Neil went on, 'is to put rat bait in their food.'

One very curious and frequently observable fact of relations between the Aborigine and the White Australian is that no matter how much the second offers to despise and denigrate the first, he will nevertheless go to great lengths to secure his regard, to earn his approval, almost, you might say, to receive his blessing. Absolutely without their realizing that they are doing so, and in the face of quite opposing impulses and attitudes, those white Australians who value the idea of 'maleness' and associate it with bush know-how and outback fearlessness – a rugged and sometimes even vaguely mystical survivalism – acknowledge in the Aborigine their highest ideal. Time and again in those country towns which can still boast an Aboriginal population, you will see enacted the same one-act social drama, in which the European seeks reassurance on the question of his manliness from the Aborigine, in which the white man is the eager petitioner for friendship – street friendship, equality, not intimacy – and the lordly bestower of it is the black. Even Hector, at the height of his rage, was forever to be seen muttering in corners with Aborigines, looking for their confidence, trusting their opinion on such matters as weather or terrain, showing that he had mastered their patois and was at least equal to their ancient certainties. There wasn't a single white man in the Boab that Friday night who didn't greet Rod Drummond, the lead singer of MANTUS, as a friend; who didn't want to talk guitars and jack plugs with him and triumph in his arm around their shoulders. And Neil too, would-be vigilante, poisoner and rat-catcher, could not, once we were out of town, go past an Aborigine without putting himself to the manliness test. The outward form of every encounter was of course contemptuous – aristocrat to serf, bank manager to window cleaner – but the compulsion to stop and talk, to be equal to any conversation about direction, danger, the whereabouts of game or fish, clearly reached down, down, into a psychology that was both private and national.

There is much talk in Australia these days about white guilt and expiation. What we observed was psychopathic not moral. Advanced schizophrenia, I'd call it.

★   ★   ★

We were in the Liveringa region, heading for Myroodah Crossing, some two hundred kilometres south of Derby, when Neil wound down his window to talk cherrabun with an elderly Aborigine who was about to cast his net into a billabong. The cherrabun is the delicacy of the area, a large freshwater prawn whose 'run', during the appropriate season, brings out every fisherman and gourmet for miles around. We'd heard a lot from Neil, since we'd set off on our two-day expedition that morning, on the subject of cherrabun and how many we could expect to catch, so it was not entirely without its discomfort for him to be told by an obvious expert, and in our hearing, that he had no chance – that this wasn't the time or the weather for them.

'No big mobs running, boss?' Neil asked again, just to be certain.

He was the only one talking pidgin. The Aborigine spoke a perfectly comprehensible standard English. He shook his head. But he didn't want to sound too final. It was clearly not a good idea to contradict a white man flatly. 'You might be lucky,' he said. 'But you've more chance with barramundi. My friend got two this morning.'

Neil dropped into his inanities again. ''M catchum big barra? 'M all along smart fulla.'

The Aborigine observed the pantomime patiently, flicking flies off his face. Behind him a middle-aged woman – presumably his wife – looked on with a kind of weary resentment. This was not the first time, clearly, a white man had pulled up in his Toyota to polish up his pidgin.

Had Myroodah Crossing been dry we would have driven over it as a short cut to Camballin, our immediate destination, an irrigation settlement where Neil had contacts, some investments, and a place for us to sleep. But the flood waters had just been through and the river was swollen. Even if the Toyota had been fitted with twenty-foot-high tyres we couldn't have made it across, but Neil still ventured out into the shallows and prodded the bottom with a stick. Three white Australian picnickers watched him with amusement from the comfort of their collapsible deckchairs. They had their car radio on, playing 'Moon River'.

Returning the way we'd come, we passed the Aboriginal couple we'd talked to. They were in the billabong now, examining their net. A small boy was with them, shading his eyes and staring at whatever it is that Aborigines see in the engrossing middle distance. I was struck again by their extraordinary capacity to create a little clearing, like the Promised Land, around themselves.

We were at some remove from the comforts that had always comprised paradise for me, for all that Neil's Toyota was fitted out with a fridge from which we could help ourselves to ice-cold beers or cokes whenever we needed them. The country was rugged and remote. The track which Neil insisted on negotiating at great speed, 'to ride the corrugations', was often barely a track at all – just an approximate clearing in the bush. Goannas frequently raced across our path. Hawks circled the sky. On the ground as on the map, Camballin seemed a long, long way from anywhere. All I'd heard about it, apart from Neil's having chosen it to invest in, was that it possessed the highest mean temperature of any inhabited spot in Australia. Something like pride waged war inside me with something like fear. I suddenly remembered how, as a student, I'd won a competition at a party to find the title of the shortest book that could ever be written with *Lives of the Jewish Explorers*. Yet now here I was, giving the lie to my race's trepidity, the only Jew for thousands of miles, penetrating further into Northern Australia, for all I knew, than any Jew in history.

With such thoughts revolving in my head I simply assumed I was mildly hallucinating when I saw the sign telling us that we had arrived in Camballin.

In the Land of Oz

LIVERINGA STATION
and CAMBALLIN FARM
WELCOME
ברוכים הבאים

It was only after we'd driven past and Neil had remarked, as it were by-the-by, 'Notice the Hebrew?' that I realized I had in actuality read what I thought in actuality I had not.

'That really *was* Hebrew?'

'Oh yeah, the Israelis own a lot of this country.'

'The Israelis?'

'Sure. It's an interesting story. I'll tell you later.'

There wasn't time now. We'd reached the house of Alan Archer, foreman of the West Australian irrigation scheme in the Liveringa and Neil's co-director in whatever project it was that Neil had going here in this corrugated-tin town of forty inhabitants, an undisclosed number of whom spoke modern Hebrew.

Alan was out, doing what irrigation foremen do early on a Sunday afternoon, but his wife, Louise, welcomed us into her house. She was carrying a naked, golden haired little boy, and was as near as damn naked herself in a skimpy singlet thrown over a bikini. Her impatience at having to wear anything communicated itself to us and made us feel intrusive. The barer the Australian body – a handy little maxim of mine, this – the broader the Australian brogue. Louise made a sound like sheet-metal garage doors (the kind you lift from the bottom) opening and closing. But that might well have had something to do with her attitude to Neil, her uncertainty as to her role, precisely, in this first actualization of one of Neil's personalized safaris. She didn't take too kindly to being part of some dubious intinerary, to being ordered about her own house, or to Neil's pulling the same suicidal tricks on her as we'd watched him pull on Robin.

'Louise knows what I'm like,' he would say.

'Louise does,' Louise would reply, bringing down her garage door.

I don't know what would have become of us all, socially, had Louise's mother not suddenly appeared from the bedroom, limping, laughing, and rubbing ointment and insect-repellent into herself. 'They've been biting me all night,' she said, without feeling it necessary to be specific. 'They started the day I landed in Australia, have been going at me continuously since then, but have increased in ferocity markedly since I arrived in Camballin.' She looked around the room, more to check what might be winging towards her than to bother with introductions, and then rubbed more repellent into herself. 'I really do sometimes wish,' she said, 'that my daughter had chosen somewhere more clement to live. Like Wymondham, in Leicestershire, where I do.'

She was good-looking, like her daughter, only in that droll self-consciously fragile style the English favour; whereas Louise had gone brittle and brown – had become a tuber not a flower – in the manner preferred by Australians. Interesting, though, to discover that Louise was herself an import and had been out here a mere six or seven years. That explained the more Aussie than Aussie off-handedness, and the impatience with vestments, and the sheet-metal timbre. Takes a Pom, as I've observed many a time, to make a genuine Australian.

Louise's mother – out here on a brief break from the environs of Melton Mowbray – reminded me of no one so much as a visiting Forsterian relation as played, say, by Beryl Reid. From time to time I would catch her standing staring in astonishment, as if she couldn't begin to work out who her daughter was, or why she had a little naked brown tadpole for a grandson, or why there were geckos darting diagonally across the walls. I don't think I've ever seen anyone so amused by what bemused them. Or vice versa.

The conversation moved from small things that bit to big

things that bit harder. Camballin, apparently, was overrun with snakes just now. Louise had found five in her garden in the last three days. She'd killed one of them and put it in a jar in her freezer. The next time she was in town she would take it over to what she called the Aggi College to find out if it was venomous. She brought it out of the freezer to show us, coiled around in white vinegar or gin. It looked venomous to me.

A couple of weeks before, a man down the street had been woken up in the night by an unfamiliar sensation, a greater than usual warmth, even for Camballin, at the bottom of his bed. Appalled to find a twenty-foot king brown sleeping with him, the man had taken fright, disturbed the snake, received three bites in his leg, and been carried off to hospital. 'That's bad luck,' one of us observed. 'It's good luck,' Louise said. 'He's still alive. Though his leg's turned completely black and grown to three times its normal size.'

Louise's mother rubbed more repellent into herself. I fell into what I suppose is meant by a brown study. In so far as I'd grasped what Neil had planned for us we would be sleeping next door, on mattresses laid on the floor, in an at-present-unoccupied house – Umpie Bong. There were still several hours to go before darkness fell, but already I could hear slitherings in the night.

I knew now – although it was too late for me to do anything about it – that we were in country far too fertile for my peace of mind. Even Louise's lounge teemed with life. Her little boy gambolled naked on the floor. An Alsatian bitch, Kalinda, did the same. Little lizards walked up the walls, unperturbed by the preserved prize cherrabun mounted, like stags' heads, on wooden shields. A ginger cat with a Persian tail appeared from outside. 'He has the body of a rat, the confidence of a German Shepherd, and the mind of a homicidal maniac,' Louise said, not without a dash of pride. 'We bought it from the Aborigines, after a bit of a haggle, for ten dollars.' The cat made a leap for

Ros, kissing her face and neck, and taking occasional playful bites out of her jugular.

'Remembering something in its feral past?' I wondered.

'Practising for something in its feral future,' Ros said, while Louise looked on with satisfaction.

For reasons best not entered into, I found myself entertaining vivid speculations as to the nature of the intimacy that prevailed between the adult Archers.

We finally met Alan – or Arch, as he was known – later that afternoon, when we all gathered for a few cold cans at a picnic spot, which also happened to be where Neil owned mining rights, some miles down the river. Our party had travelled by Toyota, but Arch arrived by boat. We stood on the bank and watched him and his two companions rowing towards us. Given the speed of the current and the number of crocodiles basking on the opposite bank, I took this to be raging torrent, so I was surprised when the three men climbed out of the boat midstream, and did the rest of the journey on foot, barely ankle high in water.

Apart from the odd twitch and yawn – signs, both, of nervousness I thought – the crocodiles took no notice. Presumably they'd spotted Humpy, the famous croc-wrestler, among the three men now carrying the boat. We'd heard about Humpy from Neil. How he was a quiet, gentle man who was none the less a match for any freshwater crocodile in the North-West. Barehanded, he took them on. And came away without a scratch himself.

It was Humpy who was the first ashore. A wiry, stocky man, with black hair turning to a steel grey, and a taciturn manner, he was also, I noticed, a touch bow-legged, and I wondered whether this was a consequence of crocodiles trying to find some way out of his powerful grip.

No physical blemish marred Arch's beauty, however, although

he too looked as though he could give anything up to three times his size a close contest. He was in fact on the diminutive side, but in perfect proportion. A pocket Atlas, I suppose you might have called him; a miniature Oz god, bronzed and muscular and piercingly blue-eyed under a peaked camouflage cap. Louise towered over him. Strong silent currents flowed between them. The third man off the boat, a shy teenager with a lowered gaze, turned out to be Arch's son from a previous marriage. Doing some quick sums I calculated that Arch had to be about ten to fifteen years Louise's senior. The presence of his nearly adult son, together with the new, naked baby on Louise's hip, the crocs, the stirring bush, the flowing river, all somehow seemed to publicize the heat of the Archers' mutual esteem.

I was standing aside, watching him upturning his boat, and imagining how he'd captured the heart of a young English girl, persuaded her to live with him in a place about as far from Wymondham as it was possible to find, when I caught sight of Ros and Pamela – Louise's mother – looking on and laughing from the river bank. 'Look at my Australian son-in-law,' I thought I heard Pamela saying. 'Look at him side by side with my daughter. Isn't he short? I *am* fond of him, Ros. I *do* love him. Look at them. Just look at them together! Isn't he short?'

Neil introduced me to Arch as an English novelist travelling around Australia with a view to writing a novel about what travelling around Australia was like. Arch shook my hand like a man who didn't want a single thing I had.

Down by the river Ros and Pamela hooted. A phrase of Norman Mailer's came back to me – 'two witches by the water's edge.'

But they weren't, of course, casting spells. They were just watching Louise and Arch, like the rest of us. And like the rest of us they were giddy with appreciation.

We drank a few more cans of beer and then followed Arch and his teeming family back to Camballin. Fast as Neil drove he couldn't keep up with Arch. In seconds they were just a cloud of dust ahead of us, a pillar of smoke on the horizon.

In pools on either side of the track crocs hung suspended, still cowering from Humpy. By the time we got back to Camballin the sun was almost gone, leaving the sky the colour of blood.

'Right,' Neil said, reversing into the drive of the unoccupied house of terrors, 'I'll unpack, you make yourselves at home.'

Home was a bare floor, a broken air-conditioning unit, a dozen lizards on the window ledge, walls full of horrendous, clinging, miniature blue frogs, and any number of holes for snakes to come in through. 'Right,' I said to Ros, 'you make yourself at home, I'll go and stand rigid in the road.'

The arrangement was that we would have a couple of hours to settle in, stretch out, spruce up and calm down before going next door to the Archers for dinner. Whether the Archers particularly wanted us for dinner was not really to the point. Arch was some kind of business partner of Neil's and we were some kind of customers. It would never have occurred to Neil that Arch might not have welcomed this lucrative new trade in human cargo tramping through his lounge. But I had observed the way Arch had looked at Neil, especially I had observed the cold eye he had cast on Neil's pastel pink crimplene shorts, and I foresaw troubles.

I did actually go and stand rigid in the street for a while, where I was eventually joined by Ros. We let Neil go on ahead of us to the Archers while we took a short turn around the township in the dark. It was on this walk that we experienced, together, our first really substantial mirage. Unless, of course, it was a vision. I was certainly in the right frame of mind for visions, myself. Though who it was that would have sent us a corporealization of two Australian youths carrying beer from a drive-in bottle-shop and Chinese food from a Chinese takeaway, I am unable to say. But we not only saw this incarnation, we actually heard it — 'Beaut night, eh?' it called to us. And we smelled it as well — the warm, sweet, slightly floral odour of shark-fin soup and steamed vegetables. In fact it was only when the Archers assured us that there was no drive-in bottle-shop for a couple of hundred kilometres and no Chinese takeaway for a couple of thousand, that we realized that what we'd encountered had not been there, was neither real flesh nor real fluid.

No such problem with the Archers themselves. You could almost see the blood pumping away below Louise's glowing skin. She had her hair down tonight as well as her garage-door accent, and wore a white singlet, glowing blue in contrast to her brown shoulders. Arch too was clean and shining, more of a dandy than I'd first thought him – a bush dandy though, in irrigation foreman's regulation khaki shirt and shorts. He managed to evoke somehow, even for me, the wild romance of working for a Water Authority. A few weeks later I was to light upon a report relating to the future of Camballin, which numbered, amongst many other optimistic forecasts for the area, the following breathless pronouncement: 'The potential of sprinkler irrigation is unlimited.' That was just the sort of zest for the practicalities of controlled inundation that Arch gave off. He took up a position in his own household to which only the word statuesque could do justice, leaning against walls of bookcases, his manhood bunched tightly in his shorts, his clear gaze surveying the multiplicity of reasons for his felicity. The little boy – the Archer union made flesh – wandered about in a state of nature, his willy a conspicuous presence and symbol. From time to time he would adopt the identical posture to his father, taking the weight of his torso on one leg and folding his arms across his chest – an expression of wholly assured, if somewhat diminutive, maleness. And all the while Louise looked on in a slow smoulder of satisfaction.

'We must exchange addresses,' Louise's mother leaned across to whisper to me at one point. 'There are things I'd like to say to you that I can't say here.'

I was excited by the note of conspiracy and wondered if she was going to tell me that her son-in-law's allure was less obvious than I thought it was.

Louise turned out to be a meticulous keeper of personal and local records, and showed us photographs of the various natural disasters which yearly shook Camballin: the floods, the cyclones, the electrical storms, the plagues of snakes and locusts. She was especially fond of a group showing the very house we were in, just its roof visible above the waters, taken from a helicopter. She had a drawer full of blackened electric plugs, the victims of lightning strikes, and albums of videos, meticulously kept and dated, a complete moving pictorial record of her extraordinary decision to come and live in so remote and harsh a place. It was both a vindication and a justification, this library of hers; not just a story of the past, but a spur for the present, a reminder to herself of just what she was here for.

'It doesn't worry you, all this?' I asked, meaning the whole catalogue of catastrophe and uncertainty.

She laughed – a clatter of sheet-metal, not unlike a lightning strike itself. 'Nah, we don't think about it.'

They kept photographing it though.

'This is Arch holding a baby crocodile,' she said.

He was too. Holding it up, with a pleased expression on his face, like a Scottish fisherman showing off a salmon. 'The croc looks docile enough,' I said.

'Look closer,' Louise said, 'and you'll see why.'

Looking closer I saw that Arch had it firmly by its windpipe. There's a trick to everything.

I sneaked a glance at Humpy, sitting quietly in an armchair, and wondered if he too resorted to cheating when subjecting the eighteen-footers to a half nelson.

'And now,' Louise said, just when I thought I'd been through all her photographs, 'I suppose you'd like to see some of the Israelis.'

Apparently, a man named Gud Ravah had purchased Liveringa Station some time ago and had brought in a group of Israeli boys — all ex-army officers — to help him develop it. Three of them in particular had become close friends of the Archers. Two called Yuron — as in 'Yuron your own', and one called Yurone — as in 'you're on Yurone'. To make it easier, there was black Yuron and white Yuron.

The presence of these Israelis had livened up not just Camballin but the whole area considerably. War games suddenly became the rage. Not war games of the kind business executives play, using plastic counters on stiffened boards, but authentic outdoor simulations, involving raids and ambushes and surprise assaults. It was common, Louise said, to be returning home quietly one evening and to find yourself suddenly waylaid by black Yuron, waiting for you on his belly in the grass, ready to toss a crumpled paper bag at you as if it were a grenade. Sometimes both Yurons raided the Boab in Derby, bursting through the doors and firing imaginary sub-machine guns at the locals. They even succeeded in making Neil forget about the condition of his trousers. 'Whenever I heard their voices outside my office,' he said, 'I knew to throw myself down flat on the floor behind my desk and spread my arms.'

Louise showed me the Yurons' favourite photograph of her little boy. He was stark naked in it, as usual, only this time he was pointing a toy Heckler and Kock automatic at the camera. 'They all loved this one,' she said. 'They all took multiple copies of it back to Israel.'

Ros remembered the various crazy offers that Australian administrations had made over the years to this and that Middle Eastern combatant: such as that they might like a little piece of Australian desert which they could call home. 'I suppose this would be a good location for the continuance of the Arab/ Israeli conflict,' she said.

'What do you mean *would* be?' Louise and Arch, not to mention Humpy and Neil, all said together. 'The next station along is in fact owned by Arabs. They had the farm at Myroodah Station before the Israelis came. Now they glower at each other across the Fitzroy River, which has been renamed the River Jordan. And those conical mountains you'll have seen on your way in – the Grant Ranges – we call the Golan Heights.'

Towards the end of the evening Humpy decided to test our nerve with shaggy snake stories. 'The pythons get very big round here,' he told us. A twenty-footer was nothing. Only the week before, one as long as that and half as long again had made a surprise call on the once-monthly Camballin outdoor barbecue and tinnie party. Wholly undaunted by the lights, the noise, or the thirty or so people present, he had slithered in, taken up a position not far from the fire, and flicked his lips. 'Snake!' someone had called out, 'But we were all too busy drinking,' Humpy said, 'to bother.'

'A favourite trick of theirs,' he went on, after Arch handed us each another can, 'is to curl around the inner rim of a toilet bowl. They like it there. And of course you just don't see 'em unless you look very carefully.'

'It's a good idea,' Arch added, 'always to check the toilet bowls in these parts.'

'Just in case,' Louise said.

'To be on the safe side,' Humpy confirmed.

'I could feel the cold beer heating up in my can. When I put it to my lips it was hot and flat. But it wasn't only my beer that they spoiled. I instantly made a decision – and never veered from it – that I would eschew all ablutions for whatever time remained to me in Camballin.

★ ★ ★

A bad night in the house. The air-conditioner was impossibly noisy, but we couldn't consider trying to sleep without it. It seemed unreasonable of Ros, to me, to consider trying to sleep at all. I believed that she owed it to me, since outback travel was her idea, to sit up all night and guard me, on python-watch.

I woke up in the middle of the night and saw something vile suspended from the ceiling. I closed my eyes but whenever I opened them again it was still there. A long brown thing, swaying, with some kind of diaphanous sac – a breeding place for more of the same – appended to its tail or underbelly. The fact that I was unable to recognize it, or know whether there was another such creature like it in the whole of Nature, only made it the more disgusting. I thought of George Grey, sitting on a rock in this frightful, alien land, contemplating the 'indifferently executed' examples of Aboriginal art around him, the ruin of his once proud expedition at his feet – the dead ponies, the parched dogs, the appalled, convulsive men – when suddenly 'a curious mis-shapen mass came advancing from some bushes with *a novel and uncouth motion*'. And I remembered how this turned out to be a boa crushing a kangaroo. Well, something equally *novel* and *uncouth*, something equally horrifically Australian, swung slowly from the ceiling, a mere three feet above my defenceless head. Out of pure terror I willed myself to sleep.

When I woke in the morning I was wrapped around in the single sheet that had covered us as in a cocoon, and I was glued, by the exudations of bodily fear, to the person who had got me into this. Above me, still swaying lightly in the air flow from the conditioning unit, was a wire flex and the brown plastic fitting of the electric light attachment. The vile diaphanous sac was the light bulb.

Still eschewing all ablutions, but attending briskly to everything else, I braced myself for a day with Neil. We were to be off early, to try the roads to the gorges, and to be back at Derby before dark. But first Neil insisted on preparing us a massive breakfast. With every rasher of bacon I swallowed I heard another item entering itself, with that dead springless click of electronic technology, into the computer.

With the single exception of snakes, nothing on this personalized trek so far had caused me as much concern as Neil's wardrobe. I couldn't work out where in the Toyota he stored so many sporty little shirts and the impeccable crimplene shorts that matched them, nor how he was able to change so often without our noticing. The night before, at the Archers, he had astonished us by turning up in a powder-blue safari suit and white Italian sandals. He had even changed his navigator's watch, which tweeted on the hour, every hour, for a gold-faced cocktail number which had the manners not to tweet at all. This morning, though, he was back in the gear which befitted a 4-wheel driver, always excepting, of course, the clinging crimplene shorts.

We called in to say goodbye to the Archers on our way out of Camballin, and had a brief conversation about the Boab tree in their front garden. Fearing for its survival in the frequent floods, Louise had trimmed its top, cut back its grizzled locks and twiggy fingers, in the hope that it would the better hold its own against the waters. For our last view of them, the Archers fell into a sort of tableau:

Louise on the verandah in her bikini, glowing; Arch, his arms crossed upon his chest, his khaki shorts bundled like a bag of marbles, manful; Pamela aerosoling herself, comically-hysterically; the baby brown and naked on the lawn; the dog Kalinda, in the sand pit, licking herself attentively; the feral Aboriginal cat up to her gums in Kalinda's jugular; a brahmin bull, just visible in the field behind, pawing the red dust; and in the foreground, as ancient as a maypole, the denuded Boab, erect, engorged, and circumcised.

★ ★ ★

So, from Camballin back to Fitzroy Crossing, and then north towards the Napier Ranges, the King Leopolds in the far distance. We were in rugged country now, not at all unlike that wherein George Grey once more encountered hostile Aborigines, 'each tree, each rock, [seeming] to give forth its black denizens, as if by enchantment'. No denizens of either colour here now, though. Just an endless, all but invisible dirt track running through broken boulders and dried-up creek beds; and fierce, forbidding outcrops of rock on either side of us, softened occasionally by the presence of punky-looking bottle trees and Boabs, smooth the whole way up the trunk and then suddenly foliated on top, like the young unemployed you meet in Sheffield.

Two or three hours out of Camballin, in the course of which we never saw a living soul, nor knew for certain whether we were even on a track at all, having driven up and down mountains and along the beds of rivers, we suddenly came upon a road sign, a twisted arrow in a neat yellow triangle, warning us of an irregularity – to wit, a sharpish bend in the rubble. This was the equivalent of getting to within six inches of the summit of Everest and finding a notice alerting you to a steep incline just ahead. I consecrated this bizarre sign and the incongruous stony ground it stood on to ourselves and to our friend Philip Cochrane, a man of fastidious intellect whom we had first met at the West Country Trade Fair in Torquay where he had sold us fetching Liberty print purses to hang around the necks of little girls – thereby illustrating the truism, as we no doubt illustrated it for him, that you never know who or what you are going to meet where.

As witness what happened in Tunnel Creek, where our caravan finally came to rest at lunchtime, on the thirteenth tweet of Neil's daytime watch precisely. An eroded limestone passage, open at either end but pitch black in the middle, Tunnel Creek was a popular spot for visitors when the roads were passable. Today we had it entirely to ourselves. A host of black butterflies, not expecting to be disturbed this early in the season, flew off the rock walls as we approached, darkening the air. Neil led us in, shining a torch so that we could see our way on what felt, beneath our feet, to be a mixture of rock and shingle. It was not unlike walking on a beach except that we weren't out in the sunshine. It was a sickening place. Bats whistled and hung upside down above us. The frills and honeycombs of stone, sculpted by millions of years of dripping and seeping, were coated with a fine slime.

After a few minutes we saw water. According to Neil a virtual river flowed through here in the Wet, though now the water seemed still; as far as we could tell, merely a standing pool. Neil left us a torch so that we might gambol a little as we pleased, while he went back to prepare a gargantuan lunch for us and his computer to ingest.

We listened to him crunching back to the daylight. Then we were alone. Ros suggested a dip. I was against the idea. The tunnel made my flesh creep. What beauty it had was all of the sinister kind. Which was why the bats liked it.

'No,' I said.

It's a word she particularly despises. But I had to leave. Speleophobia was gaining upon me. I began the crunch back myself, while she approached the water, trying its depths and temperature with her foot. What stopped her diving into the invisible pool she still doesn't know. Under normal circumstances my 'No' would have put the issue beyond doubt. She would have been in there. But this time something made her hesitate. A bad feeling. She was on her way to join me, in fact, when a loud swish! – a sound as of a crocodile's tail turning, a crocodile in a fury of frustration – made us both start. The cave echoed with the disturbance – the walls of slime wanting none of it and throwing it back, a ripple of bat restlessness high above us. Ros was quickly by my side. Even in the darkness I could feel that she was white.

We hurried out into the daylight, where once again the black butterflies materialized from the rocks, and where the smell of fried onions and sausages and lamb chops and steak and tinned tomatoes told us that our personalized bush-lunch was ready for us.

Bent over the frying pan, Neil recalled his first camping holidays with Robin, when they were happy and not near the premature fruition of a ten-year plan. He'd originally met Robin, he told us, at the bar of the Boab, where she was pausing briefly for refreshment before continuing her journey around Australia. 'Will you marry me?' he'd asked her after an acquaintance of about fifteen minutes. 'She looked at me as if I'd crawled out from under a stone, so I thought, "Hello here's a challenge," and I pursued her around the country until she agreed.'

'You'll find,' Ros told me at a later date, 'that many Australian women marry the men they do only to put an end to the curse of their petitionings.'

Not wishing to argue with an authority, I accepted her word for it. As I accepted her observation that on the night we all four ate sunshine potatoes together Robin had transferred her rings of betrothment from her left hand to her right.

After the steak, lamb chops and sausages, Neil prepared us egg-jaffles, followed by tinned fruit salad and Carnation milk, followed by biscuits and billy-tea. We sat under the shade of a huge white ghost gum and rested, the conversation turning at last, as it always will between small business people, to turnover. Turnover talk, in fact, is merely a primitive form of hierarchy jostling. Unless you are a fool you tell your turnover only to someone whose turnover you calculate to be lower than your own. In the brief preliminary tussle that took place in the shadow of the King Leopold Ranges, Neil effortlessly wrenched power, dazzling us with figures of such enormity that there wasn't the faintest likelihood thereafter of our daring to mention figures ourselves.

And so, force-fed and out-turnovered we returned to the Toyota and the drive back to Derby via Windjana Gorge, the latter a wonderful opening out of the terrain, a vast craggy ravine of steep limestone cliffs and lovely, pellucid sun-lit water. It was to see country of this kind that we'd hired the services of Neil in the first place, and we were furious that now we'd got here it was time to return.

'The trouble with Windjana Gorge,' Neil said, virtually completing the circle of our acquaintance with him, 'is that it's badly managed.'

I looked up the sheer walls of the Gorge and then across into Neil's eyes, nervous and flickering behind his thick spectacles. Scout-master's eyes, I said to myself. Cub-leader's eyes. Then I added, entirely for my own behoof, 'Beware the boy who would be a man.'

As we drove back along the Kimberley Plain Neil told us an Aboriginal Dreamtime Legend relating to the area. 'The Kangaroo and the Emu fell out, the Emu chased the Kangaroo and the Kangaroo flattened the land as he ran away. Which is why it's a plain.'

'Is that the full extent of the legend?' Ros asked.

'That about gets it,' Neil said.

'You have a real feel for Aboriginal mythology,' Ros told him.

Eighteen kilometres before Derby we came to Mowanjum, an Aboriginal township from which all alcohol was banned. 'What you'll find,' Neil said, 'is that they come back here with their bottles at night and finish them off in the road. The booze is prohibited in Mowanjum but not on the highway.'

And sure enough there were brown stubby bottles every-where. For the distance of about one kilometre on either side of the township the road glistened with broken glass, as if diamonds had suddenly risen to the surface of the bitumen.

★ ★ ★

The following morning I cashed another cheque with Stormy Collopy and went to pay Neil. The bill was half as much again as he'd said it would be. 'We did a few more kilometres than I'd calculated,' he explained.

I cast my eyes down the print-out and saw itemized, in computerese, the lamb chops and the tins of tomatoes and the steaks and the many dozens of sausages which Neil had insisted, like a hurt host, that we consume. I contested his total.

'Fine,' he said. 'Fine. I always like to make my bill out in advance and then discuss it with the client afterwards.'

He was dressed in his accountant clothes again. Ten-year-plan regulation mufti. His fingers tapped away at the soundless keys until the bill came down not quite enough to satisfy me but far enough to satisfy him. We shook hands and I promised that I would indeed make the name of the man at the information bureau dirt the minute I got to Perth. Neil gave me the addresses of a few people I could make it dirt with.

Although we'd already bought a couple of bus tickets valid from Derby to Broome we couldn't face waiting for the bus. So we hired a car instead, for all that there was an extortionate one-way drop-off fee and remote area loading and various other little hidden extras which made the two hundred and fifty kilometres to Broome the most costly in Australia, if not the world. But I didn't care. I would have given half my blood to speed us out of Derby once and for all. Which is why I responded ambiguously when, in what was meant to be our final five minutes in the town, Ros ran into Rod Drummond, the lead singer of MANTUS, in the Post Office, and arranged to meet him later that morning, at the Aboriginal Hostel, 'for a chat'. I could see that we owed it to our professional integrity not to go past an opportunity to hear about Derby as it were from the other side; I thought that we owed it to just about everything else, however, not to roam the streets of this hell-hole for eternity.

Rod Drummond was no less ambiguous himself. He couldn't work out precisely what we wanted to chat about, nor was he at all certain that he possessed the *information* he assumed we were after. He was waiting for us when we arrived at the Hostel and drove us out with him to pick up a party of seven Aboriginal children who were flying in from school at Kalgoorlie to rejoin their families in the far north. On the way to the airport I tried to sound Rod out on the tone of community relations in Derby. I knew in some detail what the whites thought of the blacks; I was curious to hear the reverse story.

'It's a lovely, friendly town,' he told me. 'The friendliest I've been in.'

I've never been much of an investigator. I have no talent for concealing the question I really want the answer to. But I did my best not to be too obvious. 'Yes, yes, some of the people are very nice and friendly,' I said. 'However, I've noticed that as soon as they get a few beers into them they start to show a – I don't know – a different aspect. A certain aggression – a sort of social belligerence, I suppose you could call it – suddenly begins to show itself.' ('They call you *coons*, Rod,' was what I wanted to say.)

He listened to me very patiently, his fine dark eyes concentrating on the road ahead. 'It's a really nice place to live, socially,' he repeated.

I wondered whether he was being evasive or had really failed to grasp my meaning. 'So everyone' – I leaned on the word *everyone*, trying to put colour into it – 'so everyone gets on here?'

'Ah, yeah. Occasionally there's a failure of communication because people are changed around every couple of years up here, and it takes a while for the new ones to become acclimatized. But that's all.'

'People get changed around every couple of years?' I thought I was on to something now. So they shipped the Abos out after twenty-four months – sent them back to the missions or out into the bush – just so they should never feel at home. The bastards!

'Yeah. You know, the public servants. They all do a couple of years up here before moving on to somewhere else.'

White men – it was white men he was talking about and the only people they shipped out were themselves. Damn!

No matter how hard I tried I failed dismally to prise Rod open on the subject of racial disharmony. Perhaps he didn't want to be prised, could not afford to be prised; or perhaps there was nothing *to* prise; either way I came under intense silent pressure from Ros to let him alone. He was an amiable man with a lovely smile and kindly eyes. A good rock musician to boot. I had no business pushing him around.

We watched the seven Aboriginal teenagers coming off the plane, behind executives travelling on expense accounts. They didn't look especially excited – the children I mean – but then shyness often constrains the expressions of Aborigines, and besides, these kids were frequently in the air. It's a big state, Western Australia, in which being bussed to school can mean being flown thousands of kilometres. They climbed into Rod's vehicle and packed in tight together. Not for the first time I noticed that Aboriginal children seemed to get closer to one another than European ones.

Back at the hostel they rushed as one person to get on the pool table. At one stage all seven of them were playing simultaneously, striking balls from all sides of the table, some of them having to use rests for cues. 'Two at a time works better,' Rod tried to explain to them, but they were unable to face the prospect of splitting up. Playing all at once was more fun. The idea of individuation appeared to hold no attractions for them.

Rod invited us back to his rooms. He was a considerate and attentive host, seeing to all our needs and taking us patiently through his collection of paintings and artefacts, many of them 'presentations' made in return for services to the community. But we could feel his discomfort mounting. 'Am I giving you the sort of information you require?' he kept checking. It was our fault entirely that he didn't know what we wanted, since we didn't know what we wanted ourselves. I made one or two more subtle essays at investigative journalism – hinting at the primeval antagonism between white and black, wondering about rivers of blood – but I never once found anything politicized in my host. 'Derby is a great place for sports,' was all I succeeded in getting him to blurt out.

The tension became unbearable for all of us at last, and we rose to go. 'If you find any good jokes on your travels,' Rod said, 'I'd be grateful if you'd send them to me. I collect them.'

'You collect jokes?'

'Yeah. Got thousands.' He went over to a cupboard and brought out a file, bulging with cartoons, clippings, jokes from magazines, obscene drawings, and those duplicated rigmaroles – parodies of official memoranda and regulations and so on – that get passed around offices.

There was material here I hadn't seen since I'd been a schoolboy. Descriptions of horse races in which the runners had such names as Big Prick and Tight Thighs, and which ended in a close finish with Fat Tits getting up a sweat and Big Prick coming up fast on the inside. Cartoons of distended organs – 'Why do my friends call me a dickhead?' asked a character who had a penis where his nose should have been and testicles for cheeks. And material I had never seen before such as the following:

We don't pay no taxes, we don't make de goods
Just real little Abos, way back in de woods.
Dey pay us to vote, and dey pay us to sin
While dem sweet Goumint men keep de cheques rollin in.
We wait every month, for de slip wid de figures
And dat's all we do, we dam lucky niggers.

'How . . . ah . . . Why . . . um . . . I take it these, er, don't cause offence,' I said to Rod.

'Only to people with a very narrow one-track mind and no sense of humour,' he said. He was in good spirits now, laughing at his collection. More relaxed than he'd been all morning. 'This is my favourite,' he said.

ABORIGINAL APPLICATION FOR EMPLOYMENT

(Note: it is not necessary to attach a photograph as you all look alike.)

ADDRESS . . . . (*If living in car, give make, model & reg no.*)

NAME OF MUVA . . . .

NAME OF FAVA (*If known.*) . . . .

LATIONS LIVING WITH YOU (*Continue list over page*) . . . .

MARITAL STATUS: (*Common law . . .*) (*Shacked up . . .*) (*Other . . .*)

APPROXIMATE ESTIMATE AND SOURCE OF INCOME: (*Unemployment benefit . . .*) (*Armed robbery . . .*) (*Theft . . .*) (*Accident compo . . .*)

PLACE OF BIRTH (*Free public hospital . . .*) (*Under gum tree . . .*) (*Zoo . . .*)

TICK ANY ILLNESS YOU HAVE HAD IN PAST YEAR (*Scabies . . .*) (*V.D. . . .*) (*Head lice . . .*)

AT WHAT DISTANCE CAN OTHERS SMELL YOU: (*800 metres . . .*) (*400 metres . . .*) (*100 metres . . .*)

YOUR GREATEST DESIRE IN LIFE . . . . (*N.B. Other than a white girl.*)

'Well,' he said, 'what do you think?'

'Certainly novel,' I said.

'Bloody funny, I reckon,' he said.

We parted amicably, all trace of the earlier tension quite vanished. It was perfectly clear that if we'd got on to dirty jokes sooner we'd have had an easier morning all round. 'I hope I've given you some useful information,' Rod said. He still wasn't entirely sure that he hadn't failed us, but we had spent half an hour copying out some of his best jokes, so he could see that we weren't exactly leaving empty-handed.

As we drove out of Derby, looking neither to the left nor to the right of us, we both noted that, whatever we had or hadn't got from Rod Drummond, our encounter with him was the only one in this town from which we had not come away with an indigestible ball of violence in our stomachs.

One thing still worried me, though. Which one of us had been the chump – him or me?

SIX

NEITHER AN ONG NOR A MO

Just as Max Bygraves had stolen a march on us to Darwin, so had Jocky Wilson – the world's no. 6 ranked darts player – beaten us to Broome. Or at least his advance publicity had. Jocky himself would be arrowing in that weekend. By then, however, we would have left. No disrespect to the pastime, but not even the world's no. 1 – not the finicky-fingered Eric Bristow himself – could have kept us in Broome a minute longer than we had to be there.

It wasn't so much that we hated Broome; more that we *recognized* it. We knew, as it were from the inside, what it was trying to be; and we knew who it was waiting for. Tintagel – that's what it reminded us of – the mock-Arthurian Cornish seaside village just a few miles from our own. Tintagel, impatient for the season to get started, and the visitors to show. Only, instead of trading off a mythical past of blemished knights and Camelottery, Broome was peddling a real and recent history of imported oriental adventures and pearl-luggery. And, instead of offering a wild windswept Atlantic shoreline, it boasted, as every travel brochure vouched, limpid azure waters and miles of breathtakingly beautiful beach. I'll return to the beach. I had my first ever nudist gambol there, and feel that I owe it the same sentimental fidelity due to all witnesses, animate or otherwise, of inaugural unveilings. But, for the rest, Broome was a shoddy pastiche.

A jumped-up Chinoiserie pervaded the town. The couple of streets that remained of old Chinatown offered a handful of pleasant architectural curiosities, queer mixed marriages of East and West, yoking hyperactive Shinto ornamentation to cool colonial functionalism. Otherwise it was all breeze-block bottle-shops and Sino/Lebanese/Italian restaurants taking cover behind movie-makers' façades of Japanese temples and Buddhist pagodas. And phoney oriental script everywhere you looked. The bay, almost entirely in the clutch of mangroves, looked poisonous – hot and still and secretive, despite the odd wrecked sailing-ship beached picturesquely to suggest high-seas romance. The poor quality of the make-believe, the half-heartedness of the opportunism – for all the publicity surrounding the shrewd developmental plans of the semi-resident English life lord, McAlpine – all this, in combination with the atmosphere of anxious early seasonal expectancy, the sounds of small financial nerves snapping, made Broome feel altogether too like the thing we'd left behind.

The truth is that once you've been on the service side of the tourist industry you can never really enjoy it from the other end again. Not because you've seen through it. Quite the opposite. It's because your heart bleeds every time you pass an empty shop, or meet the eye of a proprietor wondering if he is ever going to have a customer again. The new arcade in quasi-Chinatown, Johnny Chi Lane, echoed to our footfall as we strolled through it on our second morning in town. The man who ran the ice cream parlour paced his forecourt in an immaculate apron. The owner of the gift shop was tying balloons to her front door, 'to see if that will attract attention,' we heard her tell her assistant. The only business which could be said to be in operation was the vegetarian café, The Tamarind Seed, where we paused to slurp mango smoothies through a straw and to listen to the runaways – it was lower-middle-class drop-out territory, Broome – reading aloud to one another from the letters they'd just collected from the Post Office. I always find it salutary to be reminded that even people with rings through their noses like to get the odd newsy missive from their mums.

It was the hippies, of course, (the mung beans, as they're known up here), who had turned a section of Cable Beach into a nudist haven. But for some reason they weren't in evidence when we walked along the sand later that day. The beach was as quiet as Johnny Chi Lane had been. One very large lady, browned all over and therefore not strictly speaking naked at all, rolled in the frothing surf like a dugong. And an exceedingly handsome and well-preserved couple, half-in and half-out of their clothes, half-in and half-out of the water, bobbed up and down and waited to see what we would do. 'Well, I can't really come up with any good reason why not,' I said to Ros. I think she was surprised by this reply to a question she hadn't asked. And I know she was surprised by the alacrity with which I shed my clothes and ran twinkling into the sea, partly because I was normally reluctant even to go as far as trunks, but more especially because I couldn't swim.

In fact I had nothing more in mind than a brief frolic in the shallowest fringe of surf, and a bit of obliging bobbing to put the handsome, well-preserved couple at their ease. The surprise for my part was how much I enjoyed it. One minute I'd been a grave grown man who liked the feel of bitumen beneath his feet, the next I was a weightless water baby, snorting spume and spluttering and hallooing. Everything that naturists used to say in the 1950s, when the world was innocent, turned out to be true. Yes, I *had* been reconnected with my physical self. Yes, I *did* feel as one with the great elemental forces – sea, surf, sky and my salty privities in cosmic harmony. And yes, yes, yes, I *was* free, happy, natural, and unashamed. If I knew of one impediment to perfect bodily felicity it was only this: no one had invited us to join a game of volleyball.

As it happened, I was lucky. I might easily have had something more serious to complain about. We shouldn't have been anywhere near that water. It swarmed with stingrays and box jellyfish and all the other usual malevolent inhabitants of boiling tropical oceans whose season for an uninhibited frolic of their own this was. Somehow we'd missed the notices warning us to keep out. When I realized how close I'd been to a terrible quietus I snapped double in a spasm of imaginative self-pity and didn't straighten until teatime.

A spectacular electrical storm took over at the very moment my spasm eased. Now it was the turn of the palm trees to fold and groan. We were in the Continental Hotel at the time – the Conti, as it affectionately referred to itself – watching the regulars engaging in the same 'this-is-our-bar-why-don't-you-fuck-off-out-of-it' routine favoured by regulars everywhere but wrought to high art in North Cornwall. As indeed – since this was North Cornwall merely moved to a warmer spot – it was here. During a particularly violent passage of the storm a well-dressed and absolutely sober Aborigine ran in for cover. Apart from shelter he appeared to want nothing other than an instant lottery ticket from the dispenser on the wall, and a packet of cigarettes. But the Aborigines had their own space at the Conti, a great noisy barn of a lounge behind this one. As one man, the Rotarians at the bar swung around on their stools and stared the rogue Aborigine back where he belonged.

They would have done the same to us had we let them catch our eye. Their prejudice, you see, wasn't confined only to colour. But we stayed out of their gaze, at a window table at the far end of the room, from where we could watch the palm trees tossing their fronds like Bacchantes, and the wet, livid

sky sizzling. God, too, insisting on his territorial rights. It was
the sort of tropical night frequently evoked by writers of imaginative literature as a backdrop to great emotional upheaval or
sudden rushes of personal lucidity. So it probably wasn't at all
coincidental that the only other people in the bar who weren't
locals happened to be the handsome, well-preserved couple
whose example on Cable Beach earlier that day had very nearly
killed us. From the expression on their faces I could tell that
they were thinking the same about us. We'd each followed the
other supposing that the other knew it was safe. The deluded
leading the denuded.

Although we knew perfectly well that we were wasting our
time, that there was not the slightest likelihood of our finding
anything remotely authentic in Broome, we still tried to dig
ourselves out a Chinese meal that night, beginning our search –
with reprehensible naivety – in Chinatown itself. I don't know
how many pagoda façades we peered behind, but we never saw
or smelled a single dish which we could imagine any self-
respecting pearler tucking in to after a hard day on the ocean
bottom. Unless one side-effect of the bends is an inexplicable
craving for sliced beetroot and sweetcorn salad.

We settled at last for an establishment which had the fewest
fire-breathing dragons painted on its shutters and a promise, at
the head of its menu, that we wouldn't be disappointed in the
fresh specialities prepared by Kenny Ong and Tony Mo. A
white Caucasian Australian male wearing an aertex shirt with
rolled-up sleeves rubbed his chin when we asked for a table,
although there were about forty of them, all empty, before
agreeing that we might reasonably sit wherever we fancied.
Once in our seats we became the responsibility of the head
waitress, a tall, pinched, irremediably occidental woman who
spoke in what I took to be a Norman dialect and wore a vaguely
Nipponese nightie tied in bows across a flat French chest. Her

job was only to make us feel uncomfortable. Our actual order was taken by the under-waitress, a new girl being broken in for the season, who had clearly never handed anyone so much as a biscuit in the whole of her life until now. She too was neither an Ong nor a Mo. It's possible that Kenny and Tony were having a night off, or an off-night, but whatever the reason we were unable to detect a trace of Chinese culinary competence in anything that arrived at our table. Our fish soup was a wet prawn cocktail. Our Chinese vegetables were frozen green peas and carrots. Even the tea we ordered arrived *à l'Australien*, in breakfast tea-cups and with sugar lumps.

'China tea!' I'm afraid I shouted at the waitress. 'China tea. The way they drink it in China!'

The Frenchwoman hurried over. 'I can assure sir we serve only in ze very best china,' she assured me.

A man has to be a fool to let a bad meal depress him, but the town and the food were all of a piece. We should have known better than to try either. After all, we'd lived in North Cornwall for ten years. And we knew that you don't go looking for good Chinese food there.

On our last afternoon in Broome I sat on a bench outside the Post Office and watched a couple of Aborigines in smart, green, upper-echelon council-worker-type uniforms busying themselves in the gardens of what I took to be some sort of public or municipal building. I had already been struck by the more or less relaxed demeanour of the visible black population of Broome. They seemed to belong to the town in a way that the Kununurra and Derby Aborigines didn't. And they walked the streets with a swagger which it wouldn't have been too fanciful to call Caribbean. They dressed more cheerfully too, and went in for less of that defensive raucousness that characterized their public behaviour further north. Watching these two in their natty green uniforms only confirmed my first sketchy impressions. 'Broome might not be my cup of tea,' I said to myself, 'but there's nothing wrong with race relations here. If that's not self-respect I'm looking at I'll eat my hat.'

Ros, meanwhile, had been in a phonebox attending to some advance social arrangements. She too, while trying for a number that wouldn't answer, had been observing events in the grounds of the municipal building opposite. Only she had noticed the odd detail that I hadn't. Such as, to take a random instance, that the building was a prison. And that the Aborigines in the natty green suits were inmates, not landscape gardeners. And that the natty green suits themselves were regulation prison fatigues and not the new street fashion of liberation.

I'd heard about Broome Regional Penitentiary, mainly from Neil who reckoned it was such a soft touch that every Abo in the northwest of Australia couldn't wait to be sent there. 'They queue up to be let in,' he told us. But I had also read a newspaper story about the premature death, behind these very walls, and in circumstances which needed some explaining, of Dixon Green, a young and hitherto healthy Aboriginal inmate. According to the Government pathologist Green died as the result of a heart attack, though when his brother saw the body shortly after his death he wondered why his face was bruised, why there was sand in his mouth, and why several of his teeth were missing. Other parts of Dixon Green were to go astray also, by the time the cadaver would be returned to the family. The brain, for example. And the heart. Accidents happen, of course. Even numerical accidents like the one we observed with our own eyes at precisely that moment, when an open truck arrived at the gates of the penitentiary and all the prisoners who climbed aboard it just happened to be black.

'That doesn't *necessarily* prove,' I said to Ros, 'that there are not any white convicts in there. It might simply mean that the prison authorities think so highly of the Aborigines in their charge that only they get the trips out in the truck.'

'It might,' Ros agreed. 'Although in that case, why do you suppose the white driver is steering so close to those trees that the Aborigines in the back have to throw themselves flat on the floor of the truck to avoid decapitation?'

I considered that a tough question to answer. But it was equally difficult to be certain how far the little social drama that was unfolding in front of us – the convicts hammering on the roof of the cab and swearing violently at the driver; the driver leaning out of his window and aiming random blows, before ploughing the truck into the trees again – was anything other than the natural release of high spirits of men cooped up too long. Australian blokes have been beating one another up as a means of expressing affection or relieving tension for some time; why shouldn't the usual laws of a predominantly male society be operating here?

I wasn't trying to shirk uncomfortable truths. I'd read that Aborigines are imprisoned at twenty times the rate that white men are in Western Australia, and that Dixon Green was by no means the only Aborigine in the state to have died while in police custody. I wasn't so committed to my own colour that I needed this to be untrue. I wanted to be rational about what I saw, that was all. And this, anyway, I did see: that the convicts in the back of the truck, with their Afro-Caribbean haircuts and their pumped-up biceps and their confident aggression, presented, en masse, a possibility of politicized Aboriginality preferable to anything we'd so far witnessed outside bottle-shops, arranged in a circle on a nature-strip, or sucking on a flagon under a gum tree in the park.

There is nothing remotely contentious about my 'prefer-able', unless it would be argued that man is never worthier than when he's docile.

★　★　★

Later that afternoon Ros inveigled me into a Catholic church whose only point of interest was a mother-of-pearl altar. Native nacre-work of this kind abounds in Broome, the shell being to the West Kimberleys what Delabole slate is to North Cornwall. Since I disapprove of altars altogether I saw no particular reason to take exception to this one merely because it looked as though it had been stitched together with shirt buttons; but I was anxious to get out of the church for reasons which were no less aesthetic: I could smell a Mass coming. There was a sudden bustle about me. Women with the closed faces of believers were turning up and taking their places. From an ante-room I thought I could hear the blood of the First Fisher of Pearls being decanted. I flew to the door.

But I didn't have Ros with me. When I turned around to look for her I saw a small, furry, Irish nun entrammelling her expertly in obligation and guilt.

'And will you be staying for Mass, my dear?'

'I don't think so, sister. I think my husband wishes to leave.'

'Ah, well, there's no coming between a husband and a wife. Are you a Catholic, my dear?'

'I *was*, sister.' Apology? Did I hear apology in Ros's voice?

'I knew it. I knew at once you were a Catholic.'

'Used to be, sister. I'm not any more.'

'I'll pray for your soul, my dear. And I'll pray that you return to the church.'

'Thank you, sister.'

'But if you won't be staying for Mass I wonder if I might impose upon you to help me with these blinds. The string there – no, not that one, *that* one – seems to be all stuck. Do you think you can? – there, that's it . . . you're taller than me.'

For my own part I had always associated nuns with requests for some favour. You saw a nun, you put your hand in your pocket. But I had never fully realized until I beheld Ros standing on a pew and struggling with the cords of a blind, a new expression of beatitude on her face, a sweet obedience in her eyes, how subtle a snare those nuns could set. In seconds they had bound her, hand and foot, in her past.

The little, furry, Irish nun threw me a quick glance of triumph. From my station at the door of the church I glowered back. Just briefly it was like a struggle between good and evil for the possession of a wavering soul. But then Ros was back with me in the daylight, and good had scraped home by a whisker once again.

We spent what was left of the day packing and reading local newspapers. An ad in the personal column of the *North West Telegraph* took my eye. 'I would like to apologize,' it said, 'for my behaviour towards the Ladies Darts Team in the Hope and Anchor last weekend. I am deeply sorry for any offence I caused.'

It doesn't matter where you travel, the really good times are always somewhere else; but Australia has a special gift for tantalizing you with the possibility that they are just around the corner. I went to bed vicariously intoxicated, wondering about the sex of the penitent, and the nature of the offence caused to the Ladies Darts Team. The last image I had before sleep was of Jocky Wilson.

Instead of being thankful that this was her last night in Broome Ros slept fitfully, cursing the time she had already spent there. She was still in a bad temper in the morning and actually woke shouting. We were both having second thoughts about our decision to catch the bus directly to Perth, a journey of some two thousand kilometres lasting well over thirty hours. Originally we had intended to stop off here and there to look about us, but we had now had enough of small coastal towns in the north and hankered after the city. We could have flown, of course, but I felt obliged to *see* those two thousand kilometres even if I was content not to set foot on many of them. And it struck me that there was a nice symmetry about the timing of this journey, from Ros's point of view, since it would end in our arrival at Perth on Good Friday. There could be no better day for a Catholic to return to her home town, it seemed to me, apart from Easter Monday, and we were neither of us prepared to wait that long.

In the foyer of our hotel I listened to other disgruntled visitors waiting to board their various buses. No one had a good thing to say about Broome or its famed Chinatown. 'I expected something ornate,' a dainty girl from Melbourne complained, 'like you get in Little Bourke Street. But there was just a few tin sheds. Even the Chinamen looked wrong.'

How Wrong is a Chinaman?

Our drivers were called Max and Dutchy. Their routine was the familiar fatuous one, though Dutchy invested it with a more than usually hyper-tense theatricality. If any newly boarded passenger failed to say 'G'day' when Dutchy said 'G'day' Dutchy would stop the bus, climb out of the driver's seat, fold his arms across his chest, and wait. He was handsome in a disreputable sort of way, with long Western moustaches and a poker player's eyes. There was a suggestion of bad temper, perhaps cruelty in his face also, so he had no trouble getting his 'G'day', or even 'G'day, Dutchy'. After which he would pronounce, 'That's better', and return to the business of getting us down the coast to Perth. In the absence of a properly laid down class system such men as Dutchy perform an inestimable service for the smooth working of Australian society, enforcing the rules of day-to-day affability and politeness, and ensuring that surliness and disgruntlement are never permitted to take root. Whatever the state of things elsewhere in the country our bus was a model of good-fellowship and patriotism. Even the waste-paper basket by the driver's seat carried a smile sticker and the message, WE LOVE AUSTRALIA.

There was little to love in the landscape, though, for the first few hundred kilometres south of Broome. My map told me that there was ocean and beach to the west, and any number of capes testifying to early French interest in the region – Cape Latouche Treville, Cape Jaubert, False Cape Bossut, Poissonnier Point – but the Great Northern Highway was too far from the coast for any of this to be visible. The only thing to look at was the interminable scrub, littered with those disheartening beer bottles, the little brown stubbies, which lie by the roadside in the remotest places forming a sort of chain of mindless indulgence around the entire continent. I tried to ignore the bottles and passed the time pretending that the monotonous country hereabouts was in fact various and beautiful. Surely, I told myself, there is a vast and mysterious unchartedness about this; surely it is harsh and bewildering, majestic in its tediousness, surprising in its unsurprisingness. A flat wonderful unendingness. But I was soon asleep and only woke, hours later, when the bus suddenly turned left off the highway into a dirt-track wide enough, strictly speaking, for no more than a motorbike. Part of the excitement and charm of outback travel is that you can make your own road just about any time you feel like it. It's common to see a new track running alongside an old existing one, for no other reason, clearly, than that a driver needed to enliven the tedium. A Toyota-load of Aborigines is particularly likely to give up on the highway and to head off into the bush on a whim. I thought some such impulse had taken hold of our driver until it became clear that he knew where he was going and that we were about to enter the town of Goldsworthy.

Easy to miss – if you don't spot the dirt-track – clean, neat, methodical, and apparently deserted, Goldsworthy owes its existence entirely to iron ore. Although there was no reason to suppose it concealed any sinister secrets it reminded me, in its eerie quiet, of Jabiru, the uranium town in Kakadu. It possessed the same unsettling stillness and had imported, into a similarly inappropriate terrain, the same sterile ideal of gracious suburban living. The streets were spotless enough to eat from. The drive-in cinema was too beautifully laid out to allow the entrance of cars, so in orderly rows before the vast tilted screen deckchairs were arranged instead. Outside the factory gates a board announced a continuing 100 per cent safety record. There was no reason for anyone to come to harm in Goldsworthy, but then there was no reason for anyone to come to live in it at all. And, in truth, for all we saw of Homo sapiens in Goldsworthy it's possible that nobody did. The water sprinklers turned of their own accord. The bright material of the deckchairs flapped tenantless. The bus drove twice around the town, picking no one up and dropping no one off.

Just before we came into Port Hedland, another seventy kilometres down the highway, we were kept waiting at a railway crossing by a long train belonging to Newman Mining. It took nearly ten minutes to pass us. Like the snakes which Wayne claimed he'd run over in the Northern Territory, you could never at one time see both its head and its tail. Max was able to give us all the details: there were 180 carriages, each weighing 20 tons, the whole train being 2 kilometres long. Bearing in mind all these measurements and taking into account how far the train had to travel, I calculated that in order to bring it to a stop at its destination the driver would have to start applying the brakes before the train had actually begun moving.

We didn't leave the bus at Port Hedland, not even to stretch our legs. We were given a quick whisk around the town, told about the vast quantities of iron ore and salt that were exported from here, shown the Port Authority's Control Tower, affectionately referred to as the Pill (guess why? – because it controls all the berths in the harbour), and then back on to the highway south, first stop Whim Creek. Not far out of Port Hedland a spectacular electrical storm ripped into the night. The moon looked too big, fevered – a ghastly swollen phosphorescent yellow. As I cleaned the window of the bus to get a better look

I realized that I had been moon-watching every night since arriving in Darwin. Moon-watching and moon-fretting also. You did, you really did worry about the moon up here, so much less forbidding was it than the ice-cold divinity of European skies. It seemed, on most nights, wholly unstable, not a controlling force but itself affected and moved by the vast electrical disturbances. Over Port Hedland the moon looked decidedly ill.

Unable to sleep, I talked to a girl called Cathy from Okehampton in Devon. Cathy was travelling around Australia with her Welsh boyfriend whom she'd met at Cardiff University where they were both reading English. To see as much of the country as possible and to make the best use of their bus passes, they were scheduling their journey so that they could do nearly all of their sleeping on buses. This had exhausted the Welsh boy. Wrapped up in a tie-dyed sheet he roamed the bus in a frenzy, searching for more room to stretch out in. In the thirty-six hours we were on the bus together I never once saw him not in this sleepless furore. A sort of touristical Lady Macbeth, he raged from seat to seat in the hope that he'd overlooked one, that someone had moved or got off, and that he would at last find a space large enough to give him rest. This was by no means the first Welshman I had met who could not make up his mind where he wanted to sleep.

Oblivious to his sufferings by now, Cathy talked to me about Cardiff University; or rather I asked her questions relating to her course and her teachers, and she by and large failed to answer them. I knew, or thought I knew, several people who taught English at Cardiff and I was curious to learn how they were, but Cathy shook her head – no, no, she'd never heard of them. How very different, I thought, from me and my friends as students, who had been so obsessed by the people who taught us that we were familiar with every detail of their private lives right down to the birthdays of their children – Anna, and Birkin, and Dorothea. Cathy was not only light on the names of her lecturers, she didn't know the names of any writers either. 'Andrew's the one to talk to about that,' she said when I quizzed her on what novels she'd read. But had anyone tried to talk to Andrew he would have screamed.

'So what do you do?' Cathy asked me, after we had together exhausted every avenue of *her* ignorance.

The possibility that I could become the only writer she had ever heard of suddenly made me quite light-headed. I gave her my name, very slowly – I might even have spelled it for her – together with a list of my publications. She nodded thoughtfully after each one, in what looked to me like a serious effort to commit them to memory. But then I saw a fine film, like gauze, appear across her eyes; and I knew that she had forgotten me already. 'Pity you're not talking to Andrew,' she said. 'He's the one.'

We stopped at Nanutarra, in the early hours of the morning, where there was a roadhouse willing to serve chicken and chips to anyone who was game. I settled for coffee myself, and a short walk in the dust. The sky had cleared now, though the moon was still inflamed, a bright watery orange. You could easily believe, standing stock still in the sultry night heat, that you could get a tan from such a moon.

Back on the bus I found Andrew collapsed in my seat. He cursed me under his breath when I woke him, pulled his sheet over his head, and out of some mad impulse to self-destruction made straight for the empty seat next to the driver, a place which, as we had been many times warned, was consecrated to the ideal of sociability.

'You can't sit here, mate,' Dutchy told him, 'unless you're prepared to stay awake and talk to me for the next two hours, which I wouldn't want anyway since you're not a sheila.'

As Andrew raged back down the bus I noticed that the pupils

had vanished entirely from his eyes and that he looked like Blind Pugh from *Treasure Island*.

To the discomfort of everybody else who wanted to sleep, some sheila did take it into her head to occupy the chat seat next to Dutchy. She was an inane girl with blonde hair that stood up in perpetual surprise and one of those flat Australian drawls which owe their existence to a frantic desire to please. 'Oh yes!' and 'Oh no!' she would say, in the same sentence, to cover all eventualities. She was the sort of Oz girl that has been bred specifically to soothe Oz men. She talked to Dutchy about the difficulties of driving, the monotony of the roads, the special problems of handling a big vehicle, and the irritations of troublesome passengers. There was no minor hardship in Dutchy's life that she was not prepared to enter sympathetically into.

'I once nearly hit a camel on the Nullarbor,' Dutchy said.

'Oh no!'

'Yeah. It suddenly darted straight out. Very early in the morning it was.'

'Oh no! A camel darting out in front of you on the Nullarbor in the morning. Oh no!'

'The passengers were all deaf mutes. I was taking them back from the deaf-mute Olympics.'

'Oh yes, the deaf-mute Olympics. That must have been difficult for you.'

'Difficult for them. They didn't hear my warning.'

'Oh no!'

'Oh yes – they all ended up in a pile at the front of the bus.'

'Oh no! – Oh yes! I can imagine.'

I closed my eyes and returned to my own struggles at the Comatose Games. I wasn't doing well but I was murdering the Welsh boy.

A little after dawn we pulled into Carnarvon, a pleasant-looking tropical town of banana plantations, bougainvilleas and caravan parks, built on the Gascoyne River at more or less the very spot George Grey came ashore in 1839, having lost half his stores, broken up the majority of his boats and imperilled the lives of all his men on a sort of early surfing trip – before the days of surfboards – into the mouth of Shark Bay. Nothing daunted, with the seaweed still dripping from his hair and the groans of his men not yet abated, Lieutenant Grey looked around him, beheld a 'rich district', a 'low fertile country', and submitted to that spirit of prophecy which never abandoned him through all adversity:

> I, however, felt conscious that within a few years of the moment at which I stood there, a British population, rich in civilization, and the means of transforming an unoccupied country to one teeming with inhabitants and produce, would have followed my steps, and be eagerly and anxiously examining my charts.

I was disappointed that none of the guides to the area I was carrying contained copies of Grey's charts for enthusiasts like myself eagerly and anxiously to examine. Instead, all one learnt was that Aubrey Brown and John Monger had first settled the town in 1876, having driven 4,000 sheep from York – presumably the York on the River Avon, not far from Perth – and that the great aviator, Sir Charles Kingsford-Smith, had once run a garage and removal business here.

Perhaps because of the town's Welsh name, or because of their system of travelling at night in order to see everything they could in the daylight. Cathy and her sleepless boyfriend left the bus at Carnarvon. Dutchy dropped them at a coffee shop that wouldn't be open for another three hours, then drove us slowly twice around the town for no reason that I could understand unless it was to look for passengers who'd got lost. On the way out we passed Cathy and Andrew still sitting with their rucksacks by the side of the road. Andrew had wound his sheet even tighter around himself and in his impotent rage resembled some mythological figure who'd fallen out for eternity with the Goddess of Sleep.

By mid-morning we started to hit our first Perthites heading north for the long Easter weekend. Suddenly there were fewer 4-wheel drives on the road and more station waggons pulling trailer loads of boats and dinghies and surfboards. We stopped for morning tea just outside Wannoo at a roadhouse called the Billabong, where the men putting petrol in their motor cars were creamier to look at than those we'd become accustomed to, softer-bellied, pinker, smoother and more salaried. I found myself missing the leathery skin of the men from the north, but Ros had the whiff of home in her nostrils now and the closer we got to Perth the more she fell a victim to what Oliver Sacks calls 'incontinent nostalgia'. At Geraldton – 'The Friendliest Town in the West' – or rather at the sight of the multi-coloured clay tiles on the roofs of the houses of Geraldton, the tears began to stream from Ros's eyes. I was soon handing her tissues at the rate of three every two kilometres. 'Faster! Faster!' she implored. It wasn't only tears she was holding back – the sweat of sheer panic was now pouring out of her. Long before we'd arrived at the outskirts of Perth she had gone through her entire supply of perfumed face towels collected from motels all over North Australia. She dabbed her forehead. She mopped her throat. She thrust fresheners under her arms and wrung them out so that she might use them again.

'Nervous?' I noted.

She shook her head, spraying me with perspiration. Nervous? We were now passing homesteads she'd visited as a little girl, creeks she'd paddled in, roads into the hills she'd walked along with her parents in 1953. Nervous? *Nostalgia Incontinentissimus* was upon her.

The approach to Perth was lovely. I thought. Small farms. Market gardens. Modest wineries. Melancholy horses in green paddocks. The sense of manageable, domestic ruralism a pleasant relief after the massive stations of the north. Some of the houses were no more than tin sheds with simple verandahs around them, but even a tin shed can look charming in the late afternoon, set in a small paddock, sheltered by gums, amid signs of flourishing though unostentatious husbandry.

As we entered Perth proper, through a pleasantly amorphous and democratic tumble of suburbs, we heard on the radio that a man had blocked the traffic in the city by parking his car on the Narrows Bridge, climbing on top of it with a pair of rifles – one of them a military .22 – stripping to the waist, dousing himself and his car (marked HIGH EXPLOSIVES) in petrol, and daring anyone to move him along. The drama was unfolding now, this very minute, less than a mile from where we were. We could see the tailback of traffic and, because the Narrows Bridge is elevated, the blue revolving lights of the waiting police cars. Had the man decided to go ahead and blow himself and the picturesque bridge sky high, as a Good Friday gesture, we would have enjoyed an excellent view of it.

The other drama of our entry into Perth was also enacted against an ancient religious backdrop. Since this *was* Good Friday we could not hope to find a drop of alcohol in the entire city.

The person who informed us of this was the proprietor of the motel which Dutchy had been recommending to us as the best place to stay in Perth ever since we'd made the mistake, thousands of kilometres earlier, of seeking his advice on such matters. 'Beaut little place,' he'd told us. 'Cheap. Clean. Friendly. Well-stocked bar. It's where I always stay myself.' He'd dropped us off there on the understanding that we'd get together later for a jar and a yarn once he'd returned the coach to the Perth office. And so there we were, further out of town than we wanted to be, in the presence of a sepulchral Englishman with skin the texture of gabardine, being told, even before we'd signed in, what we were wasting our time to expect.

'When you say there's no alcohol to be had anywhere in Perth, I take it that you mean with the exception of here,' I laughed. I was halfway through filling out our registration card, but I stopped when I perceived that our host had not laughed encouragingly back.

'You've obviously never been in Western Australia over Easter,' he said, exchanging a soundless sneer with a party of disreputably overdressed Mediterraneans – three men in mohair suits and crêpe-soled shoes and two women in *Dallas*-style padded dresses – who were, against the usual practice of Australian motels, sitting at a round table in the reception area, taking tea. Something about their demeanour suggested that they were acquaintances of the management rather than guests. I was reminded of inexpensive hotels that I'd stayed at in the past in the Sussex Gardens area of West London, and queasy misgivings about having blundered into a front for the Palestine Liberation Organization.

'So you are not going to serve us with a drink even though we are residents?' Ros asked.

He shook his head. That peculiar satisfaction the English take in denying service or pleasure cast a kind of dying light, as it were from within, over his colourless features. 'And neither would any other hotel in Perth,' he added.

'I don't believe that,' Ros said.

It could have been a nasty moment. The inexplicable Good Friday tea drinkers at the table didn't look to me like the sort of people who took kindly to aspersions on their friends' reputations for honesty. I believe I even saw the calf muscles twitching inside the carefully creased trousers of the most senior of them. But Rosalin wasn't in a mood to be trifled with either. 'I don't intend to spend my first night back in Perth for twenty-eight years without the wherewithal to toast my return,' she announced.

She was exaggerating only a little bit. She had been back to

Perth a couple of times since 1958, but this was meant to be a re-entry on a grand scale. It was unthinkable without champagne. As in truth it was unthinkable in this miserable suburban motel. Run by one in such an advanced state of decomposition that you could actually hear the decalcifying crumble of his bones.

So I put up no resistance at all as she de-residented us on the spot, called a taxi, and ordered the driver to deliver us and our bags to the Parmelia Hilton. 'We're thirsty,' she told him, just in case he was thinking of taking his time.

The Parmelia Hilton had once been the most elegant hotel in Perth. Now, though, it was under pressure from the ultramodern sky-scrapers which were going up all over town in accordance with the city's new young millionaire image, and as part of the preparations for the Americas Cup. The name itself had a bit of a provincial ring about it, and provincialism was the very thing Perth was busy endeavouring to shrug off. *Parmelia?* Whatever the name's origins in naval history didn't it now sound rather too spinsterish and conventical? 'Sister Parmelia wishes to thank all ex-pupils for their good wishes on her retirement after forty years of devoted . . . .'

On the other hand you couldn't be in Australia long without knowing that the best establishments, like the best dishes, are always christened after women. I was prepared to bet that you could get an excellent Pavlova at the Parmelia.

We didn't ask whether the Parmelia had a room, only whether she had a bar. Yes, but we couldn't use it tonight – Good Friday, in case we hadn't heard – unless we had a room. 'We'll have a room,' Ros said.

We followed our luggage up in the lift, just for the look of the thing, splashed water on our faces, caught a quick glimpse through our windows of the police cars still biding their time on the approaches to the Narrows Bridge, waiting for the man to come off the roof of his vehicle or to ignite himself and have done with it, then we redescended for our raid upon the bar.

The staff punctiliously insisted on seeing our keys each time they served us a drink. All the other guests were British. A Scot in a Marks and Spencer's pullover was explaining the principles of oil-exploration to a tired-looking companion. He held his hand downwards, his fingers like teats, and made a slurping noise. I was overcome by a disappointing sensation of having taken a long time and come a long way to arrive nowhere very distant at all.

Over steak at the hotel restaurant I made my first acquaintance with the Perth custom of waiters positively harassing you to drink. (That is after they have positively harassed you for your keys.) A new beer was brought to us before we were halfway through our old. 'Another bottle of champagne, sir,' I was asked a half a dozen times, 'for when you've finished that one?'

I felt as if the whole city was pulling the old double detective trick on us, now giving us everything we wanted, now taking it all away from us again.

On television that night we discovered that the Police Station in Russell Street, Melbourne, had been bombed the day before, while we'd been dozing on the coach. The report was delivered in a tone not far removed from hysteria. It was a national catastrophe. Nazis might have been behind it. A police spokesman described it as 'the greatest ever outrage against humanity'.

Victoria's Chief Commissioner of Police, Mick Miller, blamed the Council for Civil Liberties for wearing down respect for law and order and making it difficult to grill suspects. 'I believe the civil liberties lobby has a say in Victoria out of all proportion to its numbers,' he declared. 'I'm speaking for the strong silent majority of citizens who are fed up with crime in this state and who are tired of being victimized by criminals. We are not seeking increased powers for ourselves but for the people of Victoria.'

Before we went to sleep we looted the little refrigerated bar in our room one last time, and toasted each other, our journey so far, and Perth. The extraordinary precautions that had been taken to keep the town alcohol free today, in respect to the memory of a martyred and highly articulate Semite; a distraught man pointing rifles at himself high above the Swan River; the living dead, a long way from their native England, bearing their national spirit of deprivation with them; senior policemen frothing with vitriolic righteousness – ah, it was good to be back in a Christian country again.

SEVEN

ET IN ARCADIA NOS

The first thing Ros saw through the windows of the Parmelia Hilton when she opened her eyes the next morning was the church tower of St Columba's, the Catholic primary school she had attended, with faith in her little heart, from 1948 to 1954. She sat up in bed, pointing, unable to speak, with tears streaming down her face.

Taking everything into account, I envied her. There was no impossible Moorish tower, picturesque in itself and capable of unloosing a flood of exquisite associations, mixing God and infancy and friendship, in my past. It does not harm to grow up in a blissfully clement climate, amid bells and poetical rituals, even if that means that you never fully quit your childhood. I buried mine, in Cheetham Hill, with alacrity, long before I had any business wanting to chime in with the grown-ups. Judaism doesn't encourage you to linger amongst childish things. And neither does the North of England. Had I possessed Perth it might have been different.

I stood at the window and picked out the tower as Ros directed. It rose above the white houses and apartment blocks of South Perth, on the opposite bank of the Swan River, on a hillside which, with the smallest latitude, it was just possible to imagine as Spanish or dream-Moroccan. Perth has never got around to deciding what style of architecture it should embrace, but, with so many natural advantages and such Divine Good-Will, that indecision can hardly be said to matter. It looked wholly benign to me, a metropolis and a seaside resort all at once, a city which enjoyed the furthest distance from its nearest neighbour city than any in the world, and I decided there and then to fall in love with it, since one has to be in love with somewhere, and to adopt Ros's earliest memories of it as if they were my own.

Out on the city streets it was a bright, cheerful, airy Saturday morning. Enthusiastic if not exactly exhilarating. It reminded me, in its warmth and country-town bustle, in its adolescent civic gaucherie, of a mini-Sydney – Sydney as it was when I first clapped eyes on it in 1965. So suddenly I was carrying a double burden of melancholy remembrances: Ros's and my own.

Some unlucky circumstance led us, within minutes of leaving our hotel, to Boans, a department store much associated with her past; she could remember it when it had wooden floorboards covered in sawdust and overhead tubes carrying the cash to the offices above and back again with the change. The store had been founded in 1895 and now it was closing down. We had turned up just in time to witness its death-throes.

Many floors, and many sections of floors, were roped off. I obeyed Ros's instructions to ignore the ropes. High up in the building we found a totally deserted floor with office chairs and desks and old-fashioned draper's dummies all numbered and arranged into manageable auction lots. In a doubly roped-off remote wing we came upon a solitary secretary still at work on ledgers behind a partition marked 'Reception'. Her partition had a lot number on it. So, judging from her expression, did she.

Ros led me to the top of the store where the restaurant used to be, where she and her mother took afternoon tea after a hot day's shopping. It was a large, elegant, and now quite empty space. Grand stained-glass windows commanded wide views over the city. A solitary cockroach lay on its back, its feet in the air, having given up all hope of service.

That special power which adheres to closed-down places of entertainment worked its wicked magic. And Ros was getting what she wanted.

On the lower fashion floors, where some selling was still going on, the only display materials were brown cardboard boxes, arranged in interesting shapes.

'Let's get out of here,' Ros said.

Back in the street we promptly ran into Jane and Brian Dobbie – the incomprehensible Scotsman and his wife we had met on our trip into Kakadu.

'Fansahmeatandyew,' Brian said.

'That's Perth all over,' Jane laughed.

What she was referring to was Perth's reputation for being a small town where everyone knew everyone else. It certainly looked that way to me. I knew five people in the city and already – half an hour after walking out into it – I had met two of them.

As we approached Hay Street Mall the streets became festive. On the mall itself a jazz band was playing and an assortment of buskers and hawkers fought for our attention, often in English accents. I was reminded of the numbers of stories I'd heard of English migrants stopping off at Perth en route to the Eastern States and liking what they saw so much that they couldn't be bothered to complete their journeys. Certainly it felt the most English of all the Australian cities I knew. It even boasted its own Tudor Shopping Arcade – London Court. Built in 1937, 'its unique Elizabethan architecture' (I'm quoting from its own advertising now) 'has attracted tourists from afar. Walter Raleigh and Dick Whittington are inside the arcade above the first floor level at each end. The St George's Terrace and Hay Street faces are highlighted by two unique clocks. The St George's Terrace clock tower is a reproduction of La Grosse Horloge at Rouen, and in a large mullioned window St George and the Dragon make circuits each quarter of an hour.'

I thought that London Court might have gone the whole way and sold exclusively pastiche English merchandise instead of fluffy koalas and 'I'm an Aussie bird' T-shirts, but I didn't otherwise object to it. I might have adopted Western Australia but I hadn't entirely thrown over my connection with England. And London Court was hardly more spurious in its essentials than what passes for the original. I did give a miss, though, to the Elizabethan Village in Armadale, where there are full-size replicas of Shakespeare's Birthplace and Ann Hathaway's Cottage. And where, apparently, 'The Poet's Arbor Restaurant is delightfully appointed'. I wasn't feeling *that* homesick.

Once Ros had squeezed all the sentimentality she could out of Perth's department stores she led me up to King's Park, the lovely picnic and perambulation area – part tended botanical gardens, part bush – which overlooks the city and the river. By late morning Perth was as warm in autumn as London ever gets in summer. And a lot less sticky. Young people on bicycles passed us, ringing their bells and smiling. Wherever there was a view down to the Swan and the amenable skyscrapers of the new go-ahead Perth there were Japanese posing for photographs. In so far as you can be certain with Japanese, they too seemed to be smiling.

We took an unhurried seafood lunch – I mean scallops and prawns and calimari, not Dover sole – in the King's Park restaurant, where I marvelled at the quaint formality, the awkward and unaccustomed air, of our fellow diners. I estimated that it must have been the 1950s since I'd last seen people eating out with such apparent uncertainty as to the conventions. I'd never been to New Zealand but I guessed that public dining was still like this there also. I found the slowness and the reserve rather soothing. I normally gallop my food down as if I have something terribly urgent to do afterwards. Today, surrounded by largely elderly people in Harris Tweed jackets and funereal hats, I found myself taking as long to swallow the elbow of a prawn as I would usually devote to a whole shoulder of lamb.

This was just the start of Perth's deceleration of all my functions. By the time I was ready to leave I too would be moving like a sloth, my limbs heavy with contentment, my mind drugged with the curiously satisfying knowledge that the nearest city was well over three thousand kilometres away.

While we were eating we saw the first of our Easter brides. This one arrived at the entrance to the restaurant in a taxi, hard on the heels of the groom in the taxi in front. The groom turned out to be blind and had to be led up the steps by his future wife. It is always a touching sight, a blind man dressed for a special occasion. The bride hung on to him tightly and appeared to whisper some words of encouragement in his ear. The moment they began their climb the taxi drivers removed the white bridal decorations from their cabs and drove off. There is no end to the melancholy of these sunny old-fashioned Australian cities.

After lunch we walked through the park down to the river. Cyclists continued to pass us, ringing and smiling. I was struck by how democratically landscaped the Swan was, how accessible to pedestrians it had been made, and how little justice was done it by calling it a river at all, since at this point of its journey it swelled and fingered the city like a harbour.

We followed it, anyway, until we reached the University of

Western Australia, another demi-paradise for ingrate Australian academics not to take the full measure of their extreme good fortune in. I had heard that the university was beautifully situated, amidst tropical gardens and sunken outdoor theatres around which peacocks strutted; but I was still taken aback by the sumptuousness of what I saw. On the lawn in the front of Winthrop Hall – yet one more testimony to Perth's Moorish/Tuscan origins – twelve golden Australian youths in judo outfits were bowing courteously, if somewhat indiscriminately, prior to settling down to throwing one another about. Their ceremonial costumes, against the dense jungle green of the lawn, glowed a ghostly white. At the furthest end of the lawn, beneath the Winthrop Tower, a bust of Socrates, resembling an early Australian explorer, looked on imperturbably, musing on truth. Three abstract sculptures in pastel colours, presumably meant to suggest sea life or sea monstrosity, rose from an ornamental pool.

We sat on a bench, Ros remembering how, as a girl inside that very hall, she had given her first public recital on the pianoforte, and I wishing that I were a student again, here, now, in this garden of the Hesperides.

Suddenly, and absolutely soundlessly, a couple of authentic Japanese in white suits materialized from the cool shelter of Winthrop's Spanish cloisters and stood transfixed by the sight of the twelve Australian forgeries still exchanging elaborate courtesies on the lawn. I watched the two men scratch their heads and shrug in unison. Without any other communication each took a camera from his pocket and snapped. For the first time it occurred to me that the camera was not necessarily the mere means for the avid accumulation of second-hand experience but might actually serve as a mediator between the photographer and philosophical bemusement. Understood from this angle it is not surprising that the Japanese are the most tireless of photographers. Maybe between the opening and closing of the shutter and the final development of the negative, something will come clear about occidental culture.

I didn't hold out much hope for them in this instance. Here on the lawn in front of Winthrop Hall (named after Sir John Winthrop Hackett) I was myself feeling increasingly like a phantom bit-part player in a surrealist film, a sensation not at all diminished when our second Easter bride of the day came running out from the abundant foliage of the adjoining quadrangle, pursued across the grass by two Tongan bridesmaids in pink organza *Gone with the Wind* ball gowns. Not having a camera I looked up to the heavens for help but there I saw only a pelican, fat, white and happy, gliding on warm currents of air.

I took a turn around the campus, enjoying more of its follies – the terrace library looking out over a landscaped pool bristling with tropical fish; the mock-Elizabethan theatre, an exact copy, some said, of the original Mermaid; the Sommerville Auditorium, a lovely shaded arena, surrounded by Norfolk Pines; the sunken garden where brides came to be photographed in a sylvan setting. And everywhere there would be sudden views of yachts on the Swan River, billowing spinnakers glimpsed through the swooning palms.

I lingered over the student noticeboards. 'Rage' seemed to be a buzz word right now at the University of Western Australia. There was a poster advertising AN EASTER ROCK RAGE, and beneath that an appeal to all students to RAGE AGAINST TERTIARY FEES. I was reminded of Gough Whitlam's famous injunction to all Australians at the time of his dismissal to MAINTAIN YOUR RAGE. He hadn't got very far with that and I couldn't see The Furies prospering out here either. You have to be altogether more deprived to stay angry about a principle for long. The one enraged man in Perth had blocked the Narrows Bridge and doused himself in petrol – and he, according to the morning's papers, was now in police custody, awaiting 'psychiatric assessment'.

I hired a car that evening and drove to Fremantle, changed and still changing out of all recognition to my eye in readiness for the Americas Cup. It was at Fremantle that I had first stood on Australian soil and first tasted Australian beer, twenty-one years before. If you had a few hours in port in those days you were advised to jump straight on the train and head for Perth. Freo wasn't considered to be worth a look. Now, given the extent of the restoration and refurbishment, the animation on the streets, and the proliferation of nightspots both smart and bohemian, there was a good argument, should you be flying into Perth with only a few hours to spend, for hopping on the train and heading straight for Fremantle.

I was soon to discover that there was more than one attitude to the tarting up of old Fremantle. It was spoiling the character of the place, some said. It had put up the prices of property. It was forcing long-time residents to move out. 'I AM NOT AN AMERICAS CUP PROJECT,' I read on one person's T-shirt – 'I LIVE HERE.' And there was another cause for concern – what would happen to this playground for visiting American yacht freaks when Australia lost the cup or, even worse, when America failed to reach the final?

I was already sick of seeing and hearing the name Bond. It towered over Perth in red neon, atop his newest office block. It was on every taxi driver's and every desk clerk's lips. But I always think you should make the best and briefest case for capitalists before consigning them to the flames. 'At least he's woken this dreary old port up,' I said to Ros. 'Look at it – there are markets, restaurants, Malaysian style food halls, street cafés. It's a positive Latin Quarter.'

But it seemed that I did not know whereof I spoke.

'It always was,' Ros corrected me. 'Freo was taking on this

character long before there was any talk of Americas Cups. We used to drive out here thirty years ago to get pasta and capuccino. I tasted my first ever gelato here – right here where we're standing now.'

In fact we were standing now outside a pub which boasted barbecued brotwurst and strong Fremantle lager. We gave the wurst a miss but the lager a run for its money. In the gents' lavatories I was much taken by the instructions on the hand drier.

BUDGET DRIER. HOW IT WORKS: We have achieved the best possible performance by using the available power supply and holding the air velocity to a level which will allow it to heat to the highest temperature near-dry hands could stand on a warm day. This produces the driest air giving maximum rate of evaporation.

WHY IT VARIES: Because of the initial temperature and humidity of the air and the amount of moisture on your hands.

I read this through again and again, trying to coax some meaning out of it. I'd had the same trouble, on the coach from Broome, with an introduction by Don Anderson to a collection of Australian short stories entitled *Transgressions*. 'But writing that is not located in the political-as-content,' my eyes believed they saw, 'may be no less subversive in that, as a mute transgressive text, it voices protest against the prison house of language while exploiting that very language as the vehicle of its protest. If that sounds paradoxical, it is because truly contemporary writing cuts against the *doxa* . . .' In the academy, as in the lavatory, Australian writers demand a high level of concentration from their readers. As I stood there, baffled and with wet hands, the machine emitted a paltry stream of tepid air for five seconds and then stopped. Nothing I could do would get it going again. I wiped my hands on my trousers, copied out the instructions, and left. Which was more or less what I'd done with *Transgressions* also.

The other reason people used to come to Fremantle, Ros said, was to eat fresh fried scallops and chips at the water's edge. So this we did, sitting on the jetty enjoying the twinkling lights and the view of the berths awaiting the competing boats from overseas. Something well-wrapped up said FRENCH KISS, though whether that was the yacht itself, or just the wherewithal to keep her seaworthy when she arrived, I didn't know or care. The water lapped against the jetty. Seagulls gathered round, wanting scallops but prepared to make do with chips. Sounds of people enjoying themselves at Lombardo's and Papa Luigi's floated over to us. Rage? Here? Then back to Perth and an exploration, in the dark, of some of Ros's old haunts. The houses of friends. The houses of friends of friends. And finally Ros's own house, the one she'd lived in until her fifteenth birthday when the family had moved to Melbourne.

'My father planted twenty-seven fruit trees in that garden,' she said, as we stood in the street outside, peering over the wall and trying to count. 'My dog, Nicholas Monsarrat Sadler, is buried under that huge gum tree, there.'

I fought back my irritability at a pet being named after a popular writer I didn't admire, and went along with the morbidity. 'How did he die?' I asked.

'He went for his first independent walk around the neighbourhood and got run over. My father found him. He wrapped him up in his old leather jacket – the one he'd worn on his motorbike when he took my mother on honeymoon – and then he carried him back, weeping. He buried the dog, still wrapped in the jacket, under that tree. It was a coat actually, not a jacket. A long, World War I pilot's coat. It was seeing him in that coat that made my mother fall in love with him.'

There's an argument for never going back to the city you were a child in.

Early the next morning we were out again in our rented Holden Gemini, once more haunting Morbidity Mews. Ros's house again. The house she'd lived in before that, next door to a girl who really was called Treta Wright, who lived next door to Brian Hayes. The houses of Ros's parents' friends. Even the house of Rolf Harris's mother, in the days when Rolf gave swimming lessons and taught Ros herself how to breathe under water. Then on to SMC – Santa Maria (Ladies) College – where she began her secondary education amid plaster-cast madonnas and ivied cloisters and all the rest of those special effects that Catholic authorities everywhere know the efficacy of subjecting their impressionable charges to.

In any circumstances, even without the added pangs of her backward journey through time, these were melancholy suburbs we were ghost-hunting in. Lost and leafy in the heat, they gave off a sense of lush obscurity, of ideal families and vivid child-hoods and irretrievable dreams. Increasingly, Perth was coming to seem to me the most exquisite setting for a permanently mislaid past. It was lotus land, a white man's Dreamtime, heavy with the melancholy of animation suspended in recollection. To live here would be to give oneself over to a great life's drowse. Irresistible and fatal.

Only that morning a report had been published in the papers claiming that Western Australia enjoyed the highest rate of domestic violence in the country. It was hard to imagine how anyone could find the necessary energy even to want to aim a blow in so soporific a setting. But there you are: the aggressive passions will out, howsoever leafy the suburb.

A propos of which Ros led me, as a final exercise in self-inflicted anguish, to the nunnery where as a little girl she had been encouraged to be a pianist and where, under a silvery gum tree, she had been chastised by her mother for saying 'fuck' in the hearing of the nuns. She was greatly distressed to discover that the tree was still there and flourishing.

'Fuck,' she said.

While I still had the car I decided that we ought to go back to Fremantle to take a further look at what was going on there and to call in at the Sunday market. I stopped off first at the Round House at Arthur Head, the Swan River Colony's first gaol, built by the engineer Henry Willey Reveley in 1831. Heritage has become a thriving business in Australia, especially on Sunday afternoons, and today there were history-hungry visitors everywhere, staring at old photographs of convicts and marvelling at the thickness of the walls. Buildings that are hardly more than three times older than me I generally find of limited interest, not least when they happen to be gaols, but one curious fact about Henry Willey Reveley caught my eye. He had been a friend of Shelley's before hitting Fremantle and had actually saved him from drowning in the Arno. I suppose, in truth, that it is really Shelley about whom that fact is curious. It seems to suggest that he was in the habit of getting into deep waters.

In the tunnel under the Round House we encountered a large and boisterous family of semi-Australianized Italians. There were about sixteen of them in all – the women multi-coloured and coquettish in strappy high-heeled cocktail shoes, dodging the puddles and potholes, the men barrel-chested and sonorous. There was one little boy in the party, five years old at the most, who was already a fully developed Italian male. He wore a gold chain around his podgy neck, a gold bracelet around his flabby wrist, and a gold ring on his fat forefinger. As we passed he winked confidently at me and confidentially at my wife.

The Fremantle market was as lively as we'd heard it to be. You could buy hand-painted frocks from Bali, you could eat any one of twenty flavours of gelato, you could have your palm read, or you could watch a Jewish stallholder suckling her baby. I believe we would have found plenty more things to do as well had we not been frightened away by a persistent street clown. I have an aversion to clowns anywhere. As a boy at the circus I found them mystifyingly unamusing and as a man on the streets I find them wholly dispiriting. This one seemed to sniff my distaste. He followed us around Fremantle, snapping his nose at me when I made the mistake of catching his watery eye. He materialized on the jetty at the same time we were there. His reflection mocked us in shop windows. And at last he caught up with us again on the terrace of Papa Luigi's, where we'd gone for a quiet capuccino. He was an especially virulent version of the type: difficult, determined, self-conscious, hiding his own self-dislike and awkwardness in motley in order to discountenance the rest of us; to strike where he'd been struck. The staff at Papa Luigi's tried to move him on but he wasn't prepared to go without putting up a clown's fight. Under his make-up you could see that he was hurt and embarrassed; so twenty more innocents had to get it in the neck. He mimicked people's walks, he peered into their milkshakes, he did inscrutable mimes to tables of elderly Italians. There is no blackmail more potent. Everybody laughed though nobody was amused.

I'm not sure how you can monitor these things but I have a suspicion that Australia has far more street clowns per head of population than it ought to have. Should that ever turn out to be a verifiable fact I would ascribe it to the national difficulty around aggression. Each man's everyday right to be as rude as he needs to be to someone else has been interfered with in this country, partly by the mateship fallacy, and partly by the myth of social easy-goingness – 'She'll be right. No worries.' But ordinary hostility will out, just as surely as domestic violence. Hence the harlequin. In an openly aggressive country like

England a man does not need to paint his face and wear parti-coloured overalls in order to ease his feelings.

A half-hour later, as I was driving out of Fremantle, I almost knocked him down at an intersection. He was riding a wobbly bicycle, swivelling around on the saddle to see who was look-ing at him. Some primitive impulse of which I am not entirely proud caused me to apply the brakes. It will go against me in the final count.

'When you're in Pert you gotta eat garlic prawns at te Witch's Cauldron,' Henri had advised me. 'You like garlic prawns?'

'Mad about them,' I admitted.

'You like a lotta garlic?'

'Oodles.'

Henri had cast his eyes heaven wards and kissed his lips at me. 'Then go to te Witch's Cauldron and ask to see te chef and say Henri sent you.'

Which was more or less what we intended to do, once we'd returned our hire car and cleaned up a bit, except that finding a taxi to take us to Subiaco on a Sunday evening wasn't proving all that easy. By eight-fifteen Perth was dark and deserted. I don't know whether the street lights had actually been dimmed but there was no mistaking the unvoiced preference of the city fathers for us to be at home and in bed at such a time. We walked slowly up Mill Street towards St George's Terrace where we at last saw a cab and attempted to flag it down. But it was behaving strangely. It stopped, started, reversed at speed through the traffic lights, seemed to be coming our way, and then drove abruptly off again. As we rounded the corner, curs-ing, we saw a body lying face down and motionless in the road. No one else was on the streets. Although this was a main thor-oughfare not a single car passed us, neither one way nor the other. There was just us and the body. And the ineffective street lamps.

The first thing I noticed when we got near was a smashed Sony Walkman, utterly silenced, its guts gaping, in contrast to the body which lay very still and compact, quite flat on the road as if all the shape had escaped from it as from a puncture. He was alive though, a young man in his early twenties, olive-skinned, with a bristling black moustache, not dissimilar to Henri's, and issuing a remote, metallic grief which reminded me eerily of the very sound you hear from someone else's Sony Walkman headphones. Just as suddenly as the traffic had earlier evacuated the streets, so it reoccupied them now. Which meant that we were all in danger. While Ros knelt by the injured boy to cover him with her flimsy summer jacket, I waved my arms at the oncoming vehicles. The first one to stop just happened to be a taxi. I dismissed from my mind the selfish irritation at not being able to hire it to take us to the Witch's Cauldron in Subiaco. The driver responded at first with commendable presence of mind. He parked so as to shield us from the cars, rang through on his radio for an ambulance, and ordered me – he being as much the habitual father as I am the habitual son – to rummage in his boot for a warm coat. He joined Ros by the boy and packed his coat around him. Then, for no explicable reason, except perhaps that he'd noticed that the boy wasn't Anglo-Saxon Australian white, he decided that he might not be genuinely hurt at all. 'Probably just a drunk,' he said.

Ros assured him that that was not the case. 'He's in a lot of pain,' she said.

The driver rolled a lazy, sceptical eye at her. Then he put his face close to the boy's. 'You bin drinking, mate? You 'ad a couple too many?'

The boy groaned, a low, broken cry not like that of any drunk I'd heard.

But he didn't deceive the taxi driver. 'Well, I'm going to have to turn you over anyway,' he said. Some demon had taken hold of him; he began pulling at the boy, twisting him agonizingly by the shoulders.

A wash of tears from under his closed lids suddenly wet his face.

'Don't do that,' Ros said.

'He'll be right – the bastard's got to breathe. And you don't want him choking on his vomit.'

The boy was howling now, trying to say something about his neck, and Ros was shouting too, almost in tears, 'Don't do that to him!' And to me, 'Don't let him do that!'

I stood by helplessly, hating the instinct that told me to leave what happened in someone else's town to the someone else who lived there, hating still more my ignorance, at my age, of how best to come to the aid of an injured person, and thinking what particularly bad luck it was for this one to have got himself knocked down, and found by me.

Of its own accord the situation changed. As more people gathered round, the taxi driver slipped away. A glamorous blonde in a cocktail dress, claiming to be a nurse, took his place. An ambulance rolled up. Followed, in farcical succession, by the police – first two in a car, then two more on foot, then three on motorbikes, then another one in a car, and then another two, for all I knew in a helicopter. There seemed to be no hurry to get the boy in the ambulance. We all stood about in random social groupings, not doing anything. A passer-by might have thought we were a street party still waiting for the ice to break. Only the nurse was in any communication with the person who had brought us together. She knelt by him, her cocktail dress hitched up and sparkling like a ballroom dancer's in the flashing blue lights. 'You been on the grog, mate?' she was asking him. 'Or have you been shooting up?'

Eventually the ambulance men decided that they might as well lift the body onto a stretcher. The nurse hopped back into her convertible. We wondered, since we'd been the first on the scene, whether a statement was required of us. 'Nah, no need,' the police told us. Our address? Nah. Our names? Nah. I had the distinct impression that much more of this and we would have got ourselves arrested for harassing the police or for injecting a quite inappropriate degree of urgency into an ordinarily leisurely Perth emergency.

Earlier that day Argentina had defeated Australia 9–6 in an Easter Sunday polo match at Sydney. Major Ronnie Ferguson, father of Sarah, had umpired. 'Australians have got to learn to play under pressure,' he had commented afterwards. 'Somehow they have got to learn speed.' Trust an Englishman to get the priorities wrong. An Australian journalist reporting the same match noted that the defeat 'might have been enough to turn a crowd quite nasty but they all had their mouths full of lavish food, so civilized behaviour reigned'. And Perth, as few of its residents will hesitate to tell you, knows far more about what constitutes civilized behaviour than Sydney does.

The Polish-born taxi driver who collected us from the Witch's Cauldron, where we'd made a belated but rather guilty feast of plump pink prawns in garlic, confirmed the rule by excepting himself from it. 'It's too quiet,' he said. 'It's good for families. A bit of gardening, a pool, the kids – that's Perth. You know, there are only seven or eight nightclubs in the whole town. In Poland – which, incidentally, is a communist country now – we have that many in one street. They don't know what opera is here. They don't know what theatre is.' He checked us out in his rear-view mirror. 'I can say this to you,' he felt emboldened to go on, 'because you are not Australians.'

'I didn't know it was that obvious,' Ros replied.

I paid him and wished him a busy night.

'Busy? Here? That's a laugh. The night's over. I'm going home.' It was ten thirty-five.

I managed to steal one last look at him before he drove off. He had blond curly hair and sad wet eyes and a little golden moustache, clipped like a fencing master's. At another time and in another place he might have fought duels to protect his honour and danced the mazurka with his defeated rivals' wives. Now he was cruising round a slumbering Perth with his cab windows open, trying to get rid of the smell of garlic.

There is nothing of which Western Australia is more proud than its self-made millionaires. Just how many there are, and just how much wealth each has accumulated, varies from taxi driver to taxi driver; but that the figures are impressive not even Queensland, its closest rival in nouvelle richesse, disputes. Nor is there anything meanly parochial – if one can refer to an area of more than two and a half million square kilometres as a parish – about this pride. It isn't at all necessary that you be born a West Australian for other West Australians to take satisfaction in your success; it is quite sufficient that you simply make your fortune there. Thus no one holds it against Bond – Bondy, to the people of Perth – that his place of birth and breeding was England. If anything, it rather adds to the lustre of the State that he should have chosen it to grow rich in. He confirms its reputation as a land of opportunity. And besides, a touch of genuine Anglo-Saxon still goes down well in a State that began life as a free settlement and continues to prefer straining its eyes across the water to looking over its shoulder at the uncouth territories behind. Western Australia has discussed the expedient of secession on several occasions, and many West Australians aggressively boast a more intimate knowledge of the streets of Paris or Rome than the beaches of Bondi or Port Phillip Bay. 'Sydney? Why would we want to go to Sydney?' they will ask you. 'If we're going to put ourselves to the trouble of flying five thousand kilometres we might as well go to Hong Kong. Or just stay on the plane and go to London.' It isn't easy, in the West of Australia, to argue the attractions of the East.

Of course a predilection for millionaires – there is no

escaping the subject in this part of the world – lies perilously
close to a preference for shysters, and the good citizens of W.A.
are frequently left stranded in that moral no-man's land between
disapproval of malpractice and admiration for effrontery. In
recent years local consciences have been especially vexed by a
series of financial swindles entailing the flotation (or is it the
submersion?) of phantom companies referred to, in the purlieus
of Perth, as 'bottom of the harbour' companies. The phrase
itself betrays the quandary, implying as it does a sneaking regard
for inventive exploitation of the natural resources. If you've got
a harbour, or something much like one, it's a bit unreasonable
to start complaining when someone uses it.

The millionaire with the keenest intuition for W.A.'s love of
opportunism, and who best answered, also, to its idea of flash
yet at the same time reputable foreign gentlemanliness, was
Claude Albo de Bernales, the mastermind of London Court,
that Perth pastiche I visited on my first morning in town, where
St George and the Dragon make circuits every quarter of an
hour. A Londoner himself – born in Brixton, to be exact,
though claiming to be of Spanish and even Basque descent – de
Bernales arrived in the Coolgardie goldfields in 1897, having
added an education at school in Uppingham and at university
in Heidelberg to his experience of life south of the Thames. He
was twenty-one when he showed up in Coolgardie, with less
than a pound in his pocket for every year he still hadn't become
a millionaire. But it was not as a miner that he made his first
fortune. Where there's schmutz there's schmuck, as they say at
Heidelberg. It didn't take the young Basque from Brixton long
to work out that there was easier money to be made retrieving
decrepit machinery from abandoned mines and selling it,
second-hand, to new prospectors, than there was in prospect-
ing itself. By the 1930s, he was a leading figure in the gold-mining
industry, negotiating the gold bounty with the West Australian
government and floating companies of his own on the London

Stock Exchange. 'Get in on the ground floor of a glittering Australian El Dorado,' was the characteristically cross-cultural invitation which separated thirty thousand English shareholders from their six million English pounds.

The West Australian press reported de Bernales' dealings in London with enormous pride. Under the extended heading, CLAUDE DE BERNALES – THE GENIUS BEHIND THE MINING REVIVAL – STATE'S GREATEST AMBASSADOR IN LONDON FINANCIAL CIRCLES – HOW HE MADE WILUNA A GOLDEN DREAM COME TRUE – A GREAT CREATIVE PERSONALITY, the *Mirror* reported: 'Reckoning things on the basis of practical value and wide vision, Claude de Bernales must certainly rank as one of the greatest statesmen W.A. has ever known.'

It's possible that the thirty thousand London shareholders came to view de Bernales' worth differently. Only one of his eight companies ever made any significant strike, none paid a dividend, and by 1939 all were ordered into liquidation. Illness alone – unless we would grossly speculate about good friends in high places – prevented de Bernales from facing criminal charges. But nothing that came to light about his dealings could sink him in the estimation of his adopted state. His obituary in the *West Australian* in 1963 was little short of adulatory. 'With his death passes one of the most colourful personalities associated with this State, whose name has become a legend to a post-war generation who had not seen his tall, immaculately dressed figure, complete with gloves and spats and monocle – at race meetings or along St George's Terrace, where he dominated any gathering . . . If history is correct – and it is reasonably so in this case – de Bernales emerged from each crisis with unruffled aplomb and with his creditors almost apologizing for any inconvenience they might have caused him.'

Reminiscing about him in the company of friends, a West Australian premier is reputed to have said, 'I wouldn't dare be with that man alone for half an hour for fear I'd give him the entire State.'

The bushranger turned respectable, in other words. Ned Kelly come to town. In silk socks and spats. And bringing a whiff of something European, something classical even, with him. Recalling 'his magnificent physique, his sartorial perfection and personal charm', *Smith's Weekly* pronounced him AN ADONIS OF THE GOLDEN WEST.

Today it is still possible to see the mock Italian Baronial folly he built himself overlooking the Indian Ocean, on what would be a prime site for viewing the Americas Cup. Though now it serves as the Cottesloe Civic Centre, denuded of its gilt Italianate chairs and Louis XVI desks and incense jars from the Barbary Coast and intriguing statuary from Inca ruins in the Andes. Its library and ballroom don't look much now either, only the jarrah panelling on the walls and the encircling romantic balustrade outside giving any clue to the earlier opulence.

Contemporary West Australian millionaires are less grandiose in their domestic ambitions. Spectacular seclusion would quickly call the bluff of their demotic pretensions and go down badly with the taxi drivers. None the less the opportunity to view 'Perth's famous prestigious riverfront homes' is not one that a visitor to the city with spare time on his hands is expected to forgo. Jolly Jumbuk cruises, leaving from Barrack Street Jetty, specialize in pointing out to the avidly curious the dwellings of the avidly accumulative; and indeed many a purely recreational journey on the Swan is interrupted by the voice of the skipper telling you precisely to the dollar how much that jumble of turrets and towers to starboard has just changed hands for.

Well connected as we turned out to be once Ros had made contact with one of her oldest mates in Mary, we were able to engage in this reverse slumming in some style aboard the *Queequeg*, a forty-five-foot yacht which ten or twelve years before had finished fourth or fifth in the Sydney to Hobart, but which today, on a balmy idle Easter Monday, was stowed with food, wine, children, us, and two of every profession considered meritorious in West Australia.

The old mate who had organized this jaunt for us – or at least had included us in it once she knew we were here – was Carole Gibbs (née Ochiltree), a person I had never previously met but knew of from a long and fitful correspondence, erupting into the most flagrant sentimentality on birthdays and anniversaries, which she and Ros maintained. Carole's letters could be so upsetting, with their minute allusions to convent vicissitudes of thirty years before, that Ros would dread the post on those days when there was something to commemorate. She even claimed that she knew, telepathically – so powerful was the affective charge of Carole's prose – when a letter had been sent and where it was at any time in the international postal system. Leaving aside what the reunion meant to them, I was pleased to discover in person what I already, of course, knew as a reported fact, namely that Carole was keen-eyed and vivacious with three children and a distinguished thespian husband, and didn't, for all the references in her letters to confessionals and cloistresses, wear a wimple.

By the time the thirty or so passengers (we could hardly have been called crew) had come aboard, bringing with them the dozen or so picnic hampers and the fifteen or so Eskies of cold beer and Chardonnay, Ros and Carole were deep into a dramatic re-enactment of their correspondence, which itself was a dramatic re-enactment of their past.

'How could I have told you?' I heard Ros asking, as we pulled away from the other forty-five-foot yachts berthed at the marina of the Royal Perth Yacht Club. 'You never wanted to talk about those things.'

'That's because you never wanted to talk to me about them.'

'Well, I expect you to be prepared to talk about them now.'

'Oh, "I expect". That's nice – "I expect". You haven't changed, Rossi. You always did "expect".'

They were to cry a few times before the afternoon was over, either jointly or when they thought the other wasn't looking. And they would fall into odd petulant silences, too. But never for long and never without an accompanying look of getting precisely what they'd come for.

I meanwhile stumbled about the boat, amazed by how many people it could carry and made aware, for the first time, of how it might be possible to traverse the world's oceans on a forty-five-foot yacht and never get around to meeting everyone who was on it. There were young kids down below in the galley, the permed punk offspring of the professionals above board, with whom I never even came close to exchanging a smile. There were real estate agents I didn't get to talk to either, and obstetricians. I did fall into conversation with Rod, however, the only person on the boat who had omitted to bring any wine even though he owned a 25 per cent share in Plantagenet, one of the new and highly regarded wineries in the south-west of the State. This – both having a stake in the winery and omitting to bring any wine – might have had something to do with his being a chartered accountant. Or it might just have been a matter of his feeling that by bringing himself he had already brought enough. I don't mean by that to imply that Rod was arrogant; only that he somehow had the knack, without at all carrying surplus weight or personality or intelligence, of suggesting superfluity. He was too tall, he was too brown, he possessed too many sharp angles, he flashed too many teeth, and when he swallowed – which was too frequently – he showed an Adam's apple that was too prominent. Physically, like many men I was to meet in Perth, there was something of the ballistic missile about him. He seemed at all times ready to launch himself from his own firing system in full confidence that he would land slap bang dead centre of the target.

Conversationally he was less killing. 'Where's that?' he asked me after I'd told him that I came from the U.K.

Perhaps he suffered from too much sense of humour. It certainly tickled him to think of himself as the only Protestant aboard. 'You leftfooters,' he enjoyed joshing the calmly carousing Catholics, 'you leftfooters are all the same.'

Two of the leftfooters in question (that's assuming Rod was right) were Ian, a prodigiously slow-talking general practitioner, and his wife Violet. Where Rod had dressed for the occasion in socks that were too long and too white, and shorts that were too tight and too much the colour of custard, Ian had made no nautical concessions to his wardrobe whatsoever. He sat with his back against the rail of the imperceptibly moving yacht, his knees together, in carefully pressed trousers and a neat short-sleeved khaki shirt. He told me that he was half-Indian but had never been to India. 'I want to see new places,' he said, leaving enough time to pop to India and back between each word. He had recently returned from a tour of Egypt and Israel in one of which, from atop some holy mountain or other, he and Violet had seen in the New Year. It was an experience which looked likely to spoil them for all other New Years. 'That's the only time I've felt the mystical significance of it all,' Violet said.

'You leftfooters are all the same,' Rod quipped. His Adam's apple bulged in his throat like a mongoose in the windpipe of a python.

Ian and Violet were concerned that I shouldn't suppose, just because they'd been to the Middle East, that they had money to throw away. 'It costs us ten thousand dollars a year to send our three kids to school,' they told me, both separately and in chorus, at various times throughout the day. I'm pleased to say that I knew enough about Perth already not to ask why it was necessary that their children should be educated privately.

I grew attached to Violet. She was abundant and toothily

good-looking and stuffed a mean mustard sausage – 'By hand,' she told me – and was even reckless in a careful West Australian sort of way. She too went in for a highly stylized slowness of delivery, though in her case I like to think that that was simply a technique for maintaining control over herself. I'd come across this mock moronic drawl before, especially amongst Melbourne Catholic intellectuals who like to savour superlatives, but the Perth version was even more deliberately oblivious to time. So much so that you could never be entirely certain that you weren't being treated with devastatingly measured irony. It's possible, therefore, that Ian and Violet had their way with me aboard the *Queequeg* that afternoon, and later on in their pool laughed between themselves at how much of his life an Englishman could be charmed into throwing away waiting for their simple answers to his simple questions.

One thing I can be certain of, though, is this: that, when the *Queequeg* at last drew up alongside the first of those great waterside palaces belonging to the new breed of West Australian millionaire, there was not the slightest irony in the manner of Ian's running commentary to me on whose was whose. 'See that one? That's Lang Hancock's. That one there – the one on three storeys – belongs to Dallas Dempster. And over there is Michael Edgley's. Here's an interesting one – it's owned by Alistair Norwood. He made his fortune out of selling jeans. You wouldn't think there was so much money to be made in jeans, would you?'

It was my opinion that there were a hell of a lot of jeans kicking around the place.

'A lot of competition too,' Ian said. He somehow gave me the impression that he'd put his mind to jeans quite seriously. 'Oh, but here's Bondy's – though he's reputed not to be in it much.'

'It's quite modest,' I noticed, 'relatively, that is. But then I suppose if you've got your name on skyscrapers all over the city it isn't so essential that you have the biggest house.'

Ian made me feel that this was the most awesomely complex sentence he had ever been called upon to unravel. He stared at me, he stared at the glass palaces, he stared into his wine. I suppose he might have been thinking through what he'd have found essential had he been Bondy. Whatever the reason, it took him a good ten minutes – time enough for three more trays of quiche and sausages (Olive's hand-stuffed sausages) to be passed around – before he came up with, 'That's right. I suppose it isn't.'

'Though then again,' I pursued, 'I would imagine that you, as a general practitioner in a booming state, must have somewhere pretty nice to repair to yourself.'

'Ah, yes – ah, yes – quite nice. Though we do have three children to send to school.'

He wasn't the only person on the *Queequeg* who found it hard to concentrate in proximity to so much worldly success. The ritual of gawping at the houses of the rich and famous – or rather, hereabouts, the rich *therefore* famous – was entered into with the same zombie-reverence by everyone on board. Barristers buckled at the knees. A pair of hard-bitten estate agents sitting on the prow like mastheads sighed like first-time buyers. Even Geoff Gibbs, Dean of the West Australian Academy of Performing Arts and the equal, normally, of Oscar Wilde as to wit and Charles Laughton as to presence, even he seemed to lose his theatrical drawl and to abandon his bohemianism every time we inched by another ten million dollar water ranch. Names familiar to me from Ros's stories of growing up in Perth cropped up continually; names of ordinarily clever and energetic boys who had made their way, by hook or by crook, to the water's edge. For there, achievement is at last palpable and indisputable – like a numbered seat on Olympus.

Except that where Olympus was impossibly remote, a hierarchy not for mortal men to aspire to, the Swan River is tormentingly proximate. And it is that – the sheer apparent accessibility of all the symbols of success – which holds the entire population of Perth in thrall. It seems that you need only reach out your hand to receive whatever is your fancy. 'I think I'll have that', you feel it is quite within the bounds of reason and probability to decide. It is an insidiously inviting city. 'Stop here and buy me,' it appears to say. 'Plenty of others have, why shouldn't you?'

In London it is clear what is and what is not for you. The city knows better than to rouse unrealizable desires. But Perth palters with your hopes like a provincial cocotte.

And so there we were – a bark freighted with all the professions, a boatful of those into whose laps Australia had poured its treasures, ourselves an object of envy to lesser, shorter, poorer crafts who paused to stare at us; and yet we teemed with ingratitude and discontent. We ate till we were stuffed: spinach quiche, potato salad and asparagus, curried mushrooms, roast chicken, barbecued chicken, mock chicken sandwiches made from Mrs Bernice Ochiltree's Recipe (which her daughter Carole will not divulge); we drank champagne and Chardonnay, low-alcohol beer, high-alcohol beer, and what we didn't like, what didn't suit our palates or didn't go with our avocado dip or simply didn't please us with its colour, we tossed overboard without a qualm – but still, because we'd been fatally unsettled as to our place and our degree, because we were in a city that tantalized us with the illusion of equality of attainability, we still lacked something that we wanted. We weren't bitter and disgruntled in the English fashion; we weren't sour from exclusion. We were piqued; our appetites pricked but not satisfied, our senses agitated, our imaginations teased. Funny what even a sleepy, provincial little cocotte can accomplish on a lazy bank holiday on the river.

Whatever its unrealizable dreams, however, this was a very polite gathering. No one was discomfortingly underdressed. No one got drunk. No one seriously flirted. In this way our cruise on the Swan reminded me of the very first experiences I'd had on Sydney Harbour, before Sydney had become a Rest and Recreation centre for American servicemen fighting in Vietnam, before it had a skyline like Manhattan's, before it even had an Opera House. I tried this idea out on Wendy Maund (née Buckenara), another old convent chum of Ros's, but she didn't seem to like the idea of herself as a Sydneysider before the fall. She was tanned and good-looking and wore a white blouse that fell away from a brown shoulder. She narrowed a wary eye at me. Perhaps she thought I was flirting. Or it might have been that as a convent girl she'd had enough of the burden of innocence. They'd accomplished their tasks well, those nuns. Anxiety hangs around the necks of the women of Perth like an albatross.

I exaggerated, by the way, when I said that two of every profession revered in Western Australia enjoyed representation aboard the *Queequeg* – in strict truth we lacked dentists. I was remarking on that very omission to Carole and Wendy and Ros, late in the afternoon – any excuse to muscle in on their devotions – at the very moment that Jock Burdett, our skipper, caught sight of a small motorboat in distress. The two men aboard were leaping up and down, waving their arms and hallooing, while their wives sat in sullen dejection and contempt.

'They must have run out of fuel,' someone guessed.

'Or Chardonnay,' Ros suggested.

Then Ian suddenly said, 'I know who they are. That's Travis Guest and Andrew Grono – they're dentists.'

We threw them a rope.

After we'd seen the thirst-crazed dentists safely to their jetty we returned ourselves to the Royal Perth Yacht Club. Here, by means of a few words in the right quarters, Jock secured special dispensation to show us the actual Americas Cup. To my surprise it was not on general public view. It was locked away in a sort of secured vault in the Yacht Club, protected by video cameras and highly sensitive alarms. But such was the esteem in which Jock was held in the R.P.Y.C. that we were allowed not just to see it but to hold it. The consensus of opinion was in favour of the cup: we found it bigger, grander, more precious, and more worth the winning as a prize in itself than we'd expected it to be. So I kept my own counsel. To my eyes it bore a remarkable resemblance to a gift I'd been given by my poorest and least discriminating relations on the occasion of my barmitzvah.

As we left I thanked Jock for the terrific day he'd given us. I liked Jock even though I hadn't had much to do with him on the boat, keeping my distance just in case he changed his mind about putting up the sails and expected me to pull the strings. He was quiet and gently humorous, and didn't eat or drink or envy. He was also, in so far as I am a judge of these things, a good skipper. At any rate we never hit anything. I thanked him for that, too. And told him how lucky I thought he was, having so beautiful a place as Perth to mess about with boats in. Even as we talked and strolled, the water lapped around the jetties, and the masts of innumerable yachts dipped and clinked.

He gave me a long, serious stare. 'You're the lucky ones,' he said. 'Having London.'

I told him how cold it had been when we left, how much it cost to make a phone call, and what it was like living under a government of sneering boy-accountants.

He shrugged. 'I'd be happy just walking along the Strand,' he said. 'And going to the galleries.' He looked quite heartbroken, remembering the last time he'd been in London.

I pointed to the river, rocking gently in the late afternoon, and the lovely Perth skyline, dotted with sand-coloured moorish monastery towers, and of course the prestigious riverside homes. 'You live in Paradise,' I reminded him.

He shook his head. He wasn't denying the attractions. In his imagination he was simply back in London, pushing through the crowds. Excited.

It turned out, though I hadn't realized it until now, that he had known Ros vaguely as a girl, that they had friends in common still, and that he had heard about her from time to time. 'See you in another hundred years,' he said to her as we parted.

Sometimes Australians can make you feel like a space-gaoler, responsible for leaving them marooned on some beautiful but futile star, a million light years from home.

EIGHT

LOST ORISONS

Once Easter was over we moved out of the Parmelia to a block of serviced apartments in South Perth, right opposite the zoo. From our living room window we were able to watch the pelicans gliding in on thermals, well-preserved West Australian ladies playing bowls, and in the evenings the South Perth Rugby Club having a gentle practice under floodlights. On this side of the river the city felt even more remote than usual from the business and commotion of the rest of the world.

There is something about the air in Perth, some quality of refinement or attenuation, which makes it easier to lift your foot up and put it down again. Already I'd noticed how relaxing it was to walk about the city, how little purpose or desire for purpose accompanied my steps. But in South Perth this sensation of blithe aimlessness threatened to melt away all our resolution. We put ourselves into bottom gear. We made forays to the shops for single items. I bought local newspapers, enticed by such headlines as GIANT TREES TO BE AXED. We even talked about retiring here not later, when we were old, but now, right now in the full bloom of our youth. If we retired to South Perth, we estimated, we would live till we were a hundred.

It threatened to take that long to get from South Perth to the city by ferry, a distance the slowest pelican could manage in under a minute, thanks to the exasperatingly charming assumption that no passenger was in any hurry and that no passenger would therefore object while the ferry waited, not only for hopelessly late stragglers, but even for those who weren't dressed or out of their apartments yet. I swear that on several occasions I saw people come out on to their balconies in their dressing gowns, make a sign implying 'fifteen minutes at the most' to the ferryman, and saunter down the gangplank a full half-hour later, absolutely secure in the knowledge that they would not be left behind.

Pretty soon you learn the trick of ferry-stalling yourself. On my second morning in South Perth I gave a little wave, ambled towards the water, and then sauntered back to have a look around the nearby shops. An advertisement on a public notice board outside the Foodmaster Supermarket had caught my eye. It read:

Dennis and Cheryl Stoll present colourful slides and temple dances – donation $5 (five dollars)

Thursdays 8–9.30

16 Jan   Wonders of the Nile

20 Feb   The Music and Dances of Ancient Egypt

20 March   A Thousand Treasures of the Tomb

Sunday Seminars cover Music, Dance, Temple Architecture, Sculpture and Painting, Wisdom Literature, Cosmic Astro-Archaeology, Philosophy of Living, Counselling by Eye and Light, and Star Wisdom Therapies for Healing Body and Mind.

And it was illustrated with two photographs of Cheryl – the first entitled, 'Cheryl performing a Dance of Adoration of the Light before a Sacred Lake in Australia, 1985' (I couldn't place the lake but was sure I'd seen Cheryl's nightie on sale back in

England at British Home Stores); the second, 'Cheryl leads Temple Dancers from the Sanctuary of AMUN in KARNAK, Upper Egypt, during Meditational Arts Nile Cruise, 1981.' Interested parties – and who that had read this far could not be? – were invited to visit the Perth Centre of the Academy of the Arts of Sound and Light on Adelaide Terrace, where they would find an atmosphere of peace and much intriguing literature. Alternatively, you could write, enclosing an A4 stamped addressed envelope, for an illustrated (more diaphanous snaps of Cheryl?) FREE NEWSLETTER.

Something made me think of Ian and Olive. I wondered whether they'd ever bumped into the Stolls on their Middle Eastern holidays. I might have been wrong but I had a suspicion that in Olive there was a Temple Dancer trying to get out. And I remembered how often, when I first came to Australia, I had seen posters outside church halls or social clubs or even university staff rooms, announcing that there would be a slide show that evening, put on by some couple who had just returned full of stories from Majorca or the Isle of Man. I was pleased that the tradition continued, even if in a more unorthodox form.

Then I meandered back to the wharf and jumped aboard the ferry which appeared to be on the point of pulling out, only to have to sit bobbing on the water for a further fifteen minutes while an intending passenger exercised her dog.

Later that afternoon I met Ros at the Western Australia Art Gallery, a proud, spruce, pleasing modern building with plenty of space around the exhibits and an atmosphere almost as relaxing as that which prevailed on the streets. The gallery possessed though, to my eye, a more than usually melancholy collection of Australian paintings. Here were the familiar depictions of fragile, fleeting moments – twilights, memories, aching distances, un-peopled landscapes – but almost wilfully unrelieved, it seemed to me today, both in themselves, and as a group, of one disposition. Perhaps wistfulness was, after all, the dominating spirit of Australian art. Or perhaps I was feeling excessively rueful myself. Or maybe there should just have been a few more people looking at the paintings.

We weren't the only ones in the gallery. Just ahead of us, and going at about the same speed, a small boy of five or six was taking a lively interest in everything he saw, getting his mother to read out to him every word of descriptive text. 'What does that say?' I'd already heard him ask a hundred times.

The mother, or just possibly the aunty, wore a powder-blue crimplene trouser suit of a kind you don't often see in art galleries on weekdays, and had her hair coifed *à la manière* Moonee Ponds. She was growing tired of answering but had obviously been told by some encyclopaedia salesman that curiosity in the young ought never to be discouraged. 'Nude,' she said. 'That means without your clothes on.'

'What does that say?'

'Also nude.'

'What does nude mean?'

'I've just told you.'

'What does that say?'

'Torso. That means not the whole body.'

'What does that say?'

'Nude. Look. This one's nice.' She nudged him towards a still life – fruit and flowers on a table. 'See. Some artists paint things not people.'

This distinction – I have a sneaking feeling she was actually voicing a preference – reminded me of my brother who paints nothing but things; things at the moment people have just evacuated or discarded them, or at the moment just before people pick them up or turn them on. Since it now seemed ages since I'd been out in the bush naming creeks and mountains after friends, I thought it was time to resurrect the practice, so I decided to give him the whole building – the Stephen Jacobson Art Gallery of Western Australia. A couple of hours later we were in the spanking new reference library, in which transparent lifts convey you to the upper floors where you can actually see and lay hands on the reference books themselves, a convenience which solves at a stroke the conundrum that has for so long plagued the scholar – how to order a book you don't know exists. We sat for a while browsing through documents which were of no earthly use to us, luxuriating in the easy access, enjoying not being ticked off by librarians, and taking in the fine views over Perth from the windows. Even from here Ros was able to spot the tower of her old convent school. I decided to dedicate the library to my brother's wife – herself a distinguished embroideress, of ideas as well as canvasses – so that neither she nor the building should feel left out. I can recommend anyone with a few hours to spare in Perth to forget about the prestigious water-front homes and pass the time in the Janet Haigh Reference Library of Western Australia instead.

In truth we hadn't gone to the library merely as tourists. We had gone to find *Valiant Women: Letters from the Foundation Sisters of Mercy in Western Australia, 1845–1849,* by Geraldine Byrne. Geraldine was yet another of Ros's co-cloister nymphs from the Golden Age of Perth Catholicism and was expecting us for dinner that evening. It seemed to Ros that we could only be the richer as historians and the more gracious as dinner guests if we spent the remainder of the afternoon acquainting ourselves with her friend's work. I didn't disagree. What else would ever have got me interested in the W.A. Sisters of Mercy between the years already mentioned but good old social obligation? So I sat looking out of the window on the fourth floor, imagining Perth before the millionaires had got at it, before the Aborigines had been dispossessed of it, before even the Catholics had built their convent schools all over it, while Ros whispered me extracts from Geraldine's book.

The letters told a rich, fantastic tale of misplaced missionary zeal, of heroism and altruism and impertinence, but above all of the most bizarre expectations and conjunctions. Sister Ursula, writing from the *Elizabeth* which set sail from England in 1845, described how the ship resembled a little city – a little holy city, she must have meant – having aboard a Bishop's residence, a Convent of Mercy, a Benedictine Monastery, a Congregation of French Priests of the Immaculate Heart of Mary, a College of Ecclesiastical Students, and a school of the English language, 'the duties of these establishments being regularly performed every day'. All this – one Bishop (Irish), seven priests (two Spanish, one Australian, three French, one Irish), one Sub-Deacon (English), one Novice to the Priesthood (French), seven student catechists (all Irish), three laymen (two French, one Italian), plus the six Sisters – for a colony of some three and a half thousand souls of which no more than three hundred would have been Catholic.

But then those figures do not include the Aborigines, towards whom the sacerdotal fleet harboured its most rapaciously philanthropic intentions. 'They are dear good-natured little pets,' Sister Baptist noticed of the native children. 'They have almost completely forgotten their native language which we hope will secure them from joining their people.' Fitted up with brand-new names, two Aboriginal boys, Francis Xavier Conaci and John Baptist Dirimera, accompanied Father Salvado to the Monastery of the Holy Trinity at Cava, Italy, where they were to study as Benedictine monks. Francis Xavier managed to stay alive for four years. John Baptist Dirimera a further two. But even they fared better than Mary Catherine, an Aboriginal girl taken to Rome by Sister Ursula in 1850, where she spent her time sewing and learning Italian. She died a year later in the care, for some reason, of the Earl and Countess of Shrewsbury.

By the time Ros had finished reading I had decided that I

hated missionaries above all meddlers. For what lies behind their energies is an assumption of the grossest ignorance and vanity – that others, once shown the way, must want to be as they are. The despot who silences opposition by crushing it is nothing like so inhumane: he knows only too well the vigorous diversity of human nature, the alternative attractions to him.

On our way back through town we walked into a little racial drama in Hay Street Mall. A large crowd had gathered to listen to a group of Aborigines sitting cross-legged on the ground, making music. A beautiful young man with liquid eyes and gypsy-like long soft hair was playing a didgeridoo, coaxing a variety of extraordinary sounds – ironical, almost, in their mimicry of animal and bird calls – from the hollow bark. Another boy, less lustrous and more introverted, kept his eyes down while he beat out an insistent rhythm on a simple drum. Between them, an older and more seasoned performer, full of confidence and self-consciously disreputable charm, sang and smiled and winked and from the back of his throat made wild-life noises which quite rivalled those of the didgeridoo.

But it was the composition and attitude of the crowd that interested me as much as the talents of the buskers. For nothing could more dramatically have marked how far we had travelled from the North of Australia than the respectful attention of this impromptu audience, its exhalations of admiration, its bursts of enthusiastic applause, its solemn air of deference to an exotic culture. In-between each number individuals from the crowd would step into the centre of the circle and place money in a blue plastic travel bag which served as the collecting tin. This action of stepping forward looked to be as deliberate a state-ment of liberal conscience as carrying a banner at a CND march or demonstrating outside a South African embassy.

In the meantime a couple of young policemen at opposite ends of the crowd had been growing very agitated. I had watched them communicating with each other by means of walkie-talkie radios, and I could tell from their expressions (I'd worn one like theirs myself when I was a school prefect) that they felt compelled to do something. The crowd could not have been more orderly, the Aboriginal musicians could not have been more innocuous, but still these rookie cops with boys' chests had to intervene. They pushed their way to the centre of the circle and muttered a few sentences to the senior busker. 'Give it a rest now, mate,' I heard one of them say, 'you're obstructing the mall.' The Aborigine smiled and shrugged his shoulders. The music stopped. Ten yards away a regular mall entertainer – an unfunny Englishman wearing silly clothes and a hat that had objects spinning on it – played his banjo unmolested. But then nobody could have said that his crowd constituted an obstruction.

Before the Aborigines packed up, a few more whites went over to drop coins in their bag. Ros did the same. She was struck by them and sorry for them and wanted to encourage them with a smile. The boy with the beautiful eyes and the gypsy hair thanked her, but as she turned the older man whispered an obscenity. It was a rude appraisal, not a curse, but it was still inharmonious.

'Serves you right,' I said.

A taxi driver called 'Rusty' Hammer took us to Geraldine Byrne's in Claremont. He was fuming, from the moment we entered his cab, about some young man he knew, whom he'd seen in town only half an hour before, who owed him fifty dollars, who was a millionaire before he was twenty-three, and who still wouldn't repay his debt.

'He's a little shit,' Rusty told us.

I asked him why the young man was behaving like this. In return we had to listen to a long tale of youthful entrepreneurial zest and cunning. The very qualities this town is supposed to revere. 'He doesn't sound too nice,' was all I could think of saying.

'He's a little shit.'

He had his window open as he reiterated this verdict and a couple of young financiers getting out of a Mercedes swung around thinking they'd been addressed.

'Rusty is not my real name,' he told us just before he dropped us off. 'But you know what a nickname is like — it sticks like shit.'

I'd met Geraldine Byrne once before, in London. Hearing that she was in town, attached in some capacity to the Australian Studies Centres in Bloomsbury, Ros had made contact with her and the two of them had gone out and got disgustingly drunk over reminiscences of the Sisters of Mercy. They had behaved so badly, getting from one place to another, that a taxi driver had ordered them out of his cab. Eventually I had to be called out to the famous Australian painter's house in Kensington where Geraldine was staying, to ensure Ros's safe return. Geraldine was wearing a pink nightdress when I turned up, and nursing a bruise on her forehead caused by falling down in the shower while trying to sober up. The havoc she had wreaked in the bathroom — water everywhere, a torn shower curtain, blood on the tiles — had reduced the pair of them to hysterics. They rolled on the carpet with tears rolling down their cheeks just telling me about it. This was the only time in my life that I had ever been called on to perform the duties of a Mother Superior. I ticked Geraldine off soundly, prescribed a dozen Hail Marys, and ordered my wife out of the house and into the car. I heard about the disgraceful scene in the taxi later, during Confession.

Tonight, Geraldine was in an altogether more serious vein. Everything I'd ever heard about her until our London encounter suggested that she could have been an amanuensis to a bishop, and now I was once again able to imagine her in such a role. Her hair was drawn back rigidly from her face. She wore a tweed skirt. She was very much the author of *Valiant Women*. And she had some distinguished guests to entertain – Alister Turner and his wife Stephanie (Alister was President of WASPS, that's to say the West Australian Society of Plastic Surgeons), Jan Chaney (Chaney was a name to conjure with socially in Perth, Jan herself being a doctor), her lawyer boyfriend Craig (who numbered amongst his clients, as it turned out, crimplened Neil from Derby), and of course ourselves. If Geraldine had a weakness it was her belief in the solemn importance of the people she brought together; if she had a strength it was her capacity, apparently quite unwitting and not at all to be traced back to the nuns who'd trained her, to be the cause that around her solemnity degenerated into mirth. Within half an hour of Geraldine's distinguished guests being introduced to one another her table was heaving with levity and bawdy.

It was actually Stephanie, whose refined beauty and advanced pregnancy appeared at first to confirm Geraldine's sense of the gravity of the evening, who began it. As wife of Perth's most eminent plastic surgeon she took a droll interest in the details of his profession, most particularly the do's and don'ts of moles. Even as we met she was working hard on Alister to promote a Mole Awareness Week for West Australians. 'There's absolutely no reason why he shouldn't set up a little mobile testing unit on the beach,' she said, appealing to our common sense in the matter.

Malignant moles and melanomas are a major topic of conversation in Australia. There isn't anybody who doesn't have a horrific mole or melanoma story to tell. The fear of them, and all other forms of skin cancer, has not exactly emptied the country's beaches, but there is no doubt that Australians sunbathe less obsessively than they used to. I, for example, was by far the brownest person at the table, and I hadn't been near a beach since Broome. In Perth this new fear of what the outside could do to you was especially acute because the town had been settled by so many Anglo-Saxons and Celts, fair- or ginger-skinned people not suited to sun-worship. Hence Stephanie's belief that a Mole Awareness Week was just what the populace was looking for.

What Jan Chaney wanted to know – and Jan was too confident and good-looking, even if she lacked Stephanie's pregnant glow, for us all not to want to know what she wanted to know – was whether Alister ever felt inclined, once he'd knocked his patients out, to whip off the odd unsightly mole as a bonus, a little something over and above what it had been required of him to remove. The answer was yes. And when that inclination had proved too powerful for Alister to resist, and the offending mole had turned out to be not only aesthetically unpleasing to the doctor but also malignant to the patient, well, Alister had reason to feel more than a little justified, didn't he?

It was a mere conversational hop skip and a jump to get from this to the whole delicate issue of the rights and obligations of cosmetic medicine. Very soon we were on to geriatric sexuality and where a doctor like Alister should or shouldn't stand in relation to the dry vagina question. I say *we*, but in fact I had been excluded from this discussion by Craig with whom I shared the other end of the table and who insisted on taking me through the history of British comedy – the Goons, Hancock, John Cleese, *The Young Ones* – in order to find out what I thought. 'So which writers do you like, Howard?' Craig asked me, changing tack.

I went through my usual routine. I didn't *really* think I liked anyone. (I didn't want to go as far back as Chaucer or Ben Jonson – not in Perth.)

The sentence, 'Oh, I see, it all comes back to the bloke and the rights of his pecker,' floated down to me from the interesting end of the table.

'I think it's wonderful if doctors can help people to enjoy an active sex life well into their eighties,' Stephanie said.

Craig was entirely oblivious to this rival conversation. I don't believe he heard a word of it. 'Come on, Howard,' he challenged me. He had an expression of intense, eager curiosity on his face. But there was a no-nonsense air about him as well. He looked like a man who'd heard a lot of bullshit in his young life. 'Come on,' he repeated, 'there must be *somebody* you like that's still alive.'

'If the vagina's dry, then let the vagina stay dry,' one or other woman who wasn't Stephanie pronounced.

Geraldine, I noticed, had a queer look on her face, as if she couldn't decide whether this raucous party meant that her evening was a success or not. But she was looking progressively less like a bishop's amanuensis.

'Presumably it's dry because it wants to be,' I heard Ros inveigh.

'Well?' Craig pressed.

'I suppose Bellow,' I said.

'Bellow?' He was flabbergasted.

'Well, not *all* Bellow.' I didn't want an argument. What I wanted was for our literary discussion to be over quickly so that I could be in there mixing it with the vagina disputants, among whom were numbered some of the best people in Western Australia. 'But *Humboldt's Gift* is marvellous.'

Craig shook his head disbelievingly. He'd been prepared to listen to me when I'd told him that we did not, in England, take *The Young Ones* to be serious and pointed political satire, but now he wasn't certain. 'Who else?' he demanded.

I scratched my head. 'Milan Kundera, maybe,' I said.

'Milan Kundera?'

'That's to say early Milan Kundera – not too early – maybe middle-period Milan Kundera.'

Elsewhere, Alister was stating his position. 'If you don't make it possible for the woman to go on and enjoy her body, you are left with the problem of the bloke. He can go on, you must remember, until he's eighty.'

So, I was convinced, could Craig.

With the exception of Geraldine, who was to turn up at the Grand Girls from St C's and S.M.C.'s Emotional Reunion Lunch in a couple of days' time, we weren't to meet anyone from this dinner party again. We took sentimental farewells of one another, of course, and exchanged addresses and telephone numbers, and made tentative arrangements for any amount of getting together for more lewd shouting, but in the dread light of unalcoholic day sense and not sensibility prevailed. In a manner of speaking, though, we would see more of Alister before we were through with this part of the world; or at least we would see more of his handiwork. Ros's friends were all in their forties now, and there weren't many of them who couldn't benefit, if only infinitesimally, from what Alister could do. It mattered how you looked in Perth. Maternity and the sun worked their ravages. Moles popped up like mushrooms. So Ros wasn't really exaggerating when she remarked, on the hundredth occasion she'd heard his name skittishly invoked, 'That plastic surgeon has taken something off every woman I know in Perth.'

Certainly, at a rough count, I'd say he had better figures than Don Giovanni.

On the boat to Rottnest, Ros and I fell to examining each other's fingernails. To anybody watching we must have looked like a pair of chimps on a mutual flea hunt, but in fact it was our immaculacy we were marvelling over. After only one week, Perth had picked us clean. Had I been in charge of promoting tourism in Perth (and before long, as chance would have it, I would meet people who were), that's what I'd have pushed: the detergent properties of the place. Come to Perth, where you can wear a white shirt for seven days. Where even your perspiration is nectarine. Where you can see further through washed and spotless retinas. And damn the Americas Cup.

Fat chance of that. We hadn't paid for a running commentary, as far as I knew, when we'd bought our tickets for a day trip to the Island; it was simply meant to be a journey there followed by a journey back. None the less the Rottnest ferry had scarcely pulled away from the jetty before, through blaring inescapable speakers, it was on – prestigious riverside homes, choicest bits of real estate, Bondy, and who would be sailing what where before the year was out.

Once we'd put Fremantle behind us, however, and the Italo-Australian crew had run out of marinas and waterside restaurants to enthuse over ('If any of youse wants a night out, that could be a good place to go'), we were permitted to enjoy the nineteen kilometres of ocean in silence. It was a choppy voyage. Quite a little sick-maker, Ros remembered, especially in the days before hydrofoils. But then that had all been part of the fun of the regular holidays she and her family had spent on Rottnest. You screamed, you got ill, you went ashore, and there on the Island, where no vehicular traffic was allowed, you cycled away your childhood in one long silent summer's idyll.

There is some argument as to who first discovered Rottnest. The honour normally goes to the Dutch seaman, Vlaming, who came ashore in 1696, declared it to be 'delightful above all other islands I did see', but still gave it the name Rats' Nest, not knowing that the little dark brown hoppers with short tails and rounded ears which he found in abundance there were not rodents but marsupials, not vermin but quokkas, small scrub wallabies which thrive on wattles and tourism. It's Vlaming whose rapturous descriptions of the Island are most frequently quoted – 'This Earthly Paradise' is his also – and it is to Vlaming that the memorial on View Hill is dedicated. But there is evidence that another Dutch sailor, Samuel Volkersen, beat him to it by some forty years. However, since all he reported finding were two seals, a wild cat and 'many excrements', his name has not adhered to the island.

It wasn't until the twentieth century that Rottnest became a holiday resort. Before then it had served as a native prison and boys' reformatory, Corporal L. Welch superintending the inaugural batch of ten felonious Aborigines in 1838, a mere nine years after the first white settlement of the Swan. Just how badly the Aborigines imprisoned on Rottnest over the next eighty years or so were in need of restraint and reform is a quodlibet that can be tackled variously, according to where one stands on the question of property. But, as far as I could tell from the exhibition of photographs and documents in the excellent Island Museum, punishment ran disproportionate to misdemeanour. Where the shock of exile didn't hurt, flogging and excessive chaining, to say nothing of influenza, pneumonia and measles in cramped unhygienic conditions, did. And all this as retribution for what? In Mangarmana's and Mangawalter's case, sheep stealing. They received six and twelve months respectively. Beedly was given six months for cleaning out the contents of a hut. Kyser was in for a year for assaulting a Chinaman.

In fairness to the authorities on the mainland they did on more than one occasion instigate enquiries into the treatment of native prisoners, even going so far as to appoint a certain Francis Fraser Armstrong as Storekeeper, Interpreter, and Moral Agent. The terms and responsibilities of Armstrong's Moral Agency were these: he was to be allowed free access to the Aborigines, was to be present at any bodily punishments, and was expected 'to attend to everything which may in any way tend to improving the habits and morals of the prisoners or to their advancement in civilisation and their gradually imbibing the great truths of revelation and the fundamental rules of Christianity'.

In 1922 the last Aboriginal prisoners left the Island. They were put aboard the S.S. *Bambra* and transferred to gaol in Broome. By then Rottnest was well on its way to becoming a haven for holidaymakers. Myself, despite Ros's rhapsodic recollections of the place, despite her guiding me like Virgil to its loveliest and quietest coves, I felt that something of the prison-camp atmosphere remained. The old administration buildings, painted a uniform scrambled-egg yellow, in which visitors still loved to loll away their vacations, were a bit spartan for my taste. The idea of confining the Island's traffic essentially to bicycles was obviously a good one, but again their uniform yellow and their clearly identifying numbers made me feel I was in the hands of some sinister regime, lulling me into submission with the illusion of healthy outdoor freedom. Most worrying of all was the Island-wide speaker system, ensuring that wherever you were a message could be relayed quickly to you. To be lost to civilization, walking by the edges of a deserted salt flat or looking out to Vlaming's landing place at Porpoise Bay, or merely to be feeding crusts to a quokka quizzing you from the protection of a Ti tree, and then to hear yourself addressed in nasal twang from some loudspeaker hidden in the undergrowth – is this not what Orwell has warned us of?

In the late afternoon, though, relaxing on the beach outside the hotel and watching families bringing their little boats to within three yards of the omelette-coloured cottages they'd rented, I came to understand the special place Rottnest occupies in the affections of West Australians. Its scruffiness and egalitarian restrictedness were everything. In sight of Perth, enjoying the same hard blue waters and the same climate, it was yet free of the depredations – actual and symbolic – of the millionaires. There could be no prestigious homes here. No exclusive suburbs. None of Rusty Hammer's little shits climbing out of limousines. You hired a spartan little cottage and you rode a numbered bike. Or you stayed away.

The more skyscrapers Perth threw up, I realized, the more popular Rottnest Island would become. And, once I'd seen that, I grew to like the place myself. Yes, I promised Ros, yes, we would come and spend a long slow summer here one of these years, just as she had in the 1950s with her mum and dad and brother and their oldest friends the Wises, the Jewish family who had escaped from Germany in the nick of time and who, here on Vlaming's Earthly Paradise, knew better than not to count their blessings.

On Saturday the 5th of April, starting at twelve-thirty and going on until very late in the afternoon, Ros had her famous Girls Reunion. The idea for it had grown out of a conversation she'd initiated with Carole, in-between ancient recriminations and endearments, and to the accompaniment of mock chicken sandwiches and Chardonnay, aboard the *Queequeg*. She had simply mused, as a matter of idleness, on how nice it would have been to see so-and-so and such-a-one had she only known where in the world so-and-so and such-a-one now were. 'That's easy,' Carole had said. 'They're right here.'

'In Perth?'

'Yep.'

'All of them?'

I missed this part of the conversation; I was talking to Ian and Olive at the time. But I can imagine Carole fixing her old friend with a whole battery of challenging expressions. Of course all of them. What else, Ros, would nice convent-educated girls from Perth do but stay right where they are? You, as we know, chose to go your own way, but then you always were . . . etcetera, etcetera.

So, since they were all here, they all met. I wasn't invited, naturally. But by special dispensation I was granted an audience afterwards, in the garden of the restaurant where they'd lunched. And, because I needed a guide and a companion, and because he was welcome at every gathering, Carole's husband Geoff was given a special dispensation also. I made, as it would have seemed to me absolutely unforgivable not to make, super-human efforts with my appearance. I teased my eyelashes. I trimmed my moustache in such a way as to give the impression of poetic yet vigorous youthfulness of upper lip. At any time you don't turn up to meet a dozen West Australian women in their prime looking like a dog. But when those women are the girls your wife made up rude rhymes with, just out of hearing of Sister Gertrude, thirty years before – well, you pull out all the stops.

'I can't tell you how exciting it is,' I said, as I greeted them in their arboreous setting, 'to see the legend made flesh at last. Nymphs, in your orisons be all my sins remembered.'

A dozen pairs of eyes, most of them unfamiliar, all of them awash with champagne, looked me up and down. The work I'd done on my moustache had not gone for nothing. 'Goodness me, Ros,' Margaret Hall (née Jackson) observed, 'you are married to a young husband.' The subtext to this: And he's not your first, either.

As well as being unusual (by all but Perth standards) for never having left their native city, Ros's friends were also remarkable for never having left their husbands. The nuns might have been proud of them. Vivacious, assured, well-turned out, without exception beautiful, they none the less gave off that small-town expectancy which I'd first observed on the faces of grown women in Sydney in 1965. 'You've just come from where people are bad,' they seemed to say then. 'Be bad for us. Bring a little far-away wickedness into our quiet lives.' I used to find this appeal intoxicating in 1965. I got drunk on my own untried diabolism. And here today, in the dense swooning garden of Bloom's restaurant, I experienced the same sensation. I was a young-husband, a toy boy, a mere one year older than my wife, and I had supped only recently with sinners. There wasn't anything that those convent-educated Perth girls could not make a man from overseas feel capable of. But of course I didn't mention this, later on, to Geoff Gibbs, since his wife was one of them.

Before I left – this was only a fleeting audience I'd been granted – I got Rosalin and Gillian Martin (née Garratt) to remember the little chant with which the kids from state schools had been wont to bait them.

> Condi dogs
> Sitting on logs
> Eating maggots out of frogs

And the little chant with which they were wont to bait them back.

> State school brats
> Sitting on mats
> Pulling whiskers out of rats.

It wasn't difficult, even at this distance, imagining how low those infidel state brats would have felt, listening to that. 'I certainly wouldn't like to be on the receiving end of you girls,' I said, as Geoff dragged me away.

We left just as Margaret and Ros were recalling the day Sister Gertrude had spotted them strolling across the playground arm in arm. 'Separate, girls. Separate!' Sister Gertrude had called out to either one or both of them. 'Separate at once!' Varied and ingenious had been the forms of unnaturalness the nuns had noticed amongst the girls, and various and ingenious had been their methods of stamping them out.

While Geoff drove me around Perth and its environs, show-ing me de Bernales' folly in Cottesloe, and Bondy's monstrous Observation City (for Observation of you-know-what) in

Scarborough, I mused aloud upon the phenomenon we'd just been privileged to witness. It didn't seem to me that the nuns had done their charges any lasting harm. And would modern children, I wondered, who enjoyed the careful conscientiousness of liberal-minded teachers, possess such a rich and comic store of ludicrous memories? I didn't want to argue for the return of bigoted religious education but didn't it feed and stimulate the imagination, all that mad dogmatism and lewd suspiciousness and eccentricty?

That night we came within a whisker of being formally introduced to the Governor of Western Australia. We had Geoff to thank for this. As Dean of the W.A. Academy for the Performing Arts and member of the executive committees of most of the performing arts companies in town, Geoff Gibbs – Dr Gibbs – spent a sizeable portion of his life in a dinner suit, attending first nights. That night's first night was balletic, and although I had long ago taken a sacred vow that ballet and my free evenings should never mix, I knew it would have been foolish to pass up the opportunity of seeing how cultured Perth society behaved in the presence of the Governor.

It was, of course, a black tie affair, which put some strain on the resources of my traveller's wardrobe. But it was my intention to keep in the background anyway, since I'd never been good with governors, so I found an obscure niche half-way up the foyer stairs and pretended to be absorbed in my programme.

I pretty soon felt as if I was in the North of England. It's a queer thing about dress suits but they always perform the opposite function to that which is required of them: they unfailingly make the men inside them look like hayseeds. And the women, too, in their frothy evening frocks and stoles, looked dressed for an engagement party in Huddersfield. Only Geoff Gibbs moved through the sparse throng with anything like an international theatre-goer's aplomb. From above the top of my programme

I watched him – overfed and rosy and mischievous, like a fallen cherub – charming a better deal for the arts out of the relevant Minister, whispering theatrical anecdotes just the right side of naughtiness to dentists' wives from Mount Pleasant wearing scarlet tango dresses.

Inside the auditorium the ballet could not begin until the Governor had made his official entry. We all stood while a drum rolled and the Governor took his place, bowing unostentatiously to those around him. Then we all stood a little longer until a scratchy record playing at about 22½ r.p.m. had got through 'Advance, Australia Fair.'

The first ballet was to music by Debussy. In so far as I could grasp the plot it seemed to be about the sea – the dancers being the waves or the tide, and the conflict the currents and eddies of the ocean. Appalled by the spectacle of bodies monomaniacally fashioned for a single purpose, I drifted off. The waves crashed, the tide rolled in and out, a climax was reached, and an interval followed. Geoff ushered us through a door marked PRIVATE into a room where a champagne party for the official guests was underway. From opposite ends of the room the Governor and I exchanged suspicious glances. We were to do this once or twice again before the evening was over, and several more times into the bargain before I was clear of Perth. There was no hostility between us. I simply wanted to keep him in my sights so that I couldn't without advance warning be introduced to him – not knowing whether to call him Sir, or Your Excellency, or Professor (which is what he was when he wasn't a Governor); and he was just trying to figure out why a very brown person in a shocking pink jacket and a crumpled shirt kept staring at him.

The second ballet set a pretentious modern action to music by Pergolesi. There was barbed wire on the stage. Images of Christianity blended with and then counterpoised symbols of repressive politics. A young girl with a lithe body attempted to simulate the grief of the eternal mother and widow. She rent her hair. She rived her clothing. But because she was so well honed for grace, so bodily introverted as it were, she was incapable of suggesting misery. I decided what I would say to the Governor during the next interval, should he seek me out. 'Don't you think, Your Most Worshipful,' I would say, 'that the self-absorption of the ballet dancer precludes the depiction of any passion *except* self-absorption? It is not an acting or a mimetic medium. It can render, with great beauty I will grant you, only itself.'

But I didn't meet the Governor during the next interval. I met Lucette Aldous. One of the most distinguished living figures of West Australian ballet, Lucette Aldous had once danced with Nureyev.

She was sitting on a sofa in one of the public areas, looking a little frayed both in nerves and in costume, when Geoff propelled me towards her. Her outfit, although it wouldn't have done for the stage, was still somehow unmistakably a prima ballerina's, insubstantial and not quite fresh. I could see the bones of her thin chest and gauge how extraordinarily light she was. She would be in the air before you could so much as touch her. I imagined putting out one finger and balancing her effortlessly on it. I could be the ocean bottom and she the dancing wave.

Her husband was with her. He too was theatrically attired, though in that bohemian manner which implied a sublime incompetence with money. While I wondered about his bell-bottomed trousers he told me that his wife had once danced with Nureyev. Rudi was the name he actually used.

Perhaps because I wasn't Rudi, and wasn't carrying any word from Rudi either, Lucette Aldous looked right through me when Geoff Gibbs told her who I was.

The final ballet was Stravinsky's *Firebird* which to my dismay I found I liked. You can't beat a story. Even a foolish one. It got me in where abstract impressionism had kept me out. At the end there was a highly dramatic engagement between the Evil One and the Young Man entrusted by the Firebird to save humanity. On behalf of all of us, and against all likelihood, the Young Man triumphed.

When it was all over I hung around inconspicuously, watching Geoff moving amongst the departing balletomanes with more nimbleness than any of the dancers had been capable of. The theatre seemed to empty very quickly. The moment I saw the Governor approaching I flattened myself against the wall. We exchanged a shifty glance. Then he was in Geoff's hands, being escorted to his car. Both men threw their heads back and laughed. There seemed to be a running gag between them which I imagined their picking up and embellishing from one first night to the next.

I was just thinking how like Tolstoy's Stiva Oblonsky Geoff was when I suddenly caught sight of Lucette Aldous and her husband at the bottom of the stairs. Immediately my mind turned to Dickens, to Miss Havisham and Joe Gargery. Which could be called a kind of augury, because the next occasion the Governor and I were to squinny at each other in formal attire was the first night of a new dramatization of *Great Expectations*.

What larks.

NINE

GRANNY APPLES

Although it was not a part of the country that I'd ever bothered to notice on the map or had ever had the slightest curiosity to visit, Rosalin insisted that we spend some time in the bottom left-hand corner of the State, a half-forgotten area of caves, forests, apples, and now – the reason it was only *half* forgotten – wineries. There were compelling emotional reasons, from her point of view, for doing the South-West, not the least being that her maternal grandparents were buried there, that her mother had been born, had met and married Ros's father there, that Ros herself retained exquisite memories of childhood holidays there, and that Fred Luff, whom we'd met on the bus from Darwin, had chosen it to buy a run-down hotel and forget his bitter Northern Territory experiences in.

The trip she had in mind would see us travelling due south from Perth to Augusta, taking in Bunbury and Busselton, and Donnybrook and Margaret River, and then moving east to Albany, by way of Pemberton and Northcliffe, Walpole, Denmark, and Wilson's Inlet; and I decided that we could give three days to it provided that Ros understood they ate into our West Australian allowance and that we would therefore have to make plans to leave Perth the minute we returned. I was beginning to fret about how unadventurous we'd become, how slow the thin air of Perth had made us, how much of our time seemed to be given over to people and nostalgia, instead of to – well, instead of to the harsh vagaries of the outback. Ros could have the South-West as a treat, but after that we really were going to have to get our skates on. I went off to make provisions for a little hire car – I didn't think we'd need much of a car – shaking my head and sighing, like a man who had it in him to scale mountains but was contracted to spend a week playing carpet bowls with old ladies instead.

In fact there were to be more hardships in this quick excursion than I'd bargained for, beginning with the hire car company not delivering the car to me as they'd promised, but delivering me to the car. This is liable to happen with rental firms that have depots only at airports, and can be extremely inconvenient if the airport is an hour the wrong way out of town and you don't have much of a sense of direction. It was only the affability of the young man who'd kidnapped me that kept me from losing my temper. That and the fact that when I'd said I'd only ever heard a white Kenyan accent like his once before, and that was in Kununurra, in the far north of the State, he'd replied, 'Oh, that'll be Charlie. He's my brother-in-law.'

On the way out of Perth we dropped in on some old friends of Ros's parents. It had always been her intention to pay this call but I took the timing of it to be a pointer to what lay ahead of us. Over the next few days Ros really meant to lift the lid off her past. Prams, rattles, swaddling clothes – it was her intention to go rummaging through the lot.

I kept out of the emotionalism of this brief reunion, building up my strength with tea and biscuits, and trying not to look too startled by the arrival of Lurline, the daughter of the house, and her husband Dewey. Lurline had a red face and wore a peaked cap with bird badges on it. It was clear at once that Lurline didn't only love birds but actually wished she'd been one. In the same way, Dewey clearly hankered after marsupiality. He laughed unexpectedly and patted his stomach at regular intervals. A few months later the world would rejoice over photographs of the Pope in Melbourne, holding a creature just like Dewey. He was balding but he swept the sides of his hair up into a sort of crest, so that he looked permanently startled. According to Lurline, Dewey was a real bushman, the last of his kind. 'Dewey could tell you a few stories,' she told me. 'Dewey can follow the track of any bird or animal. He can deal with anything in the bush. We call him our own bushie.'

Dewey laughed at this, patted his stomach, and lowered his crest.

I'd noticed that, when she wasn't talking to me or leafing through an illustrated bird book, Lurline watched Ros intently from underneath her cap, her head cocked to one side as if listening for danger. When Ros reminded her of how they used to play together as children out there in that very garden, how they used to climb trees and build hideaways, Lurline closed her eyes. 'No,' she said, as we rose to leave, 'no, I've never seen you before.'

Dewey the tracker gave his wife a little confirmatory twitch of the nostrils. He too reckoned that Ros had left no abiding scent hereabouts.

After this delayed and somewhat disconcerting start to our journey I pointed the car south and kept my foot on the accelerator, ignoring signs to Miami and Florida and even the intriguingly named Australind, site of what was to have been an important settlement linking Australia and India by trade. Now, Australind boasted the smallest church in Australia, a titanium oxide plant and a rock museum (minerals not music), and left the business of being an important settlement to Bunbury, itself celebrating its one hundred and fiftieth anniversary – its sesquicentenary, as Australians like to put it – this very year. We weren't looking for a party ourselves, just refreshment; and this we found, in the form of milky coffee, cold chips and scalding dim sims, in a milk bar right next door to Paulette's Bridal Palace, a large double-fronted emporium offering everything a bride could ever want in the way of veils, ribbons or royal coronets. We looked in Paulette's window, not with the intention of buying anything, but as an act of filial homage. For it was here in Bunbury that Ros's father had courted Ros's mother on his Harley Davidson. He had worn the long leather coat in which he would later wrap and bury the family dog, Nicholas Monsarrat, and no other bloke in Bunbury had got a look in. We drove around the sleepy Sunday streets where, almost fifty years before, he had revved his engine, and we fell easily into that trance of misty innocence which people of our generation invariably wrap around the romantic histories of their parents. Part country town, part industrial port, part seaside – even today, in the unsettled weather, families lay on the beach in the shadows of the refineries – Bunbury possessed those qualities of dreamlike remoteness and torpor which conjure a sad past as surely as a tinted photograph. By the time we'd driven up the hill to the Catholic church and convent – scene of Ros's mother's maidenly devotions – and looked out, as she surely had, far over the slumbering town to the harsh sunlit and scruffy harbour waters beyond, our eyes were hollow with vicarious melancholy.

And there was worse to come. Donnybrook: just a little over half an hour's drive inland, where, in a manner of speaking, it had all begun. Donnybrook: which had given the world Walter Lindrum, the billiards player; the Granny Smith Apple; and Ros.

To make it more exquisite for her I eked out the journey to Donnybrook, stopping separately for oil, petrol, and water. On the outskirts of the little town stood a fruit barn, a sort of indoor market on a garage forecourt: and we wandered about amongst the produce, taking our time admiring the persimmons and the quinces and the ruby blood plums, the sweet potatoes, the golden queen peaches, and of course the Granny Smiths, sharp and succulent and twice the familiar size but selling for only 40 cents a kilo, that's to say about 5 pence for a pound. Only in France, I remarked to Ros, had I ever seen that which grows on trees or pops up from the ground made to look so appetizing. And we wandered round again, squandering the afternoon, snatching every minute we decently could from the waiting maw of sentiment.

But at last there was no further postponing it. We loaded up the boot with more fruit than we would have been able to eat had we been staying a whole year in Donnybrook, and drove on into the town, turning left over the picturesque hump-backed bridge beneath which Ros had whiled away her childhood summers, floating twigs or building dams and catching gilgies, and coming to a halt finally at the little cottage, the last dwelling before the fields took over, where her grandparents had lived and died.

It looked for all the world as though no changes had been made to it for fifty years, as though someone else's granny was here, cultivating those fragile and old-fashioned pastel-coloured flowers that only grannies have ever known how to grow. What distressed Ros more than anything was that the old garden shed, falling down in 1948, still stood.

We drove a little way down the adjoining farm road, and parked with our windows open. Crickets and grasshoppers flicked about in the heat. A bull pawed the dust. Ros pointed to the highest hill, surmounted by a clump of stones. It was there that she had gone as a young woman to think about her first engagement. 'I sat there all afternoon and summoned up what little knowledge and experience I possessed. When I came back down I knew I didn't want to be engaged.'

Even without the colouring of early memories Donnybrook seemed to me to be a place of near intolerable sadness. It was the archetypal pastoral village of the imagination; the happy, enclosed and sheltered valley of childhood. It had always been in the past, had never and would never speak of any other time. I felt as if I'd been a child here at some time myself. The high, bleached gums, the little river, the smooth hills, the long rising roads going everywhere and nowhere, the modest row of wooden cottages, of which her grandmother's was the last, all suggested the unending, hopeful, hopeless, summer of everyone's early youth.

In this frame of mind, and while there was still light, we drove to the Donnybrook cemetery to see her grandparents' graves. We spent several hours there, wandering between the headstones as aimlessly as we'd earlier meandered around the fruit. I jotted names down in my notebook, as I always do in graveyards, for later fictional tinkerings. I especially liked Minnie Scriven, which struck me as Dickensian, Jamesian and Spike Milliganesque, all at once. Otherwise the stones told the usual distressing colonial stories of exile and separation. There were men from Iowa and Sardinia buried here. And women from Donegal and Harrow. I couldn't decide which was the sadder – the taciturn tomb of a solitary alien, unaccompanied and far from home, or the garrulous family mausoleums, commemorating the swathe death had cut through a whole dynasty of pioneers.

We were still there as the light faded. The tips of the hills and the tallest trees turned pink in the dying afternoon. There were no sounds to be heard other than those made by the soft scuffing of our feet and the whistling of birds. As we walked back towards the car Ros speculated on the ties that bound her to this place. It occurred to her that her mother thought she had got away but now lived somewhere comparable, where the birds also whistled in the late afternoon, in the south of Victoria.

And Ros herself had made a vast circuitous journey only to be landed in a Cornish fishing village which rivalled even Donnybrook for melancholy. 'Freedom?' she murmured, her head buried in her chest. 'Don't talk to me about freedom. I don't think anyone is free to spit.'

When we walked out of our motel the following morning we felt as though we'd stepped into Marvell's *Garden*. Ripe apples fell about our heads. The turf we trod on sprang back at us like a trampoline, denying all memory of our impress. Where the motel car park ended, a field of aubergines began; even as we stood and watched we could see their purple gourds increase and swell with life. Life, death; death, life: it didn't make an awful lot of difference. We were good and sandwiched between the two and there wasn't anything but anguish to look for from either of them. But at least, if you've got a little car, you can chug your way out of Weltschmerz Valley.

'Let's get out of here,' I said to Ros, 'before we start looking in real estate agents' windows.' But I only got her to agree to leave on condition that I would promise to bury her here if she died before me. So it came down to real estate after all.

We drove to Busselton, taking the Capel road through some fine tuart forests. Just outside Busselton we called in at Wonnerup House, a lonely homestead clearing in the bush, once owned by the Layman family. George Layman, the founder, had been killed by Aborigines. His family had opened the front door to him one day and he had fallen through with a spear in his back. The next man the widow married died by drowning. It was worth remembering that it had once been dangerous out here. Perhaps that was what the owner of our motel at Donnybrook had been alluding to when she'd called out, as we were driving off, that we should always stay in the car if we had a breakdown, otherwise the Abos would get us.

And some such ancient fear might also have been behind the

sign I saw in the back window of a deep blood burgundy
Toyota which overtook us as we were approaching Busselton.

ONE LAND – ONE LAW

it said,

OPPOSE LAND RIGHTS

I followed the vehicle into town in the hope of getting a look
at the driver. But he was too quick for us. All I could tell from
the thickness of his neck and the Australo-Viyella Tory shirt
he was wearing was that he must have been the equivalent of
a young farmer from Berkshire, the kind that drove a Volvo
with the legend, YOUNG FARMERS DO IT IN THE
HAY, somewhere visible. Was that, then, how one was to
understand the messages that people stuck in the windows of
their motor vehicles – were they really all political slogans in
search of a political cause? In which case there was some relation between bigotry and facetiousness that was worth the
investigating here, and I promised myself that one of these
days I would investigate it.

We didn't get much of a sense of Busselton; we were too
busy trying to catch the deep blood burgundy Toyota. But it
looked a pleasant town with wide streets, a long pier, and
beaches so accessible that you could open your car door and
tumble straight out on to them. We might have stretched out
on the sand ourselves for half an hour had I not noticed an
advertisement for an Angus Bull Sale which was proceeding
right this minute, several miles out of Busselton on the Margaret
River road. I'd never been to an Angus Bull Sale, or come to
that any kind of bull sale, and I thought that since we were in
young farmers' country – one land, one law – it might prove
instructive. Unfortunately the sale was just finishing when I got

there. The hay bales, which had been arranged like the seats of a theatre in the round, were empty; and the few farmers who were left – some sporting mutton chops, some in stetsons, but most in floppy white cricketers' hats – were making for their 4-wheel drives. A notice pinned to one of the fences made me feel that I'd missed something special. A couple of star sires had been on sale today: The Basin Palmer and The Blackrock Hercules, whose semen was none the less still available and 'highly recommended'. Ah, youth.

On the outskirts of Margaret River I called into a craft complex called the Old Settlement, to see if they had any maps or leaflets that might be of interest to hurried tourists like ourselves. The woman behind the counter, who somehow let it be known that she was from Farnham, Surrey, was engaged in a serpentine conversation (neither the head nor the tail showing) on the twin subjects of Aborigines and cleanliness.

'We've got some friends who have worked with them,' she was saying, 'and they tell us that it's a terrible business getting them to understand white men's hygiene. Just persuading them to wash their hands is a job in itself. They aren't able to understand the reasons for it. It's a real eye-opener, our friends say.'

The two people she was addressing were married, Australian, on holiday, and in their sixties. The wife wore blue slacks and a floral shirt and that expression of cross bemusement which settles on Australian women of a certain age if they're not out playing bowls. 'Well, it's a totally different culture, isn't it,' she said.

Her husband resembled her in most respects, except that like most Australian men of his generation his face blazed with the fires of unexpended pedantry. 'The white man's still got a lot to learn from those blackfellers,' he said. 'We're only just discovering some of their medicines. The white doctors have found out that they've got a contraceptive tree. Right there, growing, they've got what our scientists have been working years to discover. And they've got one that cures cancer.'

'They've got their own ways,' his wife explained.

'Yes, that's right,' the woman from Farnham said. She didn't seem to like this turn in the conversation. It's harder for you, if you come from Farnham, to concede the superior wisdom of the black man. As well as that, I could see that she didn't really like the idea of a condom tree either. On the other hand she knew she couldn't flatly contradict her customers and say, 'Oh no, they haven't.' So she had to keep saying, 'Yes, that's right, they have,' instead.

I helped myself to some free literature, including an invitation to drink the milk of Paradise at the Château Xanadu winery, and a chatty quarterly newsletter which talked about local characters like Allan and Christine who had settled down here for the quiet life but were now running the model railway, and Lu and Peter who were growing exotic vegetables and had named their property Rivendell, after the refuge for elves in *The Hobbit*.

I left just as conversation in the Old Settlement was moving on to acupuncture. 'A few years ago they called them cranks,' the rubicund opinionist was saying. Having done his best by the blackfellers he was now ready to stand up for the yeller ones. It struck me that he could easily have gone the other way. But then you never can tell what effect retirement is likely to have on these old die-hards. Long-winded lenience is as much a function of idleness as prejudice is.

Back in the car I consulted one of the several wine maps I'd taken. Wine was what Margaret River was now best known for. In Perth they'd told me that the area already rivalled the Barossa Valley in South Australia and the Hunter Valley in New South Wales for the production of high-quality table wines – Semillons and Merlots and Verdelhos and Pinots Noirs. And yet the industry was hardly twenty years old. Dr Tom Cullity, a Perth physician, had begun it all in 1967. And other Perth physicians had followed. There were so many doctors growing grapes in Margaret River, in fact, that the area had become known as the 'medical belt'. The reason for this, at least as it had been explained to me, was that Perth doctors were so wealthy they had to offset their incomes somehow. So how better than by popping down to the country and playing at being vignerons every weekend? Except that now the vineyards were successful and what was meant to be a tax loss had become a further liability. See how difficult it is to lose money in W.A.?

Because we were short of time and Château Xanadu was closed, we drove to the Leeuwin Estate, the biggest, richest, and most entrepreneurially inventive of the wineries. It was here, under the giant karri trees, that the London Philharmonic Orchestra, and more recently the Berlin Staatskapelle, had played on the lawn to audiences of over four and a half thousand people, not counting the kookaburras. The presence of these distinguished international orchestras in a tiny bush town on the far south-west peninsula of Western Australia was the result of a deal struck between the Festival of Perth and the owner of Leeuwin Estate, Denis Horgan, whereby he underwrote the tour and they played at his place. It was, of course, pretty smart publicity for the grapes. To be seen in Perth on the day of either of these concerts – to be anywhere other than Margaret River – was a sort of social suicide. I'd heard it said that any group planning a coup d'état could have achieved it quite bloodlessly by blocking the Bussell Highway with a single truck and walking unmolested into a deserted Government House.

But this isn't the only way in which art and wine serve each other on the Leeuwin Estate. There is something in it for painters also. 'The Leeuwin Estate "Art Series" labels', a gold plaque in the restaurant explains, 'are reserved for wines considered to be of outstanding quality and international standard. Each label bears a different painting which has been purchased specifically for the Leeuwin Estate Collection of Contemporary Art.' Thus, you can have a Sidney Nolan 'Dolphin Rock' on your 1982 Cabernet Sauvignon, or a John Olsen 'Frog in Riesling' on your 1983 Riesling (naturally), or a Sam Fulbrook on your 1982 Chardonnay.

Beguiled by its smoky flavour and excellent wood differentiation — I'd been told to look out for its charisma but clearly had no nose for it — we bought three bottles of Sidney Nolan to give as presents. I was disappointed to discover that, for $10.95 a bottle, they weren't signed.

We drove out, in the late afternoon, to Prevelly and Cape Mentelle, from where there were lovely views of the Margaret River estuary. Although I never particularly advertise this about myself I have a taste for estuaries. I like to think that I am, in some fundamental way, estuarine. I like the word. I like the idea of waters meeting, a current having its way against a tide. And I suppose I must like egress as a principle. If the sea is death then an estuary is a way of dying peaceably.

This evening, in the soft pearl light, the Margaret River was taking its time to expire. A bank of sand stood between it and the ocean, so that a sort of lagoon had formed. Heathers of infinite shades of green and silver grew along the valley. The coastline here was low, beautiful in its very unremarkableness. A few boys in wetsuits pretended there was a surf. A couple of fishermen stood motionless on reefs, lost in whatever trance it is that brings them night after night to water. And Ros and I congratulated ourselves on our good fortune at being here on the crumbling dunes, cold under the low-lying clouds, enjoying our exposure on this queer little promontory which somehow felt a continuation of the same beach we'd gambolled on in the tropical heat thousands of miles to the north.

In the days when the preferred means of transport between Europe and Australia was a boat, passengers used to stand on the upper decks and throw down streamers or ropes made out of knotted stockings so that they might maintain a lifeline, an unbroken connection, for as long as possible, with all that they were leaving. Scooping up the white sand at Prevelly it was as if we had hold of such a ribbon, uniting us with where we'd been. We renamed the spot Hamilton Strand, after Mark and Bill Hamilton, gents, of London, and returned in placid spirits to Margaret River.

Back in the lounge bar of our nicely tarted-up hotel in Margaret River there was so little business that we were able to engage the barman, Mark Waller, in conversation. He was one of those tall and touching Australians with straight backs and small handsome faces and shuttered eyes one imagines to have fallen by the thousand in Gallipoli. Mark's passion was trees. And we got on to those because we'd got on to rainfall. The reason there weren't many visitors in Margaret River at this time of the year was the wet. Thirty inches of rain could be expected to fall between now and October, but if we thought that was a lot we should have been here twenty years ago. Then it was sixty. So what had made the difference? Trees. 'We've cut 'em all down,' he explained to us. 'What you see when you're driving along the highway is all there is. I've talked to pilots who fly over the area, and they tell you that the forests are just a fifty-metre strip on either side of the road.'

So it wasn't only in Queensland that the ecological balance was being – as the Australian greens like to say – fucked? (Sir Joh Bjelke-Petersen was in everybody's minds again today; he had just rejected an Aboriginal sculpture for the centre of Brisbane.) Mark Waller bewitched us with a brave dying Anzac's smile; no, the problem was much more widespread. The pastoralists had been to blame, supposing pasture to be the only good. Only now were they beginning to realize the benefits of the bush they'd ravaged. Mark Waller had a little property of his own. This was his livelihood he was discussing. The bush provides shelter and roughage for your stock, he told us. When you get a weather alert you don't have to run right out to save your lambs if they've got bush to shelter under. But that was only part of it. Untold natural disasters must follow from the wholesale tree-felling that still went unchecked. We were interfering with the very way the planet breathed.

He mixed us one last gin and tonic. And tried to cheer us up. He didn't want to see us going to bed despondent. 'What you've got to remember is that we're still a young country,' he said. 'We might be able to reverse what's happening in time.' It was hard to say how convinced he was of that himself.

His apocalyptic warnings came back to us the following night as we were driving through the immense jarrah and karri forests between Northcliffe and Walpole. We'd been travelling slowly, with our windows open, enjoying the damp exhalation of the eucalypts, when suddenly the scene had changed. Now, instead of dense and overhanging foliage, instead of giant breathings, what we saw and heard was fire. Not bush fire but planned, deliberate, man-made fire. On either side of us, and for seemingly interminable distances, felled trees lay smoking like corpses on a battlefield, like the slaughtered of the Somme, charred and contorted, and in some cases glowing from within, as if fire had attacked their vitals first and was eating them away from the insides. We drove for miles through this carnage, past what must have been thousands of blackened carcasses, choking the fading light with their smoke and ashes. A sweet woody smell of death filled the car.

We'd begun the day in high spirits, looking forward to some hard driving and a variety of scenery – caves, coast, lighthouses and famous forests – not to mention, if time allowed and we could find him, Fred Luff. But I knew we couldn't leave Margaret River and its tourist cafés and craft shops, without grabbing a look at the Church of St Thomas More, the rammed earth Cathedral I'd heard so much about in Perth.

Ramming earth was big in Margaret River and appealed to the profound *nostalgie de la boue* of Perth professionals. Many solicitors and accountants I had met in town wanted nothing more than to own a few hectares in Margaret River and to get down there at weekends and in holidays to ram themselves a little something of their own. Sometimes, when you heard them discussing it, ramming sounded like the last refuge left for manliness in the State.

Its principle as a building method is this: you mix 16 parts gravel to 1 part cement and ram the mixture into formers with pneumatic hammers. You then pile former onto former until you have the wall you want, and seal it up with Bondcrete. Do that four times and you've got four walls.

From the outside, the rammed earth Cathedral at Margaret River looked like a leisure centre; within, it had the atmosphere of a craft market in a ski lodge. Exposed wooden girders, Swedish in appearance, held up the roof. Beaten copper holy pictures hung on the walls. The altar, made by Henry Kowalski, was a rough hewn table balanced on a tree stump. Kazimierz Ambroziak and George Power had polished the jarrah burls for the credence and offertory tables. The baptismal font was made by Tristram Willcox, the grand candelabra resembling natural configurations by Jean and John Everett. And special thanks for the feature wall were owing to the Palandris (including Big Carlo and Little Carlo), the Fontanas, the Anghinettis and the Folattis.

Nor did the more humble contributors to this grandiloquently rustic monument go without their commendations – 'The volunteer men who had poured all of the flooring (5 big pours) . . . and the volunteer women who made and served thousands of cups of tea, several hectares of sandwiches, and tonnes of cakes and biscuits.'

As further testimony to the power of pioneering communality it should be noted that the Cathedral was fully rammed inside a year. Work began on Australia Day 1982 and was completed, with a nice sense for patriotism and symmetry, on Australia Day 1983. The great Cathedrals of Europe had nothing like so good a record.

I wasn't much concerned, after this, to look at caves. At any time I am prepared to give caves a miss, not caring much for the crudity of their symbolism, but today, with the sun shining and the above-ground scenery ravishing, there was even less reason than usual to hang around in car parks waiting for the cave warden to turn up with the keys. So we drove down the Caves Road to Augusta, the third oldest settlement in Western Australia and as delightfully situated a little town as any we had yet found. From wherever we stood in Augusta we could see water – Hardy's Inlet, the Blackwood Estuary, Flinders Bay (for it was hereabouts that Matthew Flinders began to chart the Australian coastline), or the ocean itself. And whereas, whenever we had looked out from the coast of Western Australia before, we had stared northwards or westwards, to Indonesia or India or Africa, now we had, as it were, turned the corner; now there was nothing between us and, had our eyes been good enough, the South Pole.

To celebrate this dramatic new geographical perspective we bought a kilo of frozen prawns and a kilo of frozen oysters and cooked them up on a public barbecue in a park overlooking Hardy's Inlet. Then we drove down to see the lighthouse at Cape Leeuwin, declared the prospect to be much superior to Land's End, and set off for Pemberton through karri forests every bit as magnificent as they were reputed to be. The karri does not rival the boab for personality or friendliness; it is altogether too stately a tree to make a chum of. But it is somehow benign and protective for all that – an aloof but kindly uncle of a tree – and I could see why the Orange people had made this area their home for a while, seeking peace and property, and causing considerable consternation to non-Yogis, in the forests of the Karri Valley.

Pemberton itself was a let-down after the country that surrounded it. Knowing that timber was its beginning and its end, I expected a charming shaded town of simple shacks and sylvan prospects. I got the shack part right, and maybe even the simple, but I saw no charm. The wooden dwellings were all uniform in design and built in straight lines like state or factory housing. The timber had everywhere weathered to a drab unpainted grey. Perhaps you could have too much of trees.

But a tree was what we had come to see – the Gloucester Tree, a 300-year-old, 61-metre giant, 'the tallest fire look-out in the world' – and we dutifully followed the signs out of Pemberton to it. The Gloucester Tree no longer functioned as a look-out. Spotter-planes could now do that job more effectively. But an observation deck had been constructed for visitors who wanted to climb the tree, no more than four at a time, provided that they weren't put off by the message on a warning board: 'If you are unfit or have a heart condition you are advised to stay on the ground.'

'Since we're a bit pushed for time,' I said, 'I think we might stay on the ground.'

We watched a little girl called Tara shin expertly to the top. Natural bravery took her half-way, the screams of her younger brother stranded in fear at the bottom did the rest. 'You did well,' his mother told the boy, 'you climbed ten rungs.'

Several hundred rungs further up the minuscule red flash that was his sister called down, 'It's easy. It's *really* easy.'

The boy howled and stamped his feet. The mother made it worse by insisting on the achievement of those miserable ten rungs. And finally, to save the good name of his sex, the father had to begin the steepling climb himself. Long after he had become invisible we could hear his heavy breathing.

The mother – a chubby blonde in a pink and grey tracksuit – held the hand of her virility-violated boy and craned her neck heavenwards. Up and around the trunk of the

Gloucester Tree the whole pre-ordained domestic drama of her life unfolded incxorably. It was like watching Ibsen in an open-air performance.

'Dad there yet, Tara?' we heard her shouting as we left.

Since there was no point in hanging around Pemberton we set off for Northcliffe where, if we'd remembered right, Fred Luff had said he was going to take over an ailing pub. The minute we arrived in Northcliffe I wished we'd stayed in Pemberton. The light was fading. There seemed to be no activity in the corrugated iron shacks that lined the road. A backwoodsman wearing a denim suit cut across us on his motorbike. At the garage a frazzled-looking woman in a flowered frock and anorak served me petrol.

'You're a long way from home,' she said.

'You too,' I noticed.

'Surrey,' she said. She made it sound like an apology.

It turned out that she'd been in Australia for twenty years and in Northcliffe for six. 'It's OK really,' she said. 'It's not up to much financially, but the social life is good.'

I looked around me. All I could see were wide dusty streets disappearing into scrub, and tin houses.

'You've got to join in,' she explained. 'It's like anywhere. You've got to mix.'

I thought this was as good a time as any to ask her if there was a Fred Luff in town. Yes, he was installed over at the hotel. She wasn't sure whether the sale had gone through yet but it was certainly imminent. 'Well, he should liven things up,' I said.

She eyed me suspiciously. She seemed to think I was questioning her opinion of the social life.

It took Fred a minute or two to remember who we were, which gave us the opportunity to form an opinion of his investment from the inside. From without it hadn't looked too terrific. It seemed to be, as an estate agent might have said, in need of sympathetic if not imaginative refurbishment. It was neglected and impoverished and not situated where you were bound to see it. But these would have been the least of my worries had I been the licensee; altogether more problematical, both from the point of view of tone and of personal safety, were the wild-eyed hairy locals in cowboy boots who lounged around the cold cavernous bar laughing at things that weren't funny and spitting glass onto the filthy lino. They appeared, however, to present no kind of problem to Fred other than one of interior design. 'A lick of paint and a bit of upholstery and we'll have that room right,' he told us.

He was in the very best of spirits, as cheerful as he'd been when he was remembering swimming with Aborigines in Arnhem Land. 'And this over here,' he said, leading us into a peeling hall at the bottom of a flight of steps I would never, under pain of death, have climbed, 'is going to be an art gallery. There's a local painter who's quite good, and my sister-in-law in Perth paints on bark.'

He took us into an empty dining room furnished with straight-backed dark-stained chairs of the late thirties. The tables were all set for business but didn't look as though they'd been sat at since 1951. 'And this,' he said, as if he were now presenting the star prize, 'will be the restaurant.'

I was unable to keep myself from voicing doubts. 'Is there, um, much in the way of what you might call passing trade?' I asked.

He rubbed his hands. He was optimistic, truly jaunty, in a style which was supposed to have gone out with the First World War. Hope danced in his eyes. I could see my own reflection in the gleam of his moustache. 'Soon will be,' he said. 'Once the word's out. Our friends from Pemberton and Manjimup know we're opening, and they'll be heading down.'

His impossible high spirits lay like a dead weight on ours. It will take a hundred men a hundred years to get this place right, I thought, and even then there's no reason to believe that anyone will ever find it. Ros and I didn't so much as exchange a glance over the question of our staying for the night; it was too desolate even to consider. And the cowboys at the bar were beginning to eye us as if we were tender cuts of rump steak.

But Fred was no more disheartened by our premature departure than he was by anything else. We stood with him on the deserted street and shook his hand. 'Good luck, Fred,' we said. Tragic operatically.

'Oh, I won't be needing any luck,' he assured us. In his mind's eye the road from Manjimup was already congested.

He pointed us in the direction of Walpole and warned us, since it was getting dark, to be on the look-out for kangaroos. Then he rapped on the bonnet of our car and waved us off. 'Pop in again the next time you're in this part of the world,' he shouted.

The only other sign of life in Northcliffe was a motorcyclist wearing a fringed jacket and Hell's Angels sunglasses kick-starting his engine in the dust.

After about thirty kilometres the road between Northcliffe and Walpole becomes The Highway, route No. 1 around Australia, and is nothing other than a clearing through dense forest. It was on this road that we were to see that burning battlefield of vast uprooted trees, but until then the drive was marvellous. A warm vegetable breeze blew through the forest. With our windows open we could feel the damp on our cheeks. Low Wordsworthian breathings came after us. We couldn't only smell green, we could hear it. And then the first wisps of smoke, and the first lick of flame.

In the dark Walpole seemed determinedly uninviting, spread out straight and flat on either side of a single highway. Had it been earlier we'd have gone on, but already we'd rejected the hospitality of two towns we might have stayed in and we were beginning to tire of our own pernicketiness. I pulled in at the first motel we saw, which happened to have a pub attached, and left Ros to go to bed. Myself, I needed a beer. In the front window of the pub was a large, professionally painted cartoon depicting what I took to be one of the eternal verities of life in Walpole. A miserable little bloke holding a packet of mentholated cigarettes (not for real men) and an empty beer glass (ditto) was shown looking up pleadingly at a gigantic ocker in a blue singlet who was in turn looking down into his own frothing Fosters. 'PARDON ME,' the little bloke was apologizing. 'I'M STANDING UNDER YOUR FOOT.'

I went in, anyway, and kept a sensible distance from the only other drinker in the bar, a man in a neck-brace and a T-shirt that said, rather menacingly I thought, WALPOLE – W.A. While he and the barman discussed weapons, I read the boards on the walls recording prize catches of twenty-five different species of fish by local fishermen. Men in Walpole, I learnt, were capable of pulling in 260 pounds' worth of shark. Yet, for all this great plunder of the seas, the only food for sale at the bar was pies, pizzas, and chicken rolls.

'I tell you what I reckon's good,' the barman was saying. 'A crossbow.'

'A crossbow? For fishing?'

'That's it.' He did a little dumb show, for the bloke with the broken neck, showing how you stand in a boat, look down into the water, and fire at the fish.

'Yeah, well, I still reckon you can't beat a rifle with a flash torch attached to the barrel,' the bloke with the broken neck said.

'Yeah, yeah, it's good, it's good, I grant you. But you have trouble with batteries.'

'No, you don't, not if you've got a power pack strapped to your belt.'

'Good night,' I said.

Back in our motel room I found Ros watching T.V. and eating apples. We had eaten nothing but apples since we'd loaded up the car with them in Donnybrook. Although I wasn't hungry I polished three or four off myself. Then I double-locked the door, further secured it with a chair, and passed an uneasy night.

We left Walpole pretty smartly the next morning, for all that it looked more dramatic in daylight than it had in the dark. One of the reasons for visiting Walpole is Nornalup Inlet, a severely beautiful enclosure of water rescued from the Ocean, but we weren't prepared to give it more than a cursory look on the way out. We were going to have to move quickly today if we were to do our best by Denmark and Albany and still make it back to Perth before nightfall, so it was necessary that we become uncompromisingly terse in our evaluations.

'It seems to me that Nornalup belongs essentially to the drab-spectacular genre of landscape,' I said. 'It should be more striking than it actually is.'

'I'm against inlets,' Ros reminded me.

'I'm not in principle', I said, 'but I am in the case of this one.'

'It seems to me,' Ros went on, 'that there is altogether too little colour variation in the bush hereabouts. Olive seems to predominate.'

I thought that the trees were too uniformly gnarled also. Altogether we had it pretty sewn up between us that there was insufficient natural differentiation in and around Walpole.

After which there wasn't an awful lot to do until we got to Denmark except refuse a lift to a tattooed hitch-hiker with an eye-patch, and listen to part 20 of the Australian Broadcasting Corporation's serialization of *The Tenant of Wildfell Hall*. From the pace of the dramatization I estimated there were another 100 episodes to go. 'I have an infernal fire in my veins,' a character bearing a remarkable resemblance to Heathcliffe said, 'which all the waters of creation cannot quench.' Not having had breakfast yet, and not knowing whether we would be able to get any at Denmark, I knew how he felt.

On our arrival in Denmark (to quote *Great Expectations*), at five minutes short of nine (as they say at Wildfell Hall), we found only a pastry shop open and had to make do with a cherry and a vanilla slice, which Ros showed me how to eat without squelching the custard, on the banks of the Denmark River at a little picnic table in the Norm Thornton Park.

We discovered that we liked Denmark – its hilliness, its meandering river, its picturesque wooden bridge, its bandstand, and its equanimity about calling a park Norm. It also made Ros eat her words about inlets. ('But not the colour olive, Howard.') Wilson's Inlet, named after Dr Thomas Braidwood Wilson, and which should therefore have been called Tom Wilson's Inlet, was on a bigger scale than Nornalup and possessed all those qualities of grandeur and serenity that it lacked. A vast sheet of placid and protected water, surrounded by low-lying wooded hills, it was home to scores of black swans and pelicans. For the first time that I could remember I wished I owned binoculars. 'I think the reason I like pelicans,' I said to Ros, 'is that they can do everything I can't. They can fish, they can swim, they can fly, and they can store food.' She seemed to think this a fair explanation.

We found an excellent Tourist Bureau in Denmark, not just an office for the distribution of maps and guides, but a meeting place where you might be served coffee, where there were exhibits, extracts from old travel brochures on the walls, speci-mens of local nasties in pickle jars, and where the presiding genius of the place, a wiry Dutchman called Mr de Jongh, would tailor-make you an itinerary according to your particular interests. In the time it took us to read the label on a jar of pickled python, I heard him put together a three-day local wine and antique tour for a couple of ladies who had driven in across the Nullarbor from Adelaide.

Although the town of Denmark has nothing to do with the Scandinavian country of the same name – Tom Wilson had been responsible for the christening, having wanted to please an old naval chum, Dr Denmark – that hadn't stopped Mr de Jongh from trying to open up diplomatic relations between the two. On the wall I noticed a framed letter addressed to Mr de Jongh, from M. Wahl, Private Secretary to Her Majesty the Queen of Denmark, thanking him for his gift of a recent local history.

> Dear Mr de Jongh.
> It was very kind of you to send me some copies of 'The History of Denmark' – a township on the South Coast of Western Australia, and it was very interesting to read about this spot of the map. It's name is familiar, but otherwise Denmark is quite unknown to us.

And it went on to add that the book had been passed on to Queen Margrethe, and that one copy was now in the Royal Library and another in the Royal Reference Library.

'We are the only town to have an intimate relationship with a country,' Mr de Jongh told us.

Watching him twisting his mouth into that intelligently ironical shape that is necessary for the production of Dutch noises, I was reminded of how much I liked the semi-gargling sound Netherlanders make, brewing each word up at the back of their throats and then having to unpick it with their teeth. It all seemed of a piece to me, Mr de Jongh's pleasantness and efficiency and the work he had to put in to making sentences. Had he been an Australian drawler he wouldn't have been anything like so good at his job.

Rain. Real rain. Not counting storms in the far north, where the water was a mere incidental by-product of massive electrical disturbance, the first real rain we'd had in Australia. And Albany was a good place to have it. It had been threatening ever since we'd left Denmark, black clouds following us along the route Mr de Jongh had recommended, the whole length of the louring coast of Torbay. But it wasn't until we climbed up into Albany itself, and got our first sense of how this city had been clawed out of rock, and our first views down over King George's Sound, where there was twice as much water already as in Sydney Harbour, that the rain really fell. I hadn't read anything to suggest that this was absolutely normal for Albany, that day and night it enjoyed a warm and blinding rain, but I was unable to imagine it any other way. It was a dour, hard-won sprawling place. Vast and immovable granite boulders were littered about the streets. One, resembling a dog sniffing the air, had achieved such distinction as a natural work of sculpture that it had a brand new place of entertainment – the Dog Rock Motel – built opposite it. Two massive lookouts, Mt Melville and Mt Clarence, their summits hidden in swirling cloud, stood sentry over the town, contributing to its bleak grandeur.

We drove around for a while with our windscreen wipers going at double speed, waiting for the rain to ease. Ros wanted to run out into it, but I was able to dissuade her with the promise that as soon as we found a beach she could behave as unconventionally as she liked. Accordingly I kept driving away from water for as long as I could get away with it. Which was how we came to pass and pause at the Parish Church of St John the Evangelist, the oldest consecrated church in Western Australia, and how I came to notice just beside it the granite war memorial to the gallant sons of Albany killed in World War I. I don't normally read war memorials but something about this one caught my attention, and then my eyes played a trick upon me and made me believe I read my own name. In fact the Howard part belonged to a T. Howard, and the

Jacobson to an F. Jacobson just below him, separated only by
an Ingham, on the roll of honour. But the coincidence startled
me, as did the fact that there had ever been a Jacobson – not a
Jacobsen or a Jackobssenn – in Albany.

Softened by the association of my name with death and
bravery, I turned the car around and pointed it towards the
sea. The beach we at last found was deserted, the sand bleached
white, the prospect over the Sound to Michaelmas and
Breaksea Islands sublime. Behind us the wooden beach shacks
and the older colonial houses with balconies and verandahs
climbed the rocks to secure their views. We took our shoes
off and ran into the rain.

Then we drove up Mt Clarence to see the Desert Corps
Memorial, the Anzac statue which had originally stood in Port
Said but had taken a hammering in the Suez riots of 1956. Half-
way up Mt Clarence there is an avenue of trees, each one
dedicated to an Australian soldier who had fallen in World War
I, World War II, or Korea. I wondered whether there was a
Jacobson tree. I didn't really hold out any hope of finding one
but I felt it was my duty to look. Not many Jacobsons would
come this way. And it was such a foolish, uncommunicative,
made-up name, a mere convenience for harassed immigration
officials who couldn't get anything else out of the yammering
escapees from the pogroms except that they were so-and-so
and so-and-so son of Abraham or Isaac or Jacob. Even if you
weren't family you had to stick together with people who had
trodden that route. So I went looking for my namesake's tree
and I eventually came upon it. A small plaque carried the words
Private F. Jacobson – Killed in Action in France. His tree had a
commanding view back over the white sands of Middleton
Beach where Ros and I had just scampered barefoot. Nice for
him. I was upset and pleased, all at once.

From the top of the mountain we could see the whole
expanse of King George's Sound. It was there, below us, that

the Anzacs had gathered in their troopships, waiting to be delivered to Gallipoli. Altogether it was a good site for such an event – stern and magnificent and cruelly beautiful; grander than Sydney Harbour, more exhilarating and more fatally melancholy. But Albany itself could not be compared to Sydney. It was overpowered by its own panorama; a stone less precious than its setting.

Up here, with the wind blowing and the spectacle of the island-dotted waters far below, the Anzac statue – a bronze extravaganza of strong-jawed Aussies and rearing horses – could not fail to work its tawdry magic. They are great fraudulent *faits accomplis*, these memorials to fallen soldiers. Whatever the cause they fell in, whatever the politics of their commemoration, fall they did, and they are owed a tear out of the most primitive humanity. And so loyalty is forged and patriotism redoubled by means of a simple trespass on your decency. The paraphernalia of remembrance had its way with me, anyway, this afternoon, weakened as I already was by finding Private F. Jacobson's tree in the Avenue of Honour.

In the toilets at the bottom of the steps leading to the statue, I found the following graffito:

> Skipping through the jungle
> With my M-16
> I'm a mean mudda-fucker
> I'm a U.S. marine

Only someone had tried to obliterate the last line and substitute it with,

> I'm a typical dumbshit –

which, if it had the merit of pacifism, lacked the virtue of rhyme.

But then aggression must out, in some form or other.

It was doubtful whether Private Jacobson of Albany had fought for anything much – even if he thought he had – but I was sorry for him stretched out somewhere in France, having missed all the fun for the last seventy years. I was damned if I knew, however, which was to be preferred: being back in populous Europe as he was, never too far, wherever he lay, from a motorway or boulangerie, or lying in the unbearable stillness of Donnybrook, like Ros's grandma or the Chinaman Ah Yet, the kindly market gardener who in 1902 was murdered in his cabbage patch, just a stone's throw from the cemetery, for a five pound note, Australian currency.

TEN

THE TOWN WITH A ♥ OF GOLD

'All these bloody surveys they're doing,' the taxi driver said to me, 'it's time they did one on women's minds.'

He was furious because the woman driver in front of him was taking an eternity to move out into the traffic.

'What do you think they'd find?' I asked.

He took me to it by a roundabout route. 'You can be too safe,' he said. 'Don't get me wrong – I value caution. But you're a liability if you're too safe. Do you want to know the three most important qualities in a driver? Alertness. Concentration. And recklessness.'

So that's what a survey of women's minds would show up: irrefragable proof of their constitutional incapacity for driving recklessly.

I said, 'Maybe that's because they're used to having children in the car.'

'Not the ones I'm talking about,' he said. '*She* hasn't.'

'She hasn't *now*. But maybe her habits are formed from when she does have.'

By now he didn't like me much. 'It's a theory,' he said. But he made it pretty clear he wasn't buying it. The next passenger would almost certainly hear how it was time they did a survey on the minds of Poms.

It occurred to me, as I was paying him, that Perth might be one of the last places in the English-speaking world where you could have these sprawling conversations with taxi drivers. Melbourne and Sydney were out of the question now that the drivers only spoke Croatian. Bars and bullet-proof windows had put paid to New York. The very design of the cabs minimized communication in London, for which, given the spurious verbal vitality of London cab drivers, one had to be grateful. Only in Perth was a taxi ride still safe, philosophical, and largely in one's own language.

We seemed to live in taxis for our last two or three days in town. There were still people from Ros's past to see, and farewells to take of those we already had seen; there were more first nights in the company of Geoff and Carole Gibbs and the Governor to get to, and then there were our bags to pack and our travel arrangements to finalize. The plan was that we would cross the Nullarbor to Adelaide by train – one of the Great Train Journeys Of The World, according to people one would not in any other circumstances have trusted – stopping off at Kalgoorlie to get a quick squizz at the Goldfields. It sounded straightforward enough but turned out not to be, on account of our wanting to spend more than an hour but less than a year in Kalgoorlie, and on account of the trains being full. A twinkling little railway clerk in his sixties sat us down in the booking office for half a day and arranged our lives for us. We'd take the *Prospector* from Perth to Kalgoorlie on Sunday afternoon; we'd take the Trans-Australian from Kalgoorlie to Port Pirie at the crack of dawn on Thursday morning, changing at Port Pirie, on Friday afternoon, for Adelaide. We would travel First Class on the Trans-Australian in order to get the benefit of the piano bar, though he was sorry to tell Ros that the rear compartment with rounded windows which she remembered from earlier trips no longer existed. All this was subject, of course, to there being a couple of spare berths on the Trans-Australian, but he was prepared to guarantee us, at the last, that he personally would see to it that there would be even if that meant his having to link on an extra carriage with his own bare hands. In return for which we handed over a sizeable portion of our life savings and left.

I spent my last Sunday morning in Perth talking to a millionaire, possibly even to two. We had gone, with our luggage, to have an early lunch at the house of Ron and Sandra Wise, Ron being the son of the German family Ros had virtually grown up with. When I say that I spoke to possibly two millionaries, Ron was the possibly. The certainly was Denis Horgan, owner of the Leeuwin Estate Vineyards in Margaret River where the London Philharmonic and the Berlin Staatskapelle had played early Beethoven for the cream of West Australian society. He wasn't there, at the Wises's place, in person, but Ron led me to understand that he would have been if he could have been. 'I spoke to him only last night,' he said, 'and I mentioned that you were writing about Australia. He's expecting you to ring him.'

I thought that this meant sometime in the next thirty years, and made the sort of noises appropriate to the assumption; but Ron already had the phone off the hook. 'I'll dial the number for you now,' he said. I began to get some inkling of what made an entrepreneur.

Ron had once been an academic but hadn't enjoyed university life. Funny that. For all that he must have been in his early forties there was still a touch of gilded youth about him – a golden boy, if Jewish or half-Jewish boys can be called golden, trim and brown and dangerously handsome in tennis gear, but with a curious absence around the eyes, as if he were listening in to sounds from another room, or remembering events from another life. I had a theory about that: I believed that he was

forever preoccupied with the terms of some Faustian compact
he had made, too terrible to confide to those who loved him.
But I do veer towards melodrama when I try to put my mind
to businessmen.

Meanwhile, in another part of the city, another one was
picking up his phone. Ron didn't waste any time on preliminaries. None of the sorry to bother you's and I don't suppose
you remember but's of mere salaried telephone users. 'Denis?'
he simply said. 'This is Ron. I've got that journalist here.'

Although journalist can be a word of the keenest disapproba-
tion when one is at one's desk, it can carry a heavy charge of
responsibility when one is, so to speak, in the field. Journalist?
Weren't journalists people who asked questions? In all honesty
I could not think of a single question I wanted to hear the
owner of the most successful vineyard in West Australia answer.
But the phone was in my hands, a pleasant voice was saying,
'G'day, Howard,' and through the window I could see Ron's
friends, also in their tennis gear, sipping Pinot Blanc around the
pool. 'G'day, Denis,' I said, 'I wonder if you can tell me how
Sidney Nolan feels about having one of his paintings decorating
a wine bottle?'

I surprised myself by how prim I sounded. I knew that I was
still the proud possessor of some residual Leavisite moralizing –
the lees in the ageing cask of my maturity – but I hadn't intended
to be ungracious.

In the circumstances, Denis Horgan made a good job of staying affable. 'Fine wine and art and food go together in quite a
happy mix, Howard,' he said. 'And I'll tell you something
else – when we buy or commission these works of art, we offer
the painters the option of how they would like to be paid. And
some of them don't mind being remunerated in bottles, I can
assure you.'

The idea of Sidney Nolan driving down to Margaret River
with his latest canvas and driving back with a boot full of

Gewürztraminers was so pleasing to me that I wasn't able to concentrate as fully as I ought to have on whatever else Denis Horgan had to say. I do remember, though, that Leeuwin is a 'high-tech winery'; that 60 per cent of what it produces is consumed in the eastern states; that it is sold in the U.K. by Hobbs of South Audley Street – a shop owned by Lady McAlpine, wife of the very Lord McAlpine whose hand (I won't say whose dead hand) was all over Broome; and that Denis Horgan's own objective is and always has been excellence. 'I am used to taking up challenges and succeeding with them,' he told me.

I asked him if he was a doctor like all the other Margaret River vignerons. He was amused by that. 'No,' he said, 'a chartered accountant.'

'Get your story?' Ron asked me, after I'd put the phone down.

I threw him a rugged professional journalist's smile. But he hadn't finished doing me favours yet. Before we left he'd fixed up our accommodation in Kalgoorlie and organized us an interview with the Mayor. 'You went to school with his daughter, Leonie,' he reminded Ros, 'I was talking to her only yesterday. She's expecting you to ring her. I'll dial her number for you now.'

It took the *Prospector* 7½ hours to do the 650-odd kilometres to Kalgoorlie, which averages out at about 87 kilometres or 52 miles an hour. It felt slower. The *Prospector* consisted of two carriages and hostesses who served sandwiches made of cheese slices. For some reason each carriage had fitted carpets on the ceiling. The train suffered from a perpetual judder, an oscillation over and above what you normally expect from rail travel, as if it didn't quite fit the track.

The journey passed unremarkably. Whenever I looked out of the window I saw a field of washed-out golden wheat or a salt plain. The town site of Cunderdin stays in my mind because it was there that I saw a man standing on the little platform reading a Hungarian novel at the same time as the voice of Ann Blyth came through the speaker system, singing 'Only Make Believe'.

Ron had booked us in at the Old Australia Hotel. I can't pretend that we paid much attention to where the taxi was taking us; after the grinding tedium of the *Prospector* and the second lunch and high tea and early dinner of cheese slice sandwiches we would have been content to sleep out in the streets. But in the morning we were excited to find that our room had access to a lovely broad balcony, decorated with palms and ferns and fitted out with comfortable bamboo furniture, from where we were able to look out upon the main thoroughfare of Kalgoorlie.

Quite what we were seeing I am not sure that I have ever fully understood. Open up a map of Australia and Kalgoorlie doesn't appear too promising. If you discount Coolgardie, which is now a ghost town, and Boulder, which is just more Kalgoorlie anyway, it looks a long way from anywhere. It is a few streets in a desert. And yet by 8.30 in the morning, before the sun had been able to get in under our curving corrugated verandah roof, the crossroads on which our hotel was situated were as busy as Hyde Park Corner. Where was all that traffic going to? Where had it been?

We passed a couple of hours in this fashion, sitting amongst the tropical bamboo and fernery, trying to work out why we were exhilarated when we might have been appalled. Quickly thrown-up shanty towns can generate a marvellous temporary atmosphere of ferment and turbulence, as we were to discover in Coober Pedy, but apart from the evidence of the electricity poles marching down the very middle of the road, as if there hadn't been time to think of anywhere else to put them,

Kalgoorlie didn't really look as though it had been rattled up yesterday on the understanding that no one expected it would still be there tomorrow. If anything it had a solid, grandiose, even respectable air, notwithstanding the notices in the windows of the hotels reminding clients that Wednesday was C-THRU WAITRESS night. The hotels, in fact, seemed to hold the clue to Kalgoorlie. The town was famous for them – for how many it had and for the extravagance of their architecture. We could see several from where we sat – Speed's Criterion Hotel, just to the left of Mateo's Pizza Bar, with its small fantastical façade painted white, green, and pink, and its ramshackle balcony; the Palace, commanding and confident, built in 1897, a mere four years after Paddy Hannan's discovery of gold; and the Exchange, picture-postcard colonial quaint, a queer mix of the frontier and the ecclesiastical, with turrets and gables and a slightly tipsy look. They were ebullient and brash – that was why we liked them. They seemed to have been built, to support the colossal new wealth, not in a spirit of opportunism but as if out of an unstoppable communal optimism.

Altogether, Kalgoorlie reminded us of much that we had enjoyed in the Northern Territory. We were suddenly very glad we had left Perth. You couldn't mistake *this* for Europe. I wasn't myself all that cheered to be amongst 4-wheel drives and 'roo bars once more, the gadgetry of authentic outback-ism. But we agreed on this: it was good to see Aborigines in the streets again. Even if the Aborigines themselves didn't think much of it.

Tucked away in the Kalgoorlie Town Hall is a little jewel of a gaiety theatre, with eight tiers of tip-seated iron-framed chairs, all at dress-circle level and all sumptuously upholstered in crimson velvet. The balcony itself describes a graceful curve and has alabaster ornamentations tipped with gold. The pressed-tin roof features a fleur-de-lys design and is painted in airy pastel colours – pinks, creams, and swooning blues. On either side of the diminutive proscenium arch is a painting depicting an Arcadian, or at least a determinedly un-Australian, landscape. According to the only relevant bit of literature I could lay my hands on in the Town Hall, the theatre was built in 1908 and 'brilliantly lighted with a central electrolier of 1,500 candle power'. Thus did energy and culture come early to the infant gold town of Kalgoorlie.

I noted from the portraits of past dignitaries in the council room that the name of the Mayor officiating at the time of the theatre's construction was Mark Rosenberg. I was to try several times during our stay in Kalgoorlie to discover something about this rather melancholy, unmunicipal-looking man, but never succeeded. All I unearthed about the semitic history of the goldfields was that a pickpocket of international reputation, known as Jack the Jew, had been active in the area in the early part of the century. According to all accounts, Jack the Jew could slip the watch off your wrist and the braces out from underneath your waistcoat without your knowing the first thing about it. So it was probably a good job that his talents were regulated by a nice sense of honour; that his victims were primarily imprudent drunkards whose belongings Jack would spread amongst needy widows, or just hold in safe keeping until their owners were sober enough to deserve them back.

You would think that a place like Kalgoorlie, with its natural taste for eccentricity and lawlessness, would put up plaques to shining examples like Jack the Jew, instead of to the more conventional figures who have passed through, men such as Herbert Hoover, whose only distinction, once he'd served here as a young mining engineer at the end of the last century, was to go on and become President of the United States.

High office, however, works its potency on all of us, as I discovered when we were ushered into Mayor Finlayson's

private office. He was expecting us, naturally. I was a friend of
Ron Wise. And Rosalin was a friend of Leonie's. Such connections oil the machinery in W.A. But that didn't stop him
watching me cautiously from under the drape of his heavy,
slanting eyebrows. He had been around a long time, a force in
Kalgoorlie for years; he wasn't going to warm to the first journalist married to a friend of his daughter's to come in off the
streets. He was dressed casually, for work, with his shirtsleeves
rolled up – a short, nuggety man, who when he was younger
might have had the air of what pulp writers call a street-fighter.
He took me through the official line on Kalgoorlie. The town
was enjoying a boom incomparable to anything it had known
before. Contrary to all the pessimistic predictions of the previous decades, the price of gold was higher than it had ever been
and the production capacity of Kalgoorlie was limitless. 'The
ore zones on the Fimiston bases will never,' he told me, 'I
repeat *never* cut out.' Considering his lack of interest in me, and
my lack of interest in ore zones, he managed to make that revelation sound wonderfully thrilling. 'They're here till eternity,'
he went on. As a consequence of which, nothing but expansion
was expected. Houses were being built at the cost of a million
dollars a month. A Mint was coming. A Mint Museum would
be built. A man called Stuart Devlin, jeweller to the Queen and
a lover of Kalgoorlie, was to oversee the design and manufacture of gold and bijouterie at the new Mint. But all this could
be jeopardized, at a stroke, if Chancellor Keating was allowed
to implement his proposed tax on gold. The Federal Gold Tax –
that was the spectre at the feast.

'What part of London are you from?' Mayor Finlayson
suddenly asked me.

His eyes lit up when I told him. 'Ah, yes,' he said. 'Ah, yes.'
I assumed from this unexpected lapse into emotion that he had
lived in our very street.

'You know London then?'

'Only from maps,' he said.

Somebody rang while we were talking, and he slipped effort-lessly out of this vaguely absent-minded, almost melancholy mood into a tone of vigorous contention.

'Ah, come on, Milton,' he said – out of the blue I was struck by what a formidable opponent he would be – 'you're not going to swallow *that*!'

Before we parted he gave me his card. It was printed in red type on a gold background, and said,

RAY FINLAYSON
MAYOR OF KALGOORLIE

On the back was the caption,

THE TOWN WITH A ♥ OF GOLD

Just as Ron Wise had handed me on to Ray Finlayson, so did Ray Finlayson pass me on down the line to Stanley Brown. A sorrowing, exiled Englishman who would have been played by Peter Barkworth had his life been televised, Stanley Brown was manager of the Australian Broadcasting Corporation in Kalgoorlie. I met him in his offices where he sat surrounded by tapes and schedules. It's always intriguing to see who's just been or who's just coming into a radio station and I was pleased to notice that Geoff Gibbs had popped through only recently to discuss the current state of Australian theatre. I had the feeling that Stanley Brown would have liked there to be even more of that kind of thing on Radio 6GR, Kalgoorlie.

He talked to me about England, which he hadn't seen for twenty-five years. 'Not a deliberate decision,' he explained, 'just finances. I've got four boys to educate and they don't pay you very much here.' It felt as though he were manning a British Council outpost, and making the usual sacrifices in the name of the culture. Then he somehow got on to the years he spent as a sergeant in the British Army serving in Israel after the War. His memories seemed to upset him. He referred to the blowing up of the King David Hotel with his eyes lowered. 'I used to pass a bit of time in the Garden of Gethsemane when I could,' he said. He actually closed his eyes, remembering this, a look of faraway pain passing over his face, a high airy cloud, showing how remote he now felt he was from the first part of his life. 'There is something there in that garden, you know. Some spirituality.'

I closed my own eyes. Anyone coming into the room would have thought we were praying together.

Later on, after he'd finished work, he took us for an early evening snifter at Hannan's, the only real club in Kalgoorlie, an institution so exclusive that even the person after whom it was named – the very Paddy Hannan whose gold strike had begun it all – did not qualify for membership.

Hannan's dates from about 1896, the heyday of Kalgoorlie prosperity, and offers all the amenities expected of a social club – a bowling green, meeting rooms, bars, squash courts (which do not date from 1896) and two billiard tables described by Eddie Charlton as the finest in Australia. In order that they might stay that way an unusual degree of restraint is demanded of players. 'Members are respectfully requested,' a warning sign on the beautifully polished scoreboard reads, 'to refrain from lying on the billiard tables when playing.' Which might have been why no one was playing on the night I visited the club.

Strictly speaking we were doubly fortunate to be there at all that evening. The Rural and Industrial Bank had commandeered the club in order to rub shoulders with its local customers (15 million dollars' worth of business in investments alone that year), and we had the waitresses as well as Stanley Brown to thank for our smooth inclusion into the gathering. They winked at us and made a point of filling our beer glasses the moment

they saw them empty, as if the slight impropriety of our presence called out something rebellious in them.

Stanley introduced me to two people he thought I might
find interesting – the Head of Kalgoorlie College and a
Hospital Administrator. 'So at a stroke I meet the Arts and
Science of the town,' I said. No joke I have made has ever
gone down worse. Neither person put up so much as a
pretence of finding it funny, clever, or just plain conversationally helpful. From the corner of my eye I could see Ros
backing to the opposite corner of the room, her face frozen
into an expression of horrified perplexity. After three or four
minutes of complete silence the Hospital Administrator told
me that he had never before heard hospital administration
described as a science. 'I was assuming,' I said, in one last bid
for an urbane reversal, 'that you were the arts.' But even that
didn't win him round. He was a dismal man, filing-cabinet
grey, with a neck as thin as a pen, mislaid in what I think is
called a leisure shirt. He shook his head at me and walked
away. Which is how I came to get the chance to talk at length
to Dick Lamb, the Head of Kalgoorlie College, the Arts *and*
Science of the town if anybody was.

Dick Lamb wore his hair in the fashion favoured by Kingsley
Amis and John Wain and all those other Oxford-educated writers of the fifties – a kind of angry fall on one side, not a lock
exactly, and not strictly speaking a quiff, more a sort of brusque
cultural curlicue. He had their quality of delayed boyishness
too. He made jerky movements, wild bodily expostulations
which he would apologize for as soon as made, waving his arms
and staggering sideways and saying, 'Sorry, sorry!' and slapping
his head.

'Any day now I'm going to retire,' he told me, 'to make
room for younger bulls and heifers, and to write a science
fiction novel. Asimov's my model. I don't know how long
it's going to take me, and frankly I don't care. But in ten

years' time you should keep your eyes peeled for a decrepit but hitherto unknown science fiction writer called Richard Janus.'

He caught me looking at his name tag, which still said Dick Lamb. 'Janus,' he explained, tossing his hair and tapping his nose, 'after the Roman god who faces both ways.'

'Oh,' I said. But I wasn't able to hide my mystification. I hadn't made the connection yet between Lamb and facing both ways.

Puns and double-puns danced in his eyes like boy acrobats. 'What am I going to need to succeed?' he asked me. 'Luck. What do we call luck in Australia?'

I thought about it. 'Jam,' I finally said.

He slapped his forehead, shot out his elbows, and fell into a waitress carrying a tray of crumbed prawns. 'Arse!' he shouted. Then, realizing where he was, he apologized, brought his face close to mine, and whispered, 'Arse.'

I smiled and tried to look as though, yes, yes, I was gradually getting there.

'Arse becomes anus,' he went on. 'Anus is part of Janus. The Romans had no letter J. They called him I Anus. And that's me – Dick Janus.'

'Compared to the complexity of thinking up your pen-name the actual writing of the book should be a doddle,' I said.

I lost him after that, for a little while, or rather he lost me. I wish now that I hadn't succumbed so readily to the waitresses' jacobinical inclinations, and had been in less of a hurry to empty my beer glass. Because I never did follow Dick Lamb to the point where he was able triumphantly to affirm that the only philosophy which would take us safely into the twenty-first century was a form of classical rationality tinged with the best of contemporary mysticism. 'Cogito ergo summus,' he said. (Did that mean, I think therefore I *really, really* am?) 'Parapsychology will come into its own.'

'As in America?' I asked, because it was time I asked something.

He fell sideways, and let me know sotto voce (sotto voce for *him*) – just in case there were any American parapsychologists present here tonight in Kalgoorlie at a social given by the R&I Bank – that he didn't think all that highly of the instinctive sciences as practised in that part of the world. Reminding me once again of how like an Oxford arts graduate of the fifties he was.

But his own temerity only served to remind him of the ironies of cultural differences. 'There I was,' he said, 'trying to pass on the virtues of European scepticism – you know, the Socratic tradition of learning through questioning – to these student Aboriginal teachers, when suddenly one of them put up his hand. "This is all very well, Mr Lamb," he says, "but Aboriginal children are trained never to question their teachers."'

He threw me a wild stare, certain that I'd never looked upon a greater fool. 'See?' he said. 'See? I'd made a fundamental error. That was that. I was done for.'

'So what did you do?'

'Do?'

'About the Aboriginal teachers.'

He shrugged. And a shrug from Dick Lamb was no mere twitch of the shoulders. It was a massive contortion. He put his whole body into it. Even his toes got involved. But that was the only answer he gave to my question. The next minute he was introducing me to Ted Cockram, and elbowing his way out of the room.

Ted Cockram was Tourism Manager for the Goldfields. He related a cautionary story – a sort of tourist manager's nightmare – about the time he was promoting the Gascoyne River Area in the north of the State and suddenly discovered that Mt Augustus, a biggish but otherwise undistinguished lump of rock sitting plumb in his patch, was listed in the *Guinness Book of Records* as the world's largest monolith. Hello, thought Ted, where does that leave Ayers Rock? More specifically, where did it leave those thousands of visitors to Ayers Rock who thought they were climbing the world's largest monolith when all along they should have been shinning up Mt Augustus? A polite note to the custodians of Ayers Rock, to the effect that Ted's rock was bigger than theirs was, brought a visit to Mt Augustus by a party of geologists. Strictly speaking, they said in their report – and geologists only speak strictly – Mt Augustus was not a monolith at all; it was a cluster not an integer, a set not a singleton, a society not a celibate. Affronted by this insult to the integrity of his boulder, Ted sent the report to the compilers of the *Guinness Book of Records* so that they might roundly refute it and once and for all compel the little red nodule in the Central Australian Desert to own itself bested. Back, in due course, came a letter thanking Ted Cockram for his information, apologizing for the confusion, and promising that Mt Augustus would be removed from the *Guinness Book of Records* forthwith.

'And that's how I bulldozed my only tourist attraction off the map,' Ted said.

Talking to Mayor Finlayson again I noticed that he did not in fact have bushy eyebrows, but that the effect of hoodedness was a function of the eyelids, that the very skin had over-arched, ideology appropriating the flesh, exactly as it had with Harold Macmillan and Robert Menzies and Margaret Thatcher. But the Mayor's eyes themselves were a beautiful soft brown, and the kinder tonight for reflecting the animation of a social occasion. 'There are at least ten millionaires in this room,' he told me, 'and you wouldn't be able to pick one of them. We're not interested in flashing it the way they do in Perth.'

'You're not impressed by the Americas Cup impresarios?'

He pulled a face. He had, of course, to be circumspect. 'Good luck to them,' he said. 'But I need to be convinced that they're doing any good for Western Australia.'

The question of what was or wasn't good for Western Australia brought us back rapidly to the gold tax. Mayor Finlayson was an active member of AGIC – the Australian Goldmining Industry Council – a body pledged to bring to the attention of the Australian people the disastrous consequences of an added tax burden on gold. Publicity was everything. 'This is where people like you can help us,' the Mayor said. I felt instantly fraudulent. But I did help him out with a little campaign poem, the seeds of which he himself planted when he said, 'We will succeed in fighting this measure. Even if it means secession.'

'If at first we don't succeed, then at last we will secede,' I sang.

That wasn't quite what he wanted. 'We will succeed, and if success means that we must secede, then we will secede,' he preferred. I didn't rate his scansion but I believed him. Or at least I believed in the sincerity of his passion. It was absurdly exhilarating, standing with the Mayor of Kalgoorlie in Paddy Hannan's club plotting a breakaway. It was like sitting up late with Lenin in his flat in London, poking the fire.

Then we met the Rowes – Keith and Lesley – a striking couple from Perth come to make good in Kalgoorlie. Keith was a physiotherapist. He lustred when I observed that there must be a fair bit of call for a physio in a mining town. 'That's why I came,' he told me.

Lesley lustred also. They were a lustrous pair. Lesley, darkly ruminative and lazy-eyed; Keith, keen and piercing with a Roman nose and shoulders so taut that he looked in need of his own professional services. There was a gripping, almost alarming intensity about Keith. No one else that I had so far met in Kalgoorlie resembled him; so that I came to see him as representative of the new young spirit abroad in the goldfields. And he loved the town. He raved over its confidence and independence and vigour. He talked of 'lovely old blokes' and 'marvellous men', and alluded, just like Ray Finlayson, to the number of subfusc millionaires in the room. 'See that one there,' he said. 'He's worth ten million and lives in a house more modest than ours.' I happened already to have met the very person he was pointing at. I'd met his wife too. She was wearing a flounced acrylic party frock which wouldn't have cost more than ten dollars at the little girl's counter of Woolworths. She had refused to exchange a single word with me, concentrating instead on trying to persuade her plain plutocrat of a husband to leave the party because it was time to feed the chooks. I mentioned this to Keith. His eyes burned. 'Marvellous people,' he said. 'Rich as Croesus.'

Strictly speaking, Keith and Lesley shouldn't have been lingering themselves. They had planned to attend a public meeting, addressed by a visiting real estate expert, in the course of which they would be taught how to become property millionaires. It was a sign of how well we were all getting on that they were prepared to miss the meeting and jeopardize their futures.

They seemed to be the sort of people who got their ideas from public meetings. The last one they'd been to was given by someone who had once belonged to the Land Rights movement but had woken up in the nick of time to the fact that it was communist-inspired. This *éclaircissement* had fully convinced Keith and Lesley that a communist conspiracy lay behind Aboriginal agitation. It seemed wholly unacceptable to them that mining areas and crucial minerals should be handed over, via Aborigines, to the avowed enemies of Australia.

'Think of it like this,' Keith said, 'they could just make a present of the whole shebang to the communists.'

It would be no exaggeration to say that in the reflection of his eyes I actually saw it go, I actually saw the whole shebang being handed over. It wasn't all that difficult to understand his fears. Unreason is not mysterious. He was a young man already turning a distinguished grey about the temples. Something desirable, immeasurable but palpable, lay within his reach. He didn't want it to be taken from him before he'd even got it. He was greedy, yes; but it would be wrong to see the object of that greed as simply wealth. There used to be a time, before share-brokers discredited ambition, when it was possible to talk without disparagement about a lust or a greed or a hunger for life. Kirk Douglas made a good living playing characters who quivered under the demands of precisely such a hunger. He would have done an excellent job with the part of Keith.

'Isolation,' according to a quasi-official typed report I found in the public library, 'and the comparatively high masculinity factor of the population are the prime reasons for the development of an unusual entertainment pattern in Kalgoorlie.' For entertainment pattern read gambling and sex. For *unusual* entertainment pattern read *overt* gambling and sex.

In fact, for all the aura of infamy which surrounds its name, there isn't much that goes on in Kalgoorlie that would shock the inhabitants of a city the size of Cirencester. The illegal two-up schools, where old-timers stand around all day tossing coins into the air and waiting to see whether they come down heads or tails, are now virtually on the tourist route. As indeed are the girls in their lit-up tin boxes on Hay Street. Vice runs out of ideas almost as quickly as television, and there's a limit to what anyone can get up to in a desert.

And yet it is precisely because Kalgoorlie is a country town in the middle of nowhere that its notorious flesh market – a *tableau vivant* of whores in comfy horseboxes – is so bizarre. I took a look for myself once the R&I Bank's thank-you party at Hannan's had finally fizzled out. One minute I was walking down a broad, dusty, absolutely silent suburban road – the humming town behind me, the open bush before – the next I was being smiled at by girls in their nighties, sitting on the edges of their beds under tantalizing red lights, or pacing the porches of miniature simulacra of the ideal Australian home. More than anything else I was reminded of those garage sales that little girls from nice families put on in summer months, their old dollies and a few fairy cakes laid out on a trestle table, and not a customer in sight. The power of Australian provincialism can conquer all. The demimonde had come to Moonee Ponds.

Despite Kalgoorlie's high masculinity factor I was very nearly the only hominid on the street. Occasionally a car pulled up – caked with dust and fitted out with 'roo bars front and rear – opened its windows, and then drove off again.

'How are you?' one of the girls asked me.

I told her I was fine and asked how she was. 'Good, thanks,' she said. From the way she squeezed her vowels I thought she might have been a New Zealander.

Another one called out, 'Hello, you look intelligent.'

But I knew I couldn't trust her judgement. She had *Desiderata* hanging in her porch, and Kipling's *If*.

We gave the whole of the following day over to getting on and off tourist buses. Our morning guide was called Guy. 'G'day I'm Guy yer guide,' he told us. He made atrocious puns and then – a capital offence, I've always thought – apologized for them. But he was otherwise efficient, interspersing gossip with information and allowing just enough of his politics to show. Yes, the hand of Bondy had stretched into Kalgoorlie – you could see it right there, on the Mount Percy Open-Cut Mine – and yes, there were mixed attitudes to that; but better a West Australian own it, Guy thought, than . . . well, than anyone else.

The main problem in Kalgoorlie and Boulder was dust. In 1892 visibility in Kalgoorlie had remained at nil for a whole twenty-four hours. It wasn't so bad now. A Goldfields Dust Abatement Committee had the matter in hand, planting trees and otherwise devising methods of keeping the ground on the ground. Of especial concern still, though, were the tailing stumps – the flat hills of waste which marched across the landscape – since these contained cyanide and arsenic. Pollution altogether was a sticky issue. Before we left Kalgoorlie we were to hear the Mayor deny that there was any. But I was struck by the effect the dust had on the town's graveyard. I'm speaking aesthetically now. It had settled prettily on the headstones, softening the usual grey severity with a blush of almost roseate pink. Kalgoorlie's was the only carnation-coloured cemetery I had ever seen.

A descent of 200 feet into Hainault Mine, in the heart of the Golden Mile, was, if that isn't a contradiction in terms, the high spot of our tour. Wearing our brightly coloured hard hats – Ros and I looking remarkably like the Thatchers on a building site, I thought – we crowded into the little lift, six at a time, and began to learn what it was like to be a miner. 'If you think it's difficult to move and difficult to see, you'll soon discover how difficult it was to hear.' John Yellard told us. He had been a miner himself for forty years, originally in Cornwall but subsequently in South Africa, North America, Malaysia, and finally Kalgoorlie. Now he earned his crust the clean and easy way, scaring the living daylights out of tourists with his stories. 'We called this the widow-maker,' he explained, showing us the compressed air drill used for making holes to take explosive charges, 'on account of how it sent out so much dry dust that no miner who used it could expect to live for more than about eight years.' He threw a beer can down one of the vast empty shafts, created when the eyes between the exhausted levels had been picked out. We listened as it ricocheted in the darkness, taking an eternity to reach the bottom. 'I have to do a lot of drinking to provide those cans,' he said. He singled out a sweet old lady. 'A labour of love, though, my dear,' he told her.

He was a good operator, John Yellard. He abounded in what's called Cornish charm. Like many Cornishmen he was a curious mix of the raconteur and the recluse; there was a slight collapse, almost feminine, around his jaw, but the rest of his face was criss-crossed with hard lines of bitter experience. He frequently referred to the miner as 'a beast of burden', and made a habit of beginning his sentences, 'Of course no self-respecting mine,' by which he meant us to understand, 'Of course no profit-conscious' one.

Watching him going through his routine I was assailed by revolutionary emotions. It was hugely depressing, suddenly, being down there, thinking of the noise, the darkness, the discomfort, the risk, and the entrepreneurs on the surface, where it was light, waiting for the gold to come up. As if he'd read my thoughts – and why shouldn't he? he'd put them there – John Yellard said, 'Many people ask, after they've seen what I've just shown you, why anyone would become a miner. I'll tell you. Mateship. There's no camaraderie in the world like that between miners. All politics get forgotten. If a miner is trapped in South Africa or Ireland, no one asks if he is black or white, Protestant or Catholic – they get him out.'

Well, if he said so. But it seemed to me that what the voice pronounced, the face denied. Somewhere within himself John Yellard was more radical than sentimental. But the idea of loyalty engendered by deprivation had got him, and turned him inside out, and drawn his teeth, as it had millions of others.

Back on the surface, buying postcards in the Hainault Mine Gift Shop, we heard on the radio that President Reagan had bombed Libya. It crossed all our minds that we might be better off heading underground again.

★ ★ ★

I invented an expression, while I was in Kalgoorlie, to go alongside 'As good as gold'. It was, 'Less fickle than nickel'. Only a few years before, when gold was in the doldrums, nickel had been adjudged to be the goldfields' saviour, 'the key', as a contemporary report put it, 'to the region's and to Kalgoorlie's future'. Now you couldn't give it away. Kambalda, where the highest grade sulphide nickel ore in the world was mined, was surviving on whatever bits of gold turned up accidentally in its nickel pans. That's if it was surviving at all. When we drove out there that afternoon we found it strike-bound. Deserted. Just as earlier we'd found the smelter silent, a handful of men in hard hats pretending to be busy sweeping the access roads.

Kambalda was half old mining settlement – East Kambalda – and half new mining settlement – West Kambalda – situated about sixty kilometres down the track from Kalgoorlie. West Kambalda had to be built when it was discovered by the Western Mining Corporation that East Kambalda was sitting on nickel. Now the nickel was sitting on the Western Mining Corporation; the Western Mining Corporation was sitting on the unions; and we were sitting on the bus. From where Kambalda – either Kambalda – didn't look too promising. Its atmosphere reminded me of those uranium towns we had driven through in the Northern Territory, part comprehensive school on long vacation, part minimum security prison from which the inmates had all bolted out of boredom. The advantages of living here, according to Jill, our sweetly bigoted and bottled-up afternoon replacement for Guy, were clean shops, subsidized rents, and phenomenonally cheap electricity. 'And yet,' she sighed, 'and yet they strike. Ah well.'

Ah well was just one of the catchphrases that contributed to Jill's all-round winning charm; others she favoured included But there you are, and Ho Hum. She also crashed the gears of the bus. And expressed surprise when things took. By things taking she meant businesses prospering or ideas catching on.

On the way out of Kalgoorlie she had driven us past a new health club which everyone in town was going to. 'I never thought it would take,' Jill said, 'but there you are.'

Something in her nature was altogether more soothed by the example of a number of self-help schemes for Aborigines which had been tried out lately. 'I don't know,' she said, 'we all had high hopes for them but they just didn't take. Ah well.'

Since we couldn't get to see much at Kambalda, Jill drove us to the great salt flat of Lake Lefroy, where you could always count on a good mirage. Sure enough, a beguiling silver sea beckoned us from the horizon. 'It was here,' Jill told us, 'that Donald Campbell once tried to break his own land speed record, but the surface was too damp. Ho hum.'

'What, you mean the salt wouldn't take?' an American woman on the seat behind me asked. I wanted to hug her. I would have liked to name the lake after her. Lake Lila.

Then I realized she wasn't making a joke. That's what women like Jill do to you. They make you so desperate that you can actually forget that Americans don't have a sense of humour.

Back in Kalgoorlie Jill handed round a white plastic bucket from which we helped ourselves to a piece of stone with a glint of nickel in it. 'If you put them in vinegar for four or five days beautiful colours will appear,' she said. She was all breathless-ness and charm, a flashing prism of harmless girlish contrivances. 'Then paint them with clear nailpolish and the colours will stay, oh, for as long as you want.'

I threw my nickel into the dirt the second I left the bus.

But it wasn't a completely wasted afternoon. We had seen the country around Kalgoorlie and been surprised by it. Who would have thought that pink soil could be attractive? Or that there would be a luminescent quality about the bush, almost a glitter in the foliage? And I had found another tree to like – the gimlet tree, a twisting eucalypt with burnished leaves and a trunk which looked as though it had been dappled by the dust but was in fact its own colour, a sort of tarnished bronze, as if imbued in equal measure with the red and gilt of the Goldfields.

The following morning, while I did an interview for Stanley Brown's book programme, Ros took her courage in both hands and climbed aboard another bus. This one was going to Coolgardie, whose desertion, unlike Kambalda's, was the very reason you visited it. When I met her back at our hotel at lunchtime she wore a frazzled, slightly nauseous expression. I knew the look. It meant that she had seen a ghost. And I knew the ghost she had seen. Cornwall.

'So how was Coolgardie?' I asked her.

'Pixilated.'

'Oh, no,' I said.

There was no chance she was going to let me off. Some ghosts we had to see together. 'You will recall that stage of a town's life where it is down on its luck,' she said, 'where all its real activity is in the past, but one or two locals keep plugging on, buying up properties cheap and not having the money to renovate them properly, so that when at last it becomes visitable as a relic, they *are* the town?' (I kept my head lowered. I didn't want to be reminded.) 'Well, that's what's happened to Coolgardie. The most active local landlord seems to own about twenty houses. Which is very nearly all the houses in the town. He has painted these – and I don't just mean the woodwork, I mean the stone itself – sea green. The roofs he has painted pillar-box red. He is currently searching for a mineral which will cure cancer. He is certain it is in Coolgardie somewhere. He reckons "the outlook here is bright". There's an open-air museum, next to the petrol-station-cum-junk-shop – all of which he owns – jammed with rusting objects, of no value in themselves and of no interest as exhibits. Next door to that there's someone who collects limbs of trees which resemble human beings. He glues on gemstones where their eyes would be and sticks a school cap on their heads.'

'Oh, no,' I said.

'In the gemstone shop the entire stock, and I include fixtures and fittings in that, consists of six tiny cardboard boxes, three containing a handful of stones from West Australia, two from America. Do you want to know what was in the sixth box? Two balls of knitting wool-rusted. There is also an 'Ye Olde Bottle Shoppe.'

'Oh, no,' I said. I thought of Delabole. 'Not bottles.'

'Oh, yes.' But she had even worse to tell me. 'And the National Trust has moved in.'

'Ah well then, it's terminal,' I said.

She had however – or maybe therefore – liked the cemetery, where there was not only a small Jewish section but also the grave of Ernest Giles, the first white man to see Ayers Rock, and a couple of headstones, both facing Mecca, to Afghans. 'Sacred to the Memory of Tagh Mahomed,' says one. 'Who died by the hand of an assassin at Coolgardie, Jan 10th 1896.' What Ros wasn't able to ascertain was whether that was the same Afghan who'd been shot dead for offending against the rules of the Sunday morning communal haircut and shaving ritual. Only when it rained was anyone allowed a shower. Otherwise it was everyone in the same water: first the faces, then the tails, and last the feet. The Afghan met his when they caught him bathing his toes out of turn in a clean tank.

'Anyway, one good thing came out of this morning,' Ros said. 'All the old ladies off the bus gathered round me when they saw me taking notes. They wondered if I was doing my school project.'

'What did you tell them?'

'What do you think? I told them yes.'

★ ★ ★

We had another school project to attend to in the afternoon. Ted Cockram, the Tourism Manager who'd wiped Mt Augustus off the map, had invited us along to the Hospitality Inn to hear the official public release of the Goldfields Region Tourism Development Plan. This was a set of proposals put up by the Western Australian Tourism Commission following upon an independent assessment of the area's touristical options prepared by a Perth firm of independent consultants called Hames Sharley Australia. Setting aside the complications of which man in a blue suit represented which body, I was to find it difficult to concentrate this afternoon because I was certain that Hames Sharley Australia was something I had once heard the Queen say, by way of an encouragement, during a televised Christmas message to the Commonwealth.

It also wasn't to help the cause of clarification – though it would prove instructive in every other way – that the person sitting next to me in the audience should turn out to be no one less than Charles 'Digger' Daws, the Shire President of Boulder, Mayor Finlayson's keenest, most vocal, and most long-standing rival. The politics of co-operation and enmity between the twin towns of Kalgoorlie and Boulder are too vexed for any mere outsider ever to master; but it had already been explained to me that the reason Ray Finlayson was a Mayor while Digger Daws was only a Shire President lay in the mysterious attempted municipal putsch of 1969, in the course of which something was done to somebody by somebody else, and Kalgoorlie which had been the Shire Council became the Town Council, and Boulder which had been the Town Council became the Shire Council, though not before Kalgoorlie had looked like becoming the Town Council *and* the Shire Council, and Boulder had looked like vanishing altogether. Later on, when we'd become acquainted, Shire President Daws would give me his considered opinion of Mayor Finlayson. 'He's good. He's all right. But he'd stab you in the bloody back.' In the meantime, while we were still at the formal, getting to know you stage of interlocution, I had to make do with his opinion of me – 'Oh, a bloody Pom, are you?' – his opinion of the meeting – 'Now the bullshit starts!' – and his opinion of Mrs Thatcher – 'I admire her. She's not a left-winger like bloody Hawke. She gets things done. And she doesn't mess around trying to please coons.'

He was a mischievous, truculent, tireless little demon of a man with two tufts of white hair sticking up like horns on either side of his head. If I'd called him an incorrigible ratbag he'd have thanked me for the compliment. But he was right about a few things. I *was* a Pom. Mrs Thatcher had got things done. And pretty soon the bullshit really *did* start.

It was Brett Goodridge, Managing Director of the Western Australian Tourism Commission, who started it. 'In introducing the report I think I can promise you an end of the piecemeal, ad hoc, gut reaction type of development,' he promised. He had soft, beringed hands and wore cufflinks. He smoked, or rather *cleaned*, a pipe. And he had the look of a failed British Leyland manager. 'This report is something we've all had a hand in and an input to,' he concluded.

It fell to Steve Jennings from Hames Sharley to present the report itself. This seemed to me to suffer from (a) a distinct unoriginality of Goldfields visitor desideratum discernment, to wit its recommendation of (i) a casino, and (ii) more barbecue facilities in public places; (b) Steve Jennings' own low charisma-factor rating; and (c) his inability to exert any control over his left hand, which hovered in front of him as he spoke, like a magician's dancing ball, without reference to his meaning or his will.

'He's been affected by Halley's Comet, this bloke,' Digger Daws whispered to me.

While Steve Jennings struggled with his haunted hand, failing in all attempts to conceal it in his pocket or behind his back, the rest of the official party became deeply engrossed in the minutiae of their own persons. Brett Goodridge found things in his nose he never knew existed. Terry McVeigh, the Director of Investment and Regional Development for the Tourism Commission, lost vision in both eyes, so vigorously had he cleaned them with the pointed corners of his handkerchief. Ted Cockram stared in disbelief at what was growing from his knuckles. Then at last it was over and Steve Jennings was back in his seat. Before throwing discussion open to the floor, Terry McVeigh rose, like Samson in Gaza, to remind us of our responsibilities to the future. 'At the end of the day we've all got to live with the infrastructure that gets put on the ground,' he said.

'He's a bloody lecturer,' Digger Daws whispered.

The first person on his feet with a query was Dick Lamb. There were a few things he wanted to be clear about in relation to the proposal to extend caravan park facilities in the region. 'Bearing in mind that caravan parks are used by itinerants as well as tourists,' he said, 'I would like to ask Mr Jennings how far he has dichotomized and stratified his data.'

Not being able to understand the question was the least of Steve Jennings' worries. While he had been attending to Dick Lamb he had thought to bind his unruly hand to his side with the wires of the microphone; now the hand was back in its usual position, the microphone was out of order, and the rest of Steve Jennings was tied to his chair. A question from a woman representative of the Aboriginal Council gave him some respite. She had arrived late and so hadn't heard everything that had been said but wanted to know why no Aboriginal organizations had been consulted. She appeared a touch crestfallen when she was told that they all had. 'Well, I just want to remind you all that we have a consultable body in every town,' she said anyway. She couldn't have been more sympathetically treated. Everyone on the platform wanted to go on record as being willing to talk to any Aboriginal group anywhere at any time about any subject. In his agitation to be seen as even-handed Brett Goodridge actually dismantled his pipe into seven separate pieces.

All this was too much for Digger Daws. He rose to his feet in the full consciousness that everything until now had been a mere charade. Now the bullshit was coming to an end. 'Can I ask the gentleman two questions,' he said, 'after which I'd like to finish off with something in the nature of a comment.' He pronounced the word, com*ment*, in the time-honoured tradition of expert proceduralists. 'The first question is how long it took him to do the study. My second pertinent question – which those who know me won't be surprised by; just as I won't be surprised if I get no answer – is how much it cost.'

In fact he couldn't be bothered listening to the answer. He had just detected a certain something – he had just smelled another rat, as it were – in the accent of the now horribly scarlet Steve Jennings. 'That bloke a Pom?' he whispered to me. I told him I reckoned he was. 'Bloody place is lousy with them,' he said. And he was so struck by the fact that he clean forgot to deliver his com*ment*.

He was more gallant to Ros, though, before we left. In order that she should never forget him for as long as she lived, he handed her the name he'd worn on his lapel. 'I'll treasure it forever,' Ros said, sticking it on the top left-hand corner of the cover of her notebook –

Charles Daws
Shire President
Boulder Shire Council

He regarded what she had done for a moment, then he leaned over and wrote next to his name, J. P. Justice of the Peace.

★ ★ ★

After the meeting we ran into Dick Lamb in the forecourt of the Hospitality Inn, but to my confusion he was formal and remote. Not only was there no trace of his eccentric ebullience of the other night, but he seemed, I thought, to be wanting precisely to correct any false impression he had given then. I am a severe, co-ordinated, authoritative man, he appeared to be saying now, and it would be both naive and presumptious of you to suppose anything else. We accepted a lift back to town with him and parted in coldness.

But later that evening, as we were on our way to meet Stanley Brown at Hannans, we ran into Dick Lamb again. He was carrying several brown paper bags full of bottles under his arm and seemed to be sucking a lolly. He greeted us like long-lost friends, slapped his head, fell sideways, and otherwise exhibited all those signs of odd affability with which we were familiar. He didn't give any indication at all that he had encountered us earlier in the day.

Had we not had somewhere else to go we would no doubt have spent the evening drinking with him, and then in the morning he would have hated us for what he had shown us of himself. Funny how people will round on the best part of their own natures.

There was no such volatility around Stanley Brown. He was his usual sociably elegiac self. He took us back to meet his wife and an English couple, Chris and Deirdre, who owned an estate agency, a restaurant, and a motel in town. After dinner he showed us his most prized possession, a magnificent Steinway bought some years before from the man who used to tune the pianos for the ABC. It was signed by the various virtuosi who had played it including, to my surprise, Kamal. Had we been standing outside, at Stanley Brown's gate, we would have been able to watch the last effects of the sun on the tailing stumps, the pink hillocks of dust which closed the view from where ever you looked in Kalgoorlie. It was part of the town's distinct charm that you were never allowed to forget, not even visually, the reason for its existence. But here, gathered around the Steinway in Stanley and Valerie Brown's drawing room, there was no clue as to where we were. Only a queer ectopic sensation of being out of time and place.

We spent our last evening in the Goldfields with Stanley Brown at his grand piano, Rosalin on a cello, and the rest of us open-mouthed singing 'Danny Boy'. It wouldn't have been the first time that the pipes, the pipes, had called out from glen to glen into the Kalgoorlie night.

ELEVEN

A ROOMETTE WITH A VIEW

It appealed to my rudimentary sense of symmetry that the last voice we heard in Kalgoorlie should be Ray Finlayson's. We were sitting on the station platform waiting for the Trans-Australian to pull in when he came through on a radio news bulletin, countering the figures just released by the W.A. Conservation Council claiming to show that there were sulphur dioxide emissions of up to five times the acceptable level blowing across Kalgoorlie, making it the most polluted air in Western Australia. 'I can see no evidence at all of pollution,' the Mayor said. 'I can see no evidence at all that people are suffering from sulphur dioxide.'

I looked around me. 'Me neither,' I said to Ros.

Waiting with us on the platform were a couple of dozen middle-aged men in blue blazers. Since they were too old and portly to be a rugby team, I decided that they were a brass band – maybe English or German – on an Australia-wide tour. I looked forward to their company on the train. I had high hopes of the Trans-Australian. The great trek across the Nullarbor. A stainless steel sleeping berth – my own roomette, as it was called. A piano bar. And now, with a bit of luck, an oom-pah-pah band that we could yodel along with. It was going to be some trip.

So I was a bit disappointed when the men in blue blazers turned out to be the stewards, waiting to start their shift. But I wasn't disheartened.

We were no sooner aboard the train than we were required to make a snap decision – did we want to take breakfast at the first sitting or the second? As we'd been up since five we plumped for the first, not knowing that we had thereby signed our freedom away, that we were now first sitting passengers for life, always to be forced to eat too soon and always to be required to leave too early. The same terrible finality applied to our choice of table also. Because we sat opposite Bruce and Judith for our first breakfast, they were to be our eating companions for the rest of the journey. So I tried not to mind that Bruce had a gravelly voice, a murderer's beard, liked living in Essendon in Melbourne, and wore a transparent nylon shirt through which you could see – and indeed were meant to see – his pale blue singlet. I tried to concentrate instead on those qualities for which Judith had married him, Judith being one of those doggedly loyal girls, whose fragile good looks appear to be a function of a deprived upbringing, of the kind that Dickens liked to write about. And there was this to be said for Bruce and Judith, too – apart from us they were the only people travelling in the first-class section of the train (and I hadn't yet seen what was in the other half) who were under sixty-five.

It is common, still, to talk about Australia as a young country; but in fact it is the old who are everywhere in evidence. Senior Citizens Fortnight had coincided exactly with our sojourn in Perth. Boy scouts had been collecting for them in Kalgoorlie. And for the next few weeks – particularly when we hit the roads north to the Dead Heart – we were to meet almost no one else. The old of Australia were on the move, and because they were fit, competitive, and wealthy, there was no stopping them. They dominated the corridors of the Trans-Australian and set the tone of brave hilarity which prevailed in the dining car. 'It's like me,' I heard a steel-grey woman in a state of the most marvellous preservation laugh out, even before the first coffee of the journey had been served, 'that sounds just like me when I was learning golf.' We were beaten from the start. All I could do, while Ros and Judith smiled at each other, and Bruce made fine distinctions between the bread rolls on our table and those he normally ate in Essendon, was look out of the window, hope to catch sight of a kangaroo, and listen to episode eighty-seven of *The Tenant of Wildfell Hall*. 'But our intercourse must end here,' one of the characters was saying. 'End here?' 'End here.' They don't write them like they used to.

After breakfast we returned to our roomettes – we had one each; all the twinettes had been taken – to compose our thoughts. In the corridor a couple of stewards were discussing the fastidious dietary stipulations of one of their new passengers. 'He wants extra-strong tea, no milk in his muesli, and insists on having nuts sprinkled on his fruit compote.'

'He won't go down well.'

'He can't sleep on planes either. He reckons they let him into the cockpit.'

'He won't go down well at all.'

Now that I knew the stewards were not members of an English or German brass band I was at a loss to place them. They didn't at all look or talk like modern Australians. They had the musty air of college porters about them, or non-militant union convenors from Carlisle. Once these two had gone from the corridor I popped my nose into Ros's roomette and asked her for her opinion: did she think there might be some secret Australian town not on the map – say Maralinga way – where stewards were especially bred for the railways? No, she didn't think that. She knew precisely where the stewards came from – Australia in 1950. They were the same vintage as the food they served; they went with the tinned beetroot and the shredded lettuce. But that only half satisfied me; it didn't explain where the tinned beetroot and the shredded lettuce came from.

Some time in the middle of the morning I decided to go in search of what sounded like muffled revelry coming from the direction of the Piano Bar. It had been in order to have access to the Piano Bar that we had bought first-class tickets, so I felt badly betrayed – violated, as the raped and the robbed say – when the piano turned out to be a portable Japanese electronic organ – the sort that will give you, at the flick of a switch, any kind of rhythmic backing you want – and when the pianist, whom I'd expected to be in tails, turned out to be a bearded boy in jeans and anorak whose repertoire was limited – out of spite, it seemed – to hitherto unperformed works of atonality by the lesser-known Norwegian masters. A can of Coke sat beside him on a little table. When he saw me he stopped playing for a moment and said, 'We gotta lose a half an hour's sleep.'

I didn't understand him. 'Clocks go forward,' he said. He ran a hand through his uncombed hair and took a swig of Coke. Although he wasn't touching it, the organ kept up its terrible cheerless beat. It was as if somebody had invented music for doorbells.

An old-timer rose from his seat and shook a leg. It was impossible to tell whether he was partying or palsied. I sat in a corner, willing myself deaf and reading that morning's issue of the *Kalgoorlie Miner*. The front cover carried the story of the sulphur dioxide pollution. Inside I read about Mrs Selva Nix, the Goldfields entrant in the Mrs Australia quest, who had planned a Goodbye Halley's Comet Night that Saturday, as part of her fund-raising efforts. Had we stayed we could have gone to it. I made anagrams with her name and decided that Valse Inx was a good title for the tune that was being played on the organ, then I realized that no tune was being played on the organ and that the Piano Bar had emptied.

Bruce had changed for lunch into a pair of canary-yellow strides and a sports shirt in alternating stripes of pastel blue and peach. I could see that he still had his singlet on underneath. I kept looking out of the window. The train had stopped at Rawlinna, although there didn't appear to be anything you could call a platform there. I saw a school, a post office, and about fifteen wooden houses, all built to the same design and painted cream or green, and all, of course, with large corrugated iron water tanks. It was 1 p.m. on a cloudless day and nothing stirred. A few mongrel dogs slept in the dirt. To the north I saw a mirage – an interminable, inviting lake, showing the reflection of trees that weren't there. Otherwise Rawlinna was not easy on the eye. It seemed to exist only as a convenience for the railway, as a kind of slag heap memorial to the predacity of the train. Old sleepers were piled up as if for bonfires; whatever had been surplus to use in the excavation or restitution of tracks lay where it had been tossed. Everywhere I looked I saw litter – plastic egg boxes, beer cans, rags, even books with broken spines.

'Jeez, you'd have to be keen to live out here,' Bruce said.

Later in the afternoon I decided it was time to see what life on the Trans-Australian was like for poor people. I had a dread of discovering that they were having all the fun down there in coach class, that there would be poker schools and sing-a-longs and drinks parties in every compartment, so I was relieved to see that they were very nearly half as bored as I was. I took a seat in the cafeteria club bar and ordered the going thing – a hot apple pie served in a cardboard soup-bowl with an inverted tub of Street's vanilla ice cream slapped on top. Behind me, a woman old enough to be in first class was complaining about the table manners of people she had recently attended a stand-up dinner with. 'Some of these women eat as if they've never eaten before,' she said. Her companion was sympathetic. 'Buffets bring out the worst in people,' she observed. At the table opposite, three WRANs (the Australian equivalent of WRENs) were discussing everyone they knew. I decided they were WRANs partly because their voices were so deep, partly because they were all wearing what looked like ammunition – small rounds of shot – as earrings, but mainly because I'd observed that servicewomen were always much too short or much too tall, and that's what these were.

'She's a lovely girl,' one of them said, apropos an absent friend. 'But a bit over-concerned about her figure.'

'Waiting for Mr Right.'

'Only Mr Right never comes along.'

'I've heard she's found someone else's Mr Right.'

'Mr Rights always *are* someone else's.'

I looked out of the window. Since the journey had begun I'd counted three separate instances of cars parked half-way up a tree, at an angle of forty-five degrees to the horizontal. Now I counted a fourth. It was as if the driver, sent crazed by the sun and the isolation, had tried to drive his car up the first tree he'd seen in hours, had failed, and had left it there. Other sights on the Nullarbor surprised me. Meticulous rock piles. Sudden stone circles. Disused mine shafts. Inexplicable towers and pylons, apparently attached to nothing, feeding nothing, receiving nothing, offering a panoramic command of nothing. Despite the vast monotony of the plain, there seemed to be very little of it that hadn't at some time been turned over. But then that was only the view from the train.

The woman behind me had moved on to a description of the breakdown she'd recently suffered. 'I wasn't able to lie down *and* breathe,' she said.

The tallest of the WRANs had reached the sweepingly general stage of idle conversation. 'You'll find that New South Wales girls are the worst,' she told her companions-in-small-arms.

'Western Australian girls are friendly. Queensland girls are friendly, Tasmanian girls are very friendly, but New South Wales girls are a cut above.'

I fought down my need for another apple pie and ice cream and returned to my roomette. Where I read in my train brochure that we were now on the longest stretch of straight railway in the world – 478 kilometres without so much as a wobble. As Bruce said, you'd have to be keen.

Just off the railway sidings at Cook, South Australia, was a large metal water tank with a painted message on it for visitors – OUR HOSPITAL NEEDS YOUR HELP. GET SICK. IF YOU'RE CROOK COME TO COOK. We didn't see the tank itself; it was too dark when we pulled in to Cook. But resourceful youngsters were in a booth selling postcards of their two famous landmarks. The other was the Old Gaol. This consisted of a pair of tin sheds, the size of dunnies, standing side by side, like His and Hers, in the desert.

I had an interest in Cook. It was here, in 1920, that His Royal Highness the Prince of Wales stepped out on to a ceremonial dais made of railway sleepers and stood under a shelter of boughs transported from hundreds of miles away in order to observe the Aborigines of Ooldea perform their corroboree. Instrumental in the staging of this event was Daisy Bates, the extraordinary *Times* correspondent who at the age of forty-one came out to investigate the plight of the Australian Aborigine and stayed with them, as a kind of benign autocrat, like a head nurse at a hospice for the incurable, for thirty-five years. In her book, *The Passing of the Aborigines*, she describes how, earlier in 1920, she had been requested to prepare the Aborigines at Ooldea for the honour of dancing before the Prince of Wales, but had first to quell a mini-insurrection. 'You send paper to Gubmint and tell them we don't want white-fellow King,' a delegation of Aborigines told her. 'This country black-fellow. Waiyela (white-fellow) gubmint take dousand, dousand, dousand pound – close up five pounds! Wheat-amanning, potato-amanning, waiyela stealem our country. We take back . . . We kill waiyela!'

According to her own account, Miss Bates never left her tent until she was dressed for the day according to the simple but exact dictates of English fashion as she'd known it when Victoria was queen – in a 'neat white blouse, stiff collar and ribbon tie, a dark skirt and coat, stout and serviceable, trim shoes and neat black stockings, a sailor hat and a fly-veil'. So we must assume that she was thus attired when she addressed the insurrectionists: 'This young white King comes this country, my King, your King, too – big flour-giver . . . He tells me give you food . . . When this young King comes, he will give you plenty flour, sugar, blankets, tobacco . . . When all the flour and tobacco that you take from the white man gone, who will give you more?'

If the words didn't do the trick the sailor hat and fly-veil must have. Because on 10 July the Prince of Wales and his suite alighted at Cook and 'there was nobody in all Australia to give him a more exciting or more heart-felt welcome than the cannibal rebels of Ooldea'.

It was a cold afternoon on the Nullarbor, but one not lacking in ceremony or satisfaction:

Lord Claud Hamilton had been requested to present me to His Royal Highness, and when I made my curtsy, the Prince asked me to join him on the dais, where I explained both dance and dancers . . . The Prince, deeply interested, then came down from the platform for a closer view of the native crafts, and tried his skill at flint-chipping and spear-throwing to the delight of the natives and white residents . . .

'Thank you very much,' said His Royal Highness to each and every one, with a smile of appreciation.

'Dango berry-anujy,' they gravely replied, while the women and children lowered their heads and hid their eyes.

In the best traditions of Royal visits, the train at last pulled out across the plain with the Prince driving the engine, leaving the Aborigines to turn to the feast of roast sheep and flour and tobacco that 'their King's son' had given them. As for Daisy Bates, she returned to her goat van but was too excited by the exertions of the day to sleep. By the light of a solitary candle she sat up all night and read *Our Mutual Friend*.

Daisy Bates is out of favour today. Her humane pessimism jangles modern nerves. It feels indiscreet to delight as she did in the childlike qualities of a broken people stumbling in an alien tongue. And the essentially commiserating, elegiac nature of the task she set herself – 'I realized that they were passing from us. I must make their passing easier' – makes her an irrelevance in the politics of Aboriginal reform. But in the history of heroic English eccentrics, studying the classics a long way from home, she has her place. And she offers an alternative to being crook as a reason for stopping off at Cook.

It was the briefest of stops for us. We were allowed to stretch our legs for fifteen minutes, that was all. But at least we were able in that time to enjoy a night of the most spectacular beauty. I had never previously understood what travellers or poets meant when they described a sky as domed or vaulted; the heavens over Cook, though, were precisely that, curved and overarching, and studded like a ceiling with silver. As we were gazing upwards the sort of person who knows about such things showed us Halley's Comet. All I could see was a vague smudge in the middle of the Milky Way, but I pointed it out to other people as the Comet and they seemed satisfied. Who needed a Comet anyway? A sky of the deepest black vaulted us. A cool wind blew off the desert, ruffling our collars. We picked peppercorns off a handsome peppercorn tree and bit into their aromatic pungency. A couple of junkies from the wrong end of the train lit up in the darkness. God looked down and said that

if it wasn't exactly good it was the best we could ever expect.
So who needed Halley?

Ros had told me that for her the best part of the journey across
the Nullarbor was going to bed and watching the desert from a
horizontal position. She was right. I lay on my side and stared
interest back into the plain. I discerned strange shapes. I caught
the reflection of queer lights. I saw things move. On a long
journey, I realized, it wasn't unremitting Nature that caused
monotony, it was unremitting cultivation. And of course
human beings. I went to sleep happily, counting emus.

And I woke well, too, in time to see the dawn come up
blood red. The country was hillier now and more rocky. Mulga,
salt, and blue bush, according to my strip map. Kangaroo country, also, I suddenly realized. I hadn't noticed them at first,
camouflaged against the sandy backdrop, but now there they
were, dozens and dozens of them, standing stock still so that the
train shouldn't spot them. Immobilized by fear, with their
abbreviated front feet held out under their chins, like so many
giant bunnies.

The old but the by no means infirm had also come up well
this morning. After a shaky start around shower time – I could
hear them groaning and complaining in the corridors – they
were blooming by breakfast. They teased the stewards. They
hid the condiments from one another. They fished out teabags
from teapots with long red fingernails whose calcium suffi-
ciency a teenager would have envied. And they consulted maps.
They were on the move all right; and getting stronger with
every kilometre.

TWELVE

ICH HATT' EINST EIN
SCHÖN' VATERLAND

Staying in our hotel in Adelaide were a number of men with grey complexions and startled expressions, carrying battered suitcases or lunchboxes, and wearing Ukranian baseball hats and the sorts of suits worn by witnesses at the Nuremberg Trials. Had I not already gone so badly wrong with the English brass band that turned out to be our stewards I would have picked these for the USSR State Symphony Orchestra. Which was of course what they were.

They had a concert that very night at the Festival Theatre – Svetlanov conducting, Timofeeva on the piano. A real piano, presumably; not the portable Japanese Rhythm-Mate that emptied the Piano Bar of the Trans-Australian. I felt sorry for them; not for being in Adelaide, but for being Russians. Russians break my heart. They are the last people left on the face of the earth who think there is some merit in being serious. I travelled up and down in the hotel lifts with them at every opportunity, just so that they might see a friendly and encouraging face. Whenever any one of them left the hotel he had to write his name and intended itinerary on a sheet of foolscap paper pinned to a column near the reception desk. This didn't

strike me as too high a price to pay for living in a society free
of disc jockeys. It didn't strike me as particularly sinister either.
Clearly an orchestra has to be kept together; and you couldn't
be absolutely certain that an oboeist from Grozny wouldn't
take it into his head to go missing in Adelaide. This was a literary city; there would be girls out there who would stop at
nothing to get a conversation about Lermontov going.

We had no definite plans in relation to Adelaide ourselves. It
had never loomed significantly in our preparations, precisely I
suppose because of its reputation for culture; I didn't really see
how being in a place that had poetry readings the way other cities
had robberies with violence could be counted much of an adventure. But it was also the case that we had known from the start
that the moment we got to Adelaide we would have other fish
to fry. It was from here that we would begin our great thrust
northwards to Alice Springs and then Queensland; so it was here
that we would have to decide what we were going to thrust
northwards in. Ros favoured hiring a van and simply lighting out
in it, just us against the unknown, the marauding savages, and the
hundreds of kilometres of unsealed roads. All along I had fancied
the train, arguing that on a train you met people, but we had just
come off a train and my theory was in tatters. We would rest up
in Adelaide for a few days and consider.

In fact we were up and running the following morning.
We'd had a pleasant stroll around the city the evening before,
enjoying the bustle of late-night shopping and willingly conced-
ing that yes, Adelaide did indeed have an open, airy quality, a
something at once mellow and vibrant, as my tourist guide said,
an atmosphere of communal, lingering, street-consumerism
that one associated more with a European city than an Australian.
We had even found a red-light district, or at least a red-light
block, where, to low Balkan music, we had eaten a Serbian
mixed grill in an enticingly lurid establishment – to which
nobody but us had been enticed – called Montenegro. But it

was still all a bit too like Perth for our immediate taste. Something about the city was flat. More mellow than vibrant. And we weren't alone in feeling it. According to a report on local television, Adelaide was in the throes of post-Festival trist-esse; it lay on its bed every evening smoking cigarettes and staring dreamily out of the window, unable to find the will to stir. It was culture-sated. It didn't have a clap left in it. Not even Lauren Bacall as Bel Lago in *Sweet Bird of Youth* could get it to rise. God knows if anyone had turned out for Svetlanov. I watched the musicians returning to the hotel – this time in dinner jackets and Ukranian baseball hats – and saw no sign that they were any more animated than they'd been when they'd left it. We smiled and nodded at them again, so that they shouldn't think all Westerners were like Sid and Nancy, and in the morning we sped out of town in a little rented Pulsar.

We weren't leaving for good. This wasn't the beginning of our trek to Alice Springs. But we had been in the Festival City for a full fourteen hours now (counting the eight we'd been asleep) and we felt that we had earned a break. A weekend in the Barossa Valley, where the Rhine riesling flowed, seemed just the ticket.

There's an easy way of knowing when you've hit the Barossa Valley; approaching it from Adelaide, you look out for the piano-accordionist in his lederhosen and his little feathered hat, playing outside the Bavarian restaurant at Lyndoch. Thereafter the area need hold few surprises for you. You will take it for granted that you can buy leberwurst and lachschenken at Steinberner's butcher shop, and you will assume, as a matter of course, that your legal problems will be dealt with by Heuzenroeder and Heuzenroeder, solicitors. In fact, to be strict about it, the Bavarian restaurant and its accordionist are a bit of a tourist aberration. Because this is Lutheran country, not Catholic; the first settlers came from Prussia and Silesia, and they were dissenters not knee-slappers. But at least 'I laf to goa vandering' gives you the general idea.

The seriousness of the original settlers' intentions is more manifest in Tanunda, the geographic and spiritual heart of the valley. We drove into this charming little town from Lyndoch, gently sloping hills of vines on either side of us, and immediately counted four Lutheran churches, all apparently prospering still. Outside one of them we found a plaque bearing testimony to strong wills and extraordinary conjunctions.

Here at Langmeil on 9th October 1866, Pastors
J F Gossling and E Homann and lay missionaries
J E Jacob and H H Vogelsang set out to establish a
Lutheran Mission among the Dieri tribe of Aboriginals.
On the 31st January 1867 they established Bethesda
Mission Station at Lake Killalpanina, Cooper's Creek.

I didn't know what to marvel at most, the bravery of these indomitable proselytizers, who had been an entity in the country for scarcely more than thirty years themselves, or their presumption. And I couldn't decide who would have found the other the more bizarre: the Lutherans the Dieri, or the Dieri the Lutherans. But I knew who my heart went out to. Tramping across the mulga singing hymns was one kind of intrepidity; listening to them coming must have required altogether another.

There's a good pioneer museum at Tanunda, housed in the old telegraph office. We spent an hour or so here, looking at sepia photographs of soberly industrious Lutheran families, the founders of the industry that keeps half of Australia semi-permanently drunk and idle. And we spent a further twenty minutes trying to get away from the curious lady at the enquiry desk and book counter who reversed the usual procedure and demanded information from us. 'Where do you come from?'

she wanted to know. 'How long have you been away? How can you afford such a long trip? Have you resigned your jobs? What *are* your jobs?'

We walked out on her in the end; we simply had to turn our backs on her and leave. Then we bought ourselves some sour black bread and wurst and drove out through Bethany to Menglers Hill, where we picnicked in German style and looked down over the valley. The view was not breathtaking; perhaps it was not even beautiful. But it satisfied all the quieter emotions and went well with our lunch. It was a view of sober and successful industry in a restful spot. The vines themselves, heavy with fruit at this time of the year, soothed the eyes. Nature was not turbulent or stimulating here, but calming and provident.

The township of Bethany was where it had all begun, twenty-eight Lutheran families arriving in 1842 and dividing the land up exactly as they would have done in Silesia, in the traditional hufendorf method of narrow, elongated allotments which gave the maximum access to tracks and creeks to the maximum number of settlers. So today Bethany is whatever you see on either side of one long quiet road running up into the hills – a few stone houses, some barns, a church, the smallest hotel in South Australia, the smallest vineyard in the Barossa, and the pioneer cemetery. We lingered among the graves for a while, as had become our wont, and thought what a comforting place it was, all things considered, not only on account of its rural beneficence and the giant river gum which guarded it, but even more because the dead were allowed to lie so close to where they'd lived and worked. They were in the village still, and could smell the grapes. Where the cemetery ended, there the vines resumed. Between the past and the present, and the quick and the dead, there seemed to be some rational and amicable compact. So might a book drudge like myself, I reasoned, be spared the terrors of too peaceful a resting place by being buried under the forecourt of the British Museum.

We must have been drawn to Bethany, because whenever we got lost in the valley we found ourselves back there, and we returned to it again before the afternoon was finally over, deliberately this time, having failed to find anything in or around the larger centres of Nuriootpa and Angaston that we liked more. An accommodation sign swinging outside the High Wycombe Winery – the Smallest Vineyard in the Valley – had taken our attention earlier. Small was not necessarily beautiful, but anyone who had chanced calling a winery High Wycombe in such a place, where all around was Krondorf and Bernkastel, in our estimation deserved encouraging. So we drove in, not without some intimations of insobriety but hardly thinking that we were about to lose three whole days of our life to the bottle. But then we didn't think we'd be goose-stepping around a dinner table like John Cleese or doing Australian farmyard imitations either. I still remember what the afternoon was like before the gates of irresponsibility closed behind us – the Barossa hills turning an exquisite anguished pink in the setting sun, the bells of the Lutheran churches tolling, the light being led out like an unwilling bridegroom, and grapes beneath our feet.

Colin and Angela Davis ran the High Wycombe Winery and were also teachers. Whether the teaching supplemented the winemaking or the winemaking the teaching we never found out. But the winemaking was what gave them the pleasure. The reason they'd built a brand new row of chalets for paying guests was so that Colin could afford to give up teaching. 'In this country we pay kids to stay on at school,' Angela told us, 'as a consequence of which Colin, who is a science teacher, is expected to teach them practicalities such as how to post a letter and how to go shopping. It's an insult to his intelligence.'

'Ah, don't start that again, Ange,' Colin said.

He was a lean figure with a little grey moustache and a rather careworn look belied by the fire in his eyes. His accent was a queer nasal mix of Australian and whatever it is they speak in

High Wycombe. A Rhodesian who had spent time in Ilfracombe and Dudley would have sounded the same. His wife's name he produced from somewhere high up in his sinuses, fatalistically – not so much Ange as Enj.

Angela herself was strong and square-jawed. Pioneer stock. According to her own testimony the great-great-great-grand-daughter of the first white woman to be born in South Australia. What an earlier generation of men would have called a damned fine woman with no nonsense about her. But she had dark flashing eyes which didn't quite go with her pioneer sturdiness, suggesting a weakness for Spaniards somewhere back along the line between her and her great-great-great-grandmother.

Ten minutes after we'd installed ourselves in the chalet Colin knocked on our door with a complimentary bottle of High Wycombe Cabernet Sauvignon. Twenty minutes after that Angela turned up with a bottle of High Wycombe White Port. When Colin next appeared it wasn't to give us wine but to tell us that they would be grape-crushing early the next morning and to hope that we weren't light sleepers. But Angela, on her final visit, resurrected the tradition of which we had started to become fond and let it lightly be understood that, were we to be thinking of staying another night, they would be thinking of having us to dinner. Colin's Whitehill Crusher looked like a cross between a sewing machine, a giant liquidizer, and an old-fashioned mincer. It was worked by a rubber fan belt which turned blades similar to those on a lawnmower. And it was loaded by hand – Colin taking turns with Angela to stand in the back of a semi-trailer and toss in the grapes with a pitchfork. According to Colin, a Whitehill going at full pelt could pulver-ize twenty tons in an hour; so it will be clear from the time it took Colin to crush his grapes – two hours for three tons – that there was no sense of urgency at the High Wycombe Winery. Dressed in their oldest clothes and wellingtons they squelched thigh-high in fruit, pausing from their pitchforking to squabble, or to listen to the valley echoing with Sunday church bells, or to discuss such matters as the future of liberal education in Australia, and the relative merits of the city and the country. As regards the latter, they believed that living in the Barossa gave them the benefit of both worlds – the calm of Bethany to hand, the vitality of Adelaide a two-hour drive away. 'It was never our intention to become country bumpkins,' Colin told me.

When he thought Angela wasn't listening he took me into his confidence about the quality of the grapes. 'Not been enough rain,' he said. 'They're as dry as a Marseilles prostitute.' Only he pronounced the place Marsails, as I suppose everybody does in High Wycombe. Fortunately I was already familiar with the gross Australianism. 'As dry as a nun's nasty'; so I found Colin only marginally indelicate.

Later in the morning I accompanied Angela on an errand to her friends Janette and Fernando Martin (once Martino) who ran the Château Dorrien just outside Tanunda, a fun complex housed in the old Seppelt's Winery, famous for its towering scraggy palms and castellated storage tanks. These tanks had now been turned into tourist kiosks where you could buy knick-knacks and hamburgers and tickets for camel rides. Inside was a wonderland of Bavarian kitsch, incorporating a Wiener World Bistro, hot-nut bars, gift counters and the like. A sound of violent beating came from the kitchens. 'That'll be Fernando hammering the schnitzels,' Angela said. I met Fernando briefly. The last time I'd clapped eyes on anyone as dashingly romantic as this was in an operetta sung on a stage set identical to the room I was now standing in. Would that have been *White Horse Inn*? I exchanged a few sentences with him, being careful not to look at the forest of black hairs that sprouted from his slashed satin shirt. He told me he had just returned from a most wonderful holiday. 'Heidelberg?' I wondered. 'The Tyrol?' No – Alice Springs and Ayers Rock. I enquired – as I now enquired of everyone – about the state of the roads. 'Put it this way,' he said, 'if you go in a new car it will be old by the time you get back. That's *if* you get back. I'm glad I didn't take mine. We went on the bus' (I couldn't imagine Fernando on a bus) 'and it had eleven punctures.'

Before we returned to Bethany, Angela showed me the new Lutheran school her daughter went to. She was full of praise for it and wouldn't have countenanced her daughter attending any other. But she gave me an inkling, too, of just what it was that bound non-Germanic families such as the Davises and the Martin(o)s in friendship. 'It's hard for people like Colin and me to be accepted by the community, whatever we think of them,' she said. 'Not being Lutherans we're behind the eight ball from the start.'

Ros and I decided not to let not being Lutherans stop us from putting our nose into the Tanunda Oval that afternoon, where a BACK TO TANUNDA DAY, in celebration of South Australia's 150th birthday, was in progress. This party seemed to have two distinct and sometimes contradictory elements. Around the peripheries of the playing field people in early German settlers' dress were gathered, some of them looking defiantly natural, as is the way when you are costumed peculiarly, but others looking genuinely natural, as though this was how, spir-itually anyway, they essentially saw themselves. In the oval proper, though, a general free-for-all seemed to be taking place, a sort of *It's a Knockout* without any referee. I learnt from some-one who might or might not have been an early Lutheran pig farmer that this was called the Participatory Games – you were awarded a signed certificate just for being in them. Had I not suddenly noticed a wine-tasting tent it's just possible that I would have thrown off my jacket and participated, but the opportunity of making a few judicious assessments on a sticky afternoon was not really to be foregone. The more especially as there were only minutes left before the Tanunda Liedertafl Choir and the Tanunda Brass Band began their concert in the agricultural hall. A little something red and pungent from Yalumba, a little something even redder and more pungent from Peter Lehmann, and it was time to take our seats.

I'd read somewhere that the agricultural hall sometimes functioned as a giant church for star ecclesiastical performers, accommodating congregations of twelve or thirteen hundred. There weren't that many here today, but we were still a sizeable audience for an aluminium shed with a gravel floor, and corn mice scuttling between the plastic chairs, alarmed, as indeed I was, by the music and the sentiment. I suppose I ought to have been pleased to get my German brass band at last, but it was too late for me – all I could see now were sleeping-car stewards. They went through the usual disheartening brass band routine of thinking to surprise you with what they could do with 'pops' – a spirited 'Sweet Gingerbread Man', a less banal but still banal medley from *Cats*, and so on. Then they did something which in all truth *was* a surprise: they went straight from the 'Lincolnshire Poacher' to the 'Luftwaffe Theme' from the film *The Battle of Britain*. They let it rip too, giving it plenty of martial swagger and air space. But it wasn't that it should be played so feelingly that startled me, simply that it should be played at all. 'Trink, trink, Brüderlein trink,' the Liedertafl Choir, all neat in blue blazers and grey flannels, now rose and sang, which struck me as all very well, but. They didn't win me over with, 'In München steht ein Hofbrauhaus,' either. It was only when they got to 'Ich hatt' einst ein schön' Vaterland' – the song of the migrant, the plaint of the forever exiled – that the tears sprung out of my eyes and I was every man's brother once more.

Mind you, I had been drinking.

The Barossa hills were a flaming pink again when we called upon the Davises to dine that evening, the same colour as the crests of the cockatoos scavenging in the landscaped woodchip garden, and the same colour as the crisp short-sleeved sports shirt in which Colin welcomed us. He was unrecognizable from his daytime self. So was Angela. She wore a cream pleated skirt and a rich floral blouse and had applied her make-up so that her unspoken Spanish ancestry should blaze from her brow. It was hard to believe that they had been on the back of a semi-trailer only a few hours earlier, pitchforking grapes into a crusher. Only the indelible purple stain on Colin's hands gave any clue to what they did when they weren't entertaining. I handed him my brown paper bag with some discomfort; I wasn't at all sure about the etiquette of taking wine to the house of a vigneron, but had rejected Ros's suggestion that we take flowers instead, remembering my own invariable chagrin as a host when a guest presented me with a bouquet and not a bottle. 'Aw, that's good,' Colin said, after the most perfunctory look at what I'd brought, 'it's always a good idea to keep tabs on the opposition.' But that was the last we saw of that.

While Colin opened champagne, the whole time singing loudly to himself, Angela introduced us to her 'dearest friends', Franz and Vivien, who owned the Landhaus – a highly regarded restaurant which was also, with one room, the smallest hotel-motel in South Australia. On the face of it they looked an oddly assorted couple: Vivien, sedate in pearls and carefully coiffured; Franz, a cadaverous grey, with a goatee beard and wisps of white hair on either side of a central strip of baldness, his cable-knit sweater worn over his emaciation like a shroud. As if to allay any fears we might have had that he wasn't going to make it through the evening, Angela said, 'Franz is sometimes known as the Mad Dutchman.'

One isn't always so lucky with people who have a reputation for lunacy, but Franz did indeed turn out to lack the usual restraints. Though he began normally enough, with stories of his experiences as a businessman/chef. 'So I took over this absolutely run-down restaurant,' he explained, 'famous throughout the

Barossa for its appalling décor, atrocious cooking, and unbeliev-
able overpricing. I killed myself doing it up, changing the menu,
all that – and who do you think my first customer was? A woman
who'd been to it in the old days and had brought a whole coach-
load of people down from Queensland specifically to witness at
first hand everything that she'd described to them. She was furious when she saw what I'd done. "My God, you've changed it!"
she screamed. "I've come thousands of miles to see this again and
you've changed it!"' His next problem was staff. 'I employed an
English woman. As an assistant. Only she didn't – assist me. I had
to bribe her before she'd undertake a single task. She just
wouldn't. I had to renegotiate her wages and conditions of
employment every day, before she would. Whenever I asked her
to do anything she'd say, "Oh, oh, this could be the straw that
breaks the camel's back." So I had to do *everything* myself. She
stood at the sink, her back to the business. Drying the same fork.
First I took the orders and then it would be – ZIP – into the
kitchen, and – ZIP – buttering the scones, and – ZIP – over to
the soup, and then – ZIP ZIP – back out into the restaurant
again, and – ZIP ZIP ZIP – "Here you are, madam, I take it
everything is to your requirements?"'

These various zippings were enacted by an increasingly
demonic Franz. Second by second he grew wilder, the wisps of
white hair rising from his head, his mouth widening into a scarlet satyr's grin. And soon he was dancing on the table, stripped
down to his underpants and socks and a borrowed polka-dot
bow tie. It was at this point that Angela did the first of her
farmyard imitations – a rooster, I suppose it must have been.
'Don't do that, Enj,' Colin said. Still utterly sedate, Vivien
looked on with unconcern.

Back in his chair, Franz told us about his brother Alfonso
who spent five days a week locked up in Hillcrest – the Adelaide
lunatic asylum – but was let out at weekends. 'I ought to warn
you that he is known to be partial to a run down to the Barossa,'

he warned us. Five minutes later he left the room; and five minutes after that Alfonso turned up in Angela's nightie and a sort of yarmulka made from a crocheted doily, waving a plastic fan. 'Good evening, I'm Alfonso, the mad brother,' he said.

All in all this struck me as a novel and possibly highly remedial method of dealing with schizophrenia: one simply brought the other half of one's riven personality out with one; one took one's doppelgänger to the party. 'Good evening, Alfonso,' I said. Since I was for it, I had to go all the way with it.

Angela too had another name she wanted us to know her by. 'I'm Louis the fly,' she sang, remembering an old Australian fly-spray jingle. 'I'm big and mean and mighty unclean. Straight from rubbish tip to you. I'm Louis the fly.'

'Aw no, Enj,' Colin said.

It would be wrong to say that the evening wasn't going the way Colin wanted it; he laughed, he hummed to himself, he uncorked bottle after bottle, discoursing not upon their cheeky little personalities but their relation to the whole history of wine-making in the Barossa – 'This is one of the very last Cabernets that Henschke made before he was found murdered in his bed,' he announced at one point. But I could tell that there was an element he considered missing from the dinner party. I think it was culture. I couldn't see why else, amid so much din, he kept putting Pavarotti on the record player. It drove Angela mad at last. She tore it off the turntable and replaced it with the Rhinelanders' 'Thirty All Time German Favourites'. One thing led inevitably to another. As non-Lutherans living in a tightly knit Lutheran community, Angela (the fly) and Colin, and Vivien and Franz/Alfonso, clearly needed regular surreptitious release; notwithstanding their high regard for their neighbours, they required an outlet for their feelings. That was the only reason we all ended up doing that John Cleese impersonation I have already alluded to. As soon as we'd exhausted it, Angela remembered another one she was good at. 'Basil!' she screamed.

'Don't do that, Enj,' Colin pleaded.

Later in the evening, after the children had come down the stairs to ask us to make less noise and we were therefore in a more receptive frame of mind, Colin produced a High Wycombe Shiraz, vintage 1978, No. 0004 out of a bottling of 3,000 – one of the first wines he ever made. Although it was patently a treasure, Colin had some reservations to voice about its oaky flavour. 'Not everybody likes my oakiness,' he said.

'Don't sell yourself short,' Angela told him. There was a new weight of seriousness in her voice. Clearly, Colin selling himself short was an issue around the place.

Alfonso having returned to Hillcrest, Franz said, 'When you put your mind to it, Colin, you are one of the best winemakers in Australia.'

'It's true,' Vivien said.

Colin glowed. The burgundy dye that had been confined to his hands now suffused his whole person. He was the same colour as his Shiraz.

More special occasion bottles were opened. Not just Colin's either. We got into wines from any number of local vineyards, monuments and trophies, a veritable museum, each bearing witness in its very nose and aroma to the day-to-day tragedies or triumphs of the Barossa. It was as much a history lesson as an orgy. Had it been literature we were discussing I would have been the very first to resist so blatant an example of the sociologico-biographical fallacy; but in the case of wine I was somehow able to overlook such carelessness as to *texte*. 'Glorious,' I said, swilling it about my palate. 'Absolutely glorious. And he was dead within the hour, you say?'

How we came to discuss the subject of the excellence of German desserts, why this should have led to a resumption of unruliness, and what it was in the behaviour of the others that led Colin to whisper in my ear, 'I think you're probably a bit like me,' I cannot now recall. But I know that it felt perfectly logical at the time that Colin, who often complained how much of life had passed him by, should suddenly say, 'I've never seen a blue movie.' And should ask me, whom he considered to be a bit like him, 'Have you?'

I told him that I'd seen something that I supposed could be called, just, blueish, but that if he wanted to see for himself they were showing a cut version of *Deep Throat* in Adelaide that very week.

'What's *Deep Throat*?' he asked.

Upon which someone – and I am not going to say who – put their finger in their mouth and yodelled. And had the children not come down the stairs a second time, appalled by the racket we were making, there's no knowing what turn the conversation might have taken.

As it was, the appearance of unspotted youth reminded us that it was time we returned to our chalet. Vivien and Franz invited us to resume the indecorum at the Landhaus the following night. They had a few guests booked but they would cancel their bookings. That would cause them some satisfaction in itself. 'I'll do you a terrine of whiting and prawns, followed by a roulade of pork stuffed with smoked salmon,' Franz promised us. As we were about to leave, Angela said, 'Now I'm going to say something that Colin won't like me saying.'

The last words I remember were Colin's. 'Aw no, Enj,' he said. 'Don't do that, Enj.'

At four in the morning I woke up without a hangover and heard Ros padding about the chalet, laughing to herself. Away from the dense cluster of wineries the Barossa appears to be good sheep farming country. The gently rounded hills, pale gold in the daytime, are criss-crossed with animal tracks which from a distance look like rivulets that have forgotten which way to flow. In so far as you can tell with sheep they seem to like it here. But then it would be blank ingratitude to feel any other way. Even by the usual high standards of beneficence set by valleys the Barossa is painstakingly protective. To live in its shelter is to have a great arm around you, shielding you from every vicissitude.

Yet for all its moderation it can suddenly burgeon with almost tropical plenty. The garden path to the Landhaus, for example, is overhung with fig trees, wild cherry, weeping willow, and quince – a dense abundance of growth without, only matched by the fertility of Franz's cuisine within. Yes, we did accept the invitation to take up where we'd left off the night before, even though, in the clear light of morning, we had wondered whether anyone would ever remember having offered it. We'd ventured out of doors fairly early, careful not to wake the Davises, only to see Angela in the yard clearing away several dozen bottles. It was when she greeted us with a yodel that we knew we weren't free to leave the Barossa just yet.

We were not, of course, able to reproduce our previous uproar. Franz's commitment to the kitchen made that impossible. But out of their own house the Davises were more rampant than ever; Angela queenly and indecorous by turns, Colin unable to contain himself in the excitement of confessing everything he had never experienced. 'I've never done that,' he said. 'I don't think I would have the courage even to think about doing that.' Beneath his spectacles his eyes rolled in a riot of innocence. The world was all before him.

Over the roulade, he and Franz discussed a business idea they'd been pondering. They wanted to organize escorted trips to the Barossa for wealthy visitors and executives – escorted in the sense of in the company of a beautiful woman. Their idea was for a complete packaged weekend away from it all, a weekend of food, wine, conversation, exercise, all the civilized activities in short; after which if it was mutually agreeable, if it was what both parties without any sense of pressure felt to be appropriate – but not, absolutely not, if it wasn't – then . . .

'A bit of nooky would be all right,' Angela said.

'You could call it Vineyard Venery Safaris,' I suggested.

No one thought this snappy enough.

'Nooky Tours,' Angela proposed.

It must have been at around about this time that we knew we could not stay any longer in wine country. Pleasure was all very well, but we had a journey to continue. The Barossa was the Australian equivalent to the Valley of the Shadow of Death; no pilgrim was ever going to get where he was going if he paid too much attention to what was in it. So we said our fond farewells and in the morning headed back with heavy hearts to Adelaide.

Well, to Glenelg actually. Glenelg being the most popular of Adelaide's seaside suburbs, the birthplace itself of the State, and, according to Ros's father, the only resort in Australia that was spelt the same way backwards. Parents do not know the effect they have; the only reason we went to Glenelg was because we wanted to stay in a palindrome.

And we needed to be comfortable too. On the way back from the Barossa we had called in at a camper-van company which was prepared to rent us a vehicle one-way to Alice Springs. I hadn't definitely said yes, yet, but Ros had. She had even picked the colour van she wanted. It seemed to me that if we *were* to go ahead with this I needed to give my body two or three days of absolute rest. Some men like to compose their thoughts before an uncertain expedition; I like to repose my skeleton. So I rented a converted chapel with soft beds and a view of the sea from a fretful fugitive of Birmingham whose name was something like Donny Osmonde.

I actually found the chapel some time before I found Mr Osmonde. He was hard to locate, partly because he owned and serviced personally over thirty apartments on the seafront, and partly because he'd become a slave to the walkie-talkie system he'd installed to improve efficiency. When I finally reached him he was running in two directions at once across a fore-court, a portable telephone pressed to his ear, a three-foot aerial sticking out of the back pocket of his baggy jeans. He took me into his office to write me out a receipt for the rent he preferred that I gave him in advance. It was clear that he was anxious to improve his fortunes. A bound volume of *Think and Grow Rich* was open at page twenty on his desk, and on the floor I noticed a pile of *Entrepreneur Magazine*. Other books in the process of being worked through included *Increase Your Wealth* and *How to Get Rich in Mail Order* by Melvin Powers. The moment he learnt that I lived in London he asked me if I'd ever had any dealings with a certain firm of business consultants. He had recently sent them out fifty pounds for an advice package on estate management and was beginning to worry that he'd never hear from them again. I was surprised that he didn't consider himself a rich and successful man already, with over thirty holi-day apartments to his name, but like all Midlanders he was constitutionally incapable of self-satisfaction. To be born within a fifty-mile radius of Wolverhampton is a stain that no amount of laundering, not even a regular dip in the bracing waters of Glenelg, can ever remove. Shame sat enthroned in his soft Selly Oak eyes, even though every two or three minutes business bleeped in his back pocket.

I grew to like Glenelg in the few days we were there. It possessed a refined seediness, a snappy sort of decrepitude which came from its being part city and part seaside, part amusement park and part retirement spa. There were gaudy shops by the seafront where you could buy shells and postcards which showed naked beach girls and said, 'All the sun and all the tit,/ Is the reason why I haven't writ.' But there were also good delicatessens and boutiques patronized by smart elderly women who still retained their European accents. It rained for most of our stay, so there were no sunbathers on the beach; instead it became, as a beach should only ever be, a place for the acutely distressed. People wept on it. Priests told their beads on it. Others talked obsessively to themselves on it. Through the window of our converted chapel I even saw a young man tear his hair on it. And every morning at the same time a stern and lonely woman in her eighties – a retired headmistress indubitably – arrived with a plastic bag of crumbs which she would not distribute until all the seagulls on the beach were lined up like a class of first formers, still and silent and attentive, with their wings pinned rigidly to their sides and their beaks shut.

But the most distinctive feature of Glenelg was its trams – marvels of polished creaking timbers, inexplicable silver toggles, leather hanging straps, and seats whose swinging back rests enabled them, like the name Glenelg itself, to face in both directions. You could catch a tram from Glenelg to Adelaide or from Adelaide to Glenelg; there were no alternative routes. Though of course there was nothing to prevent you getting off at any stop in-between. I trammed it conscientiously into Adelaide each day so that the city should not charge me with indifference, but I can't say that I ever fell in love with it. I found it wedded rather too literal-mindedly to each side of its split personality. It was a writers' city and so it had too many bookshops; it was a Grand Prix circuit and so everyone drove like Alain Prost. The way to die in Adelaide is to walk out into the traffic reading.

We spent most of our time in the art gallery, or in the offices of the Royal Automobile Association of South Australia, or in Hindley Street, where the Italian coffee shops and Montenegran restaurants were clustered. In the art gallery we found H. J. Johnstone's *Evening Shadows, Backwater of the Murray*, an elegy on the passing of the Aborigines, all wistfulness and twilight, once the most reproduced of all Australian paintings. And we listened to a gallery guide who specialized in popularizing aesthetics for parties of schoolchildren – 'Whack that down in your notebooks. Picasso didn't hang about, he got stuck in.

Matisse the same – wallop!' Things were altogether more sedate at the Automobile Association on whom I called twice a day to see if there were *still* 214 kilometres of unmade track to negotiate on the road to Alice Springs. 'People do get through,' one of the girls told me, 'but we don't recommend the road.' She gave me a collection of strip maps to study and some leaflets detailing the hazards of outback motoring and wished me luck unconvincingly.

We fell into a Lebanese café in order to digest this information and do some route planning. 'Not very busy,' the proprietor said. 'Taking leetle rest after Festival.'

'You are?'

'No. They. In Festival very busy. 6,500 dollars a week. Now quiet. 3,400 dollars a week.'

'So people are having a break after the Festival?' I oughtn't really to have encouraged him. I could see him gearing up to tell us the whole story of his business life without verbs but anything was better than what I was reading. Who would study instructions for making a desert 'still' out of a tin can and a plastic sheet – enough to gather a thimbleful of water – if they could talk turnover to a Levantine instead?

'Break after Festival yes,' he said. 'At home. Television. Sandwiches. Not bothered eat out.'

'But when the Festival is on you do well?'

His face lit up. He had an intriguing scar, like a knife wound, from the left corner of his mouth down to the cleft in his chin. 'Oh, Festival! Very nice people. Like Lebanese food. Like good food.'

I asked him how he did on alternate years, when art gave way to grapes, and the Barossa staged the festivities. He screwed up his face, thereby deepening his scar, and shaped a wine glass with his hands. It was a contemptuous gesture implying fastidiousness, connoisseurship, non-liking of falafel. 'But Grand Prix . . .'

'Good?'

'Bloody good! 7,000 dollars a week.'

He took us to see a room he'd recently opened in the back of his establishment as a special facility for Grand Prix customers. He'd called it the Las Vegas coffee parlour. It was fitted out with smokey glass tables and photographs of Clint Eastwood and Sylvester Stallone on the walls. 'Good, eh?' he wanted to hear me agree. 'Beautiful, eh?'

'It's nice,' I said. 'It's got a good Grand Prix atmosphere.'

'Beautiful tables – very popular with boys.' He sat at one and gestured me to look through the glass at his knees. ''Scuse me,' he said to Ros. 'Girls sit here, boys look through. Very popular. Eh?'

Before we left he warned us to be careful of Arab terrorists on the plane back to London. There was even more scorn on his face when he pronounced the word Arab than when he'd shaped the wine glass. He gave us a demonstration of how you look out for terrorists without drawing attention to yourself. It required a drop into something between catalepsy and epilepsy – the head stayed rigid but the eyes rolled like a goanna's. Come the hijack you'd be the first to go.

'I'll try it,' I promised.

But terrorists weren't the main worry right now. I was still brooding about a particular paragraph in the Royal Automobile Association's safety and survival literature.

STAY WITH THE VEHICLE – If you have followed the standard advice of leaving word at settlements as to where you are going, a search party will come out eventually, and the vehicles will be far easier to find than isolated human beings in the vastness of the outback landscape.

Eventually?

Glenelg on the morning I went to pick up the campervan resembled Yarmouth the day Steerforth was washed ashore. A wild grey sea boomed upon the beach. A cold rain that was half salt-spray blew through the streets. On the Esplanade a couple of policemen sat in a squad car with its wipers on, watching the waves. Through the mist the tram appeared uncertainly, blinking like an old sea serpent. A number of war veterans in the regalia of remembrance staggered aboard, their medals and ribbons dripping, for this was also Anzac Day, the anniversary of the landing at Gallipoli, and survivors of that and other horrors were gathering for the great parade through the city. Had it not been for my appointment with Bill Richards, whose van I was collecting, I would have stayed in Adelaide for the morning and watched the march. Already, hours before they were due to walk to the Cross of Sacrifice, old battalions were reforming, Poles, Canadians, Maltese, Greeks in long white pleated skirts, all gathering behind their several banners. In the rain a solitary piper was tuning up. The usual feelings assailed me. There was no escape from the rhetoric. However gross the plot, you couldn't deny the players.

I turned up on Bill Richard's forecourt at the same time he did. He climbed out of a white Bentley, looking dry and jaunty. I was on foot, apprehensive, wet, and Anzac-haunted. Perfect firing-line fodder, in short, for Bill Richards' machine-gun conversation. I sat at his desk and let him spatter me with opinion. 'First law of outback motoring – don't stop for Aborigines. If they've run out of petrol it's because they've drunk it. If you stop they'll ask you for beer money. They'll steal from you. They won't do you any harm, and even if they threaten you they'll be so drunk you can blow 'em over. But they're a bloody nuisance. Punctures, of course, are your responsibility. If you drive over a bottle – even if it's in an Abo's mouth – that's your fault. I'm not a racist. I admire Aborigines – full bloods that is. They're good-looking, strong, and reliable. It's the half-castes that cause the trouble. I know we're to blame, but it's too late for us to do anything about it now. They're just pissants. Did you know that some of 'em get social security money for two wives? It's true anyway. We subsidize bigamy in this country. Mind you, I don't know how anyone can marry even one of them myself.'

He was a short, round teddy bear of a man, innocuous and bristlingly aggressive all at once, a wag, a pedant, an incorrigible joker, but shrewd, shrewd, his eyes wanted you to believe. 'I might have sold this business before you get to Alice,' he told me. 'I've got a bloke very interested. We kissed and got into bed, but then he shied at my price.'

'No way to behave,' I said. I was surprised by the sound of my own voice.

'Too right. But I think I can tickle him up a bit more. Have a good trip. Remember what I told you about the Abos. Mind the bulldust holes.'

I thought about those bulldust holes as I drove back to Glenelg to pick up Ros and the provisions for the trip. I knew the word bulldust as an Australian alternative – at once more polite and more dismissive – to bullshit. It had never before occurred to me that there actually was such a thing, that it disguised craters in the road which could break your axle if you drove through them. All along I'd been apprehensive about this leg of our journey, but only now did I understand the enormity of what we were undertaking. Real bulldust! We were going to the very source of the nation's mythology, utterly unprepared and unprotected we were heading for the white hot forge of Australian metaphor itself.

Stiffen the bloody lizards!

THIRTEEN

WHER. EDNA. LAIDE. ME

Listening to the ripping open of tent flaps even before the dawn had shown her rosy cheeks above Mt Ohlssen Bagge, high in the Flinders Ranges, I framed a nice philosophical distinction between real life and camping – real life was not held together by Velchrome.

Then, watching the earliest risers returning from their tree-hacking expeditions with armloads of firewood, it occurred to me that I, who professed no protective feelings towards Nature, had done less to damage it in a lifetime of indifference than some of these mad axemen did in a morning of enthusiasm. Yet again, I said to an incurious galah, the only truly virtuous man is the sceptic. Contented with which idea I strolled over to the shower rooms – the one person on the campsite not wearing a grey towelling tracksuit for pyjamas.

Strictly speaking we were not supposed to be in the Flinders Ranges at all. They hadn't figured in my original itinerary. The plan had been that we would motor gently out of Adelaide, getting the feel of the van and so on, spend the first night in Clare in the area known, with some shortfall of cartographic inventiveness, as Mid North South Australia, load up with necessary provisions at Port Augusta – ten litres of water each, according to the RAA, enough food for every person in the vehicle to survive five days on, several sheets of plastic, a machete, salt tablets, an aluminium space blanket, a tube of Bostik – and then head on up the Stuart Highway to Coober Pedy. Well, the Clare part had gone according to schedule, but after that the languorous landscape of Upper Mid North South Australia had begun to work a dreamy sort of charm on us. The town of Gladstone was flat and silent but we drove round and round it, transfixed. We crawled like snails through the pretty settlements of Laura, the birthplace of C. J. Dennis, author of *The Sentimental Bloke*, and Wirrabara, a honeypot surrounded by forests and overlooked by Mt Remarkable. By the time we'd come out the other end of Telowie Gorge with its hills of Black-boys, spears raised against the sky, and glowing gum trees striped like tigers where their barks had peeled and flaked, we were at the mercy of the distant mountains. A couple of kilometres before Port Augusta we took the road to Quorn instead of Woomera, and within the hour found ourselves at yet another 150th birthday party. This time in the dusty playground of the local school.

Once again the population was in fancy dress – the women in starched white aprons and mob caps, the men, according to whether they were intellectuals or businessmen, done up as bumpkins or landowners. We arrived in time to see the Federal Member handing out medals to the winners of the Open Male and Open Female Fun Run. 'I think it would be quite remiss of me not to thank the people of Quorn for showing true country hospitality,' he said, once he'd kissed Cindy Smith, the Open Female winner, on both cheeks.

This was not Tanunda though. There was no wine tasting tent and no Luftwaffe music either. Quite the contrary. In the presence of no less a person than John Bannon, the Premier of South Australia himself, the loyal schoolchildren of Quorn, dressed like little serving folk, stood to attention as the Union Jack was unfurled upon a flag pole and one of their number stifled her sense of ribaldry just long enough to deliver the original 1836 Oath of Allegiance. 'I love my country, the British Empire – I salute her flag, the Union Jack. I honour her Queen. I promise faithfully to obey her laws.'

Sitting on a box covered in red material the Premier nodded his approval. On one side of him sat his wife, on the other the Lord and Lady Mayoress of Quorn. The Lady Mayoress was in period dress; the Lord Mayor might have been. 'When I think of those pioneers trudging out into the scrub,' the Premier said, casting his eye upon a far horizon so that there should be no confusion between the scrub and Quorn, 'I'm lost in admiration.'

I was fairly far gone in wonderment myself. John Bannon looked about nineteen. Which was young for a Premier even by South Australian standards. And yet he remembered where he was – 'I predict a great future for places like Quorn'; made only two mistakes with the names of the Lord and Lady Mayoress – one with hers, one with his; and even wove a little theme – that of transportation – into his impromptu speech. Ever since he had been transported in he had been transported back, and wasn't at all looking forward to being transported out.

It was hard not to like him, he bore so strong a resemblance to the State all over which, for this interminable sesquicentenary, he had to consent to be transported. He and South Australia – they possessed the same buttoned-up juvenescence and humourless charm. You couldn't help feeling that they would both be at their best in another 150 years' time. In the meantime the State could not stop squeezing itself into period costume while its Premier kept his collar stiff and fastened tight around his neck and his black socks smooth around his ankles.

I bought a foot-long sausage on a wooden stick and drove eastwards past ruined villages – crumbling monuments to misplaced optimism – into the Flinders Ranges proper.

We camped for two nights at Wilpena Pound, making bonfires and throwing ourselves into all the other attendant rituals with as much gusto, I am ashamed to say, as the psychomotor retarded axemen in the tents around us. Except that because I had no axe to call my own, because we hadn't yet been to Port Augusta to pick up a machete, I had to rip dead trees apart for firewood with my bare hands. On one of my trips into the undergrowth a pair of feeding kangaroos stopped what they were doing to watch me, even let me gather within twenty yards of them, but didn't offer any help. Their proximity exhilarated me, though, and I kept a fraternal eye open for them, calling them *my* kangaroos until some pedant told me they were euros.

'You should allocate at least two hours to walk far enough into Wilpena Pound to appreciate the grandeur of this vast amphitheatre (16 km long × 6 km wide), surrounded by towering peaks,' a leaflet issued by the Flinders Ranges Tourist Services suggested. 'We recommend that you walk past the deserted Settlers cottage then take the track on the right which leads to the lookout area on Wangara Hill. From here you can appreciate the vastness of the Pound and obtain a peep over its outer rim.'

We did precisely as we were instructed and were rewarded at last with a peep over the outer rim of an Australian marriage as well. Even before it came into view we could hear it puffing up the hill, fracturing the silence. 'Didn't I tell you you'd be at the top before me?' we heard him say. 'I told you you'd win. I told you it'd be the case of the tortoise and the hare.' He was wearing a red shirt, grey flannel trousers and black business shoes. He was middle-aged, raw-faced, and had the indomitable complacency of a failed father, husband and friend stamped upon him. She was prematurely hunched, in slacks that were both style-less and impractical and one of those ill-fitting satin blouses that put-upon women always seem to wear, not giving her enough room even to breathe in. I take it to be the modern equiva-lent of a hair shirt, and I took it that what she was doing penance for was him. Because even she, who was of course the last to know, now *did* know that she had listened half her life away to the opinions of an oaf.

'Like a great big bloody drive-in, innit?' he said, looking out over the vast amphitheatre (16 km long × 6 km wide), surrounded by towering peaks.

She flinched – ashamed that we were there to overhear him.

He wasn't convinced that the marker indicating the best place to appreciate the Pound from had got it right. He found an alternative spot, a yard or so away, and called her to it. 'This, in my opinion, is a better view. Here. Come here. Look from my rock.' He took the binoculars she'd been using and then handed them back to her. 'Now that they're focussed you might be able to see something with them,' he said. 'That'd be the furthest point, I would suggest, of the whole bloody shebang. There – where that moss is.'

'That's not moss.'

'I don't mean moss in the sense of specifically moss – but you know what I'm talking about.'

'Yeah,' she said, 'I know what you're talking about.'

He suddenly flew into a fury with the apple he'd been eating. 'This apple core is rubbish,' he said.

We let them descend before us. 'I'll go first,' he told his wife. 'You put your feet where I put mine. No – no – NO – on the edges. I may be wrong but I think it's better.' A couple coming up asked him if it was far to go. 'No, you're nearly there. You'll find a marker telling you where to look from but there's a rock just before it. I think the view's better there, but you judge for yourself.'

At the bottom, just past the Settlers cottage, we ran into them again. He had found an unmarked track he wanted to follow. 'It's bound to lead bloody somewhere,' he was saying.

'I'm going back the way we came,' his wife said. 'I've done enough walking. I'll see you at the car-park.'

He snorted. 'You bloody hope,' he said.

Although I was not yet initiate in campsite mysteries I knew that much of what I saw men doing at this one – shaving in cold water when there was an abundance of hot, washing what wasn't dirty, wearing bobble hats – I could have seen anywhere. But there could be no doubting the specific Australian content of every conversation that concerned a gas cylinder or a barbecue or a Mitsubishi Pajero Superwagon. The knick-knackery of camping spoke unambiguously to the gender differentiation anxiety which troubles the heart of every adult male Australian not in his dotage, and the anxiety spoke loudly back, theorizing and dogmatizing and brutalizing. 'Ah, yeah,' I heard from every corner of the compound, 'Ah, yeah, I've been there . . . Ah, yeah, I once tried that . . . Ah, yeah, but I've always found . . .' But they didn't fool me. I knew a bunch of Girl Guides playing at being Boy Scouts when I saw one.

I enjoyed it for all that. We woke early in the mornings to the sounds of warfare – turquoise parrots and galahs coloured the same grey and pink as a camper's sleeping-suit, fighting for every tree. High above us the mountains were tipped blood-red like the blades of halberds. As the day wore on the red would become orange and then brown and then purple. By which time I would be ready to go looking for firewood and my friends the euros. The first smells of cooking would waft across to us, filtered through the more pungent aroma of eucalyptus. Then it was music time – pop from transistors, Beethoven from cassette players. 'What a friend I have in

Jesus' from the Christians on a holiday weekend retreat, gathered for prayers and hymns in their canvas chapel. Pulped into a thing of sentiment I wandered around the camp, between the fires, muffled, like Henry V before Agincourt. A little touch of Howie in the night.

Before finally heading out of the Flinders Ranges we thought we might head just a little further into them. Once again we took the hint from our tourist literature: 'a drive of 52 km north from Wilpena leads to the township of Blinman where copper was mined for thirty years from 1862. You may inspect the old mine workings, then call at the quaint bar of the 120-year-old North Blinman Hotel.' Blinman turned out to be 200 yards of bitumen on what was otherwise a dirt road. If we'd had the right vehicle we could have turned left and driven west for a bit, turned right and driven north for a bit, and eventually we would have come to Lake Eyre, and Sturt's Stony Desert, and Cooper's Creek. Instead we called in at the 120-year-old Hotel. There was a quaint old bar there right enough, but it was squeezed by the refurbishments – a dining lounge large enough to feed several hundred, and a pool room, I mean a *swimming* pool room, in which I saw a sign that said, 'No swinging from rafters, splashing, or bombing. Save water.' Once again I was face to face with one of the great mysteries of Australian tourism. We were in a remote spot; we had negotiated what were virtually mule tracks to make it; we had not seen another vehicle for two hours; and yet here we stood in a pub that was patently pushed to handle the considerable business that came its way. How and when did its customers get here?

Seeing me looking perplexed, a couple sitting quietly at the bar drinking south Australian lager and lime gave me a smile. 'Hot, eesn't eet?' they said. They were from West Bromwich.

Just outside Blinman was a depressingly bare and shadeless

cemetery containing a memorial to William Darton Kekwick, born London 1822, died Blinman 1872 – 'In admiration of his pluck, endurance, and loyalty to John McDouall Stuart, as 2nd in command from 1859–63 when the British Flag was placed in the Centre of Australia 22nd April, 1860 and on the shores of the Indian Ocean, 25th July, 1862.' After all that tearing about the continent Blinman seemed a cruelly quiet place for Kekwick to have finished up. Later on, and in another context, I learnt that Stuart himself is buried in Kensal Green. On the principle I formulated at Bethany, that it is preferable to lie not too distant from the living, I would say that the leader is enjoying a happier retirement than his deputy.

Since we were doing death we called in at Kanyaka, one of the many pastoral ventures of the 1850s and '60s which were destroyed by drought and whose crumbling remains are still just visible on the road between Quorn and Hawker. Some are mere piles of rubble, but Kanyaka was in the process of being restored. You could make out the men's quarters, the cart shed, the stables, even a cobbled street. Soon the window frames would be back in and the chimney stacks would be repaired, and maybe even a coffee shop would be installed – the Carysfort, perhaps, after the Earl whose son, Hugh Proby, took out the original lease. But the best part of Kanyaka would always be its doom – the signs pointing to Death Rock and the Black Hole, the creek which had once given hope but was now only a bone-dry gash in the earth, the little graveyard in the baking clay, where even the one solitary tree was dead and the forgotten headstones were simple crosses made with rotten logs fastened together with rusted fencing wire.

Back in the van we cheered ourselves up by turning on the radio. Mrs Thatcher was saying that she wouldn't bow down to dictators or truck with terrorists. I suddenly felt ashamed of the Kanyakans for giving in so easily to mere starvation. The other item of interest related to the discovery by Melbourne scientists of shellfish remains on a man-made site which they'd carbon dated as 80,000 years old. So far it had been assumed that man went back no further than about 45,000 years; now it seemed as though the Aborigines could nearly double that, making them the oldest homo sapiens in the whole world. Another first for Australia. I remembered an earlier observation of Ros's that Australians were perpetually marking themselves and writing themselves reports. So – 10 out of 10, Australia! And well done those blackfellers!

We drove into a caravan park outside Quorn and went to bed early. The following day we would be on the Stuart Highway at last, heading north. And we wanted to be fresh. Some time after midnight I was woken by what sounded like live organ music. Had I been asked to name the tune I would have said it was less a medley than a fugue, and yet somehow more like Rodgers and Hammerstein than Frescobaldi. But given that there were neither churches nor discothèques near by, that Quorn itself was fifteen minutes away across the railway track, and that only we and a couple of caravans shared the park, I had to assume that what I'd heard I'd merely dreamt. I went to sleep again, berating myself for being trivial while my brain played 'Some Enchanted Evening', confusing it spasmodically with the 'Capriccio Pastorale'.

In the morning I ran into the owners of the caravans in the shower rooms. One looked a bit like Arthur Miller and was in fact called Arthur; the other reminded me of Norman Mailer but was called Ernest. They were discussing their wives when I walked in. 'Now that mine's retired she says she's got to do something with her time,' Arthur said. 'So she bought a piano.'

'Mine too,' Ernest said.

'The trouble was she thought she'd get rusty while we were off camping, so I got her this portable Yamaha.'

'Ah, we thought we heard a Yamaha last night, but then we thought it was just some sort of echo of ours.'

'So that was *your* Yamaha that *we* heard? We thought it was a bit funny. Not that my wife really likes these little instruments.'

'No, mine doesn't either. But it's just while we're away.'

I plunged my head under the shower. When I came out Ernest was explaining how his wife specialized in playing piano accompaniment for blind square-dancers. 'You'd be amazed how good some of them can be,' he said.

Arthur said, 'My father's blind.'

'Oh, yeah.'

'And my mother's only 5 per cent sighted.'

'Oh, yeah, yeah.'

'But I've never heard them mention anything about square-dancing.'

Ernest ran his hand through his hair. He had large deposits of sleep in both his eyes. Like many elderly men he was beginning to look like a woman. 'Well, they don't all do it,' he said.

Arthur wanted to know where Ernest came from. Melbourne, Ernest told him. That seemed to be exactly as Arthur suspected. 'Do you know the blind telephone exchange people there?' he asked.

'Yeah, well, yeah, I know some.'

'No, but do you know Fat Doreen?' He measured her with his hands. There was no mistaking her once he'd finished.

'Doreen? No. Hang on. Doreen? Yeah, I think I do.'

A queer look of self-satisfaction passed over Arthur's face. He wiped his hands on the jacket of his grey track-jamas. 'Well she's my wife's niece. *She* plays a Yamaha.'

Five minutes out of Port Augusta we passed a circus rehearsing in a field. We were expecting to see wildlife on the Stuart Highway but we hadn't counted on the first animal we saw being an elephant. But an hour later we were rewarded with emus; first a family of seven, apparently aware of the hazards of the highway and actually looking left, right, and left again before dashing out directly in front of us; then a more flighty pair who danced across the road with clumsy grace, like netball players on the razzle, their knees knocking, their fur stoles ruffling at their scraggy necks. They reminded me of a girl I'd once gone out with, uncannily enough called Thin Doreen, who had worked at the pet-food counter in Boots. She had the same uncertainly balanced head, the same burning red eye, the same darting sideways look. She had even owned a black feather boa which rose and fluttered when she ran exactly as the emus' did. Thereafter I wasn't able to see an emu come lolloping out of the scrub, looking vaguely guilty as if she'd just misbehaved (surely all emus are shes), without thinking fondly of Thin Doreen.

According to our maps we were now in salt lake country – the vast Lake Torrens to the east, the smaller lakes, Finniss and Dutton and Macfarlane, to the west; but from the road there was no break in the monotony of the scrubby plains. Occasionally there would be a track and a sign pointing to a homestead, otherwise there was nowhere to go. In a clearing in the bush we suddenly saw an encampment of thirty or so Mad Max bikers. Men in beards and singlets looking up from what they were doing – mending, polishing, sharpening – disturbed by the sound of our engine. Washing was slung between the trees. Fires were burning. And outside every tent a bike was waiting, like a tethered horse. They looked like the last remnants of a marauding horde; warriors and refugees at one and the same time; all that was left to pillage and be pillaged after the final holocaust.

As they raised their faces we saw an indifferent hostility, a sort of replete malevolence, in every eye. It was as if we were being given leave to pass, permission to live another day, simply because they weren't hungry right now. 'I feel as if we're being looked at by lions,' Ros said. I would have preferred lions.

There might have been some advice on how to handle lions in
the RAA outback safety and survival literature I carried; but I
knew there was no mention of how you mollify a biker. I put
my foot down hard on the accelerator and didn't come off it
until we reached Woomera.

At one time you would have needed a permit to enter
Woomera. But by 1982 it had been officially declared a South
Australian country town and was now open to you to visit
provided you didn't intend hanging around too long. Although
the barriers were up, I assumed that the sign on the checkpoint
building was meant to be taken seriously: 'Residency restricted
to Defence Related Employees.' Not that anyone would have
wanted to reside there. It was a town of barrack-like accommodation, corrugated metal houses, drab blocks of flats built in the
town council style of the 1950s, and demolition sites. Almost the
first thing we saw when we drove in was a prettily painted
collection of bombs and rockets, variously described as a Heritage
Centre and an Aircraft and Missile Park, thereby proving that
there is no past that can't be made our proud inheritance, and no
weapon that can't be made a toy. I took a stroll around the
exhibits and found an MK-10 1,000 lb S.P. bomb fitted with a
type 117 retarding tail, a Seaslug, a dinky little MK-82 250 kg
High Drag bomb with a nifty tail section known as a 'snake-
eye', a Skylark (what larks) high-altitude research rocket with a
pencil-slim body and a silver nose, together with an assortment
of Meteor MK 7 jets and MK 12 Bofors guns and sundry small
rockets and baby bombs. After which I would have liked a lie
down. Decorated in fun colours and tilted at rollicking angles
though these objects of our heritage were, they still gave the lie
in their every lineament to any claim that they might in themselves be morally non-committal. Even without their engines
and their warheads they were malevolent. 'The playthings of
Satan,' I said to Ros, which surprised her as I am not normally
given to Biblical expression.

Looking for somewhere to have coffee we found a sort of prefabricated shopping precinct which might have been the old mess quarters. I was taken aback by the glamour of the people using it. Given the vast nothingness that surrounded Woomera, and the howling desert wind that blew through it, and its state of dilapidation and dismantlement, you didn't expect to see sleek black G.I.s with glossy moustaches and hats tilted rakishly walking through its streets. Nor were you prepared for officers' wives in high city chic or sharp subalterns with murderous creases in their pants. It was all a bit like being on a film set watching a *Twilight Zone* remake of *From Here to Eternity*.

We went into the Woomera Community Store, a long milk bar where people were eating chips from paper buckets and black American service wives sat sipping milkshakes and looking suicidal. While I was getting coffee Ros found a place next to Alitha, an eight-months-pregnant Mississippian, wife of a U.S. airman here on a three-year stint. She counted out her fate on her fingers for us. One done, two still to do. Woomera? 'It's a trip,' she told us. I'd always thought a trip was a good thing, but it wasn't the way Alitha said it. She was a big, lively eyed woman, rendered comatose by life in the desert and kept verbally inchoate by being born an American. As far as I could make out Woomera was getting worse from a social point of view because its service personnel were being cut back. There used to be about 14,000 people here, now there were only one or two. And everybody knew everybody else's business. 'You hear a whole bunch of stuff about what's happening here – I tell you,' she said. 'But I dunno. Like I said, it's a trip.' She was so bored that she couldn't get un-bored long enough to join the other wives on their big-treat shopping expeditions to Port Augusta. It was the journey she couldn't face. 'Just a whole bunch of road,' she said. And any day now her mother was due to arrive. She was dreading it. Not dreading seeing her mother but dreading her mother seeing Woomera. 'If all she sees is here, she'll think – Australia? – Wow! I'm coming from where I've got everything to where I've got nothing.'

Ros said that she had taken it for granted that American bases were always well stocked with everything Americans were used to. Alitha did something extraordinary with her lips and cast her eyes comically around the Woomera Community Store. 'Anyway,' she said, 'this isn't a base. It's classified as a site.'

We didn't get to the bottom of that distinction. All I can deduce from it is that they serve chips and dim sums at a site and that you're better off at a base. But Alitha had something else she preferred talking about. 'Do you know what I wanna do?' she said. 'I wanna go to England.'

'England?' we both said together.

'Yeah, England. Does it rain in England?'

'Yes,' we both said together.

'I wanna go to England.'

She hadn't seen any rain, to speak of, since she'd been here. She longed for rain. I could see her trying to remember what it looked like, what it felt like, what colour it was.

A couple more service wives, also black, passed our table and nodded coldly at her. You could smell small-town trouble. Then a third arrived, wheeling a pushchair. 'You wanna sit down?' Alitha asked her. The woman looked fed up. 'No, no I don't think so. I think I'm ready to leave now,' she said. She had only just come.

Alitha rose and hoped that our trip would be a trip. Together we wished her rain. She didn't know what we meant at first, then she remembered. 'Oh, wow,' she said.

Outside, a man was selling tickets for the Woomera Drama Group's production of *Blithe Spirit*. Unfortunately there was no performance that evening. As we drove out of town an impossibly handsome black G.I. standing at a bus stop flashed his expensive teeth at us and saluted. Something gold on his wrist caught the sun. Three minutes later we were in the desert.

Between Woomera and Coober Pedy there are not many diversions off the Stuart Highway you would think of taking, which is just as well since you wouldn't be allowed to take them if there were. For this is prohibited territory, rocket and atom bomb testing country. Maralinga is in there somewhere to the west, though far enough away, my guide book assured me, not to cause any contemporary traveller concern.

It was a long and tedious drive to Coober Pedy. The landscape threw up a few variations – the odd salt lake, an occasional declivity, a subtle shift of shading in the scrub – but the road itself often ran horrendously straight, showing you where you were going miles before you got there, and how little it was different from where you'd been. Apart from dead kangaroos on the roadside – a shocking nightly slaughter this, providing a day-long running buffet for crows and eagles the whole length of the Stuart Highway – we passed nothing, were passed by nothing, for three hours. Only once did we stop and that was at the Glendambo Roadhouse for fuel. The girl who served us had a neck covered in love-bites. So it was either not as isolated out here as it looked, or she had resorted to biting herself.

Fortunately we had Question Time at the Australian House of Representatives to listen to on the radio. We switched on just in time to hear Hawke handling the house with his familiar brute verbosity, his voice cutting the air like a snapped cable, his integrity untouched by 'the usual squalid bifurcations of the opposition'. The main issue of the day was the crisis in the commodity markets, for his handling of which the Government Minister, Mr Dawkins, was getting it in the neck from the Leader of the National Party, Mr Sinclair. Mr Dawkins accused Mr Sinclair of being the 'least trusted man in Australia and indeed the world'. Mr Sinclair disagreed with this. Mr Dawkins wasn't surprised. Mr Sinclair returned to the price of wheat, whereupon Mr Dawkins – to drop into the vernacular with him – did his block. 'What would you know?' he screamed. 'You're an idiot! You wouldn't know the difference between mandatory and voluntary.'

It wasn't for a stranger to take sides, but I couldn't fail to observe that, although the Australian parliament had adopted the English system of members addressing one another through a Speaker, it hadn't grasped that this entailed an adherence to third-person decorum. Where was the point of referring to someone as the Honourable Member if you were going to shout 'You're an idiot!' at him a moment later?

In social life generally Australians weren't enthusiastic about the principle of moderation inherent in the concept of a 'chair'. They preferred a more direct and informal manner of address. This meant that there were no discreetly implied 'thees' and 'thous' in the language of daily discourse either. An Australian *you* is always a *tu* or a *toi*. Not the *tu* or the *toi* that you are taught about in school – to be used in a relaxed or intimate context, when speaking to friends or family or small children; but a *tu* or a *toi* – a *you* or a *YOU* – as a small nuclear anti-personnel device, like the MK 10 1,000 lb S.P. bomb fitted with a type 117 retarding tail we'd seen in the Missile Park in Woomera.

It was Ros who put it like this, incidentally. I thought she was exaggerating rather. I thought being called YOU by an Australian was no worse than being strafed by a Meteor MK 7. But that's the other fault of Australians. They overemphasize.

Just before the broadcast ended, the member for Jagga Jagga squeezed in a proposal for 1988 to be proclaimed the first ever Earth Repair Year. It was extraordinary timing. For we were now approaching Coober Pedy – Australia's 'Opal Wonderland' – whose earth was quite beyond repair, not to be healed or mended in 1988 or any other year. The spectacle of Coober

Pedy at sunset could not be compared with anything either of us had ever seen before. It was like entering a war zone. The red desert sand, the pyramids of dirt, the dugouts, the telegraph poles everywhere, the corrugated water tanks, the tin sheds, the drills, the vacuum blowers, the thin, temporary-looking strip of bitumen that was the main street, the red rubble on either side, the whole tumult of shanty-town impermanence, as if everything that wasn't merely earth could be lifted up and transported somewhere else in an afternoon – all contributed to an atmosphere of almost unimaginable ferment. We couldn't believe our eyes. We drove round and round, astonished by the dust and the hectic pace of the trucks – many of them marked EXPLOSIVES – loving the rudimentary functionalism of it all; the mining town and the minefields indivisible, not just production evident everywhere we looked but also dealing, chalkboard signs hanging outside the hotels announcing the presence of opal buyers, experts from Hong Kong and Singapore who sat in illuminated windows with their scales beside them, waiting for business like the girls in Kalgoorlie. Then we drove out again while there was still light so that we could repeat the drama of our entry.

We took up residence in a caravan park in the very centre of Coober Pedy, a swirling dustbowl at the foot of a mine belonging to Elias Christianos. The mine was a vast sandcastle, pitted with corrugated-iron water tanks, sheds, shacks, broken-down utilities, and round tin barrels of the kind used for mixing up raffle tickets. Chimneys and air vents and coolers protruded at queer angles like the eyes of periscopes. Part of the hill was buttressed with a stone wall, presumably to stop the whole pile sliding into the caravan park, so that it looked like a ruined Aztec fortress or the remains of a Babylonian temple. An enormous windlass stood to the right of Christianos's mine, with a little battered bucket hanging from it, 120 feet in the air. Next to that was a rodeo-style sign which said COOBER PEDY

VIDEO and was visible all over town. And next to that the Australian flag fluttered, a dusty red all over. Above the opposite wall of the caravan park it was just possible to see the lights of the Italo/Australian Miners Club on Garibaldi Street.

According to Sam, who collected the camping fees, the Miners Club was the place to drink, but it seemed easier just to walk up the road and try the bar of the Opal Inn Hotel/Motel. That was after we'd vainly attempted to clean ourselves up a bit. 'Getting rid of the fucking dust,' I heard somebody remark in the shower rooms, 'that's all I fucking care about.' 'The fucking trouble is,' I heard his friend observe from the next cubicle, 'you no sooner get it fucking off you than it's fucking on you again.'

On the main street some of the underground opal caves and gift shops were still open. So was the underground Catholic church and the underground motel. There was even an underground bookshop, though in Coober Pedy that does not mean what it does elsewhere; I went in, but found no Henry Miller or de Sade. And no Orianna Ooi either. The bar at the Opal Inn was busy. I'd read that there were between forty-seven and fifty-one different nationalities in Coober Pedy and I estimated that between thirty-seven and forty-one of them were here tonight. The majority of the faces, though, were European – Greek, Polish, Hungarian, Croatian – the inured faces of last-ditch migration. Working men, gamblers, maybe even desperadoes. This, presumably, was what Darwin had been like before the social services moved in.

But it didn't feel a dangerous bar. People smiled at us. A vivacious Aborigine with a look of Sammy Davis Jnr about him, and even an eye patch, gave us a friendly nod. Then someone fell into me and said, 'Where you from?' He was ill-favoured and mischievous – a self-conscious ratbag – and very drunk.

I told him, London. 'Ah, London?' He looked at Ros to see if I was telling the truth, then he fell into her. 'London – he's a good country.'

He was Hungarian, that much he was prepared to tell us; but when I asked him what he did in Coober Pedy he dropped his voice and let the alcohol liquefy his already runny vowels. I was able to make out just one sentence – 'I'm a bludger' – and to get the general idea that he was in the second-hand business.

'Second-hand what?' I asked him.

There was a sudden return of intelligibility. 'What you want?'

I didn't have to answer. Someone he knew walked by and asked him how he was. Nothing like as well as he would be, he said, if the person gave him money. A hundred dollar note was handed over without any ado. 'See?' he laughed. 'I'm a bludger.'

He insisted on buying us beers and on our joining him at a table. We accepted the beers but insisted on staying at the bar. We didn't want to get trapped in some corner with him. He was impossible to hear and becoming impossible to bear. He could hardly stand or speak. He had a small, round, corrupt but sentimental face which he lolled against my chest. Suddenly he said, 'Yewish.'

I shrugged my shoulders. 'Yewish,' he said. He tried to improve his pronunciation. 'Shewish, shewish.' He stroked his nose.

I might have been slow but I wasn't *that* slow. 'Who?' I said. 'You?'

He let out a ghastly laugh. He showed me his brown teeth. 'You, you.'

'Yes, me,' I said. 'But not you too?' I'd decided that he could easily be. I had an uncle that looked just like him.

But he was shaking his head vehemently, half laughing and half groaning. He rubbed a hand over his face. From between his fingers a few broken, incoherent sounds escaped. 'If I tell you,' he seemed to be saying, 'if I tell you, you'll chayte me.'

'If you tell us what?'

His voice went very soft, even pathetic. 'If I tell you what I am.'

'I don't mind if you're not Jewish,' I said.

'No. What I did. If I tell you you'll chayte me.'

'Tell us and see.'

'You'll chayte me.'

'We won't.'

'You will. You will chayte me.' There were tears in the corner of his eyes. Old tears. Green tears.

'We won't.' We promised him we wouldn't. We took oaths upon everything that was holy. We were almost as amused as he was distressed, though comedy wasn't wholly absent from his mortification either. He was an extremely experienced maudlin drunk.

He formed some letters with his mouth. I strained my ears. 'You—'

'Yes?'

'You'll chayte me.'

'I swear to God I won't.'

He moved his lips again, this time very close to my face. I could smell a lifetime of rich food. 'S.S.,' I heard him say. Then he turned to Ros. 'Hungarian S.S.,' he coughed. It was such a phlegmy sound that he had to cover his mouth with his hand.

'We HATE you,' we both said together.

We discovered later that we'd been talking to Gypsy Les, Coober Pedy's foremost, in fact Coober Pedy's only, junk dealer. 'He'd rip you off as soon as look at you,' one of the young barmen told us, 'but you've got to feel for the poor bastard – his girlfriend's crook, seriously crook, and he's been chewin' the rag for months.' Which was one of the reasons we didn't put a late-night call through to Simon Wiesenthal. The other was that just about everybody else in the bar looked as though they'd worked for one S.S. or another at some time in their lives. And, if a hole in the ground in Coober Pedy was the only place they could run to, well there was a kind of justice in that.

The barman who talked to us about Gypsy Les also filled us in on a few details about the town: what it's population was – somewhere between three and six thousand; who ran it – 'We don't have police and we don't have a council – we've got a Progress Committee'; and how his opal claim was going – 'I'm still serving behind the bloody bar, aren't I?' It cost $25 for a PSPP – a Precious Stone Prospecting Permit – and once you had that there was nothing to stop you going out and buying four wooden pegs, nailing a plastic identification disc to each one, and then finding a square of dust no bigger than 50 metres by 50 metres to drive them in. If you weren't happy with your square you could try another one, and even another one after that, for the same $25. Though every time you registered a claim it would cost you a further $22. The only restrictions were these: you couldn't peg anyone else's claim; you couldn't peg in the middle of the main street; and you couldn't peg under the Stuart Highway. Coober Pedy was a town which found any restraints upon its personal freedoms irksome, but it had begrudgingly accepted this last prohibition when the main arterial highway between Adelaide and Darwin – the only pass- able road connecting the south of Australia to the north – collapsed one afternoon into someone's mine.

''Course I haven't been here long enough to be able to answer all your questions,' the barman said, once he got bored with me. 'You ought really to have been talking to Bill Stretton. Yeah, I reckon Bill Stretton'd be your man. Beaut bloke. Beard down to here. Used to patrol the dog fence. Met everybody in his time. A real character.'

'Where can I find him?'

'You can't. He died four months ago.'

It turned out that Bill Stretton wasn't the only Coober Pedy character we'd missed out on meeting by a month here or a year there. Iron Man Jim Shaw, otherwise known as the Human Buckjumper, was one we ought to have known. He had come to Coober Pedy in 1921 the hard way, pushing a wheelbarrow from Tarcoola, a distance of well over 200 kilometres. Every time he came to a hill Iron Jim had to empty his barrow, carry it over, and then go running back for his belongings. It took him a long time to complete his journey. Aeroplane George was altogether speedier. To this day no one knows what Aboriginal magic he called upon to get him from one place to another, but stories abound of motorists seeing him in Coober Pedy as they drove out of it and then finding him strolling through Kulgera, 400 kilometres up the track. My theory is twins, but the one person I put this to in Coober Pedy said that Aborigines don't come in twins.

And then there was Bert Paxton who used to go opal divining stark naked when the moon was full. Some coyness surrounds the question of what Bert went divining with. But he was also known to lie on the dust hills, still naked, and to shout, 'I'm recharging,' to passers-by. It was George Van Brugge who told us about Bert Paxton. He'd been recommended to us as the man who conducted the most informative tours around Coober Pedy and we found him in his opal showrooms wearing a Wild West hat and selling earrings to some visitors in an accent that had as much to do with Amsterdam as Australia. The next day we went out with him on his bus.

He took us up into the Stuart Ranges close to where Willie Hutchison found the first opal in 1915, so that we could 'noodle' – that's to say get down on our hands and knees and fossick in the dirt for the wherewithal to make inelegant prismatic earrings. Then we went to Rudy's mine to try our hand at fault divining – pointing a parallel pair of metal rods at the cave wall and waiting for them to open. 'It's all done by bodily electricity,' George explained, which was how we came to get on to Bert Paxton. My rods did not only not part, they actually twitched closer together. 'You don't have what it takes,' George told me.

Outside Rudy's mine a pair of dusty camels with teeth as brown as those of Gypsy Les were rubbing necks. One or other of them was being trained for the great Ayers Rock to the Gold Coast Camel Race, due to get underway, like so much else in Australia, in 1988. This would be the longest camel race ever held in the country or, for all George knew, the world. It was a pity Rudy himself wasn't here for us to meet; he too was quite some character.

This characterfulness of Coober Pedy was, in George's view, one of the reasons why so many people who were merely passing through for an afternoon ended up staying for a lifetime. As we drove around he pointed out any number of temporary tin shacks or clapped-out caravans on dust heaps or half-drilled dugouts, which were the accommodation of people just like us, innocent tourists who had not been able to bring themselves to leave. A couple he had taken out on this very bus now actually worked for him; he showed us the red hill in the side of which they were excavating their new home, miles out of town where a hot wind howled and there was nothing to look at but endless pyramids of sand. They might as soon have set up house between the Iranian and the Iraqi armies.

I didn't doubt George's story. This was frontier country right enough and it was easy to see its appeal for anyone wanting to break conclusively with their past. But it seemed to me that there was some distinction to be drawn between a decision to stay and an inability to leave. George saw only affirmation, a positive vote for Coober Pedy; it didn't enter his calculations that the very despoliation of the place, the ravaged landscape itself, could sap the resolve of anyone already flirting with uncertainty and leave him marooned as in perdition.

George rounded off all his tours with a visit to his own underground house. He was very house-proud. We sat in chintz armchairs while he served us tea or coffee, showed us his wife's opals, and talked to us about heating costs, rent costs, land costs, rates costs, and so on. I was struck by how conventionally cosy he had made his sandstone vaults. You could gouge the surface of the walls with your fingers; you let in air by pulling a wire which lifted a little tin lid on a vent sticking out above the hillside; and yet for all the world you were sitting in a semi in Delft or Dorking. Indomitable, the bland homemaking spirit of man.

On the way back he took us to see the modern hospital, presided over by a much-loved Japanese doctor and a matron who cultivated an indoor garden – you had no chance growing an outdoor garden in Coober Pedy – and who had a novel way of treating loony miners: she put them in amongst the plants. A touch of green contiguity worked wonders.

In fact, much of what passed for character and eccentricity in Coober Pedy would have gone by the name of lunacy anywhere else. The last thing George showed us was Speedo's longdrop. Speedo was a shaven-headed Italian. A longdrop was the name for the deep hole in the ground which sufficed for many people in Coober Pedy – there being no sewage facilities in town – as a lavatory. Speedo's longdrop was distinct in that the shed around it was built in the shape of a space rocket, out of 'moon rocks' brought from Oodnadatta, and was surmounted by a television mast. Whether Speedo actually watched television in his longdrop George was not able to tell us, but we did discover that generally speaking longdrops were not places to linger over. They build up foul and dangerous gases. Only recently a miner had stayed longer than he should have over his, had forgotten where he was, had lit a cigarette, and had tossed the butt in the obvious place. 'Very nasty,' George said.

Thinking he might have an interesting story to tell, I wondered where I might find him. I suppose I should have anticipated the answer. 'All over Coober Pedy,' George said.

Later that afternoon we wandered up to a cemetery squeezed between the Greek Orthodox Church and the Coober Pedy

Basketball Club. The ground was littered with beer cans and bits of plastic. The graves themselves were mostly marked out with breeze blocks and memorialized by simple wooden crosses bearing the names of the dead – Albert Miles, Horace Reed, Chas Sharp, Carl Wendt – but no other messages, and no dates. One rather more stately tomb took my eye by virtue of the inscription on its headstone: *In loving memory of our mother, Ethel McCulloch, born 1882 Adelaide, passed away August 25th 1967, remembered by Jack, Edna and family.* August 25, 1967, was my twenty-fifth birthday. I spent it on board the *Achille Lauro*, leaving Australia at the end of my first visit. I was sick with grief for the friends that I was leaving behind, for Sydney, and for my lost youth. So it was a bad day all round for me and for Ethel McCulloch.

Some dissatisfaction on her part seemed to have hung on after death, and to have given her rare powers. Because scratched roughly into the horizontal gravestone itself, as if with a barbed fingernail, was an alternative, even a recriminatory valediction:

THIS. IS. WHER. EDNA. LAIDE. ME.
UNDER. SIX. FEET. OF. SOD.
WAITING. FOR. THE. ASCENDING. DAY.
SO. I. CAN. MEET. MY. GOD.

But it couldn't all have been Edna's fault, though I saw why one needed someone to blame. God himself would have given this spot a miss, assuming it to be waste not hallowed ground, a rubble heap belonging not to the church but to the basketball club.

I took a final walk around the town. Was it my fancy, or did Coober Pedy really turn opalescent in the early evening? I watched the light soften the pink breeze blocks of Jackson Lou, Opal Buyers, anyway, as the sun set over the corrugated water tanks. And I thought I discerned a pearl lustre on the skin of the Aborigines hanging about outside the Billiard Hall. A wind still blew, covering my notebook with red dust, like the blood of a dry scholar. But it was quieter on the streets than I'd yet seen it – a sinister quiet that could have nothing to do with tranquillity in such a place, but suggested the calm between air raids.

Back at the caravan park a queer hush had descended also. Old men wearing bush hats sat immobilized in the front seats of their 4-wheel drives, thinking of the drive ahead. Others drew long lines on atlases, or knelt in the dirt in the shade of their lean-tos, zipping up equipment, not exchanging a word with their travelling companions. Even around the public areas an atmosphere of awful expectation, such as might grip a last outpost, could be sensed. I don't know how it had fallen out like this but we were all heading in the same direction at the same time; by first light the following morning we would be on the road, pointing north, going for the big one, together. So we were unified in anxiety, but also ultimately isolated, because fear, just like confidence, is a private matter.

While I'd been out walking Ros had been in the campervan, bringing her journal up to date. When I got back I found her stretched out in the back, sleeping. With what looked like a suicide note between her fingers:

George said that some people got claustrophobic inside under-ground houses like his. Not me. I am claustrophobic in *Coober Pedy*. The town is in the heart of Australia. Desert everywhere. Everywhere equally far away. I feel I can't catch my breath. Is it possible I'll never see an edge again? I long to change my ratios and angles. I must find a sum which unequals my distance from here to anywhere else. I start doing subtractions. There's no relief. I am in the middle of the desert in the middle of the dead heart of Australia. George horrified me with stories of people who arrive and never leave. He drove past their caves, pointing them out. He warned us, 'You can stay too long. It can be a mistake. The locals get you and you never leave.'

. . . Depression everywhere. A steady clinging mist. The sun is shining. The wind is icy cold.

I've been wettexing the back windows, the licence plates, our hire number – 54. (Remember that – 54!) I've cleaned the cupboards and the kettle. I've collected the dirty clothes and placed them neatly in a laundry bag with the thought that they will be washed in Alice Springs. This way I plan ahead. I think positively. I am prepared. I have made a list of groceries. I have done.

So it wasn't wanting to stay that made us tense. The cause of our concern, like everyone else's, was not regret, any more than it was distance or Mad Max bikers, it was the state of the road we were fearful of, the two stretches of unbitumenized highway which were reported to be even more 'mongrel' than usual because a brand-new road was going through and no one could be bothered spending money to grade the old. In six months' time the journey would be a doddle, in the meantime the sacrifices to progress just happened to be us. Horror stories, either in the form of rumour or personally authenticated anecdote, circulated the park. One man had suffered punctures in all four tyres plus his spare; a chassis had broken in half; an engine had fallen out; a steering column had been jolted through the roof of a Toyota, missing the brain of the driver by millimetres. In the women's shower rooms Ros overheard someone who had just driven in from Alice Springs saying that the road was 'a blot on South Australia's character'. Amongst the men the talk was all of suspension systems and types of tow bar. A queer bravado, based upon a blind loyalty to one's own vehicle, underscored every conversation.

When I went for my last shower of the day I caught a couple of Eastern states pensioners putting themselves through their paces. 'The NRMA told me not to take my caravan across under any circumstances,' the senior in stress was saying, 'but I thought that was bloody ridiculous.'

'Ah, yeah, well I've heard that as long as you take it easy you should be right. Anyway I'm retired. I'm in no hurry.'

'What have you got?'

'A Jackaroo. But I'm pulling a Statesman.'

'Ah, yeah. A Statesman's all right. I've got a Jayco. I don't expect any problems to be honest with you.'

'No, you shouldn't with a Jayco. I can't see my Statesman giving me any strife either.'

A third person who had just slipped in to clean his teeth could not resist slipping into their conversation as well. 'I've just come from there,' he said. 'Just watch the bulldust holes and you'll be right. The corrugations are the real bastard. But I got through no worries. And I never had to drop below 70 ks.'

'What have you got?' they both asked him.

I didn't catch his reply, but I guessed from their silences that what he had was so good that it told them nothing about their own chances. The minute he left, the owner of the Jayco said, 'Well, you could drive up bloody Kosciusko with *that*.' And the owner of the Statesman, seizing this fatalistic chink in all the self-congratulation, said, 'I've heard that where we're going is worse than bloody Kosciusko.'

Fortunately for them I came out of my shower cubicle sooner than I should have. And they took immediate advantage of my good manners and my youth. 'Where you off to?' they asked me. When I told them that I was going where they were, they insisted on knowing what I was hoping to go there in.

'Oh, just a campervan,' I said. 'A Shiralee.'

'A Shiralee?' They exchanged fiery glances. Even through my wet hair I could see their spirits rising again, like red dust above a Coober Pedy dug-out. Or steam from an overheated Shiralee. 'We'll look out for you,' they said. Which in Stuart Highway caravan park code meant that they expected to find me overturned in the dirt, with all four of my tyres punctured, and the steering column protruding from the broken chassis, just millimetres from my brain.

And that didn't differ in any material regard from what I was expecting myself.

FOURTEEN

'AN INTERESTING PLACE WITH
LOTS OF SANDHILLS'

Although we were on the road by 7.30 we were still the last to leave. Way ahead of us we could see a cloud of red dirt, a pillar of fire, such as only a waggon train of caravans could throw up. 'The old farts have beaten us,' I thought, but I kept the sentiment to myself. As I did the dishonourable hope that we would come upon them by and by, their tow bars splintered into a hundred pieces.

The gravel didn't start immediately. We had about an hour's grace before we reached Pootnoura Railway Siding, then the bitumen suddenly stopped and we were on bare rock. Had I been offered the choice then between jagged boulders and drifting sand I would have jumped at sand, but once the highway became a blackened beach and we began slithering from one side of it to another I found myself pining for jagged boulders. As well as being unnavigable, the country was hideous, the dust thrown up from the road having strangled the vegetation and murdered even the soil. Only occasionally did something silvery and shimmering appear before us – a mirage, not of water but of bitumen. At the speed we clocked up after our second hour out of Coober

Pedy I calculated that we'd be in Ayers Rock in a little under a fortnight.

Nothing overtook us on this stretch of dereliction, and nothing passed us coming the other way either. But a sign, nailed to a choking tree, reminded us that there was life, and even something approaching black humour, out there. It said,

GET OFF THE BEATEN TRACK
VISIT COPPER HILLS HOMESTEAD – 53 ks

Back on the beaten track the sand dunes gave way to a sort of crystalline surface composed of thousands of small sharpened nodules of flint. It was possible to dodge them only by driving over slivers of serrated shale.

At Marla, with less than a third of the worst over, we were able to pause at a roadhouse for refreshments. On the forecourt we found the owner of the Jayco making some fine adjustments to his wing mirrors. 'A centimetre out of focus,' he seemed to be implying, 'that's the full extent of the inconvenience I've suffered.' But I noticed, with some satisfaction, that his hands were shaking.

An English boy, working his way around Australia, filled me up with diesel. He told me that the Marla roadhouse got very busy in the evenings, not with travellers but with locals. I surveyed the surrounding emptiness. 'I thought you need a locality to have locals,' I said.

'You'd be surprised. They come in off the stations for a meal or a drink or just the company. And of course the Aborigines can't stay away. Things can get a bit rough with them some nights. And banning them doesn't work.'

'Why not?'

'They just stand outside and throw stones at the windows.'

'That's all right by me,' I said. 'So long as they take them from the highway.'

For some reason the next leg of the journey was rougher but also more communal. At times it was even almost festive. If anyone broke down a dozen vehicles skidded to his aid. A car coming in the opposite direction wasn't in the slightest bit surprised to see you on his side of the road, searching for some respite from the corrugations. He slid over to your side, you stayed on his, and you exchanged an understanding greeting. Getting the wave right – the merest inclination of an erect fore-finger, not too perfunctory but not too regal either – became as important as not ploughing into granite. It was not unlike being on the dodgems with your schoolfriends. Except that you stayed on the dodgems for half an hour at most, if you could afford to, whereas the road to Kulgera was interminable. And not made more supportable by the glimpses suddenly accorded you of railway line, sometimes new railway line, just a boulder's throw from the highway; the gleaming track of the Ghan – the Adelaide to Alice – mocking the desert debris on which you floundered.

Earlier in the day we had seen wedge-tailed eagles in ones or twos, scavenging by the roadside and flying off when we approached, but as the afternoon wore on and we drove further north they hunted and dined in bands of six or more and were wholly untroubled by our presence. One, who caught me comparing his feathered trousers to the leg-warmers the girls had been wearing in London when we'd left, actually outstared me through the window of the Shiralee.

About fifty kilometres out of Marla we met the famous Oodnadatta Track. For people with time, courage, an appro-priate vehicle and a pass to enter Pitjantjatjara Aboriginal Land, this could have been a moment of indecision. To our right was Mt Mystery and Mt Alberga and eventually, had we wanted them, the Finke River Flood Flats; to the left was Mt Chandler and a track leading to Indulkana and Mimili and Fregon. As if to capitalize on the temptations of a crossroads at once so inviting and so deserted – truly a place for Oedipus to have scratched his head over – Adam and Lynnie Plate of the Oodnadatta visitors centre, some 250 kilometres away, had erected a grand hand-painted sign, pointing in their direction. 'Oodnadatta sure is a horrible place,' the sign said, before going on to list such counter-attractions as living in the rough, far from garbage-disposal dumps and town councils. But it was the great ode to itself that I liked, even though I vaguely felt that I'd heard something like it somewhere else before.

OODNA-BLOODY-DATTA

This bloody town's a bloody cus,
No bloody trains, no bloody bus,
And no one cares for bloody us,
In Oodna-bloody-datta.

Just bloody heat and bloody flies,
The bloody sweat runs in your eyes,
And when it rains, what a surprise!
In Oodna-bloody-datta.

The best place is in bloody bed
With bloody ice upon your head.
You might as well be bloody dead
In Oodna-bloody-datta.

Ros took over the driving from here and decided that skipping the corrugations at speed, as Neil had done on our trip from Derby to Camballin, was in fact the only tolerable way to travel. I measured our distance from the Northern Territory border by counting off dried-up creek beds – Tarcoonyinna Creek, Agnes Creek, Eateringinna Creek, the Marryat Creek.

Not one of them looked as though it had any recollection of the feel of water. Cracks wide enough to drop a child through had opened up in the clay, like gaping wounds. But, drought or no drought, the country was changing. We could smell the Territory. The sand was becoming redder, the scenery almost various. Even our strip map waxed poetical: 'In the vicinity are numerous large rocky outcrops, some of which rise to 61 metres above the surrounding country which is lightly timbered with myall and corkwood trees.' Bloody corkwood trees! Rocky bloody outcrops!

The last few kilometres of gravel ran alongside the new as yet unopened highway. Now that we were almost home we could spare a passing contempt for all those who would do this journey after us, the easy way. In shower rooms all over South Australia I had heard men saying that, although the road was a mongrel, the adventure would go out of it once it was given its pedigree. I had listened to such nonsense with astonishment; now I knew what they'd been getting at. 'Wouldn't have missed the adventure now we've had it,' I said to Ros, as we crossed the border at last and felt the feather touch of bitumen beneath our tyres.

But her appetite, it seemed, had been merely whetted. 'Then let's not stop the night at Kulgera but drive straight through to Ayers Rock.'

I consulted my watch: it said 6 p.m. I consulted my map: it said 335 kilometres. It also warned about night driving, and straying wildlife. But Kulgera didn't look inviting, and we could always drive slowly. We had become adept at that. So we took it in turns, grinding to a halt every ten or fifteen minutes so that another mesmerized kangaroo could think again about dashing out in front of us, and at 10.30 we arrived at the lights of what we expected to be a humble camping ground at the foot of a rock but which turned out to be a little city – the Yulara Tourist Resort – with a Sheraton Hotel and an airport and a shopping precinct and banks and a campsite large enough to hold 4,000.

We weren't strong enough to take what the Americans call an attitude. We had been driving for fifteen hours. Attitudinizing would have to wait until the morning. We found ourselves a power point and went immediately to sleep. Intermittently we were woken by the howls of dingoes, sometimes close, sometimes distant, carried in on an evil wind, foreboding harm.

The money to build Yulara Tourist Resort was being raised at about the time the dingo took the Chamberlain baby. It doesn't require a fanciful imagination to guess the attitude of commercial interests to any imputation that wild beasts roamed the area they were promoting. Though of course they should have seen that the very danger would itself constitute an attraction. One ought never to underestimate the ghoulish curiosity of men and women; the murderousness of the dingo has now passed into the mythology of Ayers Rock and is another reason for visiting it.

The resort turned out to be on an even bigger scale in the daylight than we'd supposed driving in at night. It lay claim to being the third largest community in the Northern Territory, losing out only to Darwin and Alice Springs. But it always looked more like a holiday camp than a town. The central complex – the hub of all the fun – was constructed of pink stone, canvas sails (made in Switzerland for some reason) and high tension wires. The justification for these nautical references in the dead centre of Australia was lost on me, but the pink worked well enough, graduating from an almost rusty red on the buildings closest to the service roads to softer and more diminishing shades as the town receded modestly into the desert. I didn't object too strenuously to the proliferation of amenities either; perhaps an 800-seater amphitheatre which showed continuous promotional films of where we were wasn't entirely necessary, but I could see the usefulness of a tavern and a snack bar and a newsagent's and a police station. What was wrong with Yulara was not its facilities but its tone. The place was rent with faction – domestic tension, family disagreement. A staff of 500 underlings lived cheek-by-jowl with their over-seers, the officials of the Yulara Corporation. Neither side had any privacy from the other. So the usual resentments and rival-ries of the workplace were magnified; the staff muttered and conspired, the management flounced and gave itself airs. As a member of a merely transient touring public – here today and gone tomorrow – it wasn't possible to buy a newspaper with-out feeling that one had intruded.

On our first late-starting morning in Yulara we found the entire resort in a pet. The boys behind the bar of the Ernest Giles Tavern were seething. The coffee we ordered at the Old Oak Tree coffee shop ('Relax under the sails or take away') came to us cold in thumb-marked paper cups, and tasted like granulated Stuart Highway. We pushed aside polystyrene cartons of other people's untouched food, dead when it was served, and spat on the table to clean it. Overdressed women in supervisory positions ponced across the concourse, kicking up sparks with their stilettoes. Even in the Aboriginal Artefact Shop and Boutique the air crackled with remembrance of injustices past. 'And then on top of that she tried to make me wear a skirt. I said, *no way*. There's *no way* I'm going to wear a skirt when I'm doing a man's job. So I worked from 6 to 10.30 at the bar then she calls me into the office and says they're one short at the coffee shop. I had to go home at 10.30 and put on a bloody *skirt*!'

'Let's go and find the Rock,' Ros suggested.

Gosse and Giles are the names most associated with the earliest white explorations of the area encompassing what is now known as Uluru National Park. Giles led three expeditions in the 1870s, all of them financed largely by a German botanist resident in Melbourne – Baron Von Mueller – which explains Mount Liebig, Ehrenberg Range, Petermann Creek, Lake Amadeus, and of course the Olgas. But it fell to Gosse to be the first white man to be flabbergasted by the Rock itself. His famous description of it, seen from a distance of two miles, as 'an immense pebble rising abruptly from the plain' is now generally out of favour, inasmuch as it fails of reverence for the sacred *and* the scientific. 'In fact,' an information board in the Visitors Centre at the Yulara Tourist Resort states, 'both Ayers Rock and the Olgas are like exposed sections of a molar tooth. Rock material plunges underground for at least 2,500 metres, possibly 6,000 metres in the case of Ayers Rock, so the term pebble is inaccurate . . . No one is certain of the exact events involving the formation of Ayers Rock. However, it is probable that it developed from an unfractured block of arkose, isolated by rapid erosion of the fractured and cracked surround rock. The development of strong vertical jointing which enclosed a pentagon shape is probably responsible for the almost sheer walls of the monolith.'

Myself, I still thought 'an immense pebble' took some beating as an account of what you first saw and how you first felt seeing it. An immense mauve pebble – a familiar object ludicrously distended – the more wonderful for making you want to laugh even as you marvelled. It becomes more seriously beautiful, the nearer you get to it – grander, softer, rounder, steeper, more diverse, in every way more surprising than the usual banal photographs would ever lead you to expect. Close up, its texture is like the skin of an animal – creased and enfolded and a little weary, but also soft to the touch. It is as much animal as mineral in other ways too. It carries wounds, gashes in the flesh, and great clefts that remind you of lips. Not lips that can be said in any weather to smile though. The grotesquerie that is amusing from a distance becomes melancholy face to face. The Rock is sad in the way that the most prehistoric of existing creatures are sad. Elephant sad. It looks bulbous and cumbersome, anachronistic, top-heavy.

And the walk to the summit – the CLIMB, as it's called – is like the steep incline of a camel's back. If there were dinosaur rides they would begin with this: a thin line of enthusiasts in summer clothes, holding on to chains and turning to wave before they vanish into infinity, while at the bottom the old and the unadventurous crane their necks and take snaps.

The CLIMB looked too formidable to me, at least on this first weary saunter, so close to our exertions of the day before. Nor is it without its perils at any time. Five memorial stones driven into the side of the Rock where the ascent begins remember those who have so far been killed climbing it – Brian Strieff; Brian Joseph Miller (aged 25 – died from a fall in 1978); Ernest Francis Jones; Marcia Burniston (also aged 25 – from Yorkshire – died December 22, 1963); and Leslie Arthur Thwaites of Newcastle, N.S.W., 'who died on top of this Rock on 15th June 1972, aged 63. The climbing of Ayers Rock was one of his life long ambitions.'

So we took a gentle exploratory drive around its base instead, noting that it really did have a front and a behind, a sombre visage with which to confront its visitors, and three huge humpy buttocks to the rear. Further reason – since all things that have behinds are sad – for its lumpish heaviness of spirits. Then we drove back towards Yulara to a spot marked SUNSET VIEWING AREA, a site to which we were to become immoderately attached over the next few days and from which we would find it difficult to drag ourselves away, not only on account of the pleasure in itself of watching the Rock flame scarlet for a few minutes as the sun went down, but also because of the social excitement, the sheer conviviality, which the occasion generated. Whatever else was or wasn't happening in the desert, you always knew where the party was at sunset, in which direction everybody would be facing, and how aware of one another the act of marvelling at an unfractured block of arkose made them.

We were there advantageously early on our first evening, with nothing to prevent us from taking up the very best possible viewing position except not knowing which the very best possible viewing position was. We changed our parking place half a dozen times, sometimes racing into a spot vacated by a vehicle which then went racing into ours. We were all uncertain together – the automobile drivers, the jeep drivers, the patrol-van drivers, even the adventure bus drivers – that was part of the fun. Once we were within twenty minutes of the event for which we had assembled, people began to stride out into the desert with fixed expressions on their faces and their cameras cocked, as if the Rock were a powerful magnet whose influence they lacked all power to resist. Others climbed on to the roofs of their vans and fixed tripods and swigged beer. A Frenchman backed his wife into the scrub, the Rock over her right shoulder. 'Avant cinq pas, s'il te plaît.'

'Ici?'

'Oui, ça suffit.'

'Trop loin?'

His eye was to his Canon. 'Pas là-bas, pas là-bas, pas là-bas.'

'Ici?' She was now ankle-deep in spinifex, her trim shoes dusted red. 'Oui.'

'Oui. Allons. Je te photographie.'

On the roof of a jeep plastered with Queensland stickers a pretty girl teetered becomingly. Ostensibly she was focussing her binoculars, but the real drama revolved around her shorts. They were pink and very brief. Every now and then she would reach behind to try to prevent their disappearing up inside her for ever. But no sooner had she pulled them out than she would find some pretext for bending forward, and they would rise again. The setting sun, not yet crimsoning the monolith, gave us a teasing foretaste of what it could do with colour on each perfect hemisphere of her buttocks.

From a Nissan Patrol three vehicles down came one of the most heartbreaking arias from the St Matthew Passion – 'Erbame dich, mein Gott'. If I had it right they would be nailing Jesus to the cross just as the Rock reddened. I wasn't at all confident that I would be able to handle that without a drink, so I scrambled into the back of the van and uncorked a bottle of Peter Lehmann 1981 Shiraz – Barossa Valley spoils – to help me through. By the time I was back in my seat Ros had fallen into conversation with a couple we had last seen broken down, but surrounded by helpful gloating pensioners, on the Stuart Highway; and a big, high, brand new brutal navy blue Ford F100 Bronco with a white trim and giant 100 bars had driven into a space unexpectedly vacated right beside us. The driver, a true blue Territorian wearing a wicked grin and a red cowboy hat, was climbing on to his roof and hauling after him a movie camera and a sophisticated high-volume cassette deck that was already turned on and drowning out the Bach with blackfeller music – a fidgety, repetitive, half-hearted glottal stomp which none the less went better with the landscape than 'Erbame dich, mein Gott' did, notwithstanding the Teutonic legacy of Baron von Mueller. From the eminence of his Bronco the cowboy beamed down on us. There was no challenge in his expression; surely, it seemed to say, you will agree that *this* is the appropriate music to be sitting Rock-watching to. Once he'd jack-plugged his equipment together he squatted with it all before him, drew out a pair of Aboriginal music sticks from his pocket, and began to beat out an accompanying rhythm. It appeared that he was making a one-man film, but what kind of film, whether it was of a spirituality quite belied by his appearance and appurtenances, or whether he was enjoying a huge joke at everyone's expense, not least the Rock's, it was impossible to determine. Either way, he stepped up the tempo of anticipation in the Sunset Viewing Area.

Cars and campervans were still arriving. And more and more of the possessed were walking out towards the Rock like zombies. A station wagon roared in, throwing dust into everybody's lenses. An American girl called Lester, who had been standing very still for six or seven minutes, was just about to squeeze her shutter. In exasperation she kicked a clump of mulga-grass. 'Aw, shoot!' she said. The station wagon performed several more manoeuvres at speed before screeching to a halt on the roughest section of terrain. Three boys climbed out to check the tyres; they seemed surprised to discover they were bald. Sometimes the vigour of youth can remind you of a nervous ailment; these three had so much unfocussed energy[1]* they looked in need of hospitalization. They jerked their attention to the Rock for a hundredth of a second – the very period they had denied Lester – grew crazed with inactivity, and then fell to emptying the wagon of their belongings. In sight of one of the great wonders of Nature they unrolled their foam mattresses and shook out their sleeping bags and rinsed their smalls and tossed their slops into the dust and never once raised their eyes to Uluru.

The older men, meanwhile, were dithering over their cameras. They weren't sure when to take their photographs. Or how many. They were growing angry with the light. 'If I stand here I can't get out of my own shadow,' one was complaining to his wife. 'If I walk forward it follows me. Maybe I should set it to infinity. Shall I set it to infinity? I've set it to

---

* See any literary magazines coming out of Melbourne or Sydney Universities in the 1960s or early '70s for specific applications of this phrase; especially in regard to George Herbert's divine lucubrations, Emily Dickinson's sexuality, Frank Churchill's hair appointment, Captain Ahab's monomania, Blake's night-flying worm, etc.

I use the phrase in its more widely understood sense.

infinity. I think I'll take two to be on the safe side. No, I won't. It's a waste. I've taken one. Do you think I should take another? Well, I suppose we've seen it now. Not all it's cracked up to be, is it?' And all the while the wife sat white and motionless in the passenger seat, her head bandaged in a scarf, staring into an infinity of spinifex.

The couple who had broken down on the Stuart Highway were explaining to Ros how a tin of coffee had saved their lives, or at least saved their exhaust, the funny part being that they didn't normally drink that brand of coffee but had bought it in a shop at Coober Pedy because it had been on special, which just went to show. As the crucial moments of sunset approached the people in the Nissan Patrol turned up their radio. I heard an alto, two oboi da caccia, and talk of Golgotha. In the excitement I filled my plastic wine beaker more times than was recommended for optimum appreciation of colour change. But everything was looking pretty rosy to me.

Even as the story of the coffee tin continued the Rock flared. A scarlet suffusion. As if, in the same way that a face changes colour, the source of the light was within. Had it given off heat one would not have been surprised. Nor if it had sweated or hummed. But it only glowed for two or three minutes, then started to brown. The sound of cameras going off was like distant musket fire.

Seconds before it was all over a death-grey jeep drove up and parked in the space left by the man who believed it wasn't all it had been cracked up to be. It was around the need to forestall precisely such disappointment that the jeep driver had patently constructed his life – hence the colour of his jeep and the timing of his visit. This was he who shows up whenever the party is over, who scorns superfluity and conversation, and knows the precise moment that expectation turns to ashes. No post-Uluru tristesse for him. The last to arrive, he was very nearly, after one forlorn photograph, the first to leave. I noticed that the clothes he wore looked empty. As did, of course, his girlfriend's. The merest round of flesh in the life of such a man would have left his system in ruins. I watched him drive out with an incommunicable expression of ghostly satisfaction on his features: once more he had got the better of what would otherwise have bettered him. By the time he was gone the last lick of flame had vanished from the Rock and it too suggested the extinction of all hope.

Later that evening we hit the town. 'Across a thousand miles of severe and uncompromising desert the breeze travels,' the brochure said, 'before whispering into the splendour and magnificence of the Sheraton Ayers Rock Hotel.' It seemed incumbent upon us to follow the breeze and go whispering into the Sheraton ourselves.

It wasn't busy. In the Kunia Lounge they even had difficulty changing a fifty-dollar note. We took a break between drinks and strolled around the reception area where Aboriginal artefacts were displayed in discreet glass cases. A set of 'Carvings of Ancestral Figures of the Tiwi Tribe' – looking to me suspiciously like funeral poles – enjoyed prominence, pleasingly arranged on a pretty plinth. The sounds of live music drew us to the Mulgara Bar where Mr Jan Castor was entertaining no more than a handful of drinkers. A stylishly handsome German or Dutchman or Czech or maybe a combination of all three – he sat on a simple stool, one leg carelessly thrown across the other, playing a guitar to computerized electronic backing. He finished a number just as we were finding a table and he seemed to wish to dedicate the next one to us. 'Zis is a song about a didgeridoo vich I have written myself. For zose of you which didn't knowing vat a didgeridoo is, it's a long pipe vich Aborigines use for blowing.'

He flicked a switch on his computer which must have been marked 'blackfeller', because suddenly he had an identically dispiriting rhythm going to the one we'd heard earlier coming from the roof of the Ford Bronco. Then he sang the song he'd written.

> I'll be your didgeridoo
> I'll give myself to you.
> I'll be your didgeridoo,
> Give yourself to me, too.

As the song progressed I noticed from Ros's expression that she hadn't taken the full measure of the subtle modulations of its lyrics. She hadn't noticed that the *I'll* became *I'm* and promised an elegiac drop into an *I'd*. 'There's an underlying statement about Time in this song,' I explained to her.

> I was your didgeridoo,

he sang as we rose to leave;

> I gave my love to you.

We were still in the hotel foyer when we heard him following up with 'Morning Has Broken'.

The next day we came upon the Peace Train, or part of the Peace Train, in the car park at the foot of Mt Olga, the largest of that clump of rival pebbles to Ayres Rock which resemble nothing so much as a basketful of brioches. Precisely what the Peace Train was about, other than in a general sort of way sticking up for peace, I had no idea; but I was vaguely aware of it from newspaper articles as a sort of itinerant neo-hippie colony following more or less the same route around Australia as we were, only starting from the other side and getting itself into rather more trouble whenever it came within sitting distance of a uranium mine or atomic testing site. There were two peace vehicles in the car-park – a green bus loaded on top with old tyres, plastic water containers, ten-gallon fuel drums, rolls of foam, black refuse sacks, suitcases, even a wicker crib, and a rainbow-coloured truck saying PEACE TRAIN 1986, in nursery letters. Each of these pulled a trailer; in the case of the bus a yellow caravan advertising HOT & COLD FOOD AND DRINKS, not at present open for business. The nerve centre of the operation was the green bus; it was from here that people in exotic costume occasionally issued, and it was to it that they returned, bearing small arrangements of vegetation or pretty stones. After watching this gentle procession for about half an hour I surprised myself by making a decision couched in military terms: 'I'm going in,' I said to Ros.

I found Joe coming out, closing behind him a fly-screen fixed to the front passenger entrance. Tall and emaciated, with a long grey beard and a single purple stone in his ear, Joe aspired simultaneously to looking like the Ancient Mariner and not having a single thing to say. He scratched his head when I introduced myself to him, and bent his back. I couldn't tell how old he actually was but felt sure that he wanted me to think he was even older. He staggered up the steps, pushed open the fly-screen, and handed me over to Carlos, and Richard Burns, and Jackie, and Baby Harry.

I realized at once that I had seen Carlos the day before at Ayers Rock. Then he had been dressed in a pair of skin-tight cords, which from a distance had looked like hose, a sort of velvet doublet tied with a phosphorescent cord, and a matching apache band in his hair. He had just climbed the rock and was cooling himself with a leaf on the end of a long twig. Today he was reclining on foam cushions scattered on the floor of the bus, in an aquamarine sleeping suit worn over a white silk Hamlet-shirt with drawstrings. Beaten silver bangles jingled at his wrists. By way of greeting he showed me a mouthful of wonderful teeth and flashed pinpoints of light from his dark, almost oriental eyes.

Jackie nodded at me from the kitchen area. She was long and blonde and angular and occupied her clothes loosely so that there should be no suggestion of anything like female vanity on this bus. Something beatific and martyred hung in the air around her. She wore her hair piled up, spectacles, and of course no make-up. She was wholly at the service of Baby Harry and Richard. Just as Richard – the benevolent dictator of the Peace Train – was wholly at the service of me. 'That's provided you're not CIA or KGB,' he laughed. There was a clue in this. I was to understand that the Peace Train didn't waste its time distinguishing between two giant corporations identical as far as essential ideology, methodology, and understanding of each other's self-interest was concerned. 'We've seen through the rhetoric of East-West aggression,' Richard told me. 'There'll be no major outbreak of hostilities because it doesn't suit the conglomerates for there to be one. In this way we are different from other peace organizations such as CND. We're not really concerned about disarmament. We don't fear a war.'

'In that case . . . ?' I wondered. I was now squatting on foam myself, looking up.

Richard Burns smiled at me. He was wearing a grey track-suit, badly torn at the crotch, and a matching woolly hat. 'In that case what is this peace we're promoting? Peace in the heart. Peace of mind. We're putting forth a consciousness. Essentially we're all related. All one family, right? We've got identical antennae. Man as computer, yeah? Basically I use the 100th Monkey Theory. Once a thought's actioned, it's available to somebody else who's been on that wavelength.' He touched his forehead, just above his right eye, and made a sort of funnel or channel shape to show me the source of an actioned thought, and the route it was likely to take.

'So in practical terms,' I said, 'how exactly do you . . . er . . . ?'

'We drive into a town, OK? We find out what's negative in that town and give freely of positive energy waves to counter that negative—' He looked around for the word.

'Process,' Carlos said.

'Process. We send positive thoughts into what is a negative area.'

'You can really see the change in people,' Carlos said. He was spread out languorously, trimming the calluses on his small brown feet with an instrument whose like I had last seen in the hands of a dentist.

'They walk around with more pride in their step,' Richard said.

'Everyone vibing at the same time,' Carlos said. He showed me his teeth again. They gleamed like the opal fault we'd seen running across the walls of Rudy the camel driver's mine.

While Jackie was serving coffee I wondered how many people and vehicles were actually in the Train. Did I mean *now*? No – I could see that now was something of a spatially limiting concept – I meant altogether, at any time, kind of continuously.

Richard pushed his woolly hat off his face. 'There's been a lot of factionalizing,' he explained. 'But I reckon we've turned over about five hundred.'

Assuming factionalizing to be a bad thing. I sympathized. 'I suppose the proximity was always bound to generate tensions,' I said.

'No – it's great,' Richard said. 'We're a continuous giant melting pot. People pick up with us, find out what they want, where they're at, join, interact, leave. It's all a question of respecting space. Take Dudley – you should meet Dudley, but he's not here right now – Dudley, you see, is more grounded. I like him, I respect his space, but I find I'm called upon to get involved in more esoteric initiations. Let's say I'm more aquarian. I like to develop concepts that aren't already there.'

'He's always been like that,' Jackie said, from the kitchen.

'It's true. I have. I used to run my own show on Queensland television. Channel 7. *Funderland* it was called – an ecology programme for kids. I've always been a bit of a concept promoter.' I must have given a smile that implied he was a long way from all that razzmatazz now, because he added, 'I'm a mutable. I can get into everything, wherever it happens to be.'

'He means he's an old rorter,' Carlos said.

Carlos himself had previously dealt in garden supplies. 'But trying to do it honestly while everyone was ripping off every-one else round you was – you know –'

I knew. Garden supplies? Sheesh. A hotbed of corruption.

'And Jackie over there,' Richard suddenly said, bouncing Baby Harry on his knee, 'used to be a dancer at the Moulin Rouge.'

I didn't trust myself to look across at her. She might have seen me putting ostrich-feathers and spangled pasties into place. But I felt it behoved me to say something. So I said, 'Do you miss it?'

She didn't hesitate. 'No – that was another time, another space.'

Before such austerity of mutation we all fell silent for a few moments. Only Joe, who had crept into the bus five minutes earlier to do something with ropes and tarpaulin, spoke. And he said, 'I'm going out again now.'

'Do you know what I dream of?' Richard asked me at last. 'Aquarian radio. With ourselves as hi-tech transmitters. And the announcer saying, "Hi, there folks – this is Aquarian Radio. I've just received information that the people of New York City are all having a hard time today. Let's send them some good vibes." And that's how it will work – those with sending to those without.'

'And that'll be your world's problems solved,' Carlos said.

'So now you see,' Richard said, 'why we're not into marches or demonstrations. There's no need. There'll be no war, unless' – he narrowed his eyes at me here and made that little funnel again along which an air-wave might travel – 'unless the Moslems start one. They've got nothing to lose. They're coming from a total pain situation.'

'That's right,' Carlos said. He had shifted his position so that he could get at the hard skin on his other foot. In the manoeuvre one of his olive shoulders had come out of his shirt, like that of a boy posing for Caravaggio. 'I've spent two years with Persians. There's a lot of pain involved.'

I felt a new surge of respect for him. 'You've been out there?' I said.

'No, but I sold Persian carpets in Sydney for two years.'

It was getting time for me to leave. 'I now feel that I know where the Peace Train is at,' I said to Richard.

He shook me warmly by the hand. Before he let it go he related a tale which I was then, and am still, wholly unable to fathom. It went back to his entrepreneurial days and concerned the Americas Cup, the aircraft carrier *Melbourne*, Bondy from Perth, Mike Willesee's television programme (on which Richard had appeared), a proposal to buy the Royal Perth Yacht Club, a proposal to build a marina at Port Philip Bay, a proposal to enter the aircraft carrier *Melbourne* in the next Americas Cup, a series of articles appearing in the *Melbourne Herald* for Easter 1984, and a man referred to in those articles as Mr Mystery. 'I'm Mr Mystery,' he told me as I stepped off the bus.

'Well, how was that?' Ros asked me when I returned.

'Pretty boring,' I said. 'I've spent most of the time talking to a dancer from the Moulin Rouge.'

'Then why are you so pale?' she asked.

In order to get a bit of colour back I took a brisk walk into

Mt Olga Gorge, giving the Peace Train as wide a berth as possible. But where the path narrowed I found myself shoulder to shoulder with a girl who could have come from nowhere else. She had a small anxiously conscientious face. She wore harem trousers in billowing black silk shot through with silver thread. Over these she wore a burgundy cardigan and on her head a knitted hat in a muted medley of greys. She was carrying two stones, one of them as large as Baby Harry. Since she spoke to me first, commenting on the grandeur of the sheer rock face of Mt Olga – she gave it the Aboriginal name of course: Katatjuta – I felt it was all right for me to refer to the stones. 'You look as though you're taking them out to plant them,' I noted.

She took a deep breath. 'I'm returning them to where they belong,' she said. 'Someone collected them, I'm taking them back. That's the way of it.'

Aha, I thought, more factionalizing. But I let her get ahead of me so that she could perform her devoirs to the sacred spirit of Katatjuta unimpeded. On the way back I saw that she had scaled the steepest of the walls and was sitting high up on some sort of projection like a nesting bird. I recognized her only by the billow of her harem trousers and the glint of their silver thread.

'Well, how was that?' Ros asked.

'Pretty uneventful,' I said. 'I've been failing to hit it off with an odalisque for most of the time.'

When we turned up for our second sunset viewing of the Rock we were surprised to find two long trestle tables, laid with a red velvet cloth, polished champagne glasses and bowls of peanuts, standing in the desert. It was the sort of facility that God might have provided for the bellyaching Israelites in Sinai, as another proof of his powers. 'It can't be a mirage,' Ros said, 'I recognize the wine waiter from the Sheraton.'

According to a boy we knew from the bottled gas filling centre on the campsite (whose ambition it was to become a Bachelor of Natural Resources), the Yulara Corporation often came up with sales pitches like this; today it was shouting drinks for tour operators, as a way of saying thank you, on behalf of Uluru, for business past and future.

Whatever pleasure it gave the tour operators, the presence of a private champagne party in a public place brought out the worst in we Rock watchers. It seemed to unite us in a common disposition to kick up dust. Our peevishness even communicated itself to an angelic little Belgian boy who suddenly began to run amok among the mulga. 'Laurent!' his father had to shout, 'Soi tranquille dans la nature. Tu es dans le premier position de l'Australie.'

For no reason and on no errand that we could figure a very small Japanese person of either sex roared out of the spinifex on a Honda motorbike. And a couple from Todmorden, on the borders of Lancashire and Yorkshire, who had driven up beside us in a rented Daihatsu Delta, introduced a note of social sarcasm inappropriate to the occasion. The man was bearded, as it were on principle, and wore a Save the Daintree Rainforests T-shirt. He had a squeaky voice and looked after the feminine end of the relationship. So he was ultimately to blame, although it was the actual woman – I could tell she was that, even though she'd shaved her head down to a half an inch of stubble – who made the noise. She squatted on the bonnet of the jeep in a pair of serious camping shorts and a no-nonsense cut-away shirt. Her legs were sturdier and browner than his and she had more hair sprouting from a single armpit than he had on the whole of his face. It was from this position that she delivered her views on humanity in general and holidaying humanity in particular, in an accent as unaccommodating as the Pennines. 'Look at that lot thurr, gettin' out o' buzzes, doin' as they're told. They'll all scream wi' admiration at same time. Driver'll tell 'em when to take snaps and when to shout "Ooh!" and "Aah!" Thurr they go, just look, like crowds i' *Clorse Encounters A Thurrd Kaind.* Bloody 'ell, they're like lemmin's. God 'elp 'em when they 'ave to vote.'

'God 'elp uzz, you mean,' her squeaky boyfriend said.

'Right, Cyril. You're right, thurr.'

From the Yulara Corporation party came sounds as of Jehovah's Witnesses having a good time. I could see from where I stood that their champagne had red dust in it but that like the sun it was going down willy-nilly.

Someone asked Our Gracie where she came from. As if there were more than one place on earth where people spoke as she did. Suffering a temporary loss of nerve she ran a hand over her stubble and said, 'Ohr, we live i' Tasmania at t' moment.'

It was a good sunset. 'Better tonight,' I said to Ros. She nodded. She was away, lost to language, dissolved herself in the spectacular deliquescence of colour, the extraordinary fleeting fusion of rock and pigment.

From the window of a nearby automobile a boy whom I took to be both Dutch and Jewish wrinkled his nose at me in mute complicity. For his wife was lost in it too. We were both married to pebble freaks. 'Rock – schmock,' his eyes seemed to say.

I quickly checked that Ros was not watching me. 'Uluru – schmuluru,' mine said disloyally back.

We were of course only joking. I like to think that Jews have a good record in regard to Ayers Rock. I don't necessarily mean in regard to climbing it (a climb being nothing other than an act of conquest anyway), but in regard to – better still, in respect of – its wrongful impropriation. Like all people who have spent time in the wilderness Jews attach a powerful totemic significance to rising ground. *And the sight of the glory of the Lord was like devouring fire on the top of the mount.* So it was seemly that the Minister for Arts, Heritage and Environment in the Hawke government charged with returning Uluru to its traditional Aboriginal owners should have been called Barry Cohen.

In truth the hand-back was as totemic as the monolith. No sooner was the land on which it stood granted in trust to the Mutitjulu Community than it was required to be leased back for a period of 99 years at an annual rental of $75,000 plus 20 per cent of the park entrance fees. Not up to much as a business deal. But it was enough to send a thrill of apprehension through the Territory. The papers talked of 'The Final Solution'. Central Australia was rumoured to have been earmarked for a new Black Republic. Were not firearms being smuggled into the area to that very end? And on the night the Bill was debated in the House nothing less than white Australian spirituality itself was deemed to be impugned.

'Ayers Rock is a majestic, interesting place with lots of sandhills and beautiful oaks and the area is mystic to all of us, not just the Aborigines,' said Mr Ian Cameron, the Honourable Member for Maranoa.

'White Australians are not culturally deprived,' said Mr Everingham – 'Casino' Everingham as he was referred to in this debate. 'Ayers Rock is their heritage. It is Australia, just as are the Blue Mountains, the Great Barrier Reef and Sydney Harbour. All Australia is of great cultural significance to Aboriginals as it is to all Australians.'

'The rock is a monolith,' said the shadow Minister for Aboriginal Affairs, Mr Shipton, and when the Government interjected he rounded on them with scholarship: 'Honourable members opposite should listen; they might learn something. The rock is a monolith. That means that it is a rock that comes out of the ground.' He rounded on them with sentiment and patriotism also. 'We are living in very fragile times. Honourable members opposite may well laugh, but they are delicate times. The fabric of Australian society is important to this side of the house.'

'I was at Charleville on the weekend,' said Mr Cameron. 'My mate Sugar Ray is a resident of Charleville. He represents the great area of Maranoa on the National Aboriginal Conference. He gets a motor car to drive. Sugar came out with a great statement and I support him 100 per cent. I think it is the only sensible thing he has said: He said that Ayers Rock ought to be handed back to all Australians.'

'Casino' Everingham quoted from a letter published in the *Australian* on March 27, 1985. '"I never realised that Ayers Rock meant so much to me until confronted with the news that absolute title to this natural wonder is shortly to be given to a small community of Aboriginal Australians. I felt that sudden sense of shock, then grief, that comes when you are about to lose something very precious, previously taken for granted . . . The stroke of the pen that will allow people to physically possess the spiritual heart of this nation is a knife thrust that wounds every Australian."'

'No longer will the Aboriginal be seen just as socially different; he can be seen universally as having taken something that belongs to all Australians,' said the Honourable Member for O'Connor, Mr Tuckey, who conceded that he did indeed have a 'conviction for assaulting an Aboriginal person' but reminded the house that the Aboriginal person in question was a 'gangster' and that it was not in fact an iron bar but 'something else' that he assaulted him with. 'This legislation,' he went on, 'creates a lease-back which will transfer $100,000 per annum to an Aboriginal co-operative. That might help the Aboriginals in some way, but I am somewhat interested to look at how they might have been helping themselves to date.'

He wasn't the only one to have visions of Aborigines growing fat on rent and gate takings. As a matter of interest the number of beneficiaries was estimated to be about 350. Which meant that on a good year they could look forward to pocketing a cool $500 a piece. 'I believe that all these handouts to Aborigines ought to be means tested,' said Mr Cameron.

'What is it that whites object to,' asked Barry Cohen, 'about Aborigines getting money?'

Sometimes the simplest questions are the most searching. We'd been pondering this one since we'd landed in Darwin. I'm glad that Hansard shows someone with the name Barry Cohen having the nerve to ask it.

Someone with the name – or at least with the pen name – Peter B. English kept me busy the following afternoon while Rosalin succumbed to the I just want to be able to say I've done it personal achievement ethic, and climbed the Rock. Not Peter B. English in person; I spent the day with him only in the sense that I had toppled into a work of polemic he had written – *Storm Over Uluru: The Greatest Hoax of All* – and was unable to clamber out. I had bought it that morning because it was very nearly the only book with words in it for sale in the Yulara newsagency. That and *Land Rights and Birthrights: The Great Australian Hoax*, also by Peter B. English. I had been curious about his virtual monopoly of the shelves. To the point of actually asking the assistant why other books that could be considered relevant to the area – John Bryson's *Evil Angels*, for example, the bleak and brilliant study of the circumstances of Azaria Chamberlain's death, selling well everywhere else in Australia – were not in stock. It wasn't for me to have any attitude to a private newsagent's buying policy, but I thought I could spot a fairly distinct way of looking at the world in the choice of books available, that's assuming that Peter B. English's works were as scurrilous as they looked, and I wouldn't have minded finding out how far this reflected the purely idiosyncratic taste of the buyer or was in fact quasi-official corporate Yulara weltanschauung. Something was rotten in the state of Yulara but so far I hadn't quite been able to nose it out.

'Well, I don't do the ordering,' the girl said. 'But I'll mention that one to him when he gets back. *Evil* what, did you say?'

So I had no choice, really, but to buy *Storm Over Uluru* and see for myself what people were reading and thinking about in the third largest settlement in the Northern Territory.

The hoax that Peter B. English claims to have uncovered is this: that far from returning Uluru to its traditional owners on October 26, 1985, the Federal Government had in fact allowed the Rock to fall into the hands of a makeshift group of Aboriginal campers and transients who had no genuine title to the property whatsoever, but were themselves mere tools in the hands of political opportunists and activists. The Mutitjulu Community did not exist as an entity until 1981 and was merely an updated version of Uluru Community Incorporated, itself going back no further than 1975. As for the members of Uluru Community Inc. having any long-standing association with the area – other than for purposes of climbing aboard the white man's gravy train – or any verifiable tribal rights to it, the idea is preposterous. What Aborigines there were in the vicinity of the Rock before the Land Rights movement began to flex its muscles were a raggle-taggle band of ne'er-do-wells and alcoholics. As a former manager of one of the motels operating at Ayers Rock in the 1970s attests, ' "This talk about the Uluru Community Incorporated would have to be the greatest load of crap I have ever come across!" ' Caustic, the author calls this.

Just who the real owners of Uluru are then – or *were* then – is a matter to which Peter B. English assiduously addresses himself, the more especially as it might just be possible, if we could find them, that they would not approve of the Rock being handed back to themselves anyway. For Aborigines of this kind he has an unashamed affection: 'loyal and faithful', he calls them, and 'likeable and easy-going'. The favourites for having a genuine claim to ownership are the Jankuntjatjara who were dispossessed in tribal battles in 1917 by the Pitjantjatjara. And it happens to be well known ('reports are too numerous to be brushed aside') that 'Paddy Uluru', the surviving Senior Elder of the defeated Jankuntjatjara – surviving until 1979, that is – 'wouldn't have a bar' of the region of which he was a likeable and easy-going custodian being given back to anyone. So it is not only the white man whose word and trust and bond the Federal Government has betrayed.

Myself I thought it highly feasible, and a most excellent wheeze to boot, that a number of floating Aborigines had been hastily and opportunistically incorporated for the purpose of there being *somebody* the rock could be handed over to. Why not? Are the dispossessed to have a nicer morality than their despoilers? Besides, the act of restitution, like the ceremony in which it was formalized, was entirely symbolic. At the very best it only signified some good faith and a queasy conscience. So the fanatic hostility to it, whether issuing in the dumb show of spiritual disinheritance as mimed by the Australian Liberal Party, or the legal punctiliousness of Peter B. English – wanting it to go to the right Aborigines or no Aborigines at all, which means no Aborigines at all – is both inappropriate and inexplicable until one remembers what the handing over symbolizes for *them*. 'Few Australians watching the hand-over "ceremony" on their television sets in the comfort of their own homes throughout the continent will forget the scenes so vividly portrayed by the electronic Media that night,' Mr English recalls. 'For these featured prominently the red and black flag of the Land Rights campaigners, fists raised in the Black Power "salute" – and a part-white showing a three-year-old child perched on his shoulder how to ball his little fist into a salute which had its origins in the Black Panther movement in America and is synonymous with every scene depicting mob violence in troubled South Africa.'

Here then is what the fuss was really all about – mob violence, imported images of identity, and fist-raising baby blacks. The something very precious that the letter-writing white Australians thought they were going to lose when inalienable freehold title in Uluru National Park was granted to the Mutitjulus was not Ayers Rock but peace of mind. And that was the explanation for the queer unease you could smell all over the multi-milion-dollar Yulara Tourist Resort – the place was rattled. Not within the boundaries of the National Park itself, and not therefore obliged to part with any percentage of its profits to the Park's new owners, Yulara nevertheless felt as jittery as a last outpost.

It occurred to me also, as I watched them shinning up the Rock, that here too lay the reason for the number of middle-aged and even elderly Australians who were chasing across the country. They were reclaiming title to it. Prompted by a deepening national insecurity about the ownership of land they had always assumed was theirs without question, they were now having to embark upon expeditions of reconquest and recolonization. Only the night before in the shower rooms I had listened to one old pedant asking another where he was off to, prior of course to telling him how to get there. 'Alice Springs, Mt Isa, Townsville, Cairns, Borroloola, Katherine, Darwin, Broome, Perth, Albany, the Nullarbor,' the other had replied, running through the names as if the mere saying of them was incantatory; the act of pronouncing them a kind of rehearsal of occupancy; visiting them a confirmation of possession. Hence the enormous size and duration of many of these journeys, great perimeter loops around the states necessitating absences of years in some instances. So many arthritic Ulysseses in caravans they saw themselves as being, not choosing to stay at home and mete and dole unequal laws; but all along it was an old errand that they were on, staking out a birthright that was suddenly under threat.

I could see that it might have been of no earthly satisfaction to Aborigines to know it, and probably of no earthly use to them either, but it seemed to me that they had white Australians well and truly on the run.

It took Ros and me almost the same amount of time to storm our separate ways over Uluru. If anything I finished a minute or two before she did – the book being altogether less acclivitous than the Rock – which gave me time to take a stroll around the van and listen to a scrawny couple of about my age congratulating themselves on their successful climb. He was bearded and bald but for a single strand of hair which he combed in a circular motion so that it sat on his head like the sort of coiled raffia mat I had been taught to make in primary school. He might have been a lecturer in an undervalued subject at an Institute of Technology, and years before she might have been one of his brighter students. She too had a single coil of hair, only in her case it was deliberate – a short, colourless plait wound hypersensitively tight. She wore a simple empty singlet and a pair of white towelling shorts not unlike a nappy. I had watched her crawling up the Rock on her hands and knees in these shorts several hours earlier and the sight had helped me to concentrate on Peter B. English. Now the two of them were out of breath and triumphant, scanning the heights they'd scaled with a pair of binoculars each and mocking the puny efforts of others.

'Those young blokes wouldn't have a hope in hell,' he said.

'Look at that big fat one,' she said. 'There – there – hanging on to the post.'

'What about the one in shorts.'

'She won't make it.'

'That Chinese girl's sitting on the bloody edge.'

'Serve her right if she falls.' She put her binoculars down and lit herself a cigarette. 'A packet of fags a day,' she said, so that I should hear too, 'and I climbed to the top of Ayers Rock!'

I felt sorry for them. They were jubilant and didn't know what to do with their jubilation – always the problem when you do something just-so-that-you-can-say-you've-done-it. They paced about their jeep, smoking hard. Not wanting to leave, not wanting to stop looking at where they'd been or to stop talking about what they'd done, but not able to hold back the onset of futility either. At last they drove off with their windows wound down low so that she could the more easily toss fag ends out. 'Well, do you believe in me now, darling?' was the last thing I heard her say.

The moment they left the car park a coach drove in. A group of men with no time on their hands charged the Rock. Within minutes they were a third of the way up it. A man with a withered arm set the pace. He wore walking boots and appeared to be working to a pre-arranged plan. Instead of following the usual vertical route, where there is a chain to help you, he preferred to zig-zag, striding way out to the left and then cutting back, in an extravagant diagonal, to the right again. This meant that he was covering about three times as much ground as everybody else, not just walking up the hill but also walking twice across it. Yet he was yards in front in no time, and very soon he had vanished over the top altogether.

A place of unfathomable mystification, Ayers Rock.

Our third and final sunset viewing. And the pair of us in a heightened state. Ready to be off the next morning, but tragic about leaving. A ritual of which we had become faithful observants was winding down. We were feeling Last Supperish.

A Park Ranger we had come to know, through being Rock regulars, was sitting in the dust playing with Judi, his Queensland Blue Heeler bitch. It would be hard to say which of them had the more liquid gaze. Altogether I had found that the Uluru National Park Rangers were of a different order of creation from the staff at the Tourist Resort; they were taller, had skin that was more golden, eyes that were more limpid, and shone with that innocent purposiveness which seems to be the reward for working in the open with animals and trees. But of all the Rangers none was more responsive or susceptible than this Ranger. He seemed to glow when you spoke to him – 'He has a meltdown like a Russian reactor,' Ros observed, news of Chernobyl having just made it through to Yulara, 'every time anybody smiles at him he goes in the core.' And he never glowed more molten than when you spoke to him or smiled at him about his dog.

Wasn't it a bit dangerous, Ros wondered, keeping a pet when there were so many hungry dingoes around? Yes, yes it was. Which was why so few people kept pets out here. But it wasn't just for dinner that the dingoes would take them if they could. Some domestic dogs they wanted for skivvies. They actually stole them away to turn them into slaves – to hunt and work for the pack, to attend to whatever dingoes deemed menial, no breeding rights allowed. In the case of its being a bitch who was captured you could almost call it enticement. An erotic gypsy theft. Given half a chance the dingoes wouldn't hesitate to pull a Heathcliffe on Judi, for example. Let us take you away from all this soft stuff, they would say. Let us plumb together the elemental rock bottom of your nature. Come live with us and be our love and we will all the pleasures prove.

I saw Ros exchange a glance with Judi. Worse things could happen to a bitch, they appeared to agree.

While we were talking an enormous armoured truck, not unlike a vehicular Ned Kelly, pulled in behind us. It was painted a no-nonsense blue-grey – the colour of deadly weaponry. A huge spare tyre was affixed to its front like a rubber shield. Ladders ran up the sides to the roof. There were grille bars over the windows. I noted that it was a Mercedes Benz Unimog 4-wheel Drive Kestrel, and wondered what German riot police were doing in Uluru.

Then I read the words, AAT KING'S ADVENTURE TOUR – CAPE YORK, KAKADU, KIMBERLEY, AND AYERS ROCK, and at the same moment there emerged from the troop-carrying section an assortment of designer-desperadoes of both sexes, the women in frameless spectacles and pastel-coloured espadrilles, the men in executive jogging shorts and vacation beards. I gathered from the way they were still getting to know one another that they had not driven in over sandhills from CAPE YORK or KAKADU but had in fact only joined the bus in Alice Springs for a half-day excursion to the Rock.

'Yes, well, I work with a firm of management consultants in London,' I heard one girl say as she climbed up on to the roof of the Unimog.

'And what's the name of this firm you work for?' a voice from New Jersey asked her.

'I said *with* not *for*.'

'Loretta,' someone else called, 'Loretta, have you got my other lens?'

The driver of the vehicle stood apart from his party, smoking. He was done up to be on safari, with a knife and several leather pouches attached to his belt. He wore a long, frontiersman's beard which had just a touch of self-denying religiosity about it. Whatever Loretta was up to on the roof of his Unimog he wasn't allowing it to spoil the adventure of the mind that he was on.

Just as the Rock began to change colour a N.S.W.-registered Ford drew in and five little girls, ranging in age from seven to twelve, spilled out. They took one look at the phenomenon they'd rushed their supper to see and expressed a unanimous though not quite simultaneous disappointment.

'That it?'

'That it?'

'That it?'

'That it?'

'That it?'

Their father took it upon himself to come across to me to find out. 'That it?' he asked.

I gave him more than he bargained for. I was a seasoned sunset-viewing connoisseur by now. I took him through shade and shadow, through chiaroscuro and definition. I pointed out hollows and configurations he had no chance of discerning on his own. I showed him prismatic freaks and unsurpassed chromatic bravura. 'Yeah, that's it,' he called back to his kids.

'That yours?' he asked, pointing to the Unimog. I laughed and pointed to the Shiralee. 'So where've you been in that?' he wanted to know. He must have been younger than me, though he looked more tired and had more lines across his forehead on account of having fathered five disappointed girls.

I told him where I'd been, then he told me where he'd been, and we met in Coober Pedy. He'd loved it. I'd loved it. We both said we rated living underground, though whereas I didn't and was only being companionable, I had the feeling that he too was being companionable but also did.

'Been to Lightning Ridge?' he suddenly asked.

'No.'

'It's bettah.'

'Better than Coober Pedy? Lightning Ridge?'

'Yeah. They live in chook pens there. They live in car-bonnets. Tin boxes. Old tyres. Whatever they can find. Ground's no good, you see. They can't make dugouts.'

I wasn't planning to go there but I asked, anyway, 'Where's Lightning Ridge?'

He knelt down and with his finger drew me a whole map of Australia in the dust. 'There's Coober Pedy, right? There's

Broken Hill. That's the Birdsville Track. Here's us. There's Lightning Ridge.'

It was impossible to miss.

I noticed that we were being photographed from the roof of the Mercedes tank. We were what they'd come all the way from Battersea to see – a couple of dinky-di bushwhackers on their hands and knees comparing tracking techniques. We even got a look not far removed from longing out of Loretta.

'Anyway, must go,' my new friend said. 'The girls are playing up. We've got no lights on our tent.'

Even while he was saying it the girls had started.

'Dad!'

'Dad!'

'Dad!'

'Dad!'

'Dad!'

I could see why he wanted to live in a chook pen.

Back in the Yulara amphitheatre they were showing the same slides they showed every night. As we already *were* in the Northern Territory it was a bit hard to understand why we were being exposed to promotional material designed to make us want to come here. Maybe the clue was in the inane lyric which accompanied the slide show –

> That's the Northern Territory, that's the great outback.
> There's no place more Australian,
> It keeps you coming back.

We'd gone to make merry on our last night in the resort without any wholehearted anticipation of success. We would have settled for half an hour just listening to Mr Castor on his synthesized didgeridoo but even he wasn't to be found tonight. At about nine o'clock, after a couple of ruminative beers at the

Ernest Giles Tavern, we decided to drive back to the campsite, a distance of no more than a kilometre or two but along a road that was black and deserted, the dividing line between civilization and the bush. Halfway there our headlights picked up three dingoes crossing from the one into the other, returning to the wilderness, it appeared, after a night on the town; and giving themselves plenty of time to get home too, like a party of drunks in an uncertain single file. It was only when we slowed for them that we saw it was the middle one alone who was actually unsteady and that the reason for this was not alcohol but terror – sheer quivering terror – because *he* wasn't a dingo at all, he was just a dog, an ordinary domestic dog, somebody's pet mutt, being led off – literally led from the front, and nipped and harried from behind – into a lifetime of captivity. If he was lucky.

The drama unfolded with an extraordinarily protracted clarity. We had time to catch the calm cruelty in the eye of the leading dingo; we had time to see the flanks of the dog trembling; we even had time to stop the van and fling the doors open, and for Ros – running towards him – to shout. 'Here, boy! Come on, come on, make a dash for it.'

In one bound he was free is now a much discredited device for getting a hero out of a tight corner, but no other description will do for what the dog did. He saw his chance and leapt. Maybe he flew. One minute he was a captive, without a hope in Hell of making an escape, the next he was lying panting on the cushions in the back of the Shiralee, a look of undying gratitude on his face, his eyes molten, the thump of his heart audible even above our diesel engine. He was scratched and bitten. His nose had been bloodied. But I wouldn't have wanted to investigate the psychological scars.

The dingoes did not immediately concede defeat. For a moment or two they seemed to be considering a raid upon the van. Then they appeared to decide that for the kind of domestic he was likely to make anyway the dog wasn't really worth the sweat. They threw us a look of the iciest contempt and padded off into the desert.

We drove the dog round to the police station where a police-woman, or perhaps a policeman's wife, refused to believe our story. She had never heard of such a thing. Dingoes didn't do that. We must have been mistaken. I sat soothing the dog and watching Ros remonstrating with the woman in the dark. I saw the head shaking and the closed expression. It was like being in a scene in John Bryson's book. If a dingo had crept up on her from behind a bush and started to rip her arm out she would still have denied it was happening. The dingo had become a symbol of Territorian defensiveness. Any attack upon it was an attack upon them.

But we hadn't gone to the police to complain about dingoes. We weren't asking that this solitary representative of the force – officer or officer's mate – should go out single-handedly on a dingo shoot. We simply wanted her to take or at least identify the dog. Even this she was unwilling to get involved in. She didn't know any dogs, didn't know anyone who kept a dog, and had no advice to give us about what we should do with this one. Though when Ros finally persuaded her just to come and look at the thing, she instantly recognized it. 'Minder!' she said. 'How did you get out?' And then to Ros. 'I can't understand it; he is never away from his owner.' And then to Minder, 'What have you been up to?'

She wouldn't of course have believed him had he told her. But it took a full ten minutes to coax him out of the van and into the police station, so frightened was he still of what was out there.

The dingoes didn't leave us alone that night. Even before we went to bed we could see them in our torchlight prowling the wire fence which encircled the campsite. There were rich pickings for

them out there. The Belgian family we'd sunset-viewed alongside were three or four caravan spaces down from us and tossing
raw meat over the wire to entertain Laurent. They were playing a game called *cherchez le dingo*, and the dingoes were doing
well out of it. But later, when the camp was asleep, they came
in. Several times we awoke to hear, and then to see them
circling the van; looking for food essentially, but also, I liked to
think, stalking us, putting the frighteners on us for balking them
of their prey. In the morning the dust bore the imprint of their
many feet.

Part of the sadness of moving on from here was that we
would, in truth, miss them; their uncanny yip-yip-yip followed
by their wild, melancholy dingo howl, and their utterly fearless
nocturnal incursions. It was quite something waking in the
dark to see those sharp pointed eyes returning the reflection of
your torch and those small vicious faces sneering at you,
undaunted, through the windows of your makeshift home.
You wouldn't want it as a permanent condition of your life
perhaps, but a little precariousness, a little foretaste of the feral,
as long as your doors are secure, can add considerable savour to
your nights.

Most of all, though, we would miss the Rock. I hadn't got
very far with it myself as a religious totem; by and large I didn't
hold with sacred sites and was left quite cold by the various
taboos and other unspeakables vested in Uluru. I had always
experienced difficulty taking holy objects seriously in my own
faith – fringes that you kissed, thongs that you wound, walls
that you wailed at – so I was unlikely to be able to venerate
them in other people's. The best thing about Aboriginal religiosity as manifested in these parts, it seemed to me, was the
tangle into which it threw the whites. Either they went the way
of Joh Bjelke-Petersen, finding connections, where lesser men
failed to see any, between sacred sites, heathens, gays, and the
spirit of the goanna, and proclaiming, 'No goannas, no gays!'

Or they felt the shame now associated with secularity and joined the scramble to show just who could be more animistic than whom. THE AREA IS MYSTIC TO ALL OF US.

But, just as there must be thousands of ostensibly practising Christians who have long since lost their taste for worship but keep turning up at church for the company and the jumble sales, so I remained a devotee of the Rock because I liked the excuse it provided for a get-together. Sombre in itself, it was the cause that light-heartedness was in others. In a word, this was awe the way I preferred it: without having to sway back and forth or wear a yarmulka. No goannas, no yarmulkas.

Coming at it from a different angle I think Ros felt similarly. We had both been happy at Ayers Rock. It was a question we put to ourselves with some seriousness as we left: Would we ever be as happy again?

FIFTEEN

MINTJA

Leafing through the *Centralian Advocate* in an idle hour I had already picked Gone Troppo as the likely winner of the Alice Springs Cup, so when we found ourselves driving into Neville Shute's famous outback town on Cup Day, and what is more only a stone's throw from the racetrack, I hit upon the ruse of a quick flutter as the smartest way of launching ourselves at once into Alice Springs society.

Horse racing in Australia is not what it is in England. Like many other Englishmen of sober origin I was brought up to regard a racecourse as a place frequented only by disreputables or Royals, and it was enough for me to sorrow over a friend that his father had been seen entering a betting shop. Had he been seen coming out of a brothel his sin would have been nothing like so unpardonable. But a day at the races is altogether without stigma in Australia, partly I suppose because the climate makes the outing itself pleasant and provides a rational explanation, over and above impecuniousness or compulsion, why anyone would want to be there; and partly because Australians are free of that shame which in England infects any method of making or losing money other than by inheritance or drudgery. And what is true of the guiltless pleasures of race-going anywhere in urban Australia is even more true of the country.

Cup Day in Alice Springs was like being at a village fête. I wouldn't have been surprised to find a welly-throwing competition underway, except that there was no call for wellies in this part of the world. The sun shone on a brightly variegated gathering − cowboys, bank managers, Aborigines, half-whites, quarter-whites, small-town socialites, bush roughnecks not looking for trouble, teenagers in shorts and thongs, families in tropical linen suits. And all free to stroll about the course at will. There was no grandstand to speak of and nowhere seemed reserved for one section of the community to the exclusion of the other. You could even wander over to the jockeys' tent and watch them getting changed. And if little men half out of silks were not your taste you could buy a steak and onion sandwich, dripping tomato sauce and oil, for hardly more than it would cost you for an ice cream in an English cinema.

Although you will always find the Wild West look at country get-togethers − even in Cornwall there are sharp-shooters in Stetsons and Cuban heels who come out only for fêtes and barbecues − I was struck by just how many men were wearing cowboy hats here today, and not as items of self-conscious fancy dress either, but as natural accompaniments to open-neck check shirts and colonial bush beards, or in the case of more citified young men out with their girlfriends, worn with a little feather in the side and impeccable white shirts and cream trousers. There seemed to be an inevitable progression about these two looks: the latter had been like the former until they'd found true love. In Alice Springs a pretty girl was, quite literally, a feather in your cap.

Opposite the TAB counter where I went to place my ten dollars on Gone Troppo I spotted the *crème de la crème* of Alice Springs seeking refuge from the sun under a canvas canopy.

Three women in particular took my eye because of their extraordinary resemblance to James Cagney, Broderick Crawford, and Edward G. Robinson. They sat preening as if at Ascot, but in apparent readiness for the St Valentine's Day Massacre. Edward G. Robinson, in a loose blouson top and a pencil-slim skirt, had her scrawny legs crossed and puffed on a long cigarette. A severe twist of gold glinted on each ear. Jimmy Cagney screwed up her eyes in puckish delinquency, a queer spun-sugar confection on her head, plastic see-through sandals on her feet. Broderick Crawford was the least elegant, letting it all hang out of a pink and brown acrylic mobster frock. Grannies themselves, you wouldn't have let your own granny near them.

Their social fortunes rose, as did ours indeed hold, when Mr Ian Tuxworth, the Chief Minister of the Northern Territory, suddenly appeared out of the throng of punters and recognized them. He was wearing a crisp white shirt and carrying a soft green drink and seemed no match at all for the hoodlums. Edward G. Robinson offered him her cheek. Jimmy Cagney offered him two cheeks. Broderick Crawford, if I wasn't mistaken, raised her mouth.

Ian Lindsay Tuxworth, 'Casino' Everingham's immediate successor, was having a hard time of it right now over expenses he had once claimed for travelling from a place at which he no longer lived. He had admitted the offence, paid back the money, and conceded in Parliament that his action had been 'morally wrong'. Such rectitude had, if anything, worked against him. It wasn't actually required of Northern Territory politicians that they fiddle their travelling allowances, but they weren't expected to bring issues of morality into it either.

And it was easy to see why he wasn't as popular as Everingham had been. He didn't have the swagger. He didn't have the Territory tone. Out here on the racecourse, in his short-sleeved shirt and bookkeeper's spectacles, he looked more like a wages clerk than a Chief Minister. You might even have expected him to try selling you a bible. I had read somewhere that he had pawned his soul to an American positive cerebration philosophy called New Age Thinking, a system for reorganizing society along corporate lines. Whether or not that could strictly speaking be called a religion, I didn't know; but he had the washed, emotionally baptized look of someone to whom truth had only recently been revealed, albeit on corporate lines, and that made him nobody's ideal drinking partner.

I watched him do his best with the Chicago underworld and then wander off to a scene of what appeared to be passingly acrimonious domesticity with another lady in a hat. It seemed indecorous to be present, but it was all of a piece with the habitual accessibility of the Australian politician. He was around more in Australia and you got a better look at him. It was no startling coincidence that we'd run into so many of them; anybody else travelling as we were would have fared the same. Australia is a small country that only looks a big one. If you take it into your head to pop out to a garden party chances are that everyone else has taken it into their heads to do likewise. And there was a matter of principle at stake here also. Australian politicians are meant to be of the people. You're *supposed* to meet them. Which was why poor old Tuxy was wandering round the Alice Springs racecourse on Cup Day in his shirt-sleeves, nodding uncomfortably at the electorate.

Despite my certainty that I'd picked a winner, Gone Troppo came in an unimpressive fifth. The following day I read in the papers that Tuxworth had also backed it. But that was only the beginning of his bad luck. A week later he was no longer Chief Minister of the Northern Territory.

All I'd lost was ten dollars.

Stuart Caravan Park, Larapinta Drive, Alice Springs, midnight. Behold the author, sitting in a tight toilet cubicle with his notebook on his knees – I wasn't eavesdropping; I just never went anywhere without my notebook – copying out a conversation between a man in the cubicle on his left and a man in the cubicle on his right, relating, if he understood it correctly, to an incident that had occurred a couple of nights before at a place 500 kilometres from here, though he wasn't sure in which direction.

'Ah yeah, but I could see the bouncer eyeing you before then. I think he could see you were going to throw up.'

'Well, I wouldn't have minded it from him. But some wanker who was just there drinking! It wasn't even his fucking pub.'

'Look, I agree he shouldn't have thrown your drinks away.'

'No. Not at those prices.'

'Whatever it is you've done there's no justification for throwing a bloke's drinks in the bin.'

'Right.'

'He could have thrown you out, but not your drinks.'

'What gets me is he said *I'd* been drinking too much yet all those other cunts were on the floor pissed as farts.'

'You should have wiped him.'

'I know. I should have.'

'What did you do, anyway, when he threw your drinks in the bin?'

'I kicked the fucking bin.'

For one reason or another we ended up staying over a week at the Stuart Caravan Park and I spent most of my time there squeezed into the tiny toilet cubicle listening, or slinking between the tents and the campervans making notes. It wasn't just that I was in a receptive mood, although I had reached that stage of a journey where you become sick of your own observations and prefer the workings of absolutely anybody else's mind. What really turned me into a bit of a snooper was the caravan park itself. Because it wasn't like any of the others we'd stayed at, where the elders of Australia bent on reconquering their homeland, and the odd Belgian diplomat's family domiciled in Canberra, and us, dropped in for the night prior to chewing up more highway in the morning. Those were just pretend caravan parks. Here people were living semi-permanent lives. They had gravel paths leading to their caravans, small tended lawns, patios, pergolas, even dividing walls. They set off to work in the morning, some of them, waving their wives goodbye, and arrived home again at six to find an apéritif waiting for them on a table laid with a cloth under a lean-to. They sustained running feuds with neighbours, stealing an inch or two of territory whenever they drove in, and losing it again whenever they drove out. They collected mail from the front office. At the weekends they threw parties.

So I suppose what I wanted to hear from them was this: were they happy? For all its discomforts, in other words, I was getting used to the campervan and wondering whether I didn't have it in me after all to make a go of it as an itinerant myself. I'd need a more sophisticated set-up of course. A Toyota probably, pulling a Jayco. And that was something else I was doing creeping around the park with my pencil between my teeth – I was peering into people's mobile homes, getting an idea of how big they could be, how much storage space they could provide, whether there would be room for a typewriter and a small library of reference books.

I believed I'd need the typewriter. I'd stood in the queue for the open-air telephone and listened to the newly arrived describing their first impressions of the employment market to the folks they'd left back home, and I wasn't cheered by what I heard. A rather slow teenager with a diminutive girlfriend hanging on his arm shouted down the receiver to his old deaf dad in Wollongong. 'Yeah, the abattoir – the ABATTOIR! It's great, they even pay you adult wages once you're eighteen. But it's only part-time at the moment because the stockmen can't get the cattle in. The CATTLE!'

It was exciting – it gave me a little frontier thrill – thinking of everyone's wages depending on the state of the creek bed thousands of kilometres away or the whim of some drunken drover. But I didn't fancy the idea of the abattoir. While the fantasy of living like this for ever was upon me I kept half an eye open on the appointments vacant sections of the newspapers, but only three even vaguely interesting opportunities cropped up. One was for a Drug Abuse Prevention Officer to work amongst Aborigines, with special reference to petrol sniffing. The second was for a Cricket Manager to breathe a bit of confidence back into the dispirited national team. Applicants were required to have first-class cricket experience, the 'ability to coach and impart cricket knowledge in all respects', the wherewithal to 'communicate effectively', and would preferably be under fifty. I *was* under fifty. And the third was for an Actor Comedian (male or female) with 'extensive experience in Egyptian comedy theatre, radio and TV' – applications to be sent to the Egyptian Theatre in Australia, P.O. Box 41, Emu Plains 2750. I remembered an old English music-hall comedian called Nat Jackley, who used to stick a fez on his head and do the sacred neck dance of Osiris, and I wondered whether this was the sort of experience they were looking for. Not that I had that either.

I'm not sure that I ever found Alice Springs itself as interesting as I found the caravan park. The idea of it as *The* Alice – *no Town Like Alice*: wasn't that the point? – waterless, rough-mannered, isolated, equally far from everything that had become soft-centred in Australia, Alice with red dust in her hair as the promotional slide show at Yulara described her – the idea was more intriguing than the actuality. As with Darwin, part of the trouble was the clean-up, the gentrification, a cosmetic that automatically, blindly, comprised a casino and a Sheraton and a mall. 'Visas for tourists jetting into Alice Springs for a taste of some outback Aussie magic,' the journalist Ross

Irby wrote in the *Centralian Advocate* on our very first morning in town, 'should carry the warning: Alice Doesn't Live Here Any More . . . She has disappeared in the clouds of dust beneath the tracks of bulldozers.'

And the reason the bulldozers were so busy was that the tourists were pouring in, stimulating the appetite, making the town hungry by what it fed on. Mintja, the Aborigines call them – ants. The same word exactly that the Cornish use for visitors – emmets. It is a ludicrous complaint normally – one tourist bemoaning the presence of another. But there *were* too many in Alice Springs and too much of what both brought them here and kept them occupied until they left – travel agents, bus companies, and buses. Buses on every corner, reversing, shuddering, double-parking, loading up and loading off. You could live with such numbers in Florence because you were only there, after all, to see the paintings: but you went to Alice Springs to experience remoteness, to congratulate yourself on the completion of a trek, and you couldn't do that if the rest of Australia was already there before you, installed in Todd Street Mall and photographing Aborigines when you got there.

Also photographing Aborigines and just about everything else in Alice Springs when *we* got there was the film crew of *The Last Frontier*, a mini-series being made for American and Australian television, starring Linda Evans, the immobile alabaster actress made famous by *Dynasty*. According to the publicity, *The Last Frontier* was 'a classic romance', the story of an American woman struggling for survival against the harsh Australian outback. The part of the harsh Australian outback was taken, naturally, by Jack Thompson. The word was that Linda Evans had arrived with her entourage the day before and was staying at the Sheraton. The whole town was on the qui vive. Any reasonably preserved matron under fifty with a large bust and hair the colour of silver fox had the chance of creating a sensation on the streets.

Just to be on the safe side – I didn't want to be mistaken for Jack Thompson – I kept a low profile on my first morning. I sat in quiet corners of cafés and read the papers. Someone from a peace group handed me a leaflet entitled *Everything you always wanted to know about Pine Gap*. Among other things, it said, 'Pine Gap is run by the Central Intelligence Agency and the top-secret National Security Agency . . . Over 500 Americans and Australians work there. Almost all top-security staff are American . . . As the eyes and ears of the U.S. nuclear forces, it is a top-priority nuclear target . . . It is 19 km south-west of Alice.' I had two thoughts about this. One was that it helped explain why there were so many extravagantly large rodeo-type Ford utilities in town. The other had more to do with principles: not only had Linda Evans, a film company, and every other traveller beaten me to Alice Springs, it now seemed the CIA had got here before me as well.

I was all for going back to the caravan park, where things happened, when Ros drew my attention to a brown, wiry old man sitting on a bench in the mall, holding a mirror to his face and shaving himself with a pair of nail scissors. It was an ablution – if you can have a dry ablution – which implied that he had no home to go to, but it was performed with an attention to detail not normally associated with the toilet of swagmen. He clipped his cheeks, his upper lip, the cleft of his chin, his neck, with the most painstaking precision, holding the scissors flat against his flesh so that he didn't miss a fraction of a hair. I guessed that he was about sixty-five but he could easily have been more. I thought he was probably German too. There was a Stroheim look about him. The extremity of his emotional life having its way with his body. Even his crew cut looked German and I supposed that he had given it himself with his little portable tortoise-shell mirror angled above him. Why he wore socks over his shoes I didn't know. To save leather, Ros reckoned; but that seemed to me a system bound in the end to be costlier in regard to socks than the conventional one is in regard to shoes. Perhaps he was simply protecting them from falling hairs. Such fastidiousness was not impossible. Once he'd finished with his face he moved down to his fingers, shaping the nails, pushing back the cuticles. He was German all right. And I became quite sure in my mind that he was one of the many Nazis who had fled Germany at the end of the war and were now living in Australia. In the case of Gypsy Les we had only his own drunken confession to go on. But with this man we had the evidence of a fanatic personal finickiness of a kind not compatible with the existence of Jews. The very reason I couldn't take my eyes off him was that I knew it was either him or me. Quite simply there was no metaphysic which could accommodate us both. But once again I didn't ring Simon Wiesenthal. It was much more fun having my foe in blood and spirit out there on the streets of Alice Springs than having Linda Evans.

Although they were as unalike as two men still essentially Australian could be, both Tom Winter and Bill Richards had said, 'And when you get to Alice Springs don't forget to go and see Ted Egan. He's your true blue Territorian. You'll have a great night.'

Ted Egan was the Territory's best-known resident entertainer; he wrote folk songs and sang folk songs, accompanying himself on an empty box of Fosters, and told tall stories, and kept alive the names of 'characters' he'd met from Barrow Creek to Borroloola. If you were in Alice Springs you were meant to go and watch him, in the same way that you were meant to see *The Mousetrap* if you'd never previously been to London. In both cases kids in shops would look at you as if you were simple when you told them what you'd bought a ticket to.

It was in the gardens of Château Hornsby, 'Central Australia's first and only winery' – about whose wines the best is silence

– that Ted Egan was currently performing. To packed houses, we'd heard, though when we rolled up after four hours of torrential rain we found only two Americans travelling on a Fulbright, plus their child, in the audience. So it very much looked, as I tried to make them feel at home by saying, that we weren't goin'a get no show. Twenty minutes before he was due to start Ted Egan himself appeared, rubbed his face, and bought us each a beer.

I felt sorry for him. Had he been a novelist giving a reading he would have considered this a big turn-out. But he was used to better. He had a sad, sleepy quality which belied the larrikin idea of him I'd formed from Tom Winter and Bill Richards and any number of coach drivers around Australia who played his tapes and spoke his name with reverence. There was something of Dean Martin's sleek slum-brousness about him, a hint of Robert Mitchum indifferentism, a rub of Stewart Granger's insubstantial gravity. And it seemed to me that although he was known far and wide throughout the territory and famous enough beyond it for what he could do with an empty Fosters carton, he was still sad because he had not become as famous as those men. And the four and a half of us weren't helping.

Then, just as we all thought that was that, an old Ford utility pulled in, bearing a mixed but not always distinguishable family from west of the Devil's Marbles, all five of them with their hair shaved three quarters of the way up their heads. The paterfamilias nodded at Ted Egan as if they were old friends. 'Remember mad Mort from Urandangie?' he asked, without preliminaries. 'In his heyday he must have been 52 stones, wouldn't you reckon?'

I didn't catch the reply, because at that moment a small bus arrived and deposited a sorority of eleven ladies in yellow cardigans, none of them seriously ill but each exhibiting some sort of bird-like affliction or another – twisted necks, palsy, beak-rot – two of them even wearing eye-patches. The only one able to keep her head still was the driver, and instead of a yellow cardigan she had on a T-shirt which said CATZ.

'Well, that's just great,' the American on the Fulbright said, 'now we got a party.'

In fact I said it, but it's the kind of thing Americans are expected to say, and it's the kind of thing he *might* have said had he been less self-conscious, and either way it was what we all wanted to say, except of course for Ted Egan who looked as though he would much rather we went away and came back on another night when he had a larger and more normal audience.

But he made a brave fist of entertaining us. He sang us a song entitled 'You Get an Awful Lot of Characters in the Northern Territory', accompanying himself on the Foster's carton which he sat on his lap and drummed on with his fingers. After which he pretended to worry that his instrument was out of tune. He put it to his ear, peered inside it, held it to the light, and lo and behold! – a can of Fosters skulking in the corner. 'Cheers!' he said, drinking it down. The women in the yellow cardigans and the family from west of the Devil's Marbles laughed, as though there were some property of humour inherent in the very idea of beer.

After a few more songs he showed us a film that had been made about him several years before. It was called *A Drop of Rough Ted* and showed him travelling up and down the Territory with his son, encountering oddballs and 'characters' in the outback or the bar, branding cattle at Muckaty Station or playing his Foster's carton at Sexy Rexy's Piss Parlour in Tennant Creek. Seeing him younger and slimmer and more hopeful, in glowing technicolour, distressed me. I could understand why some film stars would never watch their old movies – too upsetting, too unchanging, the past made for ever flesh on film. The camera is a cruel curator of memoranda; it has made us all more melancholy than we were.

As for the oddballs and 'characters' themselves – Bill Easton who did wild pig imitations and played the spoons, Charlie Priester who had his own safety belt to hold him upright at the Ti Tree bar, Roger Jose who lived in a ten-thousand-gallon water tank – they were most of them shy, recalcitrant figures. Bachelors. Solitaries. Some very nearly hermits. Their characterfulness, in the main, an eccentricity and rawness bred out of seclusion; and what else was that seclusion but the only possible response to a prior sense of overwhelming social difficulty? So it was some paradox, boisterous Australia's love of ratbag individualism – the piss parlour idealizing the very qualities least welcome in it.

Watching these distressed men blinking at the cameras, and Ted Egan's gentle consideration of them, it became clear that he shared with them more than he knew; that he too was more reticent in the flesh than in his own mythology. Rough Ted? I didn't see it. Maybe he wasn't ready to lock himself away in a ten-thousand-gallon water tank yet but he was looking bored with all the rollicking. And I could hear a hollowness in his lager-phone.

After the film he talked to us about his 'mate', Rolf Harris. We might not have been aware of it but it was he – Ted Egan – who had originally given Rolf Harris the words for 'Two Little Boys'. He had first heard them himself on his mother's knee and had repeated them to Rolf. One night Rolf rang him from London. 'Ted,' Ted said he said, 'that song? I want it for my TV show. I can remember the tune but I have lost the words. Sing it for me.' So Ted sang it, every verse, all the way from Alice Springs – 'And fifteen million copies of the record later . . .'

He didn't mean that to sound small-spirited. He had no complaints. But there is one clang that all the goodwill and high-mindedness in creation cannot keep out of a voice. And I heard it then. It was too cruel – of course it was too cruel – the contrast between Rolf Harris's London Television Spectacular and Château Hornsby, Alice Springs; and the gap was altogether too wide between fifteen million purchasers of the record and the eleven maimed spinsters in yellow cardigans, the five shaved yokels from west of Devil's Marbles, the two Americans on a Fulbright, and us.

He sang another song or two and finished with 'Such is Life, Ned Kelly, Such is Life'. He shook my hand warmly when we left. Cheers, he said. Glad you came. Good to see you. He almost certainly called me mate. It was quite ridiculous, considering that I'd come out to be entertained, just how upset I was feeling. I wanted to put my arm around his shoulder and tell him what I thought. 'Do something else,' I wanted to say to him. 'Stuff all this beer can, Fosters carton, Northern Territory vitalistic character baloney. You've given it a fair go and you don't believe in it yourself any more, so stuff it. It's no life having to stand up in front of paltry audiences who'd laugh at anything, for a living. I know. I used to be an academic. I taught at a polytechnic. I got so bored with the audiences I had to entertain I used to fall asleep while I was talking. One of these days it's going to happen to you. Your head will just drop down inside your Fosters carton and you won't even know about it. Your fingers will go on drumming. You'll go on singing. And your fans will go on clapping. Because they won't know about it either.'

But of course I had no other career prospects to advise him on, unless he wanted the managership of the Australian cricket team and that wouldn't be free of humiliations either. All I could do was pump his hand and thank him and try not to catch any of the little points of fire which still flashed out of his somnolence.

The last thing he said to me was, 'You should come on a good night when we get ninety or a hundred.' So he was beyond help.

★ ★ ★

We spent the next few days in a desultory fashion, collecting mail, answering it, sitting in the mall watching tourists watching Aborigines watching tourists, and making short sorties into the Macdonnell Ranges to places which were invariably named, like Alice itself, after women – Emily Gap, Jessie Gap, Trephina Gorge. Had we ventured further we would have found Glen Helen, Ruby Gorge, and Claraville. I wasn't especially athirst for landscape after three solid days of guzzling Uluru, but little by little the subtler coloration of the Macdonnell Ranges tickled a bit of life back into the palate. This was paler, more luminous country than where we'd been; the rocks more orange than magenta, the spinifex blonde, the gums blanched and ghostly, appearing to hold light itself in their high foliage.

Of all things not pebbly in the vicinity of Uluru, the most lovely had been the desert oak – a casuarina, not a eucalypt, which seemed to droop in the most melancholy way when it was hot, but in the early morning, or when freshened by a breeze, would rally with a sort of silvery shudder that any ballet dancer might envy. Now it was the white gum, as made famous in Namatjira's paintings, that caught the eye. And the Aboriginal association is not fortuitous. Every now and then a species of tree and an inbreed of person hit it off well. You sit an Englishman under an oak. A Pacific Islander beneath a palm. Me beside a boab. And an Aborigine below, behind, before – the preposition eludes you because it is so often as if he simply materializes *from* – a white gum tree.

A man must always resist his taste for the picturesque, but my most vivid recollection of Alice Springs *is*: Aborigines returning home along the dried-up bed of the Todd River in the late afternoon, a slow, dusty, crepuscular glide which played tricks with perspective as well as time, so that you could never be entirely certain whether you were merely watching the same scene infinitely repeated, or whether it was the trees themselves that were moving and the men and women utterly still.

But when we weren't scrambling up the Macdonnell Ranges to look at examples of Aboriginal rock art – sometimes no more than a couple of ochre stripes on an orange stone, or a rough semi-circular gouge in a crumbling wall; and when I wasn't losing my temper with the politics of 'sacred sites', not being able to think of anything at Corroboree Rock, 'where sacred objects or tyuringe (pronounced tew-ring-ger)' were buried, except *mezzuzahs* and *tzitzits* and *tefillin* – when we weren't punishing ourselves like this with conscientiousness, I was able to get back to the more interesting business of creeping around the caravan park with my notebook.

Outside one ramshackle old van I heard the occupant currying favour with the site manager. 'Every other bugger wanted me thrown out,' he said, not knowing which upset him most, remembering the indignity or acknowledging the obligation – 'You were the only cunt who understood me.'

And from the caravan opposite – more like a nightclub, to be truthful, with bamboo blinds over the windows and coloured lights in the pergola and a pyramid of used beer cans mounting by the front door – there poured an unremitting repertoire of filthy folk songs, sung in a self-mocking nasal twang by a sort of Australian George Formby.

> Mick me mate the master farter –
> Jesus! you should have heard him fart . . .

was his favourite, the thing about Mick being that he had a 'double-jointed arse'.

But it wasn't all swearing in the park, or at least it wasn't *only* swearing. A couple of men in their middle thirties, who looked as though they might have belonged to a serious rock group, sat around in the afternoons making billy tea and smoking and tackling the big issues head on. The one who did most of the talking had screwed-up eyes and a small button nose, flattened with years of being pressed up against the wrong side of the glass of life. 'The only place in the world I'd go to,' he said, 'is New Zealand. Why go somewhere else to get shot? It's stupid. Why be blown sky high in Melbourne? All you need is a couple of hectares of scrub and you can forget the fucking world. If you get nuked, you get nuked. If you get zapped, you get zapped. You've no choice in the matter. You might as well be in New Zealand.'

His friend was quieter and more ruminative. A jazz pianist, maybe. 'It's a pretty crazy world,' he said.

'Who likes it? If I went up to Ronald Reagan tomorrow and said, "I don't like what you're doing," he'd say, "Fuck off!"'

'That's right.'

'Some silly prick presses some silly button and she goes bang! And we can't do a damn thing about it. I dunno, there's so much power in so few fucking hands. It'd be better if we went back to bows and arrows.'

'Yeah, well, I think we should abandon the whole notion of technology.'

'I'd go further. I'd say ban fucking electricity. We're an over-electrically oriented society. And you know what electricity leads to? More electricity. Some people blame the Japanese. I don't. They're doing what they've got to do. They know that there was no way in the fucking world – logistically – that they could have won that war. Not as long as New Guinea held . . .'

There were a couple of Japanese in the caravan park; one of them almost certainly the demon of self-sufficiency we'd seen chugging up the highway to Woomera, the other surely the figure who had come roaring out of the desert on his Honda, just as the sun was about to incarnadine the Rock. The second of these had turned up a few nights after us and been allocated the site next to ours. It was an awkwardly shaped patch of grass and dust whose precise boundaries were difficult to distinguish. We'd had troubles ourselves over territorial rights here and had

learnt that you had to fight for every inch. So when we saw
him scratching his head, and then pacing out what might or
might not be his, we went to his rescue. 'That's all yours – all
that there,' Ros said.

'And that,' I added.

'And that bit there,' Ros said.

He looked quite crestfallen. He had a pleasant, naturally
amused face, and the tousled hair of a comedian; but I thought
for a moment that he was going to cry. 'And if that's not enough
you can always take a bit of ours,' I said.

But we'd both misunderstood him. It wasn't the niggardli-
ness he couldn't bear. 'All this? For me?' he said. 'But I only
have little tent.' It was the waste.

In Japan they could have built a small city on this. So he was
uncomfortable – *morally* uncomfortable – with the luxury.
'Spread out,' Ros laughed. But his English wasn't up to the
phrase. Just as his Japanese was almost certainly not up to the
concept. He pitched his tent finally on an extreme corner of
the plot and never ventured thereafter more than eighteen
inches beyond it.

I grew to marvel at the compact nature of his existence.
Every afternoon, to the astonishment of the entire population
of the caravan park who would crawl out of their own bivouacs
to watch him, he would remove a number of delicate objects
from a box on the back of his motorbike, screw together a tiny
copper cooker, shake out a collapsible copper pan, and prepare
tea. This he would take formally, sitting cross-legged at the
entrance to his tent in a clean shirt. Had his English been better,
or had he looked as though he would positively have welcomed
it, we might have spent more time talking to him. As it was we
smiled at him a lot, and then, as the days went by and he seemed
to slip into intertia, we began to fret about him. The other
Japanese stayed two days and left. Other travellers far less self-
contained left also. But still our neighbour sat hugging the

corner of his sandy domain, still taking tea, still studying his atlases, but showing no sign either of enjoying being here or intending to move on. What if he'd lost his nerve in the middle of Australia and couldn't motivate himself to continue?

I felt particularly bad about this in case I'd inadvertently contributed to his debilitating cultural confusion. One night, prior to driving into town but not wanting to lose our space – it was, as I've said, a highly competitive caravan park – I had found a couple of dustbins lying about and used them to mark out my boundaries. He had watched me doing this with some concern. 'So that no one nicks my spot,' I'd explained, illustrating my meaning partly by shouting, and partly by pointing to the campervan, to the ground, and to Alice Springs. Unfortunately I am a careless pointer and had in fact signalled Heaven, Hell, and Coober Pedy. To make it even harder for him we had no sooner driven out than we had both been beset by a sudden lassitude which compelled us to drive back in again. Watching me return, remove the bins, and park the van precisely where it had been fifty seconds earlier could have been what tipped the balance for him. It was possible that he didn't have the confidence, after that, to go out again and mix with Euro-Australians.

Just as I didn't have the confidence to go out and mix with Aborigines. I don't mean that loosely. I'm not talking about casual street encounters. I had an invitation in my pocket to visit the Aboriginal community of Areyonga, 300 kilometres due west of Alice Springs, where the road finally gives out on Haasts Bluff Aboriginal Land. We'd been invited along, subject to Land Council permission, by Leanne Cook, a teacher at the Areyonga Bilingual School whom we'd met outside the amphitheatre on our last morning in Yulara. Come and see what we do, she had said, and we had considered ourselves enormously lucky to be asked. Except that, when the moment to front up to getting that permission actually came, I lost my nerve somewhat. Wasn't it a bit far? Wasn't the road a bit rough? Wasn't it a bit cheeky on our part to go nosing into an area that we had no business in?

Which is the real reason I hung around the caravan park. The longer I could go on finding interest in the unremarkable the longer I could fend off the unfamiliar. Who needed Areyonga when there was the shower block?

But I couldn't get away with this for ever. I was beginning to bore myself, for one thing. And my back was playing up. And Ros was becoming increasingly unimpressed by the dialogue I was bringing back. So the morning finally arrived when I capitulated. 'The person to talk to at Central Land Council is Merle,' Leanne had told us. 'Then Merle it is,' I said to Ros.

SIXTEEN

GHOSTBUSTING

Behind a counter marked PERMITS a heavy, handsome, self-possessed and laconic part-Aboriginal woman sat eating a sandwich. 'I'm looking for Merle,' I said, feeling pretty certain that this was she. I didn't let anything like certitude show though – not here, not in the offices of the Central Land Council. I wanted them to see that my intentions were entirely pacific. If I could reasonably have approached the counter with my hands up, I would have.

'You've found her,' she said, in-between bites. But the minute I started to explain why I was looking for her, she stopped me. 'I'm just finishing smoko,' she said, staring directly at me. It was a perfectly weighted reprimand – not a rudeness but the surest of parodies, for her own satisfaction and my education, of a white person's unhurried attitude to a black.

'Please, please take the longest of smokos there has ever been,' I would have said had I not promised Ros that I wouldn't humiliate us both by excessive deference. Which is the reason I wasn't on my knees either.

I thought Merle was going to take her smoko in front of us and go on eating her sandwich, very slowly, while we waited;

but in fact she disappeared and came back again five minutes and thirty-eight seconds later. 'OK, what can I do for you people?' she asked.

She was a deeply ironical woman, experienced, unimpressionable, politicized not in the firebrand manner of the young but as if on a slow burner, simmering evenly. She treated us both to the frankest of looks, as though she'd heard everything that we had to say a hundred times before. After a laborious account from me about who we were, where we came from, why we were here, who we'd met from Areyonga and what we hoped to do when we got there (which was mainly get the hell back again), she said, 'Look, I think I'll just give you a permit.'

It felt more like a punishment than a reward. It's possible that she had spotted how apprehensive I was of what might be waiting for me at the remote Pitjantjatjara community, how much I was secretly banking on her not letting us in. Or it might have been her way of showing how little trouble she thought me capable of causing. Either way I felt put out that her indifference was so massive that she couldn't even be bothered rolling it in our path as an obstacle. She wrote out the permit – TO ENTER ONTO AND REMAIN ON ABORIGINAL LAND OR SEAS ADJOINING ABORIGINAL LAND – and said that she would radio Areyonga to inform them that we would be there the next day. Radio? But of course – did I think there were telephones in Areyonga? Maye she didn't know the concern this information caused me; maybe she couldn't tell that she was talking to someone who had never been more than a hundred yards from a telephone – not even in Camballin – in his life. But she gave me a pretty level gaze as I thanked her, and for a laconic person did not look at all dissatisfied with her morning's business when we left.

We spent the rest of the day making preparations and the evening at the cinema. It was showing *The Gods Must Be Crazy*, a quirky little African comedy about what happens to a tribe of remote bushmen when a Coca-Cola bottle falls from an aeroplane and lands on one of their heads, which had gathered a huge cult following in Australia. This was already the umpteenth time it had been on in Alice Springs in under a year, and even before it had finished you could tell that the audience wanted to watch it again. Especially they wanted to watch again those scenes in which the bare bum of the starring pigmy bushman was shown high-tailing it from danger. Small, black, bare and frightened – that seemed to be the combination that had the large, white, clothed and fearless Australians laughing every time. One flash of prune-coloured hemisphere, the merest pusillanimous twinkle – and they were gone. I thought the couple in the seats directly in front of ours would have a double heart attack, they were so amused. But it wasn't savage laughter. This could have been a child or an animal whose simplicity they were enjoying. To stimulate the other kind of mirth the film showed other kinds of blacks – blacks *not* in a state of nature, city blacks, blacks in power, impossible dictators and hopeless revolutionaries cocking up self-determination. The audience seemed to get a kick out of making the distinction.

And the film *was* idiosyncratically humane enough for you to feel that it was all right to be amused. It appeared to release tensions that it hadn't itself generated, as if the audience of whites badly needed to laugh at blacks in a context that was not their own and in a spirit that was neither malicious nor particular. I am not aware that *The Gods Must Be Crazy* enjoyed any unusual success in England, so I can only assume that it provided something Australians required and were not otherwise getting, namely a break from the solemnity of the issue of race. Less than twenty-four hours later in a debris-strewn valley in the Krichauff Ranges we would witness an identical phenomenon, only with the colours reversed.

★ ★ ★

The next morning, early, we drove west out of Alice Springs in the direction of Areyonga. To take our minds off our apprehension we went in for drooling over the landscape, Ros choosing to notice the fine gradations of amethyst in the mulga, shading off even into lilac. I sticking with the orange of the Ranges, eroded so dramatically that a great wall seemed to run along their rim, shading off even into amber.

For the first hour almost all of the traffic we saw was touristical — occasionally a coach, more frequently a Pajero pulling a Statesman, somebody's mum with a white scarf round her head in the passenger seat, somebody's dad driving as if what was left of his life depended on it. But as we neared Hermannsburg, and the exit tracks to the beauty spots thinned out, and the condition of the road deteriorated, it became more and more just us and heavily-laden blackfeller vehicles. No couples circling the continent twinned in mute detestation here. Aborigines don't travel in such small denominations. If one goes on a journey, they all go on a journey. Piled into the back, hanging off the roof, as much of them out of the vehicle as in it, they belted along, all suspension spent, waving and hallooing, only inches from the dust. You always knew when it was a blackfeller's truck that was coming towards you, it was so much closer to the ground.

But the other side to this incorrigible sociability was evident everywhere too. Strewn by the road, sometimes still where they'd landed on the very crown of the road, beer cans and stubbies and, somehow worst of all, the cheerless green cardboard boxes of Orlando Coolabah Moselle — the most popular, because it was the least expensive Aboriginal tipple in Alice, at rather less than four dollars, not even two pounds, for a 4-litre cask. We'd counted scores of these boxes, tossed into the dirt and the scrub like so many castaway dreams, ever since leaving town, and though they became less frequent the further we drove into Aboriginal territory they by no means disappeared altogether.

We'd read that there was a serious cheap wine glut in Australia, that a more discriminating public had left behind the bulk stuff and was now progressing nicely through the vintages, as a consequence of which the country had a plonk lagoon as great as Europe's butter mountain. Sturt's inland lake found at last. But at least out here there was no paradox of the needy growing gaunt while all around them was plenty. Short of actually piping the wine in, the distributors could not have made a better job of shoving a surplus in the way of its market.

In order to make absolutely certain that none of the irony would be missed, that vulgar stage manager, life, had contrived to sit a cask of Coolabah, with its empty tin-foil skin spilling from it, right beside the red stone cairn to Albert Namatjira, the Aboriginal painter from Hermannsburg who himself had not been able to withstand either the blandishments or the anodynes of white society.

It was a plain monument – a stone pillar some sixteen or seventeen feet high – carrying a simple inscription:

> This is the landscape that inspired
> the artist, ALBERT NAMATJIRA.
> 28.7.1902–8.8.1959

It suddenly occurred to me that I knew what I was doing on the day he died. I was on holiday in the Lake District with schoolfriends, and I was throwing up. I could be sure of that because I had counted off the seventeen days to my seventeenth birthday that summer by getting drunk and throwing up on every one of them.

Albert was a full forty years older. You could argue that he should have known better by then. But I don't really see that one must attach a use-by date to the allure of self-annihilation. I was touched, as it was impossible not to be, by this modest memorial to creativity and despair, erected in a sublime and lonely place, but the story of Albert Namatjira's failure to survive success outside his own community held an exquisite satisfaction to white Australians which it seemed to me a duty to resist. Even leaving aside the sequence of prohibitions and rebuffs that led Namatjira into alcoholism (not being allowed to buy this, not being allowed to build that, not being allowed to go there), what sense did it make to talk of it as a tragedy of race, of cultural unreadiness, yet another heartbreaking example of a gifted black man unable to hold his liquor – 'Their livers are even different from ours,' Australians will tell you; 'they get drunk just looking at the bottle' – when all around were gifted white men equally unable to hold theirs?

A few kilometres before Areyonga we slowed down to read the following notice:

RESTRICTED AREA

The possession or consumption of liquor beyond
this point without a permit is a serious offence.
Vehicles carrying liquor may be seized and
forfeited and the following penalties may apply:
First offence, up to $1,000 fine or 8 months gaol.
Second and subsequent offences, up to $2,000 fine
or 12 months gaol.

The sign was faded and not all that conspicuous, and we weren't carrying any Orlando Coolabah Moselle. I did remember, though, that we still had three quarters of a bottle of High Wycombe Franklin Gray Muscat left in our store cupboard – the last remaining drop of all that Angela and Colin Davis had given us.

'Do you really think that's significant?' Ros asked.

How did I know? I stopped the van a few yards into the RESTRICTED AREA and reversed out of it again. 'Look,' I said, 'we're on somebody else's land, and we're only on that by the grace of Merle. I somehow feel that it would be only common courtesy to obey the regulations. Besides—'

'You don't want to go to gaol for eight months.'

'So, do you?'

'The sign doesn't say anything about Muscat.'

I had a vision of us trying to get away with that before a court of tribal elders. Or before Merle. I switched off the engine and went into the back of the van and brought out the bottle. When it comes to the point it is not easy to throw away your last three quarters of a bottle of Franklin Gray Muscat, the more especially when you're a long way from its source. But rules were rules.

'There is the question of litter,' Ros said.

I agreed, 'I suppose we could bury it.'

'Or drink it,' Ros suggested.

I debated the morality of that. In the end, the earliness of the hour combined with the heat of the day and the heat of the bottle of Muscat decided me against the surreptitious consumption option. So, on Ros's suggestion, we had a little ceremony. Ros stood to the left of the sign, and I honked the horn, while she very gradually upended the bottle into the desert. In honour of which occasion we named the nearest hill of the Krichauff Ranges Franklin Gray, and the more substantial twin eminences to the right of it we named Mt Angela and Mt Colin. To the whole area we gave the name High Wycombe.

Thus cleansed of all sin, like two little lambs of God, we entered the forbidden land, determinedly making no references to the sparkling brown stubbies and the cheerless green boxes which littered the road with no less frequency after the sign than they had before it. In fact, although we thought we were almost there, there would be another half-hour to go before we reached Areyonga. We kept going, the country becoming more ancient, the orange hills crumbling even as we looked, and me stopping at anything that even so much as resembled a habitation, just in case that was it. Then at last we rounded a bend and saw power lines, and a moment or so later a pool of water, set amid trees and rocks, with ropes slung from branches for swinging and jumping from. No one was there but it was easy to people the scene, to see natives up to their necks in warm water as we'd seen them in the Ord in Kununurra, to imagine them frolicking innocently like the creatures of Paradise that Captain Cook had beheld on his first view of the Aborigines of Botany Bay. Our spirits rose. A couple of wild donkeys turned to look at us. The rocks were suddenly wooded, beneficient, sparkling like gold in the sun. At last — the black man and nature restored to harmony, at last.

Our optimism was short-lived. A kilometre further on and we were in the settlement, a couple of rough stone roads of prefabricated houses, some on stilts and made of aluminium, with rusting cars and all manner of other rubbish outside, each one like a gypsy encampment in a lay-by, no charm or happy sense of permanence anywhere. Loitering in their own gardens or squatting under the trees as if they were on a nature strip in the middle of Katherine, the Aborigines resembled both in dress and demeanour those we had seen in urban settings throughout the North. The shrill sounds of domestic disharmony issued from a dozen homes at once. And the place had a litter problem too — trash everywhere, but as usual no bins to put it in, the roads themselves their own rubbish piles of loose stones and dirt and chippings. Dogs rummaged. Flies buzzed.

It would be irresponsible to give the impression that this was a shanty town comparable to the street of shame that Neil had shown us in Derby; the dereliction was not at all of those proportions and the beauty of the valley itself — great sheets of jagged bright orange cliff on either side — was still just holding out against the vandalism of its human occupants. But it was a shock to realize that we had come all this way only to find the

same old dispiriting hand–me–down slummery of fringe dwelling, albeit at a distance of about two hundred kilometres from
the fringes of the nearest town.

As an almost deliberate act of will, so as not to have to know
what I was letting myself in for, I had not bothered to enquire
what Areyonga was. All along I had been half fearing and half
hoping that we were on our way to an ancient site where we
would find barely clothed tribespeople – or at least not clothed
in jumble sale T-shirts and beanies – practising their marvellous
arts of survival and living in humpies and wurlies which figured
in my imagination as scarcely distinguishable from wigwams.
Had I taken the trouble to find out I would have discovered
that Areyonga was in fact a couple of years younger than I was,
and owed its origins – as presumably did I – to the Second
World War. Dismayed by the high incidence of native begging
and foraging for food at the military camps around Alice
Springs, the authorities saw the need to establish a rations depot
deep into Aranda and Pitjantjatjara territory in order to check
what in official language was called 'population drift'. The
advantage of Areyonga as a site – leaving aside distance – lay in
its possession of a permanent water supply already known and
used by natives, and the nearby presence of missionary influence. From the very start the Administration worked closely
with the Finke River Mission, leaving it to distribute the rations
which the Administration provided. Ten years later the Acting
Administrator spelt out the Government's policy 'to co-operate
with the Christian Missions and to give governmental support
to their work. We adopt this policy both because we place a
high value on Christian teaching and the spiritual counsel and
moral guidance of the Church in the uplifting of humanity and
because we recognize that the Missions can also make a major
contribution to those measures in health, education, and train-
ing for citizenship which open a path for the native people
towards full social acceptance within our community.' A few

things had changed since then, of course, and it would have been a brave man who dared to discuss spiritual counsel and uplift with Merle. Yet up until only a few days before we got there, the most powerful presence in Areyonga had still been the pastor – the Reverend Leo Kalleske whose tearful departure from the township after thirty-four years of moral tutelage we had read about in the newspapers back in Alice Springs. *Auf Wiedersehen*, many of the Aborigines who lined the farewell route out of Areyonga had been taught to say, *Auf Wiedersehen Frau und Herr Kalleske*.

So Areyonga was looking more or less the way it had always been intended to.

Leanne's house was the very last on the left where Areyonga pretty well ran out. She wasn't home yet but her mother and her kid sister, Geraldine and Brylynn, on holiday from Airey's Inlet in Victoria, made us comfortable and served us tea and cake – precious commodities both in a place that relied on a once-a-week plane delivery for its provisions. It was only when I learnt this that I realized what a serious error we'd made emptying the Muscat into the sand.

In the circumstances, that's to say considering no radio message from Merle had been received, Leanne's family, and then Leanne herself, managed not to look too startled or dismayed to see us here. By late afternoon we had got through all the Dundee cake and most of the Areyonga issues – these, for Leanne, relating mainly to the school, its lack of funding and staffing, and the consequences of this for her bilingual programme. The sense she gave of a small, embattled community of whites, brimming over with good intentions, but thwarted at every turn by broken promises or no promises at all from the authorities in Alice Springs and Darwin and even Canberra, was fleshed out even more when we were joined by the head teacher of Areyonga School, Neil Aird, and his wife Dawn.

Always looking down or looking away, and given to speaking into his own chest so that you caught his words as it were on the rebound, Neil explained to me that when he wasn't actually teaching, he spent his days writing letters to the Education Department and the Schools Commission, requisitioning, reasoning, asking, pleading, begging, arguing, and trying not to lose hope. He seemed very young to be a head teacher – a tall, soft-eyed, melancholy man, whose constitutional mistrust for the noisier doings of humanity, which made him the very person to brave the seclusion of Areyonga, did not, perhaps, make him the very person to be engaged in this deadly paper war of attrition with bureaucrats. He had the air, to me, of someone who was shell-shocked.

'We're at the bottom of a very long ladder of neglect,' he said, and the ridiculous thing, to his mind, was that they still were not granted Disadvantaged Status. When I asked if there was an advantage in being officially disadvantaged they all looked at me as though I might be a deserving case myself. Disadvantaged Status was the pot of gold at the end of their rainbow. Get that and there was nothing that wouldn't flow therefrom. And the corollary appeared to be: don't get it and nothing will ever flow from anywhere else.

Neil wasn't planning to go on waiting. He seemed to suffer – it truly did look like pain: a constriction of the chest and lungs – from a vast, dumb, inchoate, frustrated sympathy for the Aborigines whose children he taught. He wanted to help them. He didn't know how to help them. He wasn't sure whether the idea of help wasn't itself an impertinence. But he was coming to the end of his run. He had been in Areyonga for over two years, and had served a similar term of duty in Millingimbi, in Arnhem Land. Now he and Dawn were planning to go south, back to Victoria, to Gippsland probably, where they would run a smallholding, with Neil taking his turn to stay at home, and Dawn taking hers to go out to work. They made it sound like the sweet life and convalescence all at once – a shimmering prospect in a flimsy frame.

Leanne was at an earlier stage in her career and so more robustly angry. Her brown eyes flashed a fury that Neil's could no longer manage. Hers was a dual role at the school; she was what's called a teacher linguist, with special responsibility for building a library of research materials in the language of Pitjantjatjara. After forty years of automatic rations and force-fed Christianity the Aboriginal populations of such communities as Areyonga had been diagnosed as culturally dispossessed. 'They don't dance,' Dawn explained, 'they don't know *how* to dance any more.' (Me neither, I thought.) 'And they've lost contact with their legends,' Leanne added. (Me too, I thought.) So Leanne was involved in heritage-repair work – collecting, collating, and even re-inventing materials.

It was Whitlam, apparently, who gave the green light to the bilingual school system. Amid much optimism, over sixteen of them had opened in the Northern Territory, Areyonga being one of the very first, way back in 1973. Whitlam himself had travelled to Areyonga to give it his blessing and had stayed in the house next door – the house that Neil and Dawn now occupied. 'I sleep in the same bed he did,' Dawn said. With mixed feelings, I thought.

The next day we would see the extraordinarily sophisticated printing and duplicating equipment available to Leanne in her Production Centre – an even more bizarre technological oasis than the computerized accountancy office we'd found in Derby. The only problem being that the machinery was too complex for Leanne to use. It required its own fully trained printer, and although one had originally come with the equip-ment he had since gone down with Ross River Fever and there had been no replacement, no mention of a replacement and not one word as to whether the position had ever been advertised. In the meantime the presses lay idle and the Aboriginal children went on with their colouring books, little knowing both how close and how far they were from the wonders and ineffable benefits of man's great scientific stride.

There was to be a film show at the school that night, a video of somebody or other's choosing, with hotdogs and ice creams sold before and after, all proceeds going to Neil's current pet project – a school excursion to Melbourne, where the kids could get their first, and their last, ever look at a real city. Melbourne was where Neil himself came from and I read this scheme of his as a sort of final symbolic gesture: he would complete his circle of obligation to these children backwards instead of forwards, he would render his past to them in lieu of his future.

Before the video we went for a short walk with Leanne and Geraldine and Brylynn to the waterholes, a picnic spot of spectacular seclusion just minutes from the rubble of the road. While Geraldine talked to Ros about Airey's Inlet (she wasn't to know what I knew about Ros and inlets), and while Brylynn sat on the bank and kicked her feet in the water, I balanced on a boulder and listened to Leanne voicing her anxieties about my presence. What was I actually here *for*? Did I want to find something out in particular? Did I want to take photographs? Was I after some specific sociological low-down on the community. 'People have come here before,' she said, 'and gone away with some funny ideas about what they've seen.'

I didn't ask her to be more exact. It was easy enough to understand the reasons for her concern. She was how we came to be here. In a manner of speaking, it was she who had put the door on the latch for us. So it was she who would be respon-sible if we slipped away with the silver. I did all I could to put her mind at rest. I wasn't looking for any dirt. I didn't want to ridicule the community. I had no political axe to grind. The silver, in other words, could hardly be safer. But as for funny ideas – well, you can't stop anybody taking those.

Leanne having one or two other matters to attend to, it was Brylynn who showed us the way to the school. After a bit of a pouty patch at the waterholes, when she'd been inexplicably fuming at one of those infinitesimal family slights only discernible to the naked eye of a fifteen-year-old, she was now at her most expansive. All people of this age are of course schizophrenic; but the term has to be understood in its Darwinian, not in its Freudian, sense. They are simply selecting the personality that will give them the greatest possible chance of survival. I hoped Brylynn would select this one. She talked to us briskly about the school and the teaching she was doing there herself while she was on holiday. Wanting to work with children in the future she was treating this as serious experience, even though her own teachers back in Airey's Inlet didn't think much of the idea and believed she would have been better off putting in a couple of weeks playing ring-a-roses with the local infants.

Which is what *I* would very much have preferred to be doing from the moment Brylynn pushed open the door of the school and showed us in. A sight of a kind there was nothing in any part of my cultural background to prepare me for met my eyes. Aborigines of all ages, Aborigines of all sizes, Aborigines dressed for every possible climate, squatting on the floor of the hall on old blankets or on scraps of mouldy carpet or simply on the bare concrete itself – a hot, black huddle of wholly foreign and for that reason wholly frightening humanity ('Oh, God! Sir, look at them; look at them!') less packed and less numerous only than their dogs who were also here tonight to see the video – sleeping where there was space, prowling where there wasn't, the scabbiest curs you ever saw, fighting, scratching, sniffing, in some instances even pissing, without any sense at all that the inside was not the outside or that the school hall was not the road.

From behind a hatch a couple of bright-eyed girls, as astonished by the sight of us as we were by the sight of them, sold us hotdogs. These they presented to us, with a shy aversion of their heads, on a square of tissue. Holding mine aloft, while trying not to spill the sauce, I decided that the better part of valour was valour and plunged into the heaving mass. A dog looked at me curiously as I found a space to squat in, which caused me suddenly to be queasy about my sausage. To hell with it, I thought, meat's meat. And I sank my teeth in, thinking that I had eaten much that wasn't kosher in my life before, but that this was *trayf* and *trayf* again – this was *über-trayf*.

I'll say this for Aborigines' dogs: they are not personal nuisances. They don't want you to love them. They don't nuzzle your groin. They do not imagine that sexual congress is possible, or even desirable, between you and them. They seem to want you to be there to prowl between, and that's all.

And between their owners too – or at least between their owners and me – there was a curious absence of informality or licence: we were jammed up against one another but our eyes kept their distance. Despite my alarming conspicuousness I was almost never stared at. Even the handsome, sleek young blades who came in after us and stood against the wall, superciliously smoking, did not taunt or grace me with a look.

Once the television was switched on the smallest children settled into the front row of squats; with their unkempt hair-do's and their natural tawny streaks they looked from behind like a line-up of punk dwarfs. Then a picture flickered on to the screen and I realized that I had come this far not to see a Pitjantjatjara travelogue, or a Land Council documentary, or even *The Chant of Jimmy Blacksmith*, but *Ghostbusters* – *Ghostbusters*!! – that dead-pan college kid romp through genre-pastiche and smart-arse middle American not quite funny enough to be Jewish throw-away, second-time-round asides.

Who in this room apart from Brylynn was going to hear, let alone understand, let alone enjoy *Ghostbusters*?

I kept my eye on the kids in front. They stared at the screen as the wisecracks and put-downs began, reactionless. Elsewhere, too, although I wasn't looking, a profound unresponsiveness reigned. Then the first of the ghosts appeared and we were away. The kids put their fists in their mouths, they put their hands against the sides of their heads, they rose shouting and laughing with fear. As the action progressed and the ghosts multiplied and became more demonic – spirits and demons, of course! – they squashed themselves closer and closer together until at last they were not twenty but one, not so many separate entities of terror but a single compaction, a pure concentrated essence, of petrified child. A corporal dematerialization, 95 per cent efficient – wasn't that more spooky than anything in the movie?

But then something broke their spell and they all separated; or at least they separated sufficiently to be able to unite again, only this time not in mortal fright but mortal mirth, an amusement so in-wrought and fundamental that they could only express it by leaping into the air and throwing their arms around one another's necks and then burying their own faces in their own hands. It simultaneously joined and divided them, this thing they'd seen, it threw their functions into complete confusion; the power of their own response literally overwhelmed and even seemed to shame them. And this effect was not confined only to the youngsters either – the whole room, the whole *floor*, the dogs and Ros and I expected, behaved the same. So what was it that had done this to them? What, in *Ghostbusters* was *that* funny?

Why, a white man running away, of course. A soft, plump, pink Caucasian male frightened out of his wits and running for his life, pursued by evil spirits through the streets of downtown New York. The reverse equivalent precisely to what had had them rolling in the aisles the night before in Alice Springs. Except that to amuse the blacks the white man's bum didn't even have to be exposed. Naked terror was more than enough to be going on with. What's funnier than an horripilated black rolling his eyes in fear? An horripilated white rolling his.

So was this racism in action? Hardly. It's possible that there never is an emotion or an impulse which is usefully described by that word, even if it comes in handy sometimes to express one's abhorrence of a programme or a policy. For the truth seems to be that races, just like sexes and generations, have a positive need, a requirement of the whole system, to find one another ridiculous and to enjoy one another's discomfiture. I wouldn't be surprised if it turned out to be the case – though I haven't myself done the research – that denying yourself the relief of laughing at people who are another colour or another size, who speak peculiar languages or worship foreign idols, actually makes you ill. Certainly those who conscientiously give their lives over to removing offensive adjectives from every library book in North London, for example, don't *look* well. And, whatever else the Aboriginal population of Areyonga might have been suffering from, they seemed to be in perfect health when riven with amusement by the trepidation of somebody my colour.

I could have said, somebody my *religion*, because if I wasn't much mistaken the fleeing honkie had been circumcised, barmitzvah'd and the rest of it. But I doubt if the Aborigines would have spotted that, or that it would have made any material difference to their pleasure if they had. Given the extent of their need to ease basic otherness tension, anti-semitism would have been pure finessing.

I watched the rest of the film, or at least I watched the audience watching it, in a far easier frame of mind. They hadn't just relieved their own pressures, they had relieved mine. I felt freer, now that it was sort of openly agreed between us that we were all specimens of some type, to indulge my own humdrum taste for the human-picturesque. I couldn't have been the first person to be struck by the enormous urchin-charm of Aboriginal children – all in that state of becoming indigence that would have sent Murillo wild – but I was struck by it anyway. As I was by the theatrical gestures some of the women made when they rose to leave in the middle of the video, sweeping their blankets around themselves and their offspring as if they were the cloaks of aristocrats. Instinctual elegance? Natural grace? – Oh, what a mess it all is, the language of cross-cultural appreciation; but natural is probably never a good word to get tied up in, the more especially, in a case such as this, where no one could be oblivious to the possibility of scrutiny, where no one was unaccustomed to the experience of scrutiny, and where no one, therefore, could be expected to be unaware of their effect.

The audience was never still. People shifted their positions or left altogether, and others immediately took their places. There was no overwhelming narrative reason for coming or going; the film was a series of moving staircases which you got on or off whenever you felt like. Only the children remained settled, compressing or separating according to horror or humour. And of course the dogs, still prowling between the humans – a glint of their part-dingo ancestry occasionally showing in an uninterested eye.

And then, the very second the video finished – and I mean the actual story, not the reel; the plot, not the credits – they were gone, up and vanished all of them, without even bothering to wait for the name of the actor whose cowardice had given them so much pleasure to appear on the screen. It would be no exaggeration to say I didn't see a single one of them go, because they didn't *go*, in the accepted usage of that word, they simply and suddenly – like Prospero's palaces – dissolved. Where they once had been, there they now were not. Precisely as the earliest explorers had noticed of Aborigines, they still possessed the power to evanesce.

What they'd perhaps never possessed the power to do, though, was take their rubbish with them. It was still there on the floor – the tissues from their hotdogs and the polystyrene cups from which they'd drunk their trashy cordials, torn and broken, tossed aside without a thought – the only evidence that they'd ever been here. 'What I think it shows,' I said to Brylynn, 'is the instinctive attitude of nomadic peoples to an expended site. They are up and they are off. It's only the obsessively permanent, like ourselves, who fret about litter, and care about being house-proud and street-proud. What all that is, is neurosis of the immobile. Don't you think?'

But Brylynn was too busy sweeping up to have time to answer me.

Although there was room in Leanne's house for us to sleep, it seemed an unnecessary imposition on her given that we had our campervan outside. So we just drove it up her path and said good night and locked our doors and lay awake listening to the dogs.

Had all the dogs in London been rounded up, and every bitch been prodigiously on heat, they would not have made one quarter of the racket the dogs of Areyonga made. Earlier in the day we'd met Neil's dog and seen how, as a mere white man's ball of fluff, he knew to keep his distance from the real thing. Even in the daylight the front gate was as far as he'd go. At the first wild howl he'd prick his ears and twitch his nose, hearing some distant echo of heroic times, when the blood ran hot; but it was no more than a last, faint atavistic tug on the line. He'd stand stock still, his head ever so slightly to one side, not even bothering to weigh his needs against his safety. What the blackfellers' dogs got up to was not for him. He was out of it now. As were we all.

★ ★ ★

Neil's cockerel, confused about the dawn, woke us at 3.50 a.m. This meant that we were up and ready in good time for the proposed walk up Helicopter Hill – so called because of its flat landing-strip summit – in the company of whoever wasn't teaching, that's to say Geraldine, Dawn, and Dawn's two boys.

We had a good, invigoratingly spiral climb up the hill, from the top of which we could look out over Areyonga and see how bare and minimally purposeful it was. Ros found a geode – already worked – and declared that we were in an ochre area, but that didn't help me overcome my sense that however ruggedly beautiful the country was here there was also a quality of ruination about it. Ruination wholly independent of anything humans had done. 'The very stones lying upon the hills,' the explorer Eyre wrote of an even more desolate Australian mountain range, 'looked like the scorched and with-ered scoria of a volcanic region.' And so they did here. It wasn't just the fault of people that Areyonga always looked like some sort of accident.

Back at the bottom I decided it was time I took a look around the church. But I'd forgotten that we were between pastors. The church was locked, so I had to be satisfied with reading the missionary literature which was still pinned to the notice board. GREAT NEWS FROM CHINA, one pamphlet proclaimed, 2 NEW CHURCHES EVERY DAY! It might have been the exertion of the climb but I found myself turning giddy. Imagine there being a soul in Christendom who could conceive it to be of any interest or consolation to the Pitjantjatjara community of Areyonga – Ngura panya Utjula: that narrow place – however many new churches were opening in China.

An older handwritten sign, in whose faded script one could still read the exasperation in the fingers, retold the Easter myth for incorrigibly irreligious minds.

Easter is the time when Jesus died and rose again.

Easter Sunday is the day HE came alive again.

HE died for our sins. We remember this at Easter time.

This is why we have Easter holidays.

Easter time is *not* for parties, for hunting, for gambling and *not*
   for getting drunk.

I didn't follow that myself. Why shouldn't a return to life be
celebrated by more life? Or, to put that another way, why had
German Lutheran gloom been brought to this already excori-
ated valley?

Despite promising Leanne that the last thing I was here to do
was rake up dirt, I couldn't resist sounding out the views of the
whites of Areyonga on the usefulness of missionary Christianity
in general and the influence of the last pastor, the Reverend
Kalleske, in particular. Unfortunately everyone I spoke to was
circumspect, so I was able to piece together only a rough
impression of his long pastocracy. He had been a stern shepherd, often the only believable authority figure in Areyonga,
and therefore the only one able convincingly to administer
discipline. That somebody needed to assume such a role was
undeniable, but wouldn't it have been better for the Aborigines
to go in ultimate fear of one of their own? Where were the
tribal elders? And what chance had they of reasserting themselves when the autocracy of the church was so entrenched?

I was reading C. D. Rowley's powerful book, *The Destruction
of Aboriginal Society*, while I was in Areyonga, and it was clear
from that that the moral and legislative listlessness that prevailed
here was the common experience of artificially stable communities. '. . . the Aboriginal, once he had sat down, quickly lost
the power to do more than supplementary hunting, if only
because the processes of hard socialization in which the
Aboriginal personality was formed were so rapidly lost in
circumstances where autonomy for the process was lost. It was

not lost because of some special tyranny in the white "boss". As the history of the best-intentioned of the missions suggests, human kindness which stabilized the nomads in a dependent imitation or a dependent mendicancy had the same effect in the end.' Though Rowley also had thoughts towards a solution which were those exactly of the whites we met in Areyonga. 'Perhaps the answer lay in opportunities for stablization in situations where leadership and decision making for change rested within the Aboriginal society, the whites at the point of contact offering assistance and advice on request.'

There was a more specific grouse against the reign of Pastor Kalleske also. That part of the church service which was not read in English he invariably gave in Aranda, that being the language in standard use at Hermannsburg Mission where Pastor Kalleske had his strongest connections. But the people of Areyonga were Pitjantjatjara not Aranda, and it was in Pitjantjatjara – their own language – that the teachers at Areyonga School were endeavouring to make their charges literate. With so many other obstacles in their way they felt that they could have done without this one.

It was no longer the case that those working for the secular betterment of the Aborigines could believe that they were allies with those working for the spiritual.

On the other hand there could be no doubting the high regard in which both the Pastor and his wife had been held by the generations of Aborigines, far and wide, whose lives they'd influenced. Their departure from Areyonga, only a matter of days ago, had been even more dramatically emotional in fact than the newspaper accounts suggested. Aborigines travelled miles – from Hermannsburg, and Docker River and Kintore and Papunya – to see them go. They lined the road out of Areyonga, sitting in the dust waiting, while innumerable bulletins were relayed concerning the state of the Kalleskes' packing. They waited and waited. Then the word came that the cortège was ready. Slowly down the rubble-road the car appeared – Leo Kalleske driving. Lydia Kalleske walking behind, extending her arms to the people, and calling *auf Wiedersehen*. It was Lydia Kalleske – who had once been in charge of the Areyonga choir, taking it up to Darwin for the Eisteddfod, and down to Adelaide for a series of invitation-only concerts – who had taught many of the Aborigines lining the route the meaning of *auf Wiedersehen* and how they should sing it out in return. Even the most rigorously anti-clerical of the teachers agreed it was a most distressing farewell.

I pictured the scene for days, unable to imagine anything more extraordinary. The slow, regal procession through the narrow, rock-ridden valley – the wild donkeys staring down from the orange hills – the dogs everywhere – the bitches on heat – the wide-eyed urchins with their fists to their mouths – the rows of melancholy, black faces – and the German woman walking behind, calling goodbye to her past. *Auf Wiedersehen*!

By now they were in retirement in Tanunda. For all we knew dining at the Landhaus, sampling Franz and Vivien's roulade of pork.

Later that afternoon we were invited to look around the school. 'Hello!' we said to each class. 'Hello!' they mimicked back, raising their faces to us in mischief and curiosity and shyness. In a rare swell of promiscuous paternalism I was ready to adopt them all.

I was dismayed, I have to say, by the amount of colouring-in I saw going on, but it was Friday afternoon and you could feel time being marked before the weekend. In her Production Centre, where equipment with the capacity to produce the *Sydney Morning Herald* was languishing for want of a printer, Leanne introduced us to her teaching aid, Nyukana. It was a feature of the bilingual programme that an indigenous language speaker and member of the community should be employed as an assistant. 'Nyukana is the Pitjantjatjara model and I am the English model,' Leanne explained. I suppressed my purist loathing for that particular usage of the word model – a model was a train or it was Twiggy, it seemed to me – and I tried to introduce myself to Nyukana. But her shyness was gargantuan. The whole top half of her body fell away, her eyes raked the ground, her arms went everywhere. Infected by it, we did the same. I lost control of all my limbs. Ros's face set in an inane smile. Even Leanne had to turn away. We were all relieved when Nyukana resorted at last to Aboriginal social magic and dissolved.

I was very much taken by shyness on such a scale. I don't just mean that I was beguiled by its sweetness – though I *was* beguiled by its sweetness – but I also thought it gave a clue to another idea of privacy, that it was a true register of the great shock that meeting a stranger actually is. I felt that I shared something of this resistance to the nakedness of new encounter with Nyukana for, although I did not go quite so spectacularly awry myself when it happened, I was none the less never able to hear let alone remember the name of any new person I was meeting.

There is an argument which maintains that present-day Aboriginal delitescence and tongue-tiedness is a sign of their inadequacy and shame, a function of their being instilled with the idea of their inferiority. But this is no more than the rationalization of a culture which has by and large lost its awe of strangers and puts a high premium on social competence. We are all salesmen now and you can't sell anything if you carry on like Nyukana. The assumption is that self-respect and the confidence easily to interact must go together. What the earliest explorers noted in their journals again and again, though, was the exquisite reserve of Aborigines, their overwhelming desire to be unseen – even if that meant shinning up a tree and staying there – long before there was any instilled sense of inferiority to attribute it to.

In the playground – where she was refereeing a game of Pitjantjatjara rounders – I met Jane, another teacher at the school, who told me almost immediately, as a piece of information without which I couldn't be expected to understand her, that she came from Moree, the country town in the far north-west of New South Wales. I would have been more surprised by the degree to which Jane was 'dressed' and 'made-up' had I not had some experience in the past of country school teachers in Australia – I'd been an educational book rep in the early seventies, travelling around Victoria with a boot-load of set texts – and their greater conscientiousness, in matters of personal presentation and couture, than their equivalents in Britain. Australian teachers altogether spruced themselves up for their work in a manner that would have been unthinkable to any of the elbow-patched paupers who had passed on the values of civilization to me. But it was strange, for all that, to see Jane standing in her French high-heeled shoes in the dust bowl that was the Areyonga school playground, a silk scarf that might have come from Yves Saint-Laurent about her shoulders and a tin whistle to her scarlet lips.

'I am very much a Moree girl,' she told me. Which was meant to explain such disparities as her *comme il faut* (though not *comme il faut à l'Areyonga*) style and appearance, her sense of separateness, and her mistrust of the prevailing tone of social informality. 'People keep wanting to borrow things,' she said, 'and I just don't believe in lending them. Not even to good friends.' I took this to be outback wisdom speaking; Moree was probably even more remote than Areyonga – lend something to a person in Moree and it would be ten years before you next saw the person let alone the thing.

But she was also a Moree girl in the sense that that was where she was most happy. 'There is nothing I love more than to return to Moree in the early evening, to walk into town, and to see a pair of moleskins in front of me. Then I know I'm home.'

This was saucy: moleskins were the trousers that the menfolk of Moree wore.

Just before we parted she asked me what I did, and in that case what their titles were. 'So that I can pass an opinion,' she said. I wrote them down for her. She scrutinized the scrap of paper and then folded it neatly into her *sac*. 'Now I can pass an opinon,' she said. It sounded very deadly. I suddenly had an intimation of what it might be like to be a chap in Moree, awaiting her appraisal of his moleskins.

While I'd been talking to Jane I'd kept half an eye on a large open truck which appeared to be driving up and down the two roads of Areyonga and round and round the school playground for the sole purpose of picking up stray women and young girls. It turned out that there was nothing sinister in this. The entire female population of Areyonga was off for the weekend to Yuendumu or thereabouts – a cross-country trip of over twelve hours – to play a game of softball. The truck kept circling so that no one should be left behind. When at last it was ready to leave – Leanne had joined me outside and was my guide to this ritual – it made one more circle of the settlement with all the women piled into the back waving and shouting goodbye, before driving off at speed and in a cloud of dust in the direction of Papunya, the first stop. Half an hour later it was back. Once again it cruised the town, and once again, to the sound of even more shrill excitement, it sped off in a cloud of dust. This procedure was repeated more times than I could count. 'What happens,' Leanne explained, 'is that the women keep changing their minds about going. They get ten kilometres out and think they'd rather be back here.' And sure enough, when I looked around, there, sitting contendedly in a circle under a tree, were several of the women we'd seen waving us goodbye the first time.

There was an end to this. The truck finally did leave. Only this time it was not jammed with shouting women but shouting men. What had been intended as a girls-only excursion ended up, to absolutely nobody's surprise, as a trip away for the boys. 'They leave it to the women to arrange it,' Leanne said, 'and presumably to pay for it – then they take it over.'

Leaving aside the question of sexual politics – and it was clearly not a cut and dried case of one group exercising its tyranny over another – this event seemed to me to provide an unusual and sympathetic insight into an alternative interpretation of decision. Here was no finality. Here was no heavy burden of completion morality. Here everything remained open and flexible, not just until the last minute but even way beyond it. Simply because you embarked upon a journey was that any reason you should finish it? The whole thing suddenly struck me as intelligible and desirable. Who said a beginning was a binding contract to provide an end? Protestants, I supposed. But wouldn't Hamlet have had a happier time of it if he'd been a blackfeller sitting under a tree, or on the back of a truck, in Areyonga? How all occasions do inform against me? Not here they wouldn't. Yes, this part of being an Aborigine looked good to me. Not least because I imagined it as one in the eye for Pastor Kalleske – another failure of the missions to load their charges down with the weight of responsibility and obligation. I could see that there were problems as far as the people at the other end were concerned – those waiting for their game of softball – but then they were Aboriginal women also, and so presumably engaged in similar vacillations. It was only a game anyway. Like everything else in life.

A barbecue had been planned for us later that evening. 'A bush barbecue,' Neil had said, 'not here in Areyonga.' I'd looked surprised. Wasn't Areyonga bush? 'I mean *real* bush,' Neil said.

So we set off after school, loaded down with provisions, Neil and Dawn and Brylynn in Neil's Toyota, Ros and Geraldine and I in Leanne's Pajero. It was the first time I'd been in any relation to a Pajero except that of external satirist. Now, as a passenger, I had to eat crow. It did, what I think they call in the business, the business. Following Neil, we travelled out of Areyonga on roads that had not been there before we made them. Up mountains, through forests, along the beds of creeks, the Pajero all the while purring as if we'd taken it for a roll on an asphalt carpet. It's the same with everything I thought: get inside the object of your satire and you forget what you found ridiculous. Cars, men, institutions – the same truth held. The only safety was in distance.

The object of the first stage of our short expedition was a disused copper mine – in a place so high and so remote that it was hard to imagine how anyone had ever found it let alone thought of scratching for precious metals in it. Not for the first time it was brought home to us how little there was, even in this vast scarcely populated country, that didn't bear the marks of some earlier visitation. In this instance, although we weren't aware of it while we were there, the visitation might have been particularly distinguished. It was Ros who came upon the information later, in a book on Albert Namatjira, that towards the end of his life the painter had discovered and pegged a copper deposit in this very area, subsequently abandoning it because, like everything else in his declining fortunes, it didn't yield. So, it was not impossible that these rather beautiful empty caves we walked through, the habitation now only of bats, the signs of hope only a few blue-green chippings on the ground, had once been his.

It's probably only supervenient fancy that makes me think that some thwarted spirit, an atmosphere of forfeiture or destitution, clung to the place; but I do recall that Neil and I fell into an unaccountable despondency up here, and stood together at the edge of the high plateau of white dust, Neil shaking his head – not violently but finally, as if there could be no gainsaying what he saw – and I absently trying to kick the entire hillside down, sending sand and pebbles flying into the vast imperturbability of bush below.

What I suspect we were both thinking was this: that in another million years or so a project might just take root here with some prospect of success; until then it was folly to think you'd even get as far as failure.

Back down amongst it, with the light fading, we went in search of the ideal creek bed on which to build our barbecue. Neil was an exacting leader. Many a dry creek that would have done the rest of us nicely Neil rejected on the grounds – if I heard what he shouted through the open window of his Toyota correctly – of unevenness, over-accessibility (i.e. low inconvenience rating) or poor acoustics. We ploughed through the roughest terrain and then ploughed back out again, until even the Pajero began to work up a sweat. The later it got, the more surprised the wild horses and donkeys were to see us still looking. They raised their heads from feeding in alarm. Some, thinking we must be dangerous, decided it was best to flee. God knows how much smaller life we sent scuttling for safety through the undergrowth. In the end it was the lateness of the hour that settled it. We found a spot that looked suspiciously like the first one we'd turned down and set to work building a fire. This consisted of collecting three leaves and two twigs and tossing on a match. The match was supererogatory. On such tinder a warm breath would have done as well.

It was a wonderful night. Not quiet – the bush out here was never quiet – but utterly still. The heavens almost as vaulted as they'd been over Cook, the stars so distinct that you could calculate the millenia that separated them. Cities spare you the horror of the stars by blurring them; the melancholy of country people must be a consequence of how much time they see whenever they raise their eyes. Tonight everything was a hard silhouette of itself – the trees, the parked vehicles, us, all so sharply defined that we seemed things of outline only, without other substance.

And, if that was how I looked, it was also how I felt. It was as close as I'd so far got, on this journey, to spirituality. I imagined perpetuity for myself as being like this: my profile, a line circumscribing nothing, spinning eternally through space. Not a torment – not at all Dantesque infernal – but a supreme lightness; a sort of distillation, only of spirit into body instead of the other way around. Which might mean that it was physical I was feeling, not spiritual at all. Either way I enjoyed it, sitting swooning by the fire, oblivious to such purely temporal threats as snakes and scorpions.

Barbecues and infinity – the fact of the one leads invariably to thoughts of the other. Which is why Australians are so melancholy also.

We all swooned a bit. Hardly speaking, we sat with our legs crossed, chewing chilli sausages and pepper steaks sandwiched between thick absorbent slices of white bread; and unified in a single suspiration we washed them down with billy tea. What brought the idea of language back to our little lapsed party was Leanne's damper, rising miraculously from a cast-iron pan which she'd placed on the burning embers. Buttered and dripping marmalade or jam, it resembled an enormous Devonshire scone, an entire cream tea in a single bite.

I asked for the recipe. 'Flour and water,' Leanne said. I swooned again, in an ecstasy this time over ingredients not outline.

It must have been the sight of this bushman's scone that reminded Neil and Dawn of their whizz through the West Country on their one and only English trip. A visit that had very nearly been ruined for them at the outset by an event they still vividly remembered. 'We heard on the aeroplane,' Dawn said, 'that Mrs Thatcher had just been elected Prime Minister. But by then it was too late to turn back.'

I laughed, but they weren't of course joking. They were a serious couple, Neil and Dawn. They really did believe that you oughtn't to go merry-making in a place of whose politics you didn't approve. Thus they wouldn't go to South Africa or North America. And they hadn't yet been to Queensland. 'We'll wait for that one,' Dawn said.

'I admit it cuts your travel options down a bit,' Neil conceded.

Talk turned again to the problems of Areyonga and what they all saw as the hopeless intransigence of white attitudes to blacks. It was queer, sitting by the fire under the stars on this marvellous warm night, eating damper running with marmalade, lazily feeding the flames merely by reaching for any combustible to hand – the very ground we sat on was combustible – and tossing it on, and at the same time fuming over ocker incomprehension of Aborigines. I had a feeling that Aborigines themselves would not have wanted to be the object of our concern here, now, in this setting. 'People talk about their language as if there's just one,' Leanne said. 'And they think *that's* just a series of simple noises. They've no idea of the range of sophistication in Pitjantjatjara, for example. Simple noises? I'd like to hear them trying to make some of those simple noises!'

I curled out a finger and flicked a branch onto the fire. Our own conversation had scarcely been more than a series of simple noises for some time now – I sighing over the rising dough, Ros crooning over the bush, Neil and Dawn reiterating the fact that we'd stolen Aboriginal land and had to give it back. And that satisfied me. It was good, once in a while, knowing your role and limiting the range of your responses to a couple of syllables. It went with being all profile and no substance. And that's the other advantage of a barbecue in the bush – it isn't necessary that you have an inner life in order to enjoy it. Off, off and away I went, spinning into the immensity, my own untenanted circumference.

After another night of street theatre from the dogs of Areyonga – this time they did the Rape of the Sabine Woman *and* the

Sacking of Troy – we rose to find Leanne building a barbecue in her back garden, preparatory to making us damper as a fare-well breakfast present.

While things were still at their early stage, the damper a mere latency yet in a bowl of flour and water, I ran across the road to get more marmalade from the community store. I'd heard about the community store and wanted to see it for myself before I left. There was some issue about it in Areyonga which I hadn't been able wholly to track down. It was run by a white man for the black community, with the idea that its profits should be ploughed back into the settlement. But so far a narrow strip of cleared ground with a basketball net at either end was all the tangible benefit to the community the store had provided.

It was a great hollow barn of a place with petrol pumps outside. Within, its metal shelves were stocked with a limited range of standard junk foods – orange juice that wasn't really orange juice, bottles of cordial and cola, tins of corned beef and baked beans. Understandably, given the problems of distance and transport, everything was pre-packaged, canned or frozen. And for the same reason everything was impossibly expensive. So you got the worst of all worlds here – it wasn't cheap and it wasn't fresh and it didn't taste nice.

A large quantity of black and yellow tracksuit tops hung from a rail in the corner, near the folding mattresses and the army-surplus type blankets. The only clue to any more exotic or invigorating life lived in Areyonga was given by the shelf of cowboy boots and saddles. Every now and then, I'd heard, the local boys would go out looking for wild horses to catch and train. But I didn't see any saddles being bought. Only corned beef and hotdogs – the latter being made on one of those hot-spiked Spanish Inquisition contraptions which impales the bun.

In the main the Aborigines of Areyonga didn't look comfort-able with the conventions of purchase. They did form a sort of queue at the till, subject as it was to defections or incursions at any point, but they took no interest in the additions of the bill, just handed over a large note every time and accepted whatever change was given them. I never saw a single instance of change being checked or queried or come to that received gracefully. For their part it was a mute, difficult, unabsorbing transaction; from the point of view of the storekeeper it was like taking candy from a baby.

I assumed that the easy-going bearded white man by the till was indeed the storekeeper, and I was struck by his treatment of his women customers. It would be incorrect to say that he took liberties with them exactly, but he knew their names and patted them on the back and put his arm around their shoulders, almost in the manner of a male nurse at a home for the incurably but innocuously simple. I was not at all able to read the response of the Aborigines to this, and queried it back in Leanne's garden. 'They tolerate it,' Neil told me. 'That's about it.'

There were divisions, that much was clear, between the small number of whites in Areyonga. Too small a number for such divisions not to be costly. Which was partly why our teacher friends were sorry to see us leave; they were starved of talk. However passionately committed they were to the Aboriginal community they served there was no possibility of any real social contact there. They had one another and that was that. No wonder they were serious. Or, good job they were serious.

And we too were sorry to go. We'd been well looked after. We'd blown in out of the blue and been trusted and made welcome. We drove away with a curious premonition of anti-climax, as if we knew already that we'd have trouble over the next weeks doing anything quite so interesting. I now realize that this was a throb of wishful fidelity, that like young lovers faced with a parting we clung to the obligations of the present only because we were fearful of the enticements of the future. The more especially as the future in this case was Queensland, a state whose politics, according to Neil and Dawn, were such that we shouldn't even approach its borders.

We drove out with sadness anyway. And under the gaze of not a single pair of Aboriginal eyes. All those who were not away on the soft-ball excursion were up in the orange hills, scrambling after something – maybe a wild horse – that one of them had found. We could hear shouts of excitement coming from high up on either side of the road, and we could see the Cuban heels of the stragglers' boots, but they didn't see or hear us. They let us go without so much as a wave.

SEVENTEEN

THE TOWNSVILLE HOIST

We called in at Hermannsburg on the way back. Although it no longer functioned as a mission, being now under the administration of the Ntaria Council – Chairperson, Mr Gus Williams – the township was still dominated by a tin cross on a little hill. I walked up and read the inscription.

> This memorial to the sacrifice of the first
> missionaries and the first Aboriginal Christians
> marks the 90th anniversary of the mission's
> founding on June 8, 1877.
> Your sins are forgiven.   Matthew 9:2

The founding missionaries – Schwarz and Kempe (Schwarz being the Jewish-looking one, Kempe more Max von Sydow anguished) – started out from Bethany in fact, in 1876. The village schoolchildren turned out to see them off, singing 'Jesus Lead Thou On' under the direction of their teacher, Herr Topp. That was on Friday the 22nd of October. They had a tough journey ahead of them. On Thursday the 11th of November Kempe froze solid in his bed. A week later Schwarz fell off his horse; or rather was thrown from his horse which had been horned by a cow which Schwarz had for some reason whipped. And a week after that Kempe lost his trousers in a waterhole, 600 head of cattle suddenly appearing out of nowhere and trampling them to nothing where they'd been left to soak. Two days later Kempe wrote in his journal, 'Often I have been almost tempted to exclaim in the words of the prophet: "It is enough; now O Lord, take away my life" for I am sick at heart.' But missions are not made by men who lose their faith as easily as their breeches, and he was soon back on a heavenly course. 'But then again I tell myself that we are in the Lord's service, that he has sent us and will always be with us. He will also know why he deals with us in such a way . . .' God works, as we used to say in Salford, in Strangeways.

Some of the first mission buildings still stand in Hermannsburg, a cluster of simple whitewashed barns that look like churches, or churches that look like barns, one or two with inscriptions in both German and Aranda on stone lintels. The presence of a few slender palms softens the spot and gives it the air of a very small colonial outpost. Had I been sure that we were allowed in Hermannsburg without a permit I would have taken more time to look around; as it was I slunk about rather, scribbling hurried notes and forming surreptitious impressions.

In the graveyard across the way the most notable memorial was to Moses Uraiakuraia, 'Inspiring Leader and Teacher, Folklore Historian, Bible Translator, Travelling Evangelist – 1878–1954. "Those who turn many to righteousness shall shine like the stars for ever and ever." Dan 12:3b.' It made me think of pyramid selling.

The graveyard was a strange mix of German and Aboriginal, as – Adolf Inkamala: 'We come Lord to thy feet.' And there, too, was the grave of Mrs Kempe and her child. But if you were a non-believer, and the term included Moslem Afghans, you didn't make it into this graveyard. You lay buried in the dust somewhere outside the cemetery fence, no stone or memorial marking your remains.

We drove out, having developed no taste for the place and taken no pleasure in its atmosphere, the tin cross always visible until we were once more on the gravel track.

It was a quiet, musing, uneventful journey back to Alice Springs, broken only by our having to pull up suddenly when we came to an unmistakably low-slung Aboriginal vehicle parked at a slight twist in the dead centre of the road. A surly looking adolescent sat staring out of a rear-seat window, otherwise no one was in the car. We waved to him. He waved back. But gave no sign that he was in any trouble. I passed slowly, trying to work out where the driver was and why the car was abandoned like this, and then I saw two sets of Aboriginal limbs thrashing about in the scrub, just yards from the road, on a blanket that could have been any one of those I'd seen on the floor of Areyonga School during the showing of *Ghostbusters*.

It was a hot day. And it must have been a hot impulse whose call was so imperative that there hadn't even been time to pull the car into the verge. They'd just stopped and tumbled out, whoever they were, and were now flailing the air with their uncannily attenuated arms and legs, like some dusty Leviathan of the bush. I did what I could to resist thoughts about native spontaneity, but there was no getting away from it – you didn't see people flouting the rules of the road with such insouciance in England, merely because the primal need had taken them.

We weren't so spontaneous ourselves, naturally, as to stop in order to get a better look; but the road was straight and otherwise deserted, and for some while I could see the car in my rear view mirror, still where it had been left; and I was able to imagine the expression on the face of the gooseberry boy in the back seat, full of disdain and impatience, but troubled also by a dim sense of missing out. That could have been the last day of his childhood we'd driven through. Unless this happened whenever he got taken for a ride.

We were no sooner back in Alice Springs than we found ourselves listening to a group of evangelists wired up for a large audience but having to make do with a small one on the grass lawn outside the council buildings, where the town Aborigines like to congregate. In the main they had the usual story to tell of not finding Jesus until they were forty-five and *now* look at them; but their act livened up when a middle-aged Liverpudlian swinger in a blue country and western waistcoat worn over camel-coloured flared trousers stepped forward and took the mike. He looked so experienced that for a moment I thought he was going to toss it from hand to hand and swing it through his legs. And he *was* experienced – that was precisely the confession he had to make. 'I used to go around with the Beatles when I was younger,' he admitted. 'I used to spend all my time – every hour that the Devil sent me – with John and Paul and Ringo and George.' (I don't know why one suddenly chooses to believe a person who says this sort of thing, but I believed him utterly. He had the authentic nasal drawl. And the same sense of humour.) 'And I thought that was the whole meaning of life. John and Paul and Ringo and George – and me. If you'd asked me then what else there was to life I'd have answered, nothing. But I was wrong. Jesus is the only friend worth having.'

I thought this was a bit rough on the memory of the Fab Four. Not only did he still talk like George and look like Ringo, I believed I could detect the lingering influence of John's theologizing. And when he began singing –

> Jesus is the answer, for the world today,
> Above him there's no other; Jesus is the way

— I thought I was listening to McCartney.

Funny, the way things had turned out. They'd stayed with showbiz and he'd gone to God, and yet he was the only one of them now on the road. He might have shifted his allegiances from pop to pietism but here he was, twenty-five years on, in his old flared gear, in the middle of Alice Springs, still doing a gig.

And remembering exactly how you handle hecklers. 'Let Jesus clean your mouth out, brother,' he called to some blasphemer on the opposite side of the street. And when the language got worse he flicked on his amplifier and swung into another number. Peace, love, I've seen the light so why can't you — pure Lennon.

I watched a pair of young Aborigines come sidling down Todd Street in riding boots and crumpled jeans — a real swagger they had going — but the moment they heard the word Jesus their whole bearing altered. Shoulders dropped, eyes lost their defiance, hands slid of their own accord behind backs. For all the world they looked like a pair of recaptured truants. Feeble shadows of themselves, they joined the congregation on the grass — babies in the Lord once more.

It was only when it became clear there was to be no tucker at this mission that they faded guiltily away. As indeed — for equally non-spiritual reasons — did we.

I'd heard there was a game of footie on in town that afternoon and thought it might be fun to take in at least the final quarter. I'd become a bit of a fan of Australian Rules Football during my Melbourne years, which meant that I knew the rules and what to look for, but was rather ruined for the provincial version of the game. Once you'd watched Carlton take on Richmond there wasn't much you could hope for out of Rovers versus Westies, even if Rovers liked to call themselves the Mighty Blues. But it wasn't so much the contest that was disappointing as the supporters. They lacked ocker authenticity, or rather, since they *were* authentic, they lacked that counterfeit authenticity which I was used to, which made the real thing look merely ersatz, and which required for its production a solid body of intellectuals in the crowd. Spectatorship – thoroughly engaged spectatorship – is more demanding than it's often given credit for; in the case of spectatorship of sport, especially in Australia, a further degree is a minimum requirement.

I'm not saying that they didn't try at Traegar Park. 'Bounce it – why don't you bounce it, Squiggie, you . . . you lady!' I heard. And they had half an ear for referee abuse. 'Wanker, Smithie! Fifteen yards. Fifteen fucking yards, you mongrel!' But ultimately they lacked the vocabulary, the spleen, the vehemence, the feel for patois, the sheer pent-up rage and frustration which only academics can bring to footie watching.

The nearest I came to feeling I was back in Melbourne was when a well kitted-out Aborigine sitting on the grass beside me began to feel the sun warming up his blood. 'How am I going to get a root tonight?' he asked whoever cared to listen. 'How *am* I going to get that root?'

Although we'd only been away for a few days we were nevertheless alarmed to discover that the Japanese motor cyclist, whose nerve I might have been responsible for shattering, was still in his old place at the caravan park. So on our last morning in Alice Springs, before I returned the van to Bill Richards' agent, Ros insisted that I go over and see whether there was any assistance I could give.

'Isn't this more a job for you?' I asked.

'Yes,' she said, 'but you're the one who knows how language works.'

Which was how I came to be sitting on the ground with him outside his tent, shouting, 'Long time! You've been here long time! Is everything all right? OK? You not in trouble?' I'd toyed with heap big trouble, but held off at the last minute.

He knew what I was saying. 'Machine,' he explained. 'My machine. Parts. I'm waiting one week.'

Did that mean he *had* been waiting one week or *would* be waiting one week? I shuffled impossible conditional clauses made even more uncertain by the future-pluperfect tense. 'Today,' he said. 'Parts coming today.'

So there was absolutely nothing to worry about. He was fine. He was better than I was. Just to keep talking I asked him about his friend. Where had he gone?

'Friend?'

How do you mime friend? I pointed to where he'd camped when he'd been here.

'Oh – he. He machine in trouble also. In Ayers Rock.' He laughed, not at the misfortune of others but at this sudden picture of Japanese marooned beside their ailing bikes all over Australia. 'He parts come from Japan.'

I asked him where he'd been before Alice Springs. He took a neatly folded map from his tent and pointed to Perth. 'Fly in here. Buy bike. Go here.' His finger traced a route that actually wasn't there, along a road that had never been built. Perth to Alice via the desert.

'A difficult journey.' I said.

'Oh – exciting. Big, big desert. Meet Aboriginaries. Good men. Good men. I take wrong way. They see me. They shout, "Go back – go left – go right!" They shout me whole way. Good men, black men. Good good men.'

I wished I'd been there, in the Gibson Desert, to behold it – this extraordinary confrontation of cultures. When Aborigines saw their first white man dismounting from a horse many of them fainted clean away, imagining that here was a beast that had the power to separate. So what about our friend, in his helmet and goggles, climbing off his Honda?

I suddenly decided I wanted his name, just so that I could savour it, though I felt I could only ask for it if I explained I was a writer. But we had trouble with the word. 'Wrliter? Wrliter?' I thought of saying, 'Mishima — like Mishima.' However I could see that this might have given him entirely the wrong idea. I didn't want it to look as though I was recruiting for a private army. Then I hit on 'journalist'. 'Ah, journalist.' He did a little scribble in the air. 'For paper.' He even brought a folded Japanese newspaper out of his tent. His smile seemed to imply that he knew I was in there.

I thought this was close enough not to quibble over. 'Yes, for paper.' Whereupon he wrote his name down for me — Shigeru-Horigan — rather Irish, I thought; and his address in Omiyacity, Saitamaken.

Before we parted I asked him how much longer he planned to be in Australia, and he explained he was on a working holiday and had a six-month visa which he hoped he could extend. I wondered — I really did mean this to be my last question — what he was intending to work as.

He suddenly became very amused. His whole face crumpled. He nodded in the direction of his immobilized Honda. 'Motorbike mechanic,' he said.

Returning the campervan wasn't easy for us. It had been our home for weeks. We were even beginning to look like it, in the way that owners come to resemble their own pets, or in Australia their own children. Ros couldn't bear to be there when I actually handed it over, so I dropped her off in town and arranged to meet her later, once I'd done what had to be done, in Todd Street Mall.

Walking back, troubled by that curious sense of privation that follows parting with a set of car keys, I thought I detected a more than usually heavy traffic of Aborigine-bearing taxis on the streets, and a few more police patrols about as well.

And when I caught up with Ros I learnt that there had indeed been some hyperactivity of an Aboriginal nature in town today, caused by the heat and by alcohol and by whatever other mystery ingredient it is that makes one day more excitable than the last. The paddy wagons had been out, that's all that had really happened, and a few offenders had been bustled, protesting, into the back of them. The taxis I'd seen were simply carrying Aborigines bent on dematerializing quickly away from trouble.

But if nothing much had really occurred, it was a reminder for all that of how unresolved the black/white issue still was in Alice Springs, and how pervasively present in the town – as a matter of visible fact, not merely of politics – these second-class citizens with no jobs were. There was absolutely no escaping the issue. During our last few hours in Alice it was all around us. Even in the little art gallery in the mall, where it was above all possible, you might have thought, to subsume race under artefact, it rose like an odour from a sewer. 'These,' a young Japanese tourist wanted to know, pointing to a book which contained illustrations of ancient Aborigines sharpening sticks, 'can I take photograph of these?'

'I think he means in the street,' an English girl with him helped out. 'I think he means the ones outside.'

The woman he had shown the book to was herself part-Aboriginal. 'Ah, I dunno,' she said. 'I don't think they like it. Better ask them yourself.'

'Ask them? Ah yes.'

'Yeah, I would.'

'Is it – is it – is it, hoh, dangelos?'

'Dangerous? Ah no . . . it's not dangerous.'

'Do they expect you to pay them?' the English girl asked. I stayed away from wine bars in Clapham so as not to hear an accent like that. Now here it was, catching up on me in Alice Springs.

'Aw look,' the woman behind the counter said – and I could see her thinking that if she was forced to become any more ponderous she would crush herself beneath the dead weight of her words – 'Aw look, I'd ask them.'

So leaving Alice wasn't an especially painful rupture, though we weren't pleased to be back on a bus. After being masters of our own fate for so many weeks it was a shock to be reminded that there were such things as prohibitions. And twenty-seven hours until Townsville seemed an awfully long time to have to suffer them. Especially as neither of us had the slightest desire to go to Townsville.

But I had the proofs of a novel to read. The job wouldn't take long. Just a day or two. And the typescript would be waiting for me in Townsville. We'd pick it up from the Post Office, do what had to be done to it which would be nothing, post it back, and head up the coast to the real Queensland, to Cairns and the Daintree and the Barrier Reef. That was the plan. And Townsville was not meant to be any significant part of it. What we didn't yet know was what had been done to my manuscript. But I'll come to that – or rather, iLl caM£, TWon; *@:;%at!? – later.

'My name's Warren, but you can call me Spike,' our bus driver said, at the very moment, according to my strip map, that we crossed the tropic of Capricorn. Also according to my strip map the small settlement of Ti Tree, which we came to a couple of hours after leaving Alice, was 'mentioned in various factual novels on these parts'. It didn't ring any bells and in fact I didn't see any settlement; only a roadhouse, claiming to be 'The most Central Pub in Australia'. It was certainly the liveliest. Under a sign which said 'Flo's Bar', men with bruised and bleeding faces, with tattooed ears and pierced nostrils, wearing bandanas and, I swear, feathers, fought and shouted and poured beer unremittingly down their throats as if they were gargoyles in reverse. Warren had only allowed us a ten-minute refreshment stop at Ti Tree but we were all back on the bus in five, and that included the couple we'd originally stopped to drop off here, who returned with their suitcases pleading to be allowed back on board. As we drove out we saw police making three arrests. What puzzled me was how they chose.

It was an uncomfortable journey. The temperature in the bus kept changing, making it impossible to go to sleep. The stops were all in the wrong places and at the wrong times. And there was nobody much to talk to. The German nursery tree and shrub cultivators in the seat in front of ours were pleasant enough in their rabidly curious way; but we had to close our ears to Steve and Simon, the two English boys from Frensham Heights who'd cut their shirts off at the armpits in order to look like Aussies, and couldn't get over what a 'gid taim' they were having; and Terry, across the aisle from us, whose mind would only work associatively backwards, so that he couldn't so much as eat a chocolate bar without being reminded of the last occasion on which he'd eaten something similar. 'Reminds me of the time I was in Noosa,' he suddenly said, for no other reason than that we were now in Tennant Creek.

I looked out of the window and watched a group of young Aborigines seeing off one of their friends. I noticed that although there was plenty of social by-play while they waited for the bus to leave – pretend high spirits, awkward tomfoolery, stone-kicking and back-slapping – come the actual moment of parting the break was quite sudden. No kissing, no tears, and only the most perfunctory wave. There was not much to do on these buses except watch people getting on and off, and I believed that what I saw at Tennant Creek was generally true – that amongst Aborigines the emotion and ceremony of departure was kept to a minimum. So what did it mean? Was it residual nomadic wisdom: an old preservative instinct that, in such a vast country and where there was inevitably so much coming and going, you couldn't *afford* to make a fuss over leave-taking? And, if so, might that not also explain the origin of the great distinctive Australian expression, 'See you later,' which causes so much confusion when it's used to non-Australians who aren't expecting to see you again for another six months, if ever at all?

White Australians frequently complain that Aborigines have an unsatisfactory concept of time – they say they'll do something on such-and-such a date, and then they don't. 'Time means nothing to them,' Bill Richards had told me. 'They don't know if they were born yesterday or tomorrow.' But even for whites in Australia time is a more than usually fluid concept. No sweat; no worries; she'll be right – what is this small-change of ordinary transactional life but a sort of assurance that time stretches out infinitely and beneficently, and that no moment should ever be singled out for urgency?

It was at Tennant Creek that the idea came to me that it wasn't only the black man who was Dreaming in Australia.

'Historical studies of the role played by the Aboriginal since contact with white settlers are sparse,' says C. D. Rowley. 'In the broad scope of Australian historical studies he appears as an almost completely passive figure. Yet it is difficult to believe that long association and the most intimate personal relationships in frontier areas have failed to influence the style of Australian life.' Forget the 'frontier areas' aspect of the argument; as far as I was concerned you could trace Aboriginal influence in the very language most commonly heard on Australian lips.

The question of 'intimate personal relationships' was equally intriguing. For how many of the offspring of those early mixed relations had gone back, unnoticed, into the earliest white communities in Australia? The conclusion seemed inescapable to me: the longer the lineage the greater the chance of a drop or two of Aboriginal blood. I could think of a friend or two of mine who had a wild eye. And I went to sleep, finally, planning that I would ask them, as soon as I reached Sydney, 'Are you sure your great-great-grandfather was never in the Northern Territory?'

When I woke up we were over the Queensland border and receiving instructions from the coach captain about our breakfasting arrangements in Mt Isa. Opening my eyes I realized we were actually in it, the giant mining town which was like Kalgoorlie and Coober Pedy rolled into one and then cleaned up. No dust on the roads here, and no desperate characters on every corner. But chimneys belched smoke and there was no mistaking that the place was functional.

It had once meant a lot to me as an idea, Mt Isa. In my Melbourne years it had symbolized the options open to me should I ever have the courage to become a fugitive from conventions and relationships. I never knew what I would do if I ever actually made it there; I definitely never envisaged going underground, for example. But the town, with its reputation for hard masculine companionship, shimmered as a possibility for two whole years – a mirage I followed in my dreams, a coppery alternative to the domesticity into which I seemed incapable of not immersing myself.

Now here I was at last, having an early breakfast at the Mt Isa Hotel with a pair of German tree freaks, a bore with a rare associational disorder who was reminded of the last time he'd had breakfast, which was yesterday, and a couple of pupils from a minor experimental English public school. 'Any more tea there, Ros?' I asked.

Twelve hours and thousands of picturesquely stilted and verandahed wooden houses later we were in Townsville.

This is not the place to recite the grievances a writer feels when, without warning, he discovers that his punctuation has been fiddled with. Editorial interference has to be taken stoically. There's no point crying rape. The writer is himself the reason for the crime. Were there no mug there'd be no mugging; no paedo there'd be no paedophile. So, if we would have no editors should we flaunt no prose. A little experience teaches that there are men out there – and women too – who cannot keep their propelling pencils to themselves. It's an illness, a compulsion, a mysterious psychic disorder akin to kleptomania, except that the patient wishes not merely to take away but also to replace with something different. Emendolepsy. Tinker-ophilia.

I knew all about it – from the victim's angle. I'd been prose-violated countless times. Mangled and mutilated more often than I cared to think about, long before I turned up in Townsville. I had even been mastectomized once, been made to look on without an anaesthetic while the word breast was removed from wherever it had put in an appearance, on the grounds, I could only suppose – since my surgeon was female and Australian – that I was disqualified from using it by being male and English. But nothing had prepared me for the scale of meddling that awaited me when I went to collect my page proofs from the Post Office in Townsville – every comma changed into a semicolon; every semicolon promoted to a period, every period reduced to a comma. Not a line that didn't bear the scar of some incision; not a pause for breath that wasn't shortened or lengthened; not an interval or respite that I recognized as my own. So much for a leisurely weekend's proofreading on a hotel balcony overlooking the bay. I asked for a second table to be brought to our room, ordered a couple of dozen pencils, and requested that nobody disturb us for a fortnight.

In fact it didn't take us quite that long. Measuring time on the conventional scale, we restored the script to something like its original condition in ten days. But anyone who had seen us at the end of that period would have said we were older by a year.

We did get to look around Townsville a bit during these ten days, and given how little we were pleasure-bent it's possible that we even quite liked it. It had a waterfront, a beach, a river, a hilly hinterland, a few good nineteenth-century public buildings, a small but lovely botanic garden overlooking the sea, and some spectacular fig trees. A high, rugged outcrop of rock – Castle Hill – didn't tower over the town as spectacularly as I kept thinking it was about to, but it was picturesque enough and from some angles, especially looking up at it with your back to the beach, offered the sort of prospect that makes a man think of owning a horse and saying, 'See you later,' to his family.

In so far as Townsville could be said to have a problem, it related to its origins as a commercial centre. Because it had not been built primarily for recreation it didn't embrace its own amenities conveniently; it didn't in any inviting way, for example, front its own water. Although the sea was out there – although you *knew* the sea was out there – you went about your business with your back to it. And this needn't have mattered too much except that tourism was what Townsville now wanted to be about. Above all things it wanted to shed its country town image and rival Cairns, not just as a convenient stepping off point for the tropical paradises of the Reef, but as a sophisticated, five-star international gambling and shopping metropolis in its own right. On the very day we arrived a brand new Sheraton Hotel and Casino complex had opened its doors – an event, according to a leader in the *Townsville Bulletin*, that could 'be fairly described as marking the dawning of a new age both for Townsville and North Queensland'. And which was bound to cause some consternation up the coast – 'If anyone thought our friendly neighbour, Cairns, had the edge . . . think again.'

New age or not, the Sheraton Breakwater Complex looked a merely conventional oblong high-rise hotel to me; not all that different from a Battersea council estate. And there was no reason to believe that the casino here would fare any better than the ones in Darwin or Alice Springs, attracting far fewer tourist dollars than anticipated, despite the charms of croupiers with names like Lindelle and Leslene, and just adding to the number of ways the indigenous population could make itself miserable.

When it wasn't trying to be international and getting excited because it had a 'Gucci' shop, Townsville made a good job of being the very thing it no longer wanted to be – a charming lazily provincial tropical country town. Some of our most enjoyable times – in-between editing the editing – were those we spent sitting in Flinders Street Mall outside the fresh fruit bar, eating mangoes and paw paw and pineapple served with frozen yoghurt, watching North Queenslanders going about their business, or, and this was only marginally less strenuous, perambulating for the fun of it.

Part of the pleasure came from simply noticing how large and healthy and good-looking they were. One of Townsville's more intelligent commercial boasts was the number of outsize fashion shops for women it had. And it needed them. Women here were a good three inches taller than those we'd seen elsewhere in Australia, which means they were nine inches to a foot taller than what you'd find in Birmingham or Manchester. And without exception their br****s were fuller also. I am less likely to be reliable on inches here, but every woman we saw in Townsville, who was a native of the place or had lived in it long enough for its climate to have seeped into her hormones, had large, high, round, and perfect br****s.

The men, too, were more than satisfied with what the North Queensland sun had done for them. I noticed before too long that there was a strict way of wearing shorts in town if you were young and single – a certain brevity and tension and lift; a sort of bunching effect that wasn't a matter of the shorts being skin tight, but on the contrary a function of their being cut high and open at the leg, so that the marvel was that whatever they contained did not fall out. I called this the Townsville Hoist and noted, as the days went by, that the greater the impression of imminent catastrophe the hoister gave, the more attention he received. It goes without saying that, while this spectacle was available to be appreciated by anyone, it was ultimately *inter homines*. Hoisters hoisted first and foremost for one another.

But what really made the streets of Townsville quite distinct from any others we'd walked along in Australia was the presence of blacks who neither looked like any Aborigines we'd seen before nor behaved like them. The bus journey had already given us some intimation of this change. We'd noticed that the closer we drew to the coast the more marked became the variations in the physical appearances of the Aboriginal passengers we picked up. Skin grew progressively darker, hair curlier, features flatter, bodies stockier and shorter. By Charters Towers we had people on board who looked more like Maoris than Aborigines. I'd read that coastal tribes were not the same as inland tribes. Leichhardt himself had noted the difference. And I also knew that North Queensland had been more subject to foreign incursions, long before the English turned up, than most other parts of Australia. Melanesians had been here. Some historians speculated about Papuan colonization. But I still hadn't expected to see Townsville looking like a stage set for *South Pacific*, where handsome, vigorous, well-dressed, confident and apparently *happy* South Sea Islanders strode about the town whistling.

I'd got this sort of thing wrong in the past, of course. Most notably in Broome where I'd confused servitude with spontaneity. So I thought I'd better buy Ross Fitzgerald's *A History of Queensland* before I made another ass of myself. If these too were prisoners on day release, or just a boatload of Honolulans who happened to be in North Queensland on vacation, I thought I ought to find out about it. There wasn't much time for reading in Townsville, given the task of comma reparation to which we were committed, but a quick perusal over lychees and frozen avocado yoghurt told me what I needed to know. These were Torres Strait Islanders. They weren't in prison and they weren't on holiday; they lived here. Whether they were indeed as happy as they seemed to be Ross Fitzgerald didn't say. I looked up *Contentment, Aboriginal* in the index but didn't find any entry. It wasn't that kind of history book. If I had my facts right it very nearly hadn't been any kind of history book at all, having been pressurized, threatened, changed and in its original form even pulped – pulping being a touch more final than repunctuating – as a consequence of some heavy leaning by whoever looks after that in Queensland. I'd picked up something or other in some scandal sheet to the effect that the then Chief Justice of Queensland, Sir Walter Campbell – now the State Governor – had been behind this, but who believes what they read in a scandal sheet? Anyway, happy or not, at least I'd found out who these black men were who didn't sit in circles on nature strips looking woebegone. And Ross Fitzgerald did offer me one important clue to the undoubted confidence of their bearing. The Second World War. 'In far north Queensland the war brought Torres Strait Islanders into close contact with Australian and American servicemen and hastened their "assimilation" into white Australian society . . . The arrival of black GIs was a revelation both to the Islanders and north Queensland's white population.' I wasn't for the moment interested in the white population. 'Although the influence of black servicemen on Queensland's indigenous peoples is difficult to assess, the relative affluence of negro GIs was certainly impressive. After the war, Torres Strait Islanders displayed material ambitions similar to those of their black American brothers.'

And indubitably, by the time we blew into town forty years later, looked the better for that.

I thought of sending a telegram to Neil and Dawn in Areyonga. 'Queensland not what you think stop happy hoisters on every corner stop blacks with heads held high stop life a bugger stop never what you expect stop Joh for P.M. love Howard.'

But I realized I might have been jumping the gun a bit. There was likely to be more to race relations in North Queensland than a cheerful atmosphere around the shopping mall. And it was not at all beyond the bounds of possibility, either, that the price those Islanders paid for their external ebullience was a spiritual disinheritance, a hopelessness as far-reaching as my own when it came to knowing what you were supposed to do with sacred objects – tyuringe (pronounced tewring-ger) – and the like.

It was a puzzle and no mistake. Compounded by our taking a night off from our labours and going to see *Crocodile Dundee* in the Townsville picture theatre, where we sat stony-faced, like Lord Longford and Mrs Whitehouse on a blind date, while all around us Queenslanders with shoulders too high to see over laughed at what wasn't funny and agreed with what wasn't true. Presumably it worked differently in different venues, but in Townsville it was the moment when Paul Hogan addressed the kangaroo hunter (the ecological bad guy) as 'shit for brains' that won the audience over completely. The idea that you could update your decencies and still not have to forgo your swearing seemed to be the key to their hilarity and relief. But however much the decencies were remodelled, the *in*decencies remained where they'd always been in Australian mythology – quite beyond the grasp and comprehending, let alone the experience, of the rough-mannered, simple-hearted, but always clean-minded larrikin of a hero. Balls on a transvestite? Rudeness to a lady? Never!

It was hard enough to swallow, this cute fiction of butch naivety, even in those parts of Australia where only 25 per cent of the population was overtly homosexual. But here in the high hot north, where you could see the Townsville hoist in operation twenty-four hours a day – where you couldn't in all truth ever *not* see it – no, the gorge rose and rejected it.

For the traveller, watching something like *Crocodile Dundee* in situ is probably not a good idea. It makes you doubt the usefulness of your eyes. It seemed to me that what I saw of Australians on the street bore only an oblique relation to how it pleased them to see themselves. Here I'd been, supposedly in 1986, observing what I thought was a various and dynamic culture responding to sensitive contemporary challenges, both from within and from without, and all along it was 1958 out there, the uncultivated terrain still peopled by roving bands of amiable boof-heads whose profound ignorance of the ways of the world (poofters, foreigners and intellectuals) was, quite magically, the very thing that endeared them to the sheilas. In which case, if I *had* slipped back thirty years in time, maybe those happy-happy-talking Torres Strait Islanders really were extras from *South Pacific*.

On our last evening in Townsville – I was having second thoughts about the editing and wondering if my full stops oughtn't to have been commas after all, which meant that it was definitely getting time to leave – I ran into the greatest living Australian snooker player, Eddie Charlton, in the hotel lift. He was in town for a few days, playing exhibition matches and taking on the local hotshots, as part of a five-month tour, promoted by Fosters, of Queensland and the Northern Territory. As the hotel was only four storeys high and the lift was pretty nippy I didn't stand on ceremony. 'What's this about Joe Johnson?' I blurted out.

I'd only recently read in the papers that Steve Davis had been beaten by a rank outsider in the final of the World Championships at Sheffield. Eddie of course had played in them himself. So I wanted to hear, as it were from the horse's mouth, all about another faltering of Steve Davis's nerve.

'Joe? Didn't he play well?'

'I don't know,' I said. 'I never saw it.'

'Gee, he played well. He played very well.' He somehow managed to make this sound heartbreaking, but I knew, from having listened to him on television, that this was just his manner of delivery, and that he could sound sunk in inconsolable sorrow even when he was in the very best of spirits. And he looked in good shape today – tanned and healthy in a sports shirt and business shorts. I confess that it was strange, though, not seeing him in a waistcoat.

I didn't really care about how well Joe Johnson had played. If Eddie wasn't going to tell me that Steve Davis had wept and broken his cue and head-butted the referee, then the final wasn't interesting to me. I might as well hear about earlier rounds. So I said, 'So who knocked you out this time, then?'

The question didn't come out the way I intended it. It seemed to imply that someone was *always* knocking him out. But he took it well. 'Kirk Stevens,' he said. 'In the quarter finals. 13–12. I was leading 12–10. I should have had him. I missed a green in the 23rd, just like the last time we played. And that let him in. You don't have to give Kirk more than one opening. In the final frame I had another chance, but . . .'

He had total recall. Like a bridge player. He could remember every ball he'd ever potted. So could I remember every one of mine, come to that, but that wasn't quite the same thing. And also like a bridge player he could never have enough of post-mortems. No game was ever buried. You kept the cadaver in storage and went over it and over it. I left him on the third floor, still running through the missed chances in the final frame. He sounded heart-broken; but he always sounded heart-broken. It's an upsetting line of business, mortuary work.

After we'd parted I kicked myself for choosing the wrong

subject to discuss with him. I would have liked to hear his views on the crime wave that was currently inundating Townsville. According to the papers there were burglaries, rapes, car thefts, muggings, on a scale to rival London. There was even a story about a dog-devourer making front-page news. 'BIZARRE DOG FIND – Three dogs found chained in the heart of the city were believed to be "on the menu" of a rumoured dog eater who frequents the area.' The city in question was actually Cairns, but there was no reason to believe that once he'd got through its canine population he wouldn't come down the coast and start sinking his teeth into Townsville's. For a while I'd misread the headlines and assumed it was the dogs that were bizarre – as if we were dealing here with a highly particular gastronome who wouldn't touch anything that wasn't a chihuahua or an Alaskan malamute.

Anyway, it would have been interesting knowing what Eddie, as an ex-policeman, thought we were coming to.

On a billboard outside a newsagent's, close to the hire car company I was making my way to, I read – POLLS FAVOURING MAGGIE FACE-LIFT DISTORTED. And one across the road said – MAGGIE STORM.

This was another drawback of life in Townsville. You kept thinking you were reading about Mrs Thatcher. In fact Maggie was Magnetic Island, Townsville's popular off-shore resort, and dollar for dollar probably its chief tourist draw. The storm that was brewing, and had been ever since we'd arrived, related entirely to the issue of development. It was the same fight that was raging all over the state and indeed right across the Reef. Only a few months earlier the whole country had been in uproar over the Queensland Government's attempt to revoke the National Park status of most of Lindeman Island in order that an airline might build a resort on it. The conservationists had more or less won that one. But were losing just about everything else. Joh, of course, was the bugbear. Followed closely by Colonel Gaddaffi. If he hadn't been frightening Americans out of holidaying in Europe – that's Gaddaffi I'm talking about – there wouldn't have been so many of them coming to Australia. In fact, from what I'd seen of American tourists, they were less interested in multi-million dollar resorts and casinos than they were in staring at kangaroos and Aborigines, and meeting outback Aussies got up like Crocodile Dundee. But try telling a property developer that.

It was only as we were leaving that we realized not only that we hadn't left ourselves time to go to Magnetic Island in the finish, but that it would have been far the most sensible thing to have taken the manuscript there in the first place, and attended to it in soothing tropical insularity. On a verandah underneath a palm tree. That we never even thought of it proves to what levels of self-defeating despair the task had driven us. Now it was too late. We were both desperate to be away.

A dry, quintessentially unimpressible Queensland woman called Kay filled out the form for our hire car. She was in her mid-forties, plain – on what seemed to be intellectual grounds – with her hair pulled tightly back from her face. While she was writing I mentioned that I might want to keep the car longer than our originally agreed five days in order to drive back down the coast to Proserpine where I'd heard there was to be a rodeo. Only the slightest twitch in the finger uppermost on her pen suggested that she had heard me. 'There's a rodeo there, is there?' she finally got around to asking.

I became aware, suddenly, of her possible powers of contradiction. 'I think so,' I said, although I in fact knew so.

She went on with what she was doing, then she raised one, one only, infinitesimal eyebrow. 'You into rodeos?'

The question bore such a heavy charge of ironical indictment that I think I turned a little pink. *I* knew I wasn't a bronco-buster's bootlace, but was it *that* obvious to everybody else? And, if it was, then what did she mean to imply I might be into - saddle-sniffing? 'No,' I said. 'Good heavens, no. It's just that I'm ah . . . doing a book on the area and um . . . feel I ought to er . . .' (I nearly said, 'put my nose into everything') 'keep my eyes open.'

I always think it's quite a defeat when you have to admit you're a writer. It's like being forced to play your best card – in this case the four of clubs – first.

She made no immediate response to this. She simply went on copying out the details of my driver's licence. Then she said, as if reading out the numbers from the licence, 'A writer, eh? And how am I coming through so far?'

I think that was the moment I fell in love with Queensland. 'You're coming through marvellously,' I said. Not much of a reply, I am only too well aware. But I was in the presence of a conversational virtuoso. Somebody who did for expressionlessness what Angela Davis had done for the Australian rooster. I was licked and I knew it.

'That's good to know,' she said, about ten minutes later.

She stood at the door to see us off, utterly impassive. 'Turn left at the lights,' she said, 'and go straight. If you're not in Cairns after 370 ks you're on the wrong road.'

'Bad bitumen,' I said to Ros. 'Potholes. Savage, twisting bends. Not enough room for more than 1½ cars in either direction.'

'Thorny cork-screw trees,' she replied. 'Extreme chromatic monotony. Gnarled, evil-tempered landscape.'

We weren't playing twenty questions. We were just getting rid of our spleen while we were still within touch of Townsville. But then the country opened up. The thorny corkscrew trees gave way to banana plantations, coconut palms, and fields – did I know before now that they grew in *fields?* – of pineapples. I stopped the car so that Ros could get out to look. 'Pineapples, my dear,' I said. 'Pineapples and pineapples and pineapples.' We agreed that if she were ever to develop her allergy to Australia again (we couldn't say for certain it had gone; she hadn't been back to Melbourne yet) this is where we would bring her – to the far north-east, where she could roll amongst them by the field-full, instead of having to make do with just a couple, one hanging from her left bedpost, one from her right.

We both cheered up immeasurably thanks to those pine-apples, so that by the time we reached the cane fields we were in the right frame of mind to make ourselves over to the extravagant beauty of Queensland. I'd read that there were serious problems in the sweet-tooth industry: world overproduction, EEC subsidies, and cane farms falling into ruin through land abuse; but I fell for those cane fields for all that. I loved the way they managed to look both luxuriant and orderly, dense bamboo jungles that grew in straight lines to the very edges of the road, giving off an aroma that might have been more imaginary than actual, a giddying paradoxical something or other that made me think of dry swamps. Hawks, too, were attracted to them, and eagles, enjoying the ride. I liked to think, in the sticky currents of air that rose from them, but primarily, of course, waiting to pounce on whatever lived in that stalked, sinisterly sugary undergrowth.

The first cane town we came to was Ingham – 'Little Italy', as it's sometimes called. Apparently Italians had been here for almost a hundred years, the first boatload of migrants arriving in Townsville in 1891. They had been imported as cheap labour, mainly for the sugar industry, in which many of them were to prosper. According to Ross Fitzgerald, they aroused considerable antagonism because of 'their increasing numbers and efficient working methods. Some British workers complained that they undercut other groups by accepting lower wages and working longer hours.' What a miserable history the British have, I thought, when I read this, of carrying their querulousness into every corner of the globe, and how bad they've always been, when it comes to the logistics of labour, at working out where their own best interests lie.

'Forget Cairns for a while,' the woman at the Ingham Information Bureau recommended. 'You've got plenty of time to get to Cairns. Why don't you stay here for a while? Explore Wallaman Falls – the second longest sheer drop in Australia. And you can't leave without seeing the new cemetery. Everyone goes to the new cemetery.'

'Why's that?' I asked.

'The Italians are buried there. People like to see the mausoleums.'

She asked me to sign her visitors' book. She ran the Information Bureau as if it were her own lounge, and the vale of Herbert in which Ingham sat, as if it were her own garden. She had a sure touch. She made you feel as though you'd been welcomed into the town personally. The Italian influence, I thought. Assuredly not the British.

When she saw that I'd written 'London' in her visitors' book she said, 'I've got a penfriend there.' I could see that for a moment she wondered about asking me if I knew her. Or him. 'And I've got one in Bournemouth, one in Rochester, and two in Torquay.'

'You've got a lot of penfriends,' I said.

She was one of those people who, out of nervousness, have to use the language of contradiction even when they're agreeing with you. 'No,' she said. 'I've got ten. And two in America.'

'That's an awful lot of people to write to.'

'No, yes. I write to them all once a month. I'd like to write more often, but the postage is too expensive.'

I did a quick calculation. If she wrote to them all air mail once a week it would cost her $700, about $350, a year. The other calculation I did was that that added up to more letters than I'd written in the whole of my life.

As I left I saw her studying my address in her visitors' book. I wondered if that was where she found her penfriends. And if there might be a letter full of friendly contradictions waiting for me when I got home.

We decided against the second longest sheer drop in Australia – had it been the first longest we might have thought differently – and headed in the direction she'd shown me for the Italian cemetery.

No one who finds himself in Ingham should ever miss it. You drive 5 ks out of town on a winding route, through the sugar cane, past unmistakably Italianate villas of the modern style, the sun all the while streaming through the car windows, until you come to a sudden bend in the road and there it is – what you might have taken, had you been unprepared, for a miniature mediaeval village or a field of dolls' houses. Rows and rows of tiled shower rooms, little greenhouses with sliding doors, mini-chapels, containing altars and memorabilia, to the beloved Italian dead. In some cases even to the not-yet or the not-entirely dead.

I chose one to examine in some detail, because I was struck by its gothic windows, on which were transfers, meant to look like glass engravings, depicting a holy scene, and because I was impressed by the tiling. Highly polished black tiles preserved the mausoleum's exterior; inside, a mosaic of blue and black and puce with raised surfaces covered not just the floor but also ran up the walls of the altar. A colour photograph of the deceased above the altar was flanked by an alabaster Our Lord and an alabaster Our Lady. Our Lord was pointing to his bleeding heart. On the walls were preserved flowers mounted in glass or perspex domes. Artificial grasses and ferns were strewn everywhere. A fresh bouquet was placed at the feet of a plaster cast miniature of the Pietà – the one you can buy outside St Peter's. A cross made of ceramic roses rested by the other end of the statue. The memorial stone read:

QUI GIACE
LA MORTALE SPOGLIE DI
GIOVANNI SPINA
NATO A GIARRE IL 23.11.1898
MORTO 8.12.1970
MARITO AFFETUOSO E PADRE ESSEMPLARE

It's worth dying if you're an Italian. Take Antonio Patane. Who could not envy him what he left behind in the bosom of his grieving family? – *Inconsolabile dolore*.

I envied him his resting place, too. It was a lovely setting for a cemetery, seemingly doubly protected – first, and at a discreet distance, by the warm surrounding hills, then, in a much closer embrace, by the cane field. As high as the manusoleums them-selves, the bamboo stopped, or simply paused, at the very fringes of the estate, sweet to its very doors. For the dead it was no more than a clearing, a benign glade made architecturally fantastical, amidst the sugar.

As we drove back out of Ingham we noticed a poster in a shop window advertising Mario's Disco, and a performance of *Robin the Hood* at the Arts Theatre, directed by Monica Vitale. Then on to Cardwell, looking out over the granite peaks of Hinchinbrook Island, where we paused to walk on the beach – the mud rather – of Hinchinbrook Channel, and to stare at the bulging-eyed mud hoppers, gulping the element they lived in. On the foreshore a small yellow letterbox affair was affixed to a post, containing 'Vinegar for Sea Stings', courtesy of Tully Rotary Club. It was becoming dangerous out there.

At Tully itself we cut in to Mission Beach, along a tortuous road of tropical forests, where we saw a sign which said, CAUTION – CASSOWARIES FOR 10 KS. I was excited. I had never seen a cassowary before, not even in captivity. Now here we were in North-East Queensland, their natural and only habitat, and at any moment, if we were lucky, one was going to come charging out of the jungle with its head lowered – they had casques on their heads, like crash helmets, for this very purpose – meaning to terrify us with its loud booming grunt. It was Ros who possessed this information on them, though she had never encountered one in the wild either. In fact not many people had. They were private birds and not very easy to approach. If they didn't scare you off with their crash helmets and their gruntings and their size – they had no trouble grow-ing to heights of over five feet – they were capable of ripping you apart with their big toenail. For all that they were obvi-ously just emus gone troppo and turned technicolour, they were lethal, not floozies like their southern relations. But it wasn't for its aggressiveness that I wished to see one. What I liked was what Ros told me about their eating habits. I liked the simplicity. What they wanted to eat they just tossed in the air and swallowed down in one gulp. It didn't matter how large or unpeeled the fruit was – up it went and a fraction of a second later it hit the stomach with a thud. We had a back seat full of pineapples and coconuts and paw paws that we'd bought at a kiosk outside Ingham. It would have been fun to throw a few out of the window at a charging cassowary and see what happened. But no cassowary showed. We had to settle for seeing one a few days later at Hartley's Creek Zoo, where we'd actually gone to watch a live crocodile attack – 'See the keepers in with the 11 and 14 foot crocs. AUSTRALIA'S ONLY CROCODILE ATTACK SHOW' – and got the cassowary only as a supporting act.

As a consolation we ate our own lunch, more convention-ally, on Mission Beach, with our feet in the warm blue water, palms shading us from the sun, Dunk Island beguiling through a heat haze across Brammo Bay.

Then north to Clump Point and Bingil Bay, rejoining the highway at El Arish (El Arish?) from where it was a half-hour's drive to Innisfail. It was at Innisfail, on the junction of the

North and the South Johnstone Rivers, that Ros bought for $7 a kilo – call that a bit more than a pound a pound – the prawns of her life; the prawns for which all her existence so far had been merely a preparation; the plumpest, sweetest, tenderest, pinkest prawns that anyone can have ever driven into Cairns at sunset devouring, without bothering even to free them from their shells.

EIGHTEEN

GONE TROPPO

'Well, how do you like it?' the young man at the petrol pump asked me.

'It' was obviously Cairns. I tried to explain that I had only just this minute driven in, but he didn't have an ear for that sort of prevarication.

'I've been everywhere,' he went on. 'Sydney, Melbourne, Brisbane, Townsville – I've seen the lot. And you can keep 'em. As far as I'm concerned this has got it all.'

'Well, it certainly *looks* good,' I said, as though there might be some other way of measuring what a town's got.

'No worries,' he said. And when I asked him for a receipt he said it again. Only this time very slowly – 'No – worries – at – all –' – because in Cairns there – really – weren't – any –.

In fact you didn't have to be in Cairns for much more than a minute to see that Townsville was kidding itself if it thought it could seriously compete. It wasn't that Cairns was at all beautiful. Or homogenous. If anything it seemed to have less idea how it should develop – whether upwards or outwards, whether for the rich or the not-so-rich, whether for celebrities who were here to catch marlin or for beach-bums who simply wanted to island hop – than Townsville did. But it was spectacularly set and you could not mistake what you were here for. With the rainforests behind you, half-obscured by the mist that appeared to be of their own breathing, you looked outwards to the harbour and the Coral Sea and the Reef itself beyond. And you watched the Reef traffic – the planes, the speed boats, the passenger ferries, the cruisers entertaining party-loads of weekend scuba divers – in perpetual motion, day and night.

The hotel we chose to stay at, although like most of the new buildings in Cairns exceedingly ugly, offered the twin advantages of a large balcony overlooking the bay, and proximity to the two blocks of esplanade where all the action seemed to be. There was a bustling youth hostel here, and several cheap motels and boarding houses, and a couple of fish restaurants whose tables spilled out onto the pavement and very nearly onto the roads. It wasn't Marseilles or Nice exactly, but there was an excitement in the air, a sort of marine raffishness, a suggestion of slipped moorings, albeit that the majority of people out on the streets were young – American and European college kids having an 'amazing' adventure, Australian students taking a year off uni in order to hitch-hike to the sun, professional unattached bums who wanted to laze around close to islands.

I would have liked to spend a few hours here, eating on the pavement, but Ros reckoned we still had plenty of fruit to get through; so we sat out on our balcony instead, chewing on coconut and listening for what was stirring in the waters of Trinity Bay, while behind us on our hotel television the State Premier, Joh Bjelke-Petersen, tried to bully his way through an explanation of what was wrong with the figures that showed Queensland to have the highest number of bankruptcies, the highest unemployment, and the highest budget deficit of any state in Australia.

What was wrong with them, of course, was that they spoiled everybody's fun.

I was out again on the balcony early next morning, watching the sun rising from behind the Nisbet Ranges, where Aborigines on the Yarrabah reserve would have seen it first. Fishing boats were returning, looking laden. Large white shapes, whose outlines I could not recognize in the half-light but which eventually turned into pelicans, cruised up and down, observing the fish leaping out of the water. There was no sweat. No worries. The seas teemed with breakfast. What the pelicans especially fancied, they took.

Joggers were soon out on the esplanade. All around the sea fronts of Australia someone was running. From a satellite the country must have looked as though its entire perimeter was a moving tracksuit. On the horizon an island – perhaps Green Island – appeared and then immediately shimmered. Straight into business. The hawks too were not sure what they thought about this no worries stuff. They twitched in disbelief at the pelicans' insouciance. Ever since leaving Townsville we'd noticed that it was hawks that hovered over the beaches, not seagulls. They were a reminder that this was man's country. Lee Marvin came here for the marlin and threw back anything under 1,000 pounds. This was no place for seagulls.

After our breakfast – which differed in no essentials from the previous night's dinner – we took a Hayles Cruise to Green Island and Michaelmas Cay. I'd done a small amount of homework and found out that from the point of view of style, of reef-cred, it was just about all right to visit Green Island. You have to be very careful when claiming that you've visited the Great Barrier Reef because not all the islands are made of coral – and you look pretty foolish saying that you've been on one that is when in fact you've been on one that isn't. In the main those that are closest to the shore, with the most developed tourist facilities, aren't; while those further out, often inaccessible and sometimes invisible to the naked eye, are. Green Island, although a bit too close to be exclusive, was acceptable on the basis of its being a true cay – that's to say an aggregate of coral and sand. I'm speaking purely from the angle of snobbery now; from the point of view of conservation, and with regard to environmental sensitivity, Green Island wasn't reckoned to be very acceptable at all. But I didn't know that at the time. As I didn't know several other things about the island which had I known might have saved us no small amount of grief in the days to come.

We sat on the upper deck of the boat where, like every other passenger on that section, we had no option but to watch an American woman, whose name badge said MARIE, rub oil into herself. She must have been about fifty, dating from the last time that whiteness was considered attractive in a woman, and was going in still for the sort of half-awakened pubescence that made Debbie Reynolds famous. She was dressed in the way I remembered it upsetting me to see Debbie Reynolds dressed, in cute off-white hayseed shorts and a pink spotted halter top and a straw hat with blue ribbons. She had been pretty once – was pretty still, feature for feature – and had almost certainly been the second-string moll of a minor mafi-oso. Now, with no hoodlum to watch her oiling, she oiled, in a Brooklyn accent – 'I need protecshun, honey' – for us.

I tried to look at something else. Behind me Cairns was receding from view. It had no elegance at all from the water. It was low and squat and indeterminate, and could have been mistaken for an oil refinery or a series of customs buildings. Green Island, though, which I had to look past Marie to see, was beginning to take the shape expected of a tropical paradise – a flat green saucer with a sandy rim, a sectional view of a spinach pizza.

'Would you do my back?' She wasn't talking specifically to

me. If we have to deal in specifics she was talking to another American woman in her party. But in actuality she was addressing all of us. The American friend was just a proxy. It was in order that the entire upper deck might get to work on her that she handed over the lotion, turned around, arched her back, and held up her hair with both hands. Thus, with nothing to impede us, we were able to oil her very slowly, starting at the neck and working our way down over each shoulder blade, taking care not to miss a millimetre of damageable skin, lingering over every spinal stud, even slipping the tips of our fingers just inside the strap of her halter, so that should it perchance slide in the sun, Marie would still stay for ever white.

'Hey,' she said, just as we were wondering about the band of her shorts, 'this suntan lotion smells like pina colada. Anybody wanna drink?'

On the red plastic seats to my left a pale, fashionably dressed English couple in the black and black Joseph uniform of aggressive introspection, held on to each other tightly. By carefully keeping his eyes lowered the boy had not gagged on Marie's flesh, but now the girl was beginning to look sickly. I had to fight back a rush of loathing myself, for the nerveless distaste of the young.

We disembarked at the jetty, pausing only fractionally at the underwater observatory where they piped Tchaikowsky's *Romeo and Juliet* overture through loudspeakers to get you in the mood for paying to watch fish. Yet another American girl steered her boyfriend past the entrance. 'Aw no, not there,' she said. 'That's pure kitschville.'

It almost made me want to go in.

We spent a couple of hours on the island, Ros snorkelling, I lying on the beach. And then we were back on the boat again, speeding across the water to Michaelmas Cay, where we were transferred to what they called a submarine, though it was only we who were submerged, through the glass sides and bottom of which we were able to behold the wonders of the Reef. And wonders, to my absolute astonishment – I who had the greatest scorn for underwater gawping – they turned out to be. Fish every bit as multicoloured as the postcards suggested swam by us. Fish as bright and as neurotically gaudy as pop singers. Shirley Bassey fish. Boy George fish. Clown fish. Harlequin tusk fish. Fish that were striped and fringed, bejewelled and earringed, bearded and even caped. Batfish that were all cloak and no face, just a pout like Charles Laughton's. Banded humbugs. Mottled reef eels. Fish that danced. Fish that told jokes. Horrid stove fish. Even, in the lugubrious turquoise giant wrasse, fish that I would have sworn were Jewish.

And worse, far worse for my self-respect as a passingly sceptical citizen of the upper world, I actually marvelled over coral too. Precisely as if I'd just that very moment come screeching into the universe, I gasped at its variety, its prodigious size, its extraordinary forms and colours. We nudged our way through coral canyons, past infinite ravines and potholes gaping to eternity. We saw cliffs of mushrooms – fungia acitiniformis – staghorns, flower arrangements, bath sponges, and giant brains, like the spilled cranial innards of one whole year's intake of Oxford and Cambridge put together. I found myself making noises like David Attenborough. 'It's a miracle of natural engineering and architecture,' I said. 'A testimony to nature's most inventive builder and creator both – the tiny coral polyp.' We sat, Ros and I, with our noses to the glass of the ersatz submarine, as fish-fixated, as reef-drunk, as Hans and Lottie Haas.

The idea even assailed me that I would like to be a scuba diver. I was a long way from home. Nobody need ever find out. I made enquiries as to the cost and duration of the course and was put off only when I learnt that you were expected to be able to swim first.

We were returned from the sub to the boat for a buffet lunch, prior to being dropped on Michaelmas Cay itself for the afternoon. We were a smaller and more intimate party now than the one that had left Cairns earlier in the day; some of those had stayed on Green Island or been whisked off to other reefs; we were now down to about thirty, most of us bent on some serious snorkelling.

I thought that for lunch people were in the main dressed too scantily. A beautiful but intensely solemn German girl glided between the tables of prawns and beetroot in nothing but three small triangles and a slave anklet in matching colours. Although she was only carrying a small plastic bag she was to produce five changes of triangle, together with appropriate slave anklets, before the day was out. An unfortunate American girl, with thick-lensed spectacles and protruding teeth, wore something that looked like a cut-down baby's romper suit, which transgressed the bounds of what I think the women's magazines mean by the bikini line. And the two male diving instructors who were superintending us had stripped down to tiny green pouches. Altogether, between the excrescences and the triangulations and the stubble, it was hard for either of us to know where to look. I was relieved when we were finally let onto the island so that I could stretch out face down on the beach, leave Ros to play with the fish, and go to sleep.

It turned out to be an extremely noisy island. Michaelmas Cay was a protected bird sanctuary. Not even Joh Bjelke-Petersen would have found it easy to get permission to build a five-star resort on this speck of real estate. You had to leave those birds alone. But nobody had contrived a way of protecting them from one another. They fought and screamed and exhibited all the other symptoms of paranoid anxiety that you expect of nature when it's left to itself. Except of course that it wasn't entirely left to itself, because we were there. Not that I was anything to fear. I scarcely moved. Every now and then I looked up to make sure that I could still see Ros's snorkel, then I dropped back down again. It was bliss having so much space to myself. Ever since Townsville Rosalin and I had been getting fractious and clumsy, walking into each other, talking at the same time, answering, 'Just look at that', with, 'Yes, but look at *this*.' A few hours doing nothing on my own on a coral island, not looking at anything, was just what I needed, let the monotonous seabirds – terns or whatever – shriek all they like.

On the boat back to Cairns Ros was all excitement about the fish she'd swum with. She'd made friends with eels and a sting ray. She'd rubbed noses with baby sharks. She'd even cheered up a Depressed Gorgonian Crab. One of our diving instructors, Paul, joined in our conversation. I gathered that he was something else Ros had played with in the water. But he wanted to caution her against too relaxed an attitude to the deep. 'The sea is no respecter of persons,' he warned. (Now there were two of us sounding like David Attenborough.) 'The sea is unforgiving.'

He was handsome, in an innocent, soldierly sort of way, with golden hair and a trim moustache; but so similar to all the other diving instructors we'd come across today that I wondered whether, like the fungia acitiniformis and the staghorn coral, he wasn't yet one more miracle of polyp engineering. He claimed more conventional origins himself. New South Wales he told us he came from, and he had been in Cairns only six months. 'Though I don't expect ever to leave. Where else is there?'

None the less he still continued to harp on his theme of the dangerousness of the Reef. 'Your worst enemy can be yourself,' he said. 'Panic kills more people than sharks do. You must never panic – or at least, if you do, you must recognize it for panic. Say "OK, this is panic. I'll give it five seconds." Then you say, "Right, Paul, that's it. Panic over."'

'Right, Paul, that's it. Panic over,' I repeated, to show that I had got the hang of it.

'That's it. Except that you wouldn't say Paul, you'd say—'

'Howard,' I said.

'G'day, Howard. Paul.' He gave me his hand. It didn't feel like a polyp.

'And this is Ros.' I said.

'G'day, Ros. Paul.'

We stood on the upper deck, with the breeze ruffling our hair. Behind us the islands of the Reef were beginning to lose their distinctness in the pale light of early evening. Dolphins leapt from the water. Reflections of banded snake eels and azure demoiselles still played in Ros's eyes. I was red from the sun and sleepy. A sudden gust blew spray on us and winnowed Paul's mustard-coloured moustache. When he asked us why we didn't stay in Cairns and scuba dive our lives away, as he was doing, I was truly stuck for a rational reply.

The following morning Ros discovered that she had a coral wound on her ankle. Coral wounds can become very quickly infected. The day before, on the way back from Michaelmas Cay, everyone had lined up to have theirs treated; the German girl required iodine dabs over very nearly the entire surface of her body. But Ros had not noticed hers then. We sat out at a street café and, while I read more details about the bizarre dog-eater, she bathed her ankle in Betadine. I could see that she was proud of her injury; that she was feeling good being an Australian again. 'If this keeps up I'll have scabs on my ears soon, with a bit of luck,' she hoped. I noticed that her wound excited the envy of passers-by also. You were no one in Cairns if you couldn't show that you'd been attacked by a polyp.

I helped her, hobbling like a starlet, to the car. Then we drove out of Cairns northwards along the Cook Highway in the direction of Cooktown. We weren't leaving Cairns for ever, just for a day or two. Nor did I intend to try for Cooktown itself. There were problems with car ferries and roads, and I was running out of patience for any kind of travel that wasn't utterly painless. Daintree, where the highway strictly speaking ran out, would do fine. Any adventurous little folderols we'd fight over on the spot.

It was a wonderful drive: tropical forests, running between the coast and the tablelands, steaming high up to our left; on our right, miles of deserted beaches, and beyond them the reefs. We stopped for lunch at Mossman, the most northerly of the sugar cane towns. Since this too, though not to quite the same degree as Ingham, was an Italian town – the Di Bartolos and the Contarions (and perhaps I just imagined the Figaros) were big here – I opted for a counter lunch of calamari and chips. Good, but not as good as what Ros found in a shop specializing in 'Rare and Exotic Tropical Fruits': grandillas and babacos and rambatans and black sapote and carambola – otherwise known as 'four corners', a fruit that resembled a starfish – and sour sops and, best of all, custard apples. I fell for custard apples in a big way. They were the only fruit I'd ever eaten that tasted like an artificial dessert. They instilled in me a whole new regard for growing things. Could it be that somewhere out there was natural organic produce that had the taste of sherry trifle or crème caramel? The question was only marginally fantastic. Before we left Queensland we would eat a fruit that had been specially cultivated to taste like pink champagne.

The Aborigines I saw in Mossman were not the confident exotic Islanders I'd admired in Townsville. Nor did they seem to occupy the town in the manner of their brothers in the Northern Territory or the north of Western Australia. There wasn't that mute sit-down, as if by right, I'd grown accustomed to. Things were jumpier here. They clung to the outskirts of the town and generally kept their distance. It was also my impression, as indeed it was Ros's, that a number of them looked distinctly Italianate.

Why wouldn't they. We'd come across an Adolf Inkamala in Hermannsburg; why not a Romeo Rubuntja in Mossman?

Half an hour later we were in Daintree – the end of the line

– a small slumbrous settlement with an almost sinisterly enticing end of the line atmosphere. Probably no more than about sixty people lived in and around Daintree but they had only recently been at the centre of two intensely bitter and highly publicized feuds. The first related to the creation of what the local Shire Council chose to refer to in its publications as 'That Road', thereby giving it a harmless, tabloid-type storm in a teacup notoriety. Whereas what 'That Road' in fact entailed was 32 kilometres of fiercely contested construction through an area of National Park, already itself unstable and having serious ecological bearing on the World Heritage Great Barrier Reef Marine Park. Its ostensible purpose was to link Cape Tribulation to Bloomfield, thereby completing the coastal route between Cooktown and Cairns; though it didn't escape the notice of conservationists (a) that other adequate roads already existed, and (b) that the main advantage of this one would be the provision of access to valuable chunks of real estate. They sat down in front of bulldozers in large numbers, and in large numbers were arrested. 'The actions of protestors, although determined,' the Shire Council pamphlet in my possession crowed, 'proved to be of little more than nuisance value, and failed to delay the project.' 'That Road' went through, large tracts of rare coastal rainforest came down, and the community was left divided.

In the meantime Daintree had become a sort of sanctuary and reliquary that pilgrims such as Carlos from the Peace Train had to visit – 'I just can't wait to get up there and, you know, just suss its vibes,' he'd told me – a pagan holy place, a shrine for wilderness freaks and tree-worshippers. Amongst whom, now that I had done obeisance through the windows of a submarine to the Tritons, I was prepared to number myself.

The second cause of even still more recent ill feeling in Daintree was the eighteen-foot crocodile in whose belly only the fingernails of his female victim had been found. We'd read about the case in the newspapers while we were still in England, but we came to hear some of its more frightful details from one of the actors in the ensuing drama, an urbane middle-aged European with a polished forehead and a gold chain around his neck, who ran the Daintree souvenir shop and had spoken out against the wanton destruction of crocodiles which had followed the accident. Why blame them? he had asked. The crocs were just being crocs, doing what any croc would do. Anyone fooling about in that river, known to be infested with crocodiles, was asking for trouble. 'I'd been out in it after a party myself, only a few days before,' he told us. 'A few of us had gone for a swim. I was the last. It's a known fact that a crocodile will only ever take the last person in a group. I suddenly became frightened. I had bad feelings. I knew I had to get out of that water fast. Drunk as I was I knew I shouldn't have been in there. If anything had got me it would have been entirely my own fault.'

Beryl Wruck hadn't been swimming. She'd simply been larking about on the jetty after a barbecue. She had a drink in her hand. And a few of her friends were by her. It was low tide and maybe her feet were in an inch or so of river on the bottom steps of the jetty. Then there was a sudden violent agitation of water, though not a sound from the woman, and that was the last anyone saw of her until her fingernails showed up three weeks later.

The shooting began early the very next morning, men arriving from miles around with guns and rifles. Ready to shoot up anything in the river that moved. They called themselves the 'Daintree vigilantes'. By the time the patrols had finished – and the night-time ones had been especially exciting, full of wild talk and booze – upwards of twenty crocodiles had been accounted for.

The man at the souvenir shop had not been the only one to raise his voice against the slaughter. 'It divided the town down the middle,' he said. The old hands against the new. I knew the scenario. I knew how the sides would have fallen out in North

Cornwall. 'There was even talk one night,' he said, 'of them lynching me. But that was just drink.'

The drinking would have been going on at the general store that doubled as the bar. It was the owner of the store, David Martin, who had been the boyfriend of Beryl Wruck, and the main instigator of the violence. 'We still don't speak. But it doesn't bother me. We never really mixed with them.'

David Martin himself became something of a national celebrity for a while. A sort of anti-Crocodile Dundee. He appeared on television explaining how he simply liked killing crocodiles. He boasted of his exploits during the building of 'That Road', when he attached himself to the police force, free of charge, and spent a week plucking Greenies out of the trees they wanted to save. Returning to the croc killings, he explained to a newspaper that 'People were screaming for someone to show honesty and guts. We are just little old country boys doing the right thing.'

The rhythm reminded me of something. It was the poem that Rod Drummond had showed me in Derby:

> We don't pay no taxes, we don't make de goods
> Just real little Abos, way back in de woods.

To make the brew even stronger there were now drug trafficking problems in Daintree also. The body found on the Upper Daintree Road with shotgun wounds in its chest and heroin in its pockets was definitely not the victim of a crocodile.

'Well, this seems a nice sort of place,' I said to Ros. 'Why don't we stay the night?'

As if she could never sup on too many horrors, the woman who ran the caravan park greeted us with a wide-eyed, panting expectation. While she showed us around a couple of on-site vans she frisked us, visually, for guns or microphones. I thought she looked quite disappointed when she found only a notebook in my top pocket.

I called on her, in her office, a little later to see if she had a corkscrew, but she was busy with other guests so her husband dealt with me. Surprised by the business they were doing, off season, I asked if the publicity had increased tourism. 'First there was the rain forest affair,' he said, 'then the croc topped it off.'

Our eyes met briefly over the ghoulishness of human nature. 'But it'd be a pity if the place got spoiled,' he said.

I decided not to press on with this. I felt that my curiosity as to the degree of other people's morbidity was a form of morbidity in itself. I asked him for a corkscrew and when he said he didn't have one I joked that he didn't look teetotal. 'I'm not,' he said. 'I'm a confirmed alcoholic. The only way I can handle the stuff is to stay away from it altogether.'

More wildness. More teetering on the brink. I stumbled back to the caravan thinking what a spectacularly steamy spot Daintree was, and how you could actually smell in the trees the knowledge that there was only one way in and one way out.

The river – That River – was just visible from our back window. In the early evening we walked down to it through the camping ground, past a man in a pure white Balinese shirt chanting a simplified mantra. We stood on the jetty, where there was a sign warning us to beware the very things we'd come to see. And where a couple of steel passenger boats, finished with business for the day, were moored. We strolled along the bank, warily, watching for sudden movements in the water, mistaking bits of floating twig or debris for snouts.

The river wound through country which reminded me, in this season and at this time of evening, of Devon. High, lush and confidently various. But it was the greeny-grey of the river itself, its still menace, that told you you were a long way from

Chulmleigh and Totnes. That and the mosquitoes and the sea eagles and the thundering of lizards' feet in the undergrowth. We stayed down there longer than we should, and strayed too close to the water, half mesmerized by the danger. Then we climbed back up the grassy bank to the caravan park.

Outside the office a couple of soft-voiced desperadoes on motorbikes were conferring about camp prices. One of them was Irish and spoke with a chilling melodious lilt. I remembered the play *Night Must Fall*, and the use it made of the song 'Danny Boy', associating murder with mellifluence. The Irish boy thought $2.50 was quite a bit to pay for a strip of grass to unfurl his sleeping roll on. 'Do you get a shower and toilet block for that?' he wanted to know. The woman with the wild expectant stare X-rayed his saddle bags. And seemed to like what she saw. Instead of telling them to go somewhere else, a million miles from here, she was intent on making them feel at home. 'Of course you do,' she said. 'How far into the bush do you think you've come?'

She smiled at me, as I was passing. I smiled back, quickly and faintly. I didn't want the inadequates on the bikes to think I was smiling at them.

We stood outside our caravan and watched the sky go pink over the Dagmar Ranges. Palm leaves swayed and creaked against parked vehicles. The undergrowth began to stir. We waited until the last reflection of light had gone from the evil river, then we went inside.

Just before bedtime, from a house that couldn't have been very far away, we heard the sounds of an electric organ. It gave us 'Beautiful Day' three times, a few tunes I didn't recognize, and finished up with 'You Are My Sunshine'. After that the sounds of the tropical rainforests took over. Piercing screams of living things in anguish in the trees. I'd heard that crocodiles made barking noises, and I lay awake a long time listening, wondering if there was any reason to suppose that one wouldn't come out of the water and head in the direction of our on-site van. There was only a flimsy catch on our door. Not one that would keep out the Irish motorcyclist either. I went to sleep at last entrusting my fate to chance, unable to tolerate any longer the sounds of Nature's nightly tearing of itself apart.

In the morning we took a safari cruise down the Daintree River. Us and about twenty other people: a motley collection including three smart-talking kids from Sydney Uni; a middle-aged couple from Melbourne (he silent, she vibrant) and their fat, comatose daughter; a handsome and sophisticated American/Japanese pair, neither carrying a camera; and a discordantly blue-collar family from Port Kembla, comprising a fleshly pouting wife, a fleshly pouting baby, and a tattooed husband in a blue singlet who turned out to know more about birds, plants and crocodiles than any of us except David, our guide and captain.

Carefully controlled and bearded, a judicious weigher of every statement and emotion, a man who at all times gave the impression of someone who had come up here to get away from people but still hadn't got far away enough, David had clearly not been on the side of those who pulled Greenies out of trees and pumped bullets into crocodiles. That the two issues were intimately related he didn't at all doubt; according to him, those who had lined up on one side for the first lined up identically for the second. To chop or not to chop, to shoot or not to shoot – they came down to more or less the same thing. He was full of passions about all that had catapulted sleepy little Daintree into public prominence, but he was weary of it too. Every day he had to answer questions such as ours, and every day he had to look away when he passed the other faction in the street – except that Daintree didn't have a street.

The botany was what really interested him. He would steer the tin boat towards the bank having discerned a single pale blue flower or purple berry that hadn't been there the day before. To my eyes it wasn't there today either. I couldn't keep up with him. I simply couldn't *see* what he saw. And, when I could, I couldn't like it. It was good to be back in pandanus country again, for all that the pandanus here was of the climbing variety, like everything else in the fiercely competitive world of the rainforest, a clamberer and leap-frogger. And I formed a special attachment to the egrets with their question mark heads and necks – a perfect shape for all Australians, I thought; one that would sort perfectly with their inflexions. But the rest was all brutality; one long tale of parasitism and strangulation. 'That's Wait-a-while, otherwise known as Lawyer Cane, because once you become entangled in its hooks . . . And that over there is a strangler fig . . .' Throttling. Suffocation. Death by mangrove. It was pure Darwinism out there. It was like being back in England.

And at last, to cap it all – to top it off, as the man at the caravan park put it – we found our crocodile. A twelve- or fourteen-foot brute, that had done well to escape the slaughter, sunbathing on a muddy bank with its jaws open. What is the fascination with creatures that can saw you in half in seconds? We steered as close as we could and stared and stared. And then a little while later we found a baby one – 'Ah!' everybody said – and we stared again.

He grew lyrical, David, on our return to the jetty, describing the sights and sounds he loved most on this murderous river. 'My favourite is the Orange Footed Jungle Fowl, otherwise known as the large-footed mound builder,' he said. 'It has a lovely melancholy call.' His eyes went misty, his voice actually trailed off in a melancholy way itself, just recalling it. 'Very much the sound of the Daintree rainforest, I always think.'

I envied him. He is a lucky man who can hear a sweet plangency in the furious life and death struggle of a tropical rainforest.

Before we left the boat a little mute contest was fought out between that not so rara avis, the bright-as-a-button Sydney

Uni student and the fat comatose girl from Melbourne, the latter having for too long now allowed the boyfriend of the Sydney student to feast his eyes upon the creamy softness of her idle inner thigh. Ostensibly the girl from Sydney was only showing affection to her lover, putting an arm around his shoulder and letting her hair caress his cheek. But I had learnt a few lessons on the Daintree River. I now knew a strangler fig when I saw one.

We had a choice to make immediately as we disembarked. We could try heading further north and take our chance with the wayward opening and closing times of the Cape Tribulation road. We could go in entirely the opposite direction and attempt to make Proserpine for nightfall, in order to be there for the Rodeo the following day. Or we could go to the Peace Expo at Atherton, an event we'd only just got to hear about and which promised two whole days of tree planting, folk dancing, ethnic food eating, book and pamphlet browsing, Tropical North Tai Chi and Eurythmics watching, madrigals, Welsh singing, Caribbean music, fancy dress, to say nothing of workshops, forums and plenary discussion sessions, speakers for which included the actress Diane Cilento who now lived, directed plays and ran a restaurant in these parts. The advantage of the Atherton option was the positioning of Atherton itself – no more than an easy two-and-a-half-hour drive from Daintree across the Tablelands. Though what made us settle for it in the end, I like to think, was stringency not softness. We needed a break from coastal pleasures. Something called A Peace Exposition, taking place somewhere called the Tablelands, sounded like serious endeavour all round. The stuffed Polish cucumbers and the Sri Lankan sambal were mere incidentals. We pointed the car in the direction of Atherton, lowered our voices, furrowed our brows, and felt like mature students off to a university conference.

'This looks good, rich dairy country,' I said to Ros, once we hit the Tablelands proper. 'The cows are happy and fat but the price paid is patently an excessive deforestation.'

'Yes, well, I'm worried about pastoralists,' Ros said.

I couldn't have agreed more. 'Me too,' I said. I was rusty, but I could feel it coming back.

'When you think of their record in Australia,' she went on, 'what have they ever done except push people around, chop down trees, spread Irish-Catholic puritanism, shoot Aborigines, stuff chemicals into everything, and ask for special fiscal consideration?'

What else had they done? I couldn't think of anything.

Later that evening as we were settling into a chalet on a pleasantly wooded camping ground on the fringes of Atherton, I found a frog in the toilet bowl. Or rather it found me. I flushed the cistern and it leapt out of the water, hung in the air for a second bulging its eyes and kicking its legs, then dropped back into the bowl and disappeared. As far as I could tell it had a hiding place under the rim. The very location that Arch and Humpy had told me pythons were inclined to favour. Because I didn't like frogs all that much and wasn't certain that I would be able to sit down with one quite so close to me, I put it to Ros that it was her responsibility to remove it. She was Australian, the frog was Australian – and it seemed to me that they ought to have been able to work something out between them.

She contrived to catch it in the end, after several botched attempts which had the frog, and me, leaping in opposite directions, by flushing it into a polythene sandwich bag, which she then carried not a sufficient distance from the chalet to my mind, where she granted its occupant a freedom it probably went and squandered.

The incident was significant only in that it compromised the judgmatical temper which I'd been preparing for the Peace

Expo. After you've been frightened by a small frog there isn't a lot you can say about anything that is likely to sound just or wise, least of all on the subject of war and peace. So I kept my own counsel and adjourned for the night.

Saturday the 24th of May. Queen Victoria's birthday. I knew this from Dr Ludwig Leichhardt's *Journal of an Overland Expedition in Australia from Moreton Bay to Port Essington*.

> May 24th. It was the Queen's birthday and we celebrated it with what – as our only remaining luxury – we were accustomed to call a fat cake, made of four pounds of flour and some suet, which we had saved for the express purpose, and with a pot of sugared tea.

This picture of the great Prussian scientist and explorer sitting his little bedraggled party down in the bush for a loyal repast of sweet tea and fat cake had made a vivid impression on me, and I had vowed that wherever I happened to be on the 24th of May I would do something similar. It was purely fortuitous that I found myself in a field in the north of Queensland, not that many miles from where Leichhardt would have spread his cloth upon the ground, but where today food from every country that had once been a part of Queen Victoria's Empire was being prepared before my eyes. A man must take what the Gods send him. The Queen would have been 166 today. It was appropriate that I should be able to celebrate not with fat cake but Tongan hangi-hangi, Sri Lankan dahl, Malaysian somosas, Indian chilli chicken, moo-moo from New Guinea, marinaded fish from Papua, and two Australian meat and potato pies floating in a gravy of tomato sauce.

I hadn't at first thought that I was going to find such consolations. The fence around the Atherton Showground was festooned with schoolchildren's paintings when we arrived, all variations on the theme of peace, so that it was hard not to feel that one was turning up for a PTA meeting at the local kindergarten. An exceedingly polite Persian – the Atherton Tablelands baker – welcomed us in, asked us if we had any exhibits to unload, showed us where to park, repeated how pleased he was to see us, and wished us each, separately, and in slightly different language – a personalized message, so to speak – as nice a day as we had any right to expect.

'All this peace is going to be quite a little test for you,' Ros opined.

'I can handle it.' I said. But the truth is I had a few ticklish moments. I made it through the women's tent reasonably well, finding much to admire, in the photographs of women screaming and shouting outside military bases all over the world, in the finely judged camera angles. And it *was* interesting to see a section of real Greenham fence, decorated by Greenham women, and to discover that samples were being sent to interested parties everywhere, like moon rock. I smiled at the people wearing orange togas and expressions of highly offensive beatitude on the yoga stall. I didn't take an axe to the right-to-lifers showing foetal videos. And I managed not to take umbrage when somebody offered me a badge saying. PLANT A TREE – MAKE PEACE WITH THE EARTH – FREE TREES. But the baby-talk tone of the place got me down. MAKE YOUR OWN MESSAGE, AND THEN PIN IT ON THE GROWING TREE, I read. And the serenity, which we were to suppose was a consequence of the proximity of babies and children, affected me adversely also. In fairness, although it goes against the grain, I must say that the extravagantly concessionary tone that was taken with children throughout the Peace Exposition did not result in any juvenile deliquency beyond the usual. Babies cried and they were soothed. Infants asked and they were given. Morally and behaviourally this was undoubtedly exemplary. But aesthetically it was intolerable. Parental serenity – I don't care how many great painters have made it their subject – is hideous to the eye.

We took a break from it, in the late morning, just as Alison Bird was beginning the folk dancing, and drove into town for a beer. We chose, quite deliberately, the most open and noisy pub we could find. It was packed with bearded farmers' boys and wild bushmen, scowling Aborigines, drunken Islanders, men with faces like splintered razor blades and teeth like daggers. Although it wasn't yet midday the passions had all been unloosed: malevolence, mistrust, menace, a commitment of the whole individual and corporate identity to the idea of violence. Violence emotional and, should you have dared to catch an eye, violence actual. Communication back at the Showground had been wilfully amicable; an eye met an eye and if it was humanly possible both eyes had a go at a smile. Here, the window to the soul was nothing other than an entrance-hall to Hell. Be seen to see and you were doomed.

''Course I didn't talk to you, you stupid bastard,' a man covered with hair was saying to a huge, swaying Islander, 'you were too fucking busy – you were up that Tongan.'

'Buy me a drink now then, cunt.'

I still wasn't ready to rush *straight* back to the Expo. There were a few sights that were supposed to be worth looking at in the area, including the famous Curtain Fig Tree just outside Yungaburra, no more than twenty minutes away. We could spend a couple of hours as leisurely tourists and still be back at the Showgrounds in time for the Tableland Twinklers Round Dance Group and the Cairns and District Chinese Association's Lion Dance. We could even miss those at a pinch as long as we made it for *Love Test* – a jazz dance by Ibina Cundell that had been arousing a lot of early interest.

The Curtain Fig Tree (ficus virens) proved to be a spectacularly beautiful example of the sort of parasitism – death by long embrace – we'd witnessed on the Daintree River. It had climbed the trunk and branches of the host tree and then sent its own roots downwards in a slow but certain strangulation. In this way had the means of murder become the veil to shield the murder, the downward trailing roots hanging like a bamboo curtain behind which you could barely see the bent and shadowy form of the original tree.

Yungaburra itself, although less famous than its landmark, was a pretty, melancholy, arty little village built around something very like a village green. It had a lovely timber hotel – the Lake Eacham – better cared for inside than out, an Alternative General Store, a coffee shop that sold pottery and woodcraft, and a gallery that was as garrulous as any I'd ever come across. On an old renovated mangle in the garden a sign said, 'Welcome to the finest art gallery in North Queensland . . . The Artists' Gallery was designed to show art for art's sake, not a quick quid . . .' Inside were further notices telling you what you were expected not to do: eat, drink, smoke (we respect your blah blah . . . but applaud your blah blah), make inappropriate assumptions about art, think you knew what you were looking at when you didn't, and so on. But you had to get to the antique escritoire and read what was on that before you could count yourself a fit judge of what was hanging on the walls.

Art is an experience. We feel the movement of ballet, the intensity of painting, the emotion of music. This is the joy of art.

What many of us never feel is the pain. The agony of perfection. The discipline of trying again and again. The pain of working past one's own limits to reach that level of acclaim. The pain of disapproval, the pain of failure.

The pain of struggling so hard for so long only to find you have to start all over again. This is the pain of art that only the artists themselves can endure. Because their motivations come from within.

The next time you experience Art, applaud the joy – and the pain.

The young man who might very well have been responsible for this – I believe I glimpsed the pain – saw me copying it out. 'Oh,' he said, 'I'm glad *someone's* taking notice of that.'

We arrived back at the Exposition just in time for me to have to run right out again. We'd walked into a peace conga, and if there's one thing I've never been able to join it's a line of people snaking in and out of rooms and kicking their legs up. As a boy I'd learnt to time my exits from family functions with masterly precision; I had unusually conga-prone aunties and had come to recognize all the early signs of imminent flexuousness. But I was given no warning here. I simply walked in, saw them coming, and ran for it.

When I returned, half an hour and two servings of hangi-hangi later, Ibina Cundell was three quarters of the way through her *Love Test*. I was surprised to discover that Ibina Cundell was a woman I'd seen wandering about the hall for most of the day, looking quietly satisfied and wearing a rainbow-coloured woolly Rasta hat. Now her hair was free, in an intricate plait, and the rest of her was liberated also, disciplined only by the Isadora Duncanish conventions of the dance. That quality of overt personality suppression I had earlier taken to be primness, proved now to be a sort of self-sufficient rhapsodicality; she writhed and undulated and suggested emotions which did not seem to be entirely commensurate with peace or at all suitable for children. I was not able to deduce from her finale, which was sudden and supplicatory, whether she had passed the love test or failed it.

After Ibina Cundell a couple of bored Maori girls in national costumes they looked neither proud nor comfortable to be in sang 'Tiny Ball On End Of String', and did what Maoris usually do when they sing that song or are presented to royalty: twirled fluffy balls. Then Tropical Tai Chi demonstrated how you channel your aggressions into inner peace by making violent movements in slow motion, and looked too gratified for the good of their philosophies, I thought, by the applause they received. Before tea – moo-moo which had been baking in the ground all day was my choice – we watched a group of young Aborigines performing their extraordinarily abrupt corroborees, sudden bursts of animation, eruptions of foot stomping and herb or twig waving, lightning animal imitations, finished as soon as started on what, to the uninitiated, appeared to be a spontaneous and unanimous decision that that was enough of that for a game of soldiers. Whatever else there is to say, no one can accuse an Aborigine of being prolix.

We wandered out into the Showgrounds where the food stalls were congregated and did our best by the memory of Queen Victoria. On my recommendation – I knew she liked sweet potatoes, pumpkin, marinaded lamb, cabbage and coconut milk cooked in vine leaves – Ros had the hangi-hangi. I found the moo-moo a touch earthy and swapped to Chinese pasties and Swiss sausage. Then we returned for the evening concert which began with children from the local song and dance academy doing routines which I, in my naivety, considered to be wholly alien to the spirit of the occasion. I thought they were dressed like little harlots, aped wholly unacceptable forms of grown-up femininity, competed with a ferocity way beyond anything required by the normal conventions of upstaging, and sang American or Americanized songs which, while they might not in themselves have been warlike, belonged without question to the bitter sweet of capitalist personal amelioration trauma. If 'Put On A Happy Face' – sung the way they sang it – was not Reaganism put to music I didn't know what it was. They wore Hollywood-musical-style costumes, smiled Hollywood-musical-style smiles, and brought Hollywood-musical-style ruthlessness to the jungle known as self-expression. They were little Shirley Temples of the Tablelands, every one of them. And yet they were cheered to the rafters by an audience who were gathered for the sole purpose of proclaiming peace, and who would, in any other context, have detected menace to the world's stability in the destruction of a single acorn.

'It beats me,' I leaned across to Ros and whispered. 'And I'm not even a peacenik.'

'No, but you're a puritan.'

A puritan? I wasn't a puritan. I didn't have anything against fun. I just disapproved of ideological inconsistency and congas.

The concert never got any better to my mind. A couple of Filipino women in Imelda Marcos frocks stood and swayed on the stage, unable to remember the steps of their national dance and unable to see why it was at all necessary that they should, given how nice they looked. A Welsh folk singer in a lugubrious black bonnet sang three dirges that made one think of mist and dripping valleys. The boys of St Barnabas School rang a few bells. Mabel Dean presented an eurythmic version of *War and Peace* – pure bodily fascism set to *Finlandia*, which nobody seemed to object to. And the Torres Strait Islanders spoilt what would otherwise have been the most exciting event of the night by keeping their white vests on while performing a war dance.

Back at the chalet, once I'd checked for frogs, sleep came as a blessed respite from peace.

But we were back at the hall the following morning for the more serious stuff: the forum and the keynote addresses and the plenary discussions. A stick of a man with an authoritative manner – a retired ex-army infantry officer who had seen the light – introduced the speakers, the first of whom, and the one we most wanted to hear, was Diane Cilento. A Queensland girl originally, she was back home now and well-known in the area for her work for causes such as these. She too, I'd heard, had joined in the protests over 'That Road'.

I hadn't seen a Diane Cilento movie for years, but the voice was immediately familiar. The lovely throatiness seeming to give an almost Scandinavian timbre to a not quite standard English. And the dying fall. She was good-looking still, if a little more fleshly than in her films, and she had that tinge of sadness about her that is always the legacy of a glowing past. 'Peace has to be worked at,' she told us, working the modulations of her voice beautifully, 'it has to be earned. It cannot be found in any kind of mushroom or hallucinogenic pill.' Private peace, it soon became clear her subject was. Peace unto thyself. She spoke of that 'right and necessary third force of love and compassion which neutralizes that aggression which is in all of us'. But the aggression she alluded to was a watered-down version of the great quarrelsome impulse, a small-town nuisance of a passion, such as people exhibit when someone steals their parking place or the bank manager refuses them a loan. I thought we were here to think of ways of minimizing the danger when mighty opposites clashed, and all along we were just looking at how we might lower our blood pressure. 'Let's see if we can begin to trust our adaptation to misfortune and the Godhead in all of us,' she concluded. The whole speech had been an extension of her natural cadence – one long plaintive dying away. A throaty voice, I realized, was bound to determine your view of the world.

Dr John Waiko – the first Papua New Guinean ever to become a full professor – introduced himself in a novel manner. 'If I have to describe myself,' he said, 'I'd say I was the son of a cannibal.' He was the most intelligent person we'd heard all weekend – a passionate, blazing man with a wonderful storyteller's gift and an indomitable resentment. A credit to the cannibal who'd fathered him. Describing life in the village he came from and the commitment of his people to sociability, their need to talk, to have out communally every detail of what they'd dreamt individually the night before, he made the only convincing case I have ever heard for the inviolability of human relations.

Then Roxanne Terrel stood up and undid all his good work. A sort of ne'er-frocked nun, what you might have called a lay martyr, Roxanne Terrel was an American Baha'i with an inner glow of self-satisfaction who seemed to make a living letting people see it. The Baha'is had sponsored the Peace Expo, and as I didn't know anything about them I tried to listen hard for any clues Roxanne Terrel might give me as to what they believed. But it sounded like simple American evangelism most of the time. 'We are learning to get inside ourselves. We have locked up our hearts, we have locked up our feelings . . . Didn't you feel something yesterday? I did. Many people came to me and said, "I feel something. I don't know what it is I feel, but it is *something!*"'

The something I felt was that maybe the Baha'is were in it with the CIA. There was so much talk of the personal here today, so strong an assumption of how much we were all to blame, how necessary it was to look within and find the peace we needed *there* – the strategy for disarmament, in other words, was so exclusively limited to an interior geography – that no representative of any belligerent nation secreted in the audience need have felt that there was pressure here on his government not to go on shooting as before.

'What we need is affirmation,' Roxanne Terrel said, 'we need each other's affirmation. We mustn't be afraid of personal commitment.'

She touched her chest and talked of feelings of 'new dimensions'. As for example when a toothless Chinese girl with an ugly communist haircut tugged at her dress (did she mean vestments?) and showed her some indiscriminate affection – 'It really was like a gift for me – this simplicity.'

It was when she began crying through her squint, scarcely able to go on reading from the book about Vietnam, written by a friend of hers, which she just happened to have about her person, that Ros and I rose with that simultaneity which had eluded the

Filipino women the night before. I'd noticed that in her irritation Ros had been polishing her bag with a tissue. Although it
was made of a naturally dull nappa leather, it now shone like
steel. As we left the hall the sun caught it, so that it sent out shafts
of broken light, like those from a revolving glass ball on the ceiling of a *palais de danse*, or a dagger in the hand of an assassin. The
last words we heard were those of Roxanne Terrel. Tearful and
sticky. Like candy floss that had been wept into. 'It really takes
pain,' she was saying, 'to have compassion.'

So much for stringency. We had only one immediate objective
now, and that was to get back to the coast. Ros wanted to swim
with rainbow-coloured fish again. And I wanted to stretch out
flat, with cotton wool in my ears, beneath a palm tree. Not
wishing to appear to be in retreat, however, we took the
leisurely route, going the long way down before returning the
long way up, through the cheese towns of Malanda and Millaa
Millaa and the decimated rainforests of the Palmerston National
Park. Which gave me the opportunity to rename a few places
after people I liked; most notably the clear waterfall outside
Millaa Millaa which I called the Janson-Smith Falls, after Patrick
Janson-Smith of London; and the marvellous view from the
Palmerston Highway down over the North Johnstone River,
which I called Terry Lane Lookout, after the lucid and magnani-
mous Melbourne radio interviewer of that name. The North
Johnstone itself I changed to the Kitson River, in honour of Jill
Kitson also of Melbourne, Mr Terry Lane's producer. And to
the area in general we both gave the name the Meredith Levy
Ranges, as a gesture of affection to our friend Meredith Levy of
Sydney, and as a reminder to ourselves that there was life after
Roxanne Terrel.

We didn't spend the night at Cairns. We drove in and then
out again on an impulse. Travelling north on the road to
Mossman a few days before, we had called in at an impossibly

paradisal beach resort called Palm Cove. It had golden sands, slender swaying palm trees, a gentle Coral Sea surf, and any number of lethargy-inducing hotel/motels. 'A good place to disappear to for a while when you're feeling frazzled,' we'd observed at the time. So we took another look to see if that was how it still struck us. We walked in the surf, watching the sun go down over the Reef. Behind us we could hear the sound of coconuts dropping onto the sand. 'Beware of falling coconuts,' signs said, at regular intervals between the palms. At dusk the fruit bats came. The moon rose silver through the trees, duplicating itself upon the water. The mermaids shook their hair. I didn't know whether to swear or cry.

I postponed my decision until we'd booked into a hotel with a balcony. We sat out and watched the bats. And listened to the surf rustling like tin foil. And the intermittent thud of coconuts. Then I turned my face to the moon and, howling, swore like an Alice Springs camper.

NINETEEN

THE EXPULSION FROM PARADISE

We rose to a stormy day. An ill-tempered wind whipped across
the beach. The Coral Sea looked like the English Channel.
Behind us the clouds were low on the hills, giving the impression that the rainforests were smoking, choking on their own
exhalations.

But things were jolly enough in the garden of our hotel.
We leaned out over the balcony and greeted the handsome,
Spanish-looking woman who had welcomed us the night
before. She was collecting coconuts that had fallen from her
own palms in the storm, gathering them into a basket which
she carried like a mulatto woman in a male fantasy. She waved
back. Then went on collecting. We were interested in what
she would do next because Ros had earlier tossed down a
coconut that we'd been travelling with since Townsville and
been unable to open. When the woman came to it she
appeared baffled by the knife marks all over it, and the screw-
driver gouges, and the bruises from where I'd tried to jam it
in the door of the car. She turned it around in her hand and
then saw the price sticker. She stared at it for a long time and
then stared at the tree it had lain beneath. Then she

disappeared. Five minutes later there was a knock on our door. She was carrying a plate and several slices of coconut. And smiling. 'Like a little of this for breakfast?' she asked.

We said yes, of course.

The plan was to spend some time – one whole day and a night would do – back on Green Island. Whatever else we could squeeze into our rapidly contracting itinerary, Ros was determined to have one last snorkel. She had made friends with many of those fish. She wanted to see them again. As this was not a suitable island day we made a booking for the next. Then we drove back to Mossman to stock up with custard apples, took a look around Port Douglas, where we found Diane Cilento's restaurant closed but a frolicsome Bavarian coffee shop open and for sale, and turned up at Hartley's Creek Zoo in good time to catch the famous crocodile attack show and otherwise enjoy 'North Queensland's unique wildlife in a lush tropical setting, alongside a real crocodile inhabited creek and Australia's only walk-in dingo enclosure'.

It was here, incidentally, that I received my first and only serious wound of the entire journey. I was bitten, just below the left knee, by a goose.

None of the animals at Hartley's Creek Zoo went in for being welcoming. Crocs of all sizes hid in the mud behind wire fences, trying to look like old logs. Dingoes prowled their walk-in enclosures. The cassowaries – yes, cassowaries at last – looked murderous. And the geese bit. This might have had something to do with the general scruffiness of their environment. 'Lush' and 'tropical' though the zoo was, it was also cramped and dingy. Or it might have been that they resented having drawn the short straw and landed in a performance park rather than in any of the more conventional forms of captivity. Hard as this would have been for the children of the Tablelands Dance Academy to believe, it appeared that there were some animals who didn't find their ultimate fulfilment in vaudeville.

The show proper began at 3 p.m., when someone who wasn't the 'Most Experienced and Entertaining Guide in Australia' as pictured on our brochure, but a self-confessed, though highly Australianized, Pom called Peter said 'G'day', and pretended to go through the roof when we didn't, with sufficient enthusiasm, say 'G'day, Peter' back. It wasn't entirely unlike being on the bus again, except that Peter was not, other than in his punchy extroversion and determination to have our undivided attention, a Dutchy or a Clay. He wasn't spruce and difficult the way they were. He was an outdoor performer, softly bearded, with a highly articulated bush slouch. Culturally too he had far more in common with the eco-religionists who had set up stalls at the Expo, people like the Tablelands branch members of SGAP – the Society for Growing Australian Plants. The bus drivers we'd encountered in the early stages of our journey had all been individual survivalists; social Darwinists; existentially speaking they came fitted out with jutting jaws and roo-bars. Whereas Peter's allegiances were wholly to the Great Chain of Being theory, currently revamped into the idea of the planet as a giant and mutually beneficial allotment. 'We've pushed the croc back all the way from Bundaberg,' he told us, as he climbed into their enclosure. 'Now all he's got is north of Cairns. It's not much and we should leave him with it. For our sake as well as his. If there was no reason for there to be crocs, crocs wouldn't be here. Crocs are here because they're needed. If we didn't have crocs we wouldn't have barramundi. If we didn't have barramundi . . .' And so on, until there was a providence in the fall of a megapode.

As crocodile attack shows go, there was no reason to suppose this wasn't a good one. He prodded a few twelve-footers, lying invisible in twenty inches of stagnant water, into rearing up and showing us their teeth. By means of a large piece of meat on the end of a very long rope he enticed the meanest croc in the place – an eighteen-footer this one – into a simulated death roll – the method whereby, prior to ingestion, the croc subaqueously subdues his victim. And altogether he put on a convincing demonstration – should anyone have needed to be convinced – of why an Australian crocodile was to the human body what an American Baha'i was to the human nervous system.

Nevertheless he confessed himself to be even more frightened of the cassowary. 'Don't be fooled,' he warned us, 'these birds are accomplished killers. Just north of here is a creek called Cassowary Creek. So named because it was there that a cassowary killed three dogs and a boy in a single encounter. It's the toe that does the damage – that thing, there, that looks like a scimitar.'

I wasn't interested in any of that. Lethal animals are ten a penny. Even geese would kill you if they could. What impressed me about the cassowary was its digestive system. No messing about with gastric juices here. As soon as the bird had tossed down his apples and bananas whole and unpeeled he went looking for rocks to swallow: small stones, pebbles, whatever was laying around – he wasn't particular. Then he'd go off on a short galumphing run so that the stones could bounce up and down and pulverize the fruit. Primitive, but according to Peter, highly efficient. Certainly we saw no cassowary looking dyspeptic while we were there. And the rocks and stones? Passed quite effortlessly through the system and lying there on the ground waiting for the next time. The cassowary his own little eco-miraculous Great Chain of Being.

Before we left, Peter delivered us a small oration on the subject of wild pigs. Apparently the damage caused to the Queensland rainforests by unscrupulous developers was as nothing compared to the havoc wreaked by the wild pigs. 'They're not native, you see,' he explained. 'The Poms brought them in. I know – I know – my fault. But I'm not ashamed to say so. Now the politicians in Canberra won't let them be shot. That's the wrong kind of conservation. They're "monitoring the situation", they say, but by the time the situation's been monitored the pigs will have destroyed the forest.'

These were the only animals Peter spoke slightingly of. I had no reason to doubt the truth of his diagnosis but I put his special passion against them down to their being Pommy pigs. It's common and natural for the English to turn against their own when they come to Australia. The country somehow shames you.

But for everything native Australian, no matter how low it crawled on its belly, Peter had nothing but good to say. Even the deadly taipan, which injects enough poison into its victim to kill it 118 times, he asked us to consider from its own point of view. 'There it is, hiding behind a rock, minding its own business, and you come stomping along . . .' He pushed his bush hat back off his forehead and scratched his beard, trying to look like a frightened but otherwise well-meaning taipan.

It was a good try. It just didn't explain the 117 times over the odds the taipan poisons you for disturbing him.

It might have been for this thought that the Natural Order paid me back the next day on Green Island. Or rather – man and wife being one flesh until it comes to pain – paid Ros back.

The weather didn't improve. For the second morning running we walked out on to our balcony at Palm Cove and thought we might as well have been in Folkestone. A palm tree is a miserable-looking thing in the rain; as is a fallen coconut. The beach – no longer golden but dun-coloured – was full of them: wet and shapeless, like deflated footballs, or rejects washed ashore from some head-shrinking colony across the waters.

We drove down the coast to Cairns and returned our hire-car. We had only booked in one night as house guests on Green

Island, but we were keeping our options open. If we felt like spending the rest of our lives there, we would.

It was an unpleasant, choppy boat ride. Almost no one on the upper decks because of the wind and drizzle, and not that many of us below either. People weren't taking any chances on the day. There were later boats they could catch. If it brightened up they would pack their five changes of bikini and head for the wharf. Meanwhile it looked as though we were going to have the Great Barrier Reef very nearly to ourselves.

There seemed to be a perfect circle of blue sky over Green Island as we approached; not so much a gap in the clouds as a sort of superimposition on them, an apparently free-floating disc emanating warmth and light. But either it was a mirage or a Will-o'-the-wisp, because no sooner did we reach the island than it was gone.

We'd been told to introduce ourselves to Mark, the Activity Officer, the minute we disembarked. 'How will I know him?' I'd asked the girls who'd processed me. 'You'll know him,' they promised. And I did. He was tall and dark and very clean – too clean: you could have eaten off him. And he was wearing a T-shirt which said MARK on his chest, and ACTIVITY OFFICER on his back. 'You must be Mark,' I said, 'I'm . . .'

He only needed telling once. Thereafter, wherever I ran into him on the island, he would ask 'How's it going, Howard?' or 'You right, Howard?' or 'Wanna join us on the reef at low tide, Howard?' The only time he didn't stop whatever he was doing to look up at me and use my name was when I saw him in the bar later that night. He was off duty then, I gathered, because he was not wearing his Activity Officer T-shirt. And he stared right through me.

Because our room, it was in fact called a 'Tropical', was not quite ready for us when we arrived – girls of several nationalities running in and out of it with fan-shaped towel and face-cloth arrangements – we decided we would have a preliminary walk around the island, the cold and the soft drizzle notwithstanding. The beaches looked as though they'd had even rougher treatment in the night than Palm Cove. A few trees had come down and there was debris everywhere. We picked our way between it, determined to find marvels even amongst the ruination. We oohed at every shell; we aahed at every twist of coral. Then we both espied, lying palpitating on the sand, a brilliantly coloured fish. Perhaps an euxiphipops xanthometapon – a yellow face angel fish. What it was doing here, still alive, several yards from the water but with no apparent plans for getting back to it, we didn't understand. Ros, however, turned out to know something about resuscitating fish. It was the sort of knowledge that West Australian girls just somehow picked up. She lifted it gently and carried it in both hands back to its own element, passing it again and again through the water, 'to force oxygen into its gills,' she explained. I looked on, astonished. You can live with a person a long time and never have an inkling of what they know. After two or three minutes of this she knelt down on the sand and released the fish into the water. It made a spirited dash for the open sea, then, seeming to lose its nerve or its bearings, it suddenly leapt into the air, performed a triple backward somersault, and landed with a plop at her feet. I would have called it a day at that, but she re-commenced the whole procedure, running it through the water the way a child propels a rubber duck, all the while exhorting it with words of encouragement and affirmation. From the fish's standpoint it must have been like a telephone conversation with the Samaritans so weighted in favour of staying alive was the advice.

And eventually it did the trick. The fish started to gulp and look positive. Its eyes bulged. It even wriggled.

This time Ros took no chances; instead of trusting it to the fringe of grubby surf it had funked already, she threw it high into the air, a great arc-like throw which made sure that sink or swim the sea was where it had to stay. And this time the fish responded. We could even see the channel it made, like a torpedo's, as it sped towards it future.

At the moment of effecting the throw, however, her hand had been cut open by the sharp edge of the fish's fin, and now it bled onto the beach. And also at that very moment, even before the fish had hit the water, she had heard the sharp, infuriated cry of a bird. It was a sea eagle, fanning the air above us, and looking to see what had become of its catch. Now we knew what the fish had been doing where we found it. It was the eagle's. The eagle had dropped it and was coming back for it just as we happened along. Now he would have to start all over again. He looked bitterly put out, only marginally avenged in Ros's bleeding hand. He glided low over us, giving us a glimpse of the lovely reddish brown of his wing tips, and an idea of how nice it would have been to have had him for a friend. I thought of the albatross. *And we had done an hellish thing and it would work us woe.* Or rather, Ros had. She might have saved a life instead of taking one; but she had still interfered in the ways of Nature. She had severed a link in the Great Chain of Being, and there was no saying who might suffer as a consequence of that. Was blood to be just the start of it?

It wasn't a drastic wound. There's a limit to how much damage a half-dead angel fish can inflict. And in normal circumstances Ros would have thought no more about it. But we had been warned countless times about the possibility of a coral-associated cut turning septic, and recommended always to go along with any injury to the Dive Shop, where supplies of iodine were kept.

We left the beach, the eagle still circling above us, and made our way to the shop. I sat out in the garden snack bar and grill while Ros went to get herself dabbed. At a table near to mine a party of workmen, on the island to build more 'Tropicals', were taking a teabreak and ogling the girls. The most voluble

of them wore a T-shirt which carried the words TAFFY'S
HOMES – WE'LL DO YOU . . . A HOME; and since he was
Welsh I decided that he was Taffy. Though to call him simply
Welsh hardly does justice to the sort of Welsh he was. He was
super-Welsh, hyper-Welsh, orotund and oratorically Welsh –
altogether too rich a collection of sounds and sentiments for
this fragile little cay floating in the sensitive waters of the Coral
Sea. 'Eh, eh, eh!' he sang to his men, as a pair of only moder-
ately voluptuous Australian girls came flouncing through the
gardens, braving the cold in their bikinis. 'Eh, boys? Look what
comes here, then. When did you ever see such a couple of
lovely little fruit cocktails as these?' His voice rose and dipped,
his appreciation deeper than any mine shaft. Not since Richard
Burton's funeral, I thought, could so much deliberated vitality,
such lyrical lilting rhapsodical love of life have been assembled.
Only here on Green Island it was assembled in the single person
of Taffy.

Was Nature striking back already then? Was Taffy to be the
price I paid for Ros's throwing back of the fish?

I went to see how she was getting along with the iodine and
found her coming to the end of what had been a violent argument with the man who ran the Dive Shop. He hadn't cared
for her tone. He hadn't liked the way she'd come barging in
demanding medication. 'I'd have told you iodine was painful
and not the favoured treatment anyway,' I arrived just in time
to hear him saying, 'had you not been so *pushy* when you came
in here.'

There was a little telltale quiver still, although it was all over
now, about the bottom of his face. Closet jaw. No man who is
on reasonable terms with his own nature will ever upset himself
calling a woman pushy, even if pushy is what she is. Ditto ball-
breaker. That whole cast of threatening women from damned
whores through to termagants has no more than a shadowy
existence in reality; like bugaboos and hobgoblins they stalk a

mental landscape. Ros the fish-saver had ambled vaguely bleeding into what she thought was a Dive Shop and Dispensary on Paradise Island – to seek a little medication and hire a snorkel – only to discover that she'd blundered inadvertently into the pitted continent of somebody's private terror.

It wasn't until we got outside that I realized Ros was carrying flippers and goggles and the rest of it not merely for herself but also had a set marked GIANT (this referred to foot size) for me. Given that I couldn't swim I wondered how I would benefit from these, but she was too angry from her encounter still to tell me. I gathered that I would lie face down in twenty inches of water – which was enough after all for an eighteen-foot crocodile to be content in – and at least get a look at the wonders of the shallows as a kind of compensation for missing out on the wonders of the deep. We trudged across the island, ruminating; past dripping ferns and dropping palms and signs explaining that this area or that area was set aside for regeneration and would we therefore stay out of them, until we reached the water.

It looked cold and inhospitable. Not the translucent blue of our previous visit but a dirty disconsolate grey. I stepped into my flippers and looked about me, hoping that no one was watching, just as the rain fell. Real rain this time, heavy gobs of it, not so much falling as thrown. From more distant reefs came the rumble of thunder. We trudged back to our 'Tropical', using one of my GIANT flippers each in lieu of umbrellas. We must have looked like bird-men in a Voodoo mystery play.

Once we had dried ourselves with the fans and flowers and conch shells which it took me a while to believe were really our towels, we decided it might be pleasant to sit out under our verandah, where there was a table and chairs, and watch the rain from there. We could read, put our feet up, catch up with our journals, write postcards, and otherwise contrive to squeeze some enjoyment yet out of the island.

This worked fine for about ten minutes, then we heard Taffy and his men returning through the jungle from their tea break. Singing. Like the Seven Dwarfs. Ours was the last completed 'Tropical' on the row. Work was proceeding on the next one, ten yards away. I didn't mind the sawing too much. Or the hammering. Or the noise of the electric drills. It was the cursing I couldn't take. The *Welsh* cursing. Of all the inharmonious sounds in the world there can be none that has so little in the way of saving grace or compensating virtue as a Welshman shouting, 'Ohh, fack!' on a tropical island. Cruel anywhere, but too cruel here.

We stuck it for as long as we could, but the minute the rain stopped we tried the beach again. The same thing happened. No sooner was I rubberized than down it came. And we had to dash for it once more. Given that we were intending to go into water anyway I can't now work out why we were so frightened of the rain. But I suppose we chose to be the masters of our fate; we wanted to get wet our own way.

In this fashion, between Taffy's sonorous swearing and these fruitless flippered forays to the beach, our afternoon in paradise was frittered away. We buried what was left of it in Marineland Melanesia, a crocodile and reptile house on the island, run by a man who wore dark glasses and kept a coloured jungle bird on his shoulder. It was a rich, intoxicating collection of tropical excesses: creatures that grew too big, like sharks and giant turtles and of course crocodiles; and artefacts associated with overheated rituals, from Papua New Guinea and the forests of Borneo.

Ros talked to the man with the bird on his shoulder; although like all people who wear dark glasses indoors he would rather not have talked to anybody. He caught his own crocodiles. Harpooned them. He wanted that to sound more brutal a method than it in fact was. It was just a small dart he used. And unlike the cullers and farmers sent by Canberra, for whom he expressed a consummate scorn, he didn't botch his job. They tried to catch them in nets and almost invariably ended up drowning them. He used his harpoon and brought them in alive. Just talking about it made him bitter. I couldn't see his eyes, but I stood within his field of electricity and felt the charge. He was bottled-up, pent; like the giant turtles which swam back and forth, back and forth, in their too-small pool.

'What'll happen if I try to touch your bird?' Ros asked him.

'He'll bite,' the man said.

Having a bird on your shoulder, I decided, was the aggressive equivalent to taking your mad brother Alfonso to a dinner party; it was another way of carrying your alter ego around with you.

We left him to feed his ravening reptiles, and since our dinner was still an hour or so away, and the weather had cleared a little and the tide was out, we took a long walk over the exposed dying coral, startling eels and small sharks in pools, and causing velvety pulsating clams to shut up tight on our approach. Only the star jelly fish, coloured the richest blue imaginable, were indifferent to us. And of course the coral itself. I'd been much taken by the brain coral I'd seen through the windows of the submarine, but out here the polyps had created simulacra of the whole organic system of man; here was the large and small intestine, the gut, the heart, the soul, the seats of good and evil even – all in bright greens and flaming purples and lurid pinks.

After an amiably but inexpertly served dinner, we joined the other house guests in a stroll down the pier to the Underwater Observatory, where we passed a further hour fish-gazing. Mark gave us five minutes of his time each, sharing our portholes and remembering our names. 'Look, Howard,' he said, when it came to my turn, 'an azure demoiselle.'

These were the last words he ever addressed to me.

Back at the bar a frenzied atmosphere was building up, because New South Wales and Queensland were playing each other in the first of the State of Origin rugby series and the match was being shown live on TV. Along with all the other guests, Ros decided this was not for her; but I wanted one more beer and something for my notebook. I soon saw that it was distinctly a staff-only venue. A place for the exploited to turn up after work and swap gossip and complaints. It reminded me of a bar at a language school. Everyone was over-tired from too many late nights and too much drinking and day-long duty rotas which were not sufficiently distinguished from social life. It was a sealed community, excited by rumour, rent with dissension, entire unto itself.

A Canadian girl with green eyes noted my presence with surprise. 'Most guests don't come here,' she told me.

I asked her why that was. She shrugged. Because most guests are boring farts, she seemed to want to say. Without exactly meaning to except me from that judgement. She looked sorry, actually, to have even bothered talking to me. She was attentive only to what was passing between the other kids who worked here.

I asked her how she liked it. 'Yah,' she said, 'yah, OK Some of the people complain about the conditions—'

'The conditions?'

'Yah, you know – the state of the rooms, the amount of sharing, all that. But I don't mind. I'm only here for a while. Shooting through before university. I think travel gives you experience and teaches you a lot.'

I agreed with her. How to agree with people was what travel had taught me. I looked around the bar. A girl a couple of stools along was crying. A boy who hadn't slept for a month was rubbing his eyes and willing himself to stay awake for more. Mark had arrived, not wearing his T-shirt and therefore not obliged to remember who I was. And Taffy was there too, shining with expectation, ready for the rugby and whatever else life might throw at him.

'Of course this is not a rave island,' the girl with the green eyes was saying to me.

'No,' I said. 'No, I've noticed that.'

'Anyone seen Geoff?' she suddenly called out across the bar.

No one wanted to answer. She rose to go and find him, whoever he was. No one could be bothered to tell her that that probably wasn't a good idea.

I watched five minutes of the rugby, but my position as the solitary guest was becoming too conspicuous. And I felt a bit of a nuisance being there: a small carbuncle on the nose of everyone else's fun. Mark, I noticed, was not merely not acknowledging me – he actually disliked me. And yet only an hour or two before he had put his hand on my shoulder and pointed me out an azure demoiselle. Queer. I made my way back through the slithery ferns to our 'Tropical' where I found Ros sitting up in bed writing messages on the back of Green Island postcards. Within a week friends back in England would receive irrefragable evidence that we'd succumbed to the mindless hedonism to which they'd always supposed us susceptible, and were now blissfully whiling away what was left of our youth in a state of nature on a sun-soaked tropical pleasure isle in the Coral Sea.

In fact we left the island at the same time our postcards did. The continguing vengeful weather had something to do with our snap decision, the refusal of the staff to serve us breakfast, having kept us waiting until the breakfast serving hour was over, had more. On the coral island which we'd had a mind to disappear to, dusky youths and maidens poured you coconut cocktails by night and rubbed musky unguents into your city-fevered brows by day. We hadn't bargained on sulky treatment from kids who couldn't be bothered frying you a piece of bacon, so worn out were they from propping up the bar with

Taffy the night before. 'We might as well be in Birmingham,' Ros said. I agreed with her. We dashed out of the dining room, threw our clothes into our bags, returned our un-flapped flippers to the Dive Shop, and just made it to the jetty for the first boat back to Cairns.

Also travelling with us was the Canadian girl with the green eyes. She was in tears and didn't look as though she'd slept. I took it that she'd found Geoff.

We didn't waste any time in Cairns, though the woman taxi driver who took us from the wharf to the airport wasted some for us. She didn't think we should leave town without seeing at least the outside of the new hospital. 'It's a beauty,' she said, 'really lovely, like an international hotel.'

She had a bad case of the rising interrogatives, so that when I asked about the level of in-house caring – 'Good service?' – she naturally assumed that I was making an assertion. 'That's right,' she said, 'that's what I've heard, too.'

By mid-afternoon we were 2,000 kilometres down the coast. If we were going to be made to feel we were in Birmingham we reckoned we might as well *be* in Birmingham. Both Birminghams. The one in the West Midlands *and* the one in Alabama.

So we'd flown to Brisbane.

To tell the truth, apart from the amount of inner-city freeway (none of it as hideous as what loops around the Bull Ring), and the number of cops on every corner (none of them, while we were there, publicly pistol-whipping blacks), and discounting all the evidence of the brutal imposition of utterly unnecessary shopping precincts – for this was the place above all others in Australia where bulldozers were sent in under cover of darkness, like tanks, to settle the finer points of preservation orders – leaving aside, in other words, the personality of the Premier as graven on the forehead of his capital city, I rather

liked it. It had a queer old-fashioned frisky air. A nutty exuber-
ance which countless times caused me to laugh aloud in the
streets. A country town like Perth, surprised by how rich how
quickly it had grown, it didn't have Perth's anglophile sedate-
ness. It wasn't remotely interested in refinement. It behaved
like a hillbilly that had just come into a whopping inheritance
and didn't mind who knew it. Looking at people going about
their business or drinking cappucinos in the mall, I felt I'd gate-
crashed a party that had been going on since somewhere round
about V.E. Day, when coachloads of cockies had come whoop-
ing into town and been reluctant, ever since, to go back to their
properties.

The men had red faces and round chests and looked tickled
pink to be out. You could see their politics in the broken veins
beneath their skin, like an apoplexy waiting to break out. The
women were a curious mix of bowling ladies with leathery
complexions and sirens of the early talkies – Marlene Dietrich
and Greta Garbo especially. I don't think I've ever seen elderly
women dressed with such bad intent. Crones of eighty-five,
wearing skirts three inches above the knee, shoes with deadly
stiletto heels and open toes, and rakish white and blue bowling
hats, stood in doorways of department stores at 9.30 in the
morning, waiting for something to happen. There were old lips
slashed with lipstick in every café, old legs, no thicker than my
finger, in sheer black stockings riding every escalator. Pickled
into a long preservation by the country climate, they were now
content to go off rapidly in the city. It was like watching delinquency seize a retirement home.

A higher standard of behaviour was expected of the young.
Outside every hotel were dress and appearance restrictions so
complicated that you needed to check yourself out in a mirror
to be certain you conformed. In the far north it had been sufficient to stipulate no thongs and no tank tops, but in Brisbane
the texture of your trousers and the precise grooming of your

hair determined your right to drink. Uneven turn-ups, too little ear showing, the wrong conditioner, and you were out.

Although there were reputed to be bars in town where suspected hoisters were given the third degree, I have to say that we were never questioned, perhaps because we were together, as to the nature of our relational preferences. But in the lavatories of one hotel I did find evidence of Queensland's notorious anxiety about the spread of the spirit of the Gay and the Goanna. It was a stainless steel machine which offered you your own Germshield Disposable Seat Cover for a mere 20 cents a throw. There was even a little diagram explaining how you pulled out the tab and affixed it to the seat. If you left the tab on, and dangling in the bowl, the cover would be swept away when the toilet was flushed, thus ensuring that the next person would not be able to shield himself from germs for free.

Otherwise, though, there seemed on the surface not to be too much fear of what was catching. I saw my first ever Australian edition of *Pravda* for sale on the streets of Brisbane. I saw two on-duty policemen browsing through the modern fiction section of a pavement bookstore, and after serious deliberation make a purchase of a volume of Frank Moorhouse stories and a new novel by David Malouf. And although I'd heard that some shops in Queensland wouldn't stock my books because of the illustrations on their covers (as some feminist bookshops, mistaking depiction for incitement, even in non-censorious London won't), I saw them shown prominently, one might almost say flagrantly and abundantly, all over Brisbane. As indeed I saw at last, in a section devoted entirely to the Australian contribution to the genre, the collected poems of Orianna Ooi.

There is always hope for a city prepared to make accommodations such as these to the life of the intellect in action.

★ ★ ★

We didn't spend long in Brisbane for all that. I made the mistake of dragging us off to see *Hannah and her Sisters* on our first night in town, as a way of getting Green Island out of the system, and it worked so well for me that it tolled the death knell over my interest in anywhere that wasn't New York. I came out of the cinema in a fury with where I happened at that moment to be. Queensland! Brisbane! What was I, as a Jew, as a European, as a depressive, as a gourmandizer of the quasi-kosher, as a connoisseur of social experimentation and disappointment – what was *I*, as a seeker after urban exhilaration, doing in Brisbane? New York was where I should have been. Not the real New York; I wasn't dealing in *real* anywheres. But New York as portrayed in Woody Allen movies – full of allure and illusory amenities, all Gershwin street-throb and dangerous conviviality, beguiling, trashy, tumultuously lyrical. So badly did I want to *be* Woody Allen (who was always wanting to be someone else himself), pushing my barrow-load of confused and disbelieving hopefulness up *that* hill, that I didn't just turn on Brisbane, I turned on Australia altogether and couldn't understand what had brought me back here so many times when it had so little that I wanted.

The truth of all this, of course, is that I wouldn't have felt any of it had I watched *Hannah and her Sisters* in Kalgoorlie or in the school at Areyonga, or even, had they had an outdoor cinema, a Tropicana, on the beach at Green Island; what accounted for my restless dissatisfaction was anti-climax – my knowledge that our journey was very nearly over and that we were back now in the Australia that had been long familiar to us, and which was indeed but a poor imitation of a poor American imitation of a European model. New York or Brisbane? The question never arose when we were chatting to the euros in the Flinders Ranges, or listening to the dingoes in Yulara.

As for what it was that kept me coming back to the eastern seaboard cities, even though they weren't New York, I was given a sharp reminder of it on our last evening in Brisbane. At the house of an acquaintance of an acquaintance I found myself sitting opposite a publisher I'd vaguely known in my book repping days in Melbourne. Left to my own devices I might very well not have recognized him. He was perched on the edge of his seat, ginger-haired and bearded, wringing his hands and looking arch, like a well-connected sprite. He *seemed* familiar, but I had been travelling for months and I was seeing what I thought were the faces of old friends everywhere now. So it needed him to say, 'So you're back then,' – as if I were a recurrence of some pestiferous minor ailment – for me to remember that I remembered him.

He wanted to know what I was doing here. I told him. 'Well if you're writing about Australia I hope you make it funny,' he said.

I pulled a face. I wasn't feeling in a very funny mood. 'Funny but not farcical,' I said.

'Why not farcical? The country is a farce.'

He poured me a red wine, although he was only a guest at the house himself. 'It's a nation of fuckwits,' he reminded me.

He took me through the details of Australia's national fuck-wittedness. Its reliance on American and Pommy money-men. Its lack of an independent policy on anything. Its parochialism. Its fear of the Melbourne establishment. 'The only good things in Australia are happening in Perth,' he told me. 'Take Holmes à Court, who just happens to be South African-born. He's got the Melbourne establishment by the scruff of the neck. What he's doing to those fuckwits is the nearest modern equivalent to the Eureka spirit.' (That's Eureka as in Stockade, not Eureka as in Archimedes.)

I raised an eyebrow at the idea of Holmes à Court as a revolutionary, but he went on twinkling wickedly and pouring me more wine. 'Anyway, so who else have you looked up in Brisbane?' he asked.

'No one,' I said. 'Just you.'

He must have thought I was being ironical. 'You bastard, Jacobson,' he said.

A warm glow instantly suffused my whole being. I felt as though a dozen little lights had been turned on inside me all at once. 'You bastard, Jacobson' – that was it, the very thing, the reason above all others I kept coming back. They were so damned complimentary, Australians. They made you feel you possessed such reserves of badness. 'You bastard, Jacobson.' Who else but an eastern states Australian was ever going to say that to me? Certainly no New Yorker ever would.

At the other end of the room I saw Ros looking anxious. She'd heard the word bastard and heard the word Jacobson and feared the worst. I threw her a mute signal that everything was all right, that I was getting what I always came for and could never get enough of: the ultimate male compliment, the asseveration of one's dangerousness, bloke to bloke.

'It's true,' I said. 'Anyway, who else is there to see in Brisbane?'

'You'd be surprised.'

'Surprise me.'

He did surprise me too. Any number of people I hadn't heard of for years – personalities, public figures, show folk, many I'd assumed had quietly passed away – were all the while living the good life in Brisbane, sitting on Germshield Disposable Seat Covers, and reading *Pravda*. But the most intriguing by far was the figure on whom Brando's part in *Apocalypse Now* had been based. The Mr Kurtz of Vietnam.

'What, here?' I found it hard to believe. I don't know why; I suppose it seemed a bit of a let-down. After the Horror! the Horror! – the cannibalism and all the rest of it – you expected somewhere rather more metaphysically testing than the Gold Coast. 'Here in Brisbane?'

'Yep.'

'Do you know him?'

'I'm not saying.'

'What's his name?'

'I'm not going to tell you.'

'Why not? What do you think I'm going to do with it?'

He smiled and sat further forward, occupying even less seat. There was intense sardonic activity in his eyes. As if to imply, 'I know you, Jacobson you bastard. I know what *you'd* do.' Which was the very thing I wanted him to imply. There was absolutely nothing I would do with any information relating to Mr Kurtz. The last thing I'd have the courage for was a visit. I don't interview men who've gone up the river. But I didn't choose to let my old publisher mate know that. I wanted to hear him call me a bastard again – just one more time before I left.

'Give me a little clue.'

He shook his head.

'His initials.'

'No. I'm not telling you.'

'Just the suburb, then. St Lucia? Fortitude Valley?'

'No. Absolutely no.'

'Suit yourself,' I said. I took my notebook out and scribbled a few words on it. 'I'm going tomorrow,' I went on; 'I've got to have someone for the Brisbane section. If I can't have Mister Kurtz I'll have to have you. Publishers don't normally make for interesting reading, but I can jazz you up a bit. What was that about fuckwits again?'

The tense angles of his body somewhat belied the wicked twinkle, or vice versa. 'You bastard, Jacobson,' he said.

'Good to see you again, anyway,' he lied, as I rose to leave.

'You too,' I pretended to agree.

We gripped each other's hand firmly. It was like the locking of horns. In the old days I used to arm wrestle all my friends, and had we both been younger we could easily have gone in for a bit of that now. In the English-speaking world there really is only Australia where you can get that from your mates.

As we parted it occurred to me that I didn't in fact know who he was and that we might never have met in Melbourne after all. The more I thought about it the more likely I decided it was that we'd never addressed a word to each other until tonight.

Not that it seemed to matter.

We went on from this encounter to hear Hemi sing at the Port Office Hotel in Edward Street. Hemi was a nice, quiet, plump, bespectacled Jewish boy from Tel Aviv who used to be a tank commander in the Israeli army and was now the hottest rock sensation in Brisbane. I'd read about him in the local newspaper; how he'd turned up in Queensland three and a half years previously, supporting himself on a round the world trip by doing odd jobs, a spot of cleaning, some busking, that sort of thing, and then, virtually overnight, had become a pop idol – not anywhere else, just here in Brissie.

We had to fight our way through the crowds at the Port Office to get to the bar, and we had to fight even harder to get anywhere near the stage. I was surprised at how young the audience was. Given that Hemi's repertoire included 'Hava Nagila' and 'American Pie' you would have thought his fans would have all been my age. But no; he had found a way through to the kids of Brisbane and they cheered and stomped and did as they were told when he waved his guitar around and shouted, 'Everybody sing – I can't get no – o – o . . .'

The girls clawed the air. They pushed one another over to get a touch of his yellow pants or to tug on his Israeli beach shirt. He smiled at them benignly, a bit puzzled himself. He had tight curly hair and a double chin and reminded me not so much of the soft Jewish boys who were regularly beaten up in the playground after school, as their mothers. There was something comfortable and caring about him; something homely – *haimisheh*. It needed no imagination at all to see him in a *shaytl* with his arms covered and maybe just a dab of lipstick, blessing the *challa* on a Friday night.

Well, this was a Friday night, *shabbas* already, and we were in Queensland, sweating, while somebody who looked very like *my* mother, too, was slaying them with his Menachem Begin accent, and what his chubby fingers could do on a guitar. I couldn't get over it. It was too risible. But it was a good note to leave Brisbane on. It balanced *Hannah and her Sisters* nicely. Hemi proved, if anybody did, that the New York I hankered after – a noisy refuge for a wandering urban soul – was just a construct. He'd built his own – a condo with a busy view – right in the very heartlands of the most unpromising of all territories. As far as Hemi was concerned he was *in* New York.

Just in case there was any chance of my suffering a similar delusion, the young woman at the reception desk of the hotel we'd been staying at, the Carlton, handed me a couple of Brisbane horror stories along with my bill. We'd enjoyed the Carlton; it was a handsome wooden building with lacy balconies, large, high-ceilinged rooms, and a marvellous lounge in which we'd sat by the hour, watching Marlene Dietrich and Greta Garbo come and go, as well as marginally less elderly ladies done up to resemble tropical wildlife – a banded snake eel, a couple of pelicans, any number of fruit bats, and on one occasion a cassowary, complete with a technicolour neck, a casque, and, for all we knew, a five-inch lethal toenail. Now, it seemed, the hotel was to be demolished. The very best that could be hoped for was that the façade might be retained. But everything else would go. For?

The woman smiled a slow sad smile at me and made a gesture which was meant to embrace everything that I could see going on in Brisbane with my own eyes. The preparations for EXPO

'88. And – it was vainly hoped – The Olympic Games, 1992. Like the rest of Australia Brisbane was caught up in a madness to pull down and rebuild – except that here the only things they could think of rebuilding to entice visitors with were malls and precincts.

'Not more shops?'

She nodded. 'Shops, shops and shops. And maybe, just maybe, a tavern. But no more accommodation. They assume people want to stay in Sheratons.'

'Can't the National Trust be trusted to take it on?'

'No. They say there's too much timber in it. It would cost too much to repair and maintain.'

'Couldn't they at least slap a preservation order on it?'

As soon as I said it I realized how naive I sounded. She looked at me as if I were a two-year-old. 'Preservation orders don't count for much in Queensland,' she said.

Well, if she thought *that* was babyish she'd heard nothing yet. 'Doesn't anybody protest?' I asked.

Looking back on it I can see that it was good of her even to have bothered to reply. But she did. 'You don't protest for long in Brisbane,' she told me.

She had, once. When she was a student. As a consequence of which her car mysteriously went missing one night. When she rang the police to report its theft they said they'd impounded it for being illegally parked; and when she went to collect it she found it wrecked. Not our responsibility, they'd told her. Teach you not to park illegally.

It made her tired, just remembering the event. Creases appeared under her eyes where I hadn't seen any before. 'You get to find out what's going on,' she said. 'You get to know once the Special Branch are looking out for you.'

She was not the kind of person you expected to hear such a sentence from. She didn't look an activist. In any other town she would have been a model citizen. But over-zealous police – assuming she was telling the truth – can rattle the respectability out of anyone. And there was no doubt about the size of the police presence in Brisbane; they were everywhere you looked. Always in groups of three or four, often quite young men, lounging on street corners, privately amused, more trouble than the trouble-makers. It's my most abiding memory of Brisbane: boy cops hanging around shopping precincts, laughing.

We didn't fly out of Brisbane, as our ragged spirits might have justified, but hired a comfortable car so that we could take a leisurely look at the Gold Coast and chug down the Pacific Highway to Sydney at whatever speed we fancied.

I found that I liked (liked for other people, that is) the absurd resorts of Surfers Paradise and Burleigh Heads and Coolangatta. Grant the desires and appetites they catered for and they made sense. The way they looked and what they were there for enjoyed a perfect harmony. People wanted to come here to see the sea – very well, they would *see* the sea. If that meant more and higher skyscrapers than you'd find in the rest of Australia put together, what then? How else was everyone going to get their own triangle of placid blue? Within the limits set by affordability, the Gold Coast was democracy in action. Everybody got a look in.

And the consequence of such dense high-rise waterfrontage, for mere passers-by such as us, was an urban/marine landscape so surreal as to take the breath away. Stand on a beach anywhere between Southport and Tweed Heads looking up the coast or down it and you would see dreaming cities poised perilously on the last millimetre of land, impregnable batteries of luxury apartments rising like the topless towers of Ilium and shimmer-ing in a sea haze as though they had no foundations but simply floated, like hanging gardens. Australian Venices for sunbathers and surfers, they seemed not to have been designed the way they were but to have fallen out like that, as if some freakish

cataclysm had severed a metropolis, sinking one half and dump-
ing a golden strand on the very doorsteps of the other.

There was sand everywhere. It was what you saw from every
overleaping window. It was the feature that concluded every
aspect – sand, a roll of foaming surf, and the Pacific – the reward
at the end of every little street.

It was in a car park by the beach at Surfers itself that I was
accosted by a tired, lonely looking man with cut-price tattoos
on his arms who wanted to know whether the traffic lights up
here had television cameras in them the way they had down
there. He had driven all the way from Melbourne without
stopping and in his fatigue had shot straight through a set of
lights. Before I had any opportunity to offer my opinion he put
himself on trial for this offence, appealing to me as jury, and
insisting on his innocence. 'Actually it was only an orange light,
and even then it had only just *turned* orange,' he said, relieved
to be acquitted.

It was just as well. I could see that he wouldn't have had the
money to pay the fine.

'So where are you from?' he asked me. He reminded me of
someone I had once shared a filthy bathroom with in a mould-
ering house in Wolverhampton. He suffered the same
blue-collar sadness and isolation. And he made me feel the
same way; I wanted to kick him, then I wanted to bathe his
wounds. He wore cheap trousers enlivened by a thick leather
belt and a silver cowboy buckle. Had he been a character in a
nineteenth-century novel he'd have said, 'Aw a muddle,' and
not lived long.

'London,' I answered. I felt it would have been more compas-
sionate to have said, 'Wolverhampton.'

'Geez, you'd notice the difference.'

'I'll say.'

But of course the one who was noticing the difference was
him. He had accosted me because he needed someone to talk

to now that he'd finally made it after days of driving. He had to hear his own voice in Surfers just to be certain it was he who was here. He stood by my side, looking out over the untouched sand and the blinding sea. 'It's like bloody Hawaii,' he said at last. Then in case that gave me the wrong impression of him, in case I thought he was skiting, he added, 'Not that I've ever been to Hawaii, but I bet it's like this.'

There's no helping the poor. They just can't lie like the rich.

I asked him if he intended to stay long.

'Here? Might stay all summer. I've got nothing else to do. There's no work down there. That's why I came away. If I'm going to do nothing I thought I might as well do it up here.'

'No point in not staying, then,' I said.

He gave me the sad smile of the habitually isolated – wary but eager. He'd been on his own in his big, ugly, beaten-up Holden for days. Mine was the first non-radio voice he'd heard. I the only living soul he so far knew in Surfers Paradise. I was only sorry that I couldn't, in my own person, encapsulate more that was paradisal for him.

I wished him well and watched him walk off towards the beach in his stained olive-green trousers – strides if ever I'd seen a pair – his silver buckle catching the sun. Directly in his path a young woman was coming out of the surf. Apart from a twist of string about her loins she was naked, and as she walked she shook the water from her breasts, droplet by droplet. He had his back to me now but I could see the tension of the long drive and the worry about unemployment flowing out of his shoulders.

We, on the other hand, were growing heavier with every kilometre. Somewhere in-between the twin towns of Coolangatta and Tweed Heads we crossed the border into New South Wales. The grand, expensive-looking Services Club, at which Gene Pitney was currently appearing, provided our farewell glimpse of the mess that was Queensland morality; for it was to this club that Queenslanders trailed in their thousands after dark, to play the poker machines they were denied, for the good of their immortal souls, in their own state.

But that didn't mean we were pleased to leave it. 'Now that I'm in New South Wales I feel I'm safe,' Ros kept saying. 'I feel as though I'm home.'

I'd never heard the words 'safe' and 'home' sound so desolate.

TWENTY

FOUND! – THE SPANGLED DRONGO

Although it is not possible, once you have set eyes on Sydney
Harbour, not to want to spend the rest of your life there, taking
the ferry from one shore to the other – a Flying Dutchman
with a happy ending – we had made a solemn and binding
agreement at the outset that on this visit at least we would not
let it steal our hearts. It could caress and flatter us for a few days,
while we unwound, but it was not otherwise to be allowed
into our affections. This was the Australia we knew, the
Australia of our separate pineapple-requiring pasts, and we did
not want to have it stamping quite so soon on the still impressionable wax of our more recent experiences.

For my part I was content just to put my feet up and watch
the Bridge. I say watch, not look at, because the Bridge is no
static spectacle; unlike the Eiffel Tower or the Empire State
Building or any other of those irresistibly banal landmarks whose
chief attraction is their vulgar height, the Harbour Bridge is
never still; just when you think you have it pinned, understand
its angles and believe you know where it must be in relation to
the rest of the glowing city, it rears up at you from an entirely
unexpected and in truth entirely impossible location. That's

what it did to us as we drove in from the north along the Pacific Highway: it reared quite suddenly, rose and arched and swung, and then just as suddenly disappeared. When we next saw it, it was somewhere else, no longer showing us the grandeur of its span but its steep humped back, like the last and most terrifying run of a roller coaster.

Sydney Harbour would still be magnificent without the Bridge, but it is the Bridge which transforms its beauties from the merely actual to the symbolic. It joins and unifies and dominates and over-arches in the spirit of its own design – not stylish, not streamlined, not at all sleek or sophisticated, but spectacularly functional, a lumbering artisan somehow learnt in the ways of necromancy.

So we set out to find a flat where for five or six days we could do nothing but keep an eye on it. And Blues Point Tower, the first of Sydney's high-rise luxury developments, where Rupert Murdoch had once owned a nuptial suite and Gough Whitlam had partaken of the notorious Iraqi Breakfast, seemed to be just the thing. The estate agents managing a number of flats in the building sent a 'boy' along to show us around. He was sixty-three and suffered from an unusual stutter. It affected him only when it came to place names. It needn't, therefore, in the normal course of things, have played too large a part in our negotiations, except that something prompted him to take us on a conversational tour of Australia, and to pause in every town that he had lived in, passed through, or thought about. An even more unusual feature of this stutter was that it affected his pronunciation of place names only when they began with a preposition. Thus he was fine on Narrandera and Rockhampton, but no good at all on By – By – By – Byron Bay and In – In – In – Innisfail.

It was in the lift going up to the fifteenth floor that he gave us our most trying time. He was remembering how he'd been happy in Up – Up – Up – Upway and To – To – To

— Toowoomba but had given up on On — On — On — Onslow in favour of Over — Over — Over — Over — Over —

Ros could stand it no longer: 'Overton?' she said.

He looked at her as if she was crazy. 'No,' he snapped, 'Overseas.'

We did make one or two tentative outings from our comfortable Bridge-bound eyrie, sometimes to see friends to whom we were careful to explain that we weren't really here on this occasion, and could they please not jolt or in any other way disturb us as we were overflowing vessels, brimful of where we *had* been. And once we went to watch Judy Davis hamming it up terribly as a post-Virago Australian neurotofeministical Hedda Gabler with a Fenella Fielding snort. 'Mankind cannot bear too much reality,' the programme for some reason quoted. Reality didn't seem to be the problem to me, but I was probably biased. It was a pretty intimate theatre, balanced precariously on the edge of a wharf, and I hadn't liked the way Judy Davis looked at me when delivering Hedda's line, 'Academics do not make entertaining travelling companions.'

Our only other brush with the culture of the city came when we found ourselves embroiled in a mêlée, sponsored by the Lebanese Christian community of Sydney, outside the cinema showing Jean-Luc Godard's *Hail Mary*. And that — our embroilment, not the mêlée — was quite accidental. We had gone to have lunch with Mez Levy, after whom we had renamed the more spectacular part of the Atherton Tablelands, and Elizabeth Brown, a North Shore Sydney girl of exquisite looks who had worked for Ros five or six years earlier in Cornwall. In those days Ros ran a tea gardens and Elizabeth Brown — Miss Brown, as she was called — saw to the chips. 'What does it mean, Mr Jacobson,' she used to ask me whenever I popped into the kitchens for a chip and a chat, 'that, although I left Sydney over a year ago now to see the world, I spend my time frying mountains of chips which are no sooner devoured than I have to fry mountains more?'

'Miss Brown, everyone must have a project in life,' I used to tell her. 'You should be pleased that yours is so clearly defined.'

She became famous in the village in the end not for her chips but for the slug incident. Seeing her carrying a tray through the gardens on a balmy Saturday afternoon, an enraged customer had beckoned her over, complaining in a loud voice that there was a slug eating the same lettuce from the inside that she was eating from the out. Miss Brown glided across the trodden turf, her fine profile tilted at an angle of almost anguished solicitude. 'Oh no,' she said as she approached the table and was shown the slimy offender. 'Oh no. The poor little thing.' And, taking the slug on her finger and whispering every manner of comfort and endearment to it, she returned it to the bushes where it more naturally belonged. 'There, there,' she said, all the while remembering to keep smiling at the woman in whose lettuce the poor little thing had come so very close to perishing, 'there, there.'

Now Miss Brown was back in Sydney, back on the North Shore indeed, working for a television company, missing the chips, and this afternoon intending to see *Hail Mary*, which was being shown as part of the Sydney Film Festival. We accompanied her to the cinema after lunch, puzzled as to the amount of noise we could hear in that part of the city and wondering why there were so many policemen on the streets and why so many thoroughfares were cordoned off. Then we turned into Market Street and might have been excused believing we were in Beirut. Women wearing shawls and veils were on their knees in the roadway outside the cinema, rocking to and fro and wailing. Some tore their hair. Some screamed. 'They should take this movie to Lebanon,' one woman was shouting, 'they would eat him there – they would drink his blood!'

'Our eyes are faced towards Heaven,' one of them said to me as I approached, 'where do you cast yours?'

I looked to a nearby policeman for help. He shrugged and stared at the pavement. I did the same.

We took our farewell of Elizabeth, and watched her brave the fury of the Christian mob. It was frightening enough to be on the road, but the real threat was to those blasphemers who were actually entering the cinema. Despite the line of policemen, abuse of the most violent kind rained down on her, she who in North Cornwall still was held to be a paradigm of loving kindness, an example to us all of gentleness to slugs. 'You should be dead!' a handsome, well-dressed Italian woman in furs called after her. 'All of you in there should be dead!'

Someone chanted, 'Hail Mary full of grace – a virgin always.'

A more cultivated voice called out, 'Blasphemy is NOT art.'

I removed myself a little from the crowd to get a better look at it. There weren't only followers of our Lady of Lebanon here; it was just that they were the most hysterically vociferous. But the Italians ran them close. And then of course the Greeks. Followed by the Irish. Nor were there only women. I saw priests and mafiosi, thug-believers of several southern European nationalities, and hag-ridden boys, one of them bawling through a megaphone, 'Everyone has got a mother!'

More's the pity, you had to be insane not to think, watching a spectacle such as this. The moment the word spread that the film had started, that only a few yards away the blasphemy was afoot, a new hysteria grabbed them. Those who were not already on their knees fell to them. Some beat their chests. Others looked to Heaven, holding their palms open, their faces contorted into ghastly expressions of beggarly supplication, their eyes cast piteously upwards, in imitation of the suffering depicted in two thousand years of largely tawdry religious art.

A Lebanese woman with a transfixed gaze pleaded with the policemen in the name of *their* mothers. She wore grey socks under her sandals and carried a candle, rejoicing in the pain the molten wax caused her, dripping down over her wrists and fingers. 'Would Godard allow a film to be made about his mother?' she cried. 'No, no, he would be out here with us.'

I was struck again by the sheer tat that went by the name of religious artefact – tyuringe. The old books they were wailing from, the gaudy crucifixes, the rubbishy pictures, the snotty candles, the dead flowers, the gift-wrap ribbons, the worn beads, the mindless literature on cheap paper. An hour before I had been walking through Kings Cross with Ros and Mez Levy and Elizabeth Brown when an incensed midget touting for business outside a strip joint had leapt out at me and shouted, 'C'mon, gigolo – you've got three women, can you handle them or not? Eh? Eh? Eh, gigolo?' He had come after me in the street, crazed, driven, still shouting, 'Eh, gigolo? Eh?' At the time I thought he was as depraved a creature as I had ever set eyes on, as lost to humanity as anyone that still bore the outward semblance of a man could be. Now, after these scenes outside the film festival, I understood what Dostoevsky had been up to having Father Zossima drop to his knees before the most debauched of all the Karamazovs. Compared to the holy the depraved were certainly divine.

That was pretty much the last thought I had in Sydney. We kept to our apartment for a couple more days, steering clear of street trouble, watching the Bridge change shape and form and even colour, bearing infinite, unbearable promise in its bow – man's convenant to man – then we got the hell out.

It had never been our intention to search for anything on this journey, apart from Orianna Ooi's poems, and we had given those up unconscionably early on. But as the last of our time trickled through our fingers, first in Sydney then in Melbourne, and those familiar places willy-nilly exerted their old sway again, we submitted to a shared but largely unspoken impulse to find and take away some image, an emblematic figure or tableau, absurd preferably, that would epitomize what was known and stale to us and stand as a sort of memorial contrast to all we had recently seen that was virgin and unprecedented.

We settled on the Spangled Drongo (Chibia bracteata) as the idea to which the image we required would be as flesh. No other Australian beast that we could think of made a better job of reconciling contrarieties. It's a bit of a lumpen bird, the drongo, a fly-catching crow-like thing whose name has become a byword for clumsiness and slowness, for harmless ineptitude. A *Spangled* drongo, though, must surely be another bird again. If there's no escaping the idea of dim-wit still, at least one thinks of a high-wire circus dim-wit, a flash of glittering light, a coruscation of dancing sequins, a froth of gaudy plumes and feathers – before the fall.

Since we never went so far as actually to propose a Spangled Drongo hunt, our interest in finding one was intermittent and eventually disappeared altogether in social responsibilities and last-minute plans for departure. We went to see the film *Kangaroo* on our final night in Australia. It was a special occasion. The opening of the Melbourne Film Festival and the film's own world première. A heady night for Melbourne.

Feeling that we were merely ghosts in the country now, in every sense but the grossly bodily one already back in London, we stood in the shadows and watched the guests arrive: the cream of the Victorian arts, television producers, academics, bar-room reviewers, Catholic poets, Catholic novelists, Catholic critics, the more enlightened figures of politics and journalism, and lastly the director of the film himself, who years before in a Carlton pub had accused me of submitting language to the heel of the enemy. I had been wondering what he meant for over a decade.

We took our places and listened to some speeches. It was a full house, only two seats, a few rows down from us, unoccupied. Just as the lights were being dimmed a couple of tall young men came flouncing down the aisle to claim them. They were both dressed entirely in black, though with an enpurpled sheen, each wearing some sort of clerical collar and a short cloak which billowed out theatrically – boy-theatrically on one of them, making one think of doomed princelings or passionately androgynous Shakespearean youths; vampire-theatrically on the other, making one think of dripping teeth and soft punctured necks. I believed I saw something gold swing and glitter on each chest. They were priests – probably Jesuits – and they were gay. Dandies in the service of Jesus.

Ros dug me at the very moment I dug her. 'Found!' she whispered.

'The Spangled Drongo!' I whispered back.

'Drong*oes*,' she corrected me. 'We've bagged a pair.'

But that was how our whole trip had gone – we'd been blessed at every turn with a surfeit of good fortune.

★　★　★

Back in London we felt we had only one failure to reproach ourselves for – Tasmania. I blamed Ros that we hadn't made it across the Tasman. She blamed me. So several months later, when I happened to be in Australia – the old Australia – for purposes not unassociated with the book we'd spent all that time re-comma'ing in Townsville, I decided I would do Tasmania solo, and append it to our travels in the same way the state itself is appended to the mainland – have it spinning away independently, held in check only by a force that even on an atlas looks like a diminishing magnetic field.

I did the job thoroughly too. I secured introduction. I made appointments. I spent my first night in Hobart having dinner at Parliament House, a guest of Neil Batt, the Tasmanian Opposition Leader. I attended a sitting of the House and heard about the case of the local police officer caught selling undersized crayfish to Hobart nightclubs. I met Bob Brown, the hero of the Franklin River Blockade, now an Independent parliamentarian, and I was a witness to his offering Neil Batt support, in the event of a hung Parliament, in return for a Ministry of Forests and Wildernesses. Then I set out for the forests and wildernesses myself, travelling in a state of mind not far removed from that of George Grey's Aboriginal servant, Warrup, as described in his own words:

1st day: At Dundulap we eat fish; then onwards, onwards, onwards, till we slept at Nerroba.
2nd day: Onwards, onwards, till we reached Nowergoop, where the horses drank water; then onwards, onwards, onwards . . .
5th day: We go onwards, onwards, onwards, onwards . . .
6th day: Onwards through the forest, onwards through the forest, onwards through the forest . . . We see the sea; then onwards, onwards, onwards, along the sea shore onwards, along the sea shore onwards, along the sea shore onwards. Then we turn back again, away we go back again, back again away; through the forest away, through the forest away, through the forest away; back again through . . .

Onwards, onwards, onwards to Launceston I went; then along, along, along to Burnie; then down, down, down to the south-west, pausing at the village of Strahan where all the Greenies great and small had gathered; then on a boat along, along, along the Gordon River; and out again, back out again, back out again through Hells Gates. I visited the lovely old Gaiety Theatre at Zeehan, and saw the shocking despoliation of Queenstown; too many dams, too many dams, too much hydro-electricity, too much, too much . . . Then back through any number of placid settlements, sensitively restored, to Hobart, where after standing outside the oldest Synagogue in Tasmania (fancy there being more than one) I took a turn around the university, recalling the scandal that had ruined Professor Sydney Sparkes Orr in the 1950s, and reading on the wall of the present Department of Philosophy the chalked advice: